NEW DIRECTIONS IN LATINO AMERICAN CULTURES

A Series Edited by Licia Fiol-Matta and José Quiroga

None of the Above: Puerto Ricans in the Global Era,
edited by Frances Negrón-Muntaner

An Intellectual History of the Caribbean,
by Silvio Torres-Saillant

New Tendencies in Mexican Art,
by Rubén Gallo

Jose Martí: An Introduction,
by Oscar Montero

The Letter of Violence: Essays on Narrative and Theory,
by Idelber Avelar

The Masters and the Slaves: Plantation Relations and Mestizaje in American Imaginaries,
edited by Alexandra Isfahani-Hammond

Bilingual Games: Some Literary Investigations,
edited by Doris Sommer

Tongue Ties: Logo-Eroticism in Anglo-Hispanic Literature,
by Gustavo Perez-Firmat

Velvet Barrios: Popular Culture & Chicana/o Sexualities,
edited by Alicia Gaspar de Alba, with a foreword by Tomás Ybarra Frausto

The Famous 41: Sexuality and Social Control in Mexico, 1901,
edited by Robert McKee Irwin, Edward J. McCaughan, and Michele Rocío Nasser

New York Ricans from the Hip Hop Zone,
by Raquel Z. Rivera

Forthcoming titles

Puerto Ricans in America: 30 Years of Activism and Change,
edited by Xavier F. Totti and Félix Matos Rodríguez

New Concepts in Latino American Cultures

Cosmopolitanisms and Latin America: Against the Destiny of Place,
by Jacqueline Loss

Ciphers of History: Latin American Readings for a "Cultural" Age,
by Enrico Mario Santí

Remembering Maternal Bodies: Melancholy in Latina and Latin American Women's Writing,
by Benigno Trigo

None of the Above: Puerto Ricans in the Global Era

Edited by

Frances Negrón-Muntaner

palgrave
macmillan

NONE OF THE ABOVE

First published in 2007 by
PALGRAVE MACMILLAN™
175 Fifth Avenue, New York, N.Y. 10010 and
Houndmills, Basingstoke, Hampshire, England RG21 6XS
Companies and representatives throughout the world.

PALGRAVE MACMILLAN is the global academic imprint of the Palgrave Macmillan division of St. Martin's Press, LLC and of Palgrave Macmillan Ltd. Macmillan® is a registered trademark in the United States, United Kingdom and other countries. Palgrave is a registered trademark in the European Union and other countries.

ISBN-13: 978–1–4039–6245–4 hard back
ISBN-10: 1–4039–6245–6 hard back
ISBN-13: 978–1–4039–6246–1 paper back
ISBN-10: 1–4039–6246–4 paper back

Library of Congress Cataloging-in-Publication Data

None of the above : Puerto Ricans in the global era / edited by Frances Negrón-Muntaner.
p. cm. — (New directions in Latino American cultures)
Includes bibliographical references and index.
ISBN 1–4039–6245–6 (alk. paper) — ISBN 1–4039–6246–4
1. Puerto Rico—Politics and government—1952– 2. Puerto Rico—Relations—United States. 3. United States—Relations—Puerto Rico. 4. Political culture—Puerto Rico. 5. Nationalism—Puerto Rico. 6. Identity (Psychology)—Puerto Rico. I. Negrón-Muntaner, Frances. II. Series.

F1976.N66 2006
306.2097295—dc22 2005057421

A catalogue record for this book is available from the British Library.

Design by Newgen Imaging Systems (P) Ltd., Chennai, India.

First edition: April 2007

10 9 8 7 6 5 4 3 2 1

Printed in the United States of America.

Contents

Part III *Boricua* Borderlines

Part IV Coda

List of Figures

Preface

". . . no nation now but the imagination."

Derek Walcott, "The Schooner Flight"

Since the mid-1980s, I have lived in and out of four different cities that form part of what could be thought of as a Puerto Rican archipelago: San Juan, Philadelphia, Miami, and New York. In New York, however, the unexpected happened. I heard something crack. Loud. Even if throughout my many years as an intellectual migrant worker, I have felt home sick, or unsettled, this was different. It was as if once I arrived to this new, post-9/11 and re-Latinized Nueva York, I had lost pieces of my prior self in the move and never bothered to claim this baggage. I felt like a Caribbean Humpty Dumpty, broken and disoriented, with my yolk slowly oozing out onto the thumping sidewalk.

Until one day a colleague invited me to lunch. We talked about the university where we both taught, how I was (or was not) adapting to New York and the incongruities of life in general. Perhaps because my colleague is also part of a different diaspora, I felt free to inquire about my anxiety: "How are people to survive when they no longer essentially see themselves as nationals, ethnics, or natives?" My colleague suggested that we get some chocolate after lunch, but before we left the restaurant, he put it simply: "When you get to that point, you start needing friends."

Tellingly, this book is based on efforts to carve out new spaces for intellectual dialogue, a form of friendship. From 2000 to 2004, I organized a series of symposia on Puerto Rico, Puerto Ricans, and U.S. Latinos at Rutgers University, University of Miami, and Columbia University. The main purpose of these gatherings was to pose alternative questions and develop innovative approaches to the study of Puerto Rican and Latino cultural and political practices. In contrast to other similar events, there was no ideological, disciplinary, or methodological litmus tests. The conferences hosted participants who were journalists, filmmakers, dancers, politicians, public servants, writers, and academics across the political spectrum. The main criterion for inviting participants was their willingness to take a risk, including sitting next to people who they ordinarily would not want to.

Each conference had a different emphasis that also marked a level of dissatisfaction with the still-prevalent tendency of framing Puerto Rican practices as a fixed contest between nationalist and colonialist ideologies.[1]

The first one, titled "None of the Above," sought to redefine the political itself as well as promote dialogue between scholars residing in and out of Puerto Rico. The second, "The Puerto Rican Vacilón," built on the prior effort by considering trends in migration and how these relate to Puerto Rican practices in the current global juncture. The last gathering, "Latinos Inside," strove to promote comparative scholarship about Latino migration and contextualize matters such as citizenship, colonial power relations, and transculturation within the broader framework of globalization studies.

Inspired by these exchanges, the current volume travels through the promises and perils of Puerto Rican life in the global era, and offers new ways of defining what "Puerto Rican" politics is. Structurally, the anthology includes an introduction, three sections, and a concluding coda. The introduction considers the unexpected win of the "none of the above" alternative in the island's last plebiscite on status and its possible implications to rethinking politics. In the first section, "The Politics of Ambiguity," contributors explore the question of how the state, the incorporation of Puerto Rico into the United States' globalized economic circuits, juridical subordination, and consumption practices shape the political sphere. The second section, "Politics as Spectacle and the Spectacle of Politics," engages with the implications of blurring boundaries between politics and the mass media for the fulfillment of personal and collective desires. The third section, "*Boricua* Borderlines," and the coda examine the changing terrain of Puerto Rican cultural and subject production in the present juncture.

Although the conferences included more than 50 participants discussing a broad range of topics, it was not possible to adequately document all presentations and audience interventions. Yet everyone involved contributed significantly to this volume, and I would like to offer a special thank you to all participants, including Silvia Alvarez-Curbelo, Luis Aponte-Parés, Amílcar Antonio Barreto, Jaime Benson Arias, Thomas Boswell, Christina Duffy Burnett, Pedro Cabán, Teo Castellanos, Max Castro, Héctor Cordero-Guzmán, Luis Dávila-Colón, Rodolfo de la Garza, Junot Díaz, Arcadio Díaz Quiñones, Jorge Duany, Juan Duchesne Winter, Jeffrey Farrow, Maurice Ferré, Rosario Ferré, Aurora Flores, Juan Flores, Sonia Fritz, Sarah Garland, Félix Jiménez, Miriam Jiménez Román, Lawrence La Fountain-Stokes, Agustín Lao Montes, Raysa Martínez, Yolanda Martínez-San Miguel, Nicole Marwell, Félix Matos-Rodríguez, Mario Murillo, Katherine McCaffrey, Suzanne Oboler, Angel R. Oquendo, Carlos Pabón, Dino Pacio Lindín, Gustavo Pérez-Firmat, Fernando Picó, Dolores Prida, Gloria D. Prosper-Sánchez, Robert Rabin Siegal, Ana Yolanda Ramos-Zayas, Raquel Z. Rivera, Efrén Rivera Ramos, Jorge Rodríguez Beruff, José Quiroga, Alberto Sandoval-Sánchez, Ilan Stavans, Marian Soto, Roberto Suro, Bonnie Urciuoli, Pablo Vila, and George Yúdice.

In addition, my deep appreciation goes to my organizing partners at the three host institutions: Luis Martínez-Fernández, then chair of the Department of Puerto Rican Studies at Rutgers; the late Robert Levine, founding director of the Latin American Studies Center at the University of Miami; Gary Okihiro, director of Columbia University's Center for the Study of Ethnicity and Race; and Jonathan Arac, former chair of the Department of English and Comparative Literature at Columbia. I would also like to thank each institution's staff, particularly Johnny Roldán-Chacón, Arleny Guerrero, Joy Hayton, Monica Licourt, Yanet Baldares, and Dianne Just, without whom any organizing efforts would have been impossible. A deep-felt thank you goes to Raúl Duany and the Puerto Rican Professional Association of South Florida for their significant support to the second conference held in Miami, and to Judith Escalona, director of the award-winning website PR.Dream, for documenting both the Rutgers and Columbia conferences.

It would be impossible to conclude without expressing my profound appreciation to the anonymous donor whose intellectual curiosity and generosity made the conferences possible: You are truly one of a kind. I would also like to thank Gabriella Georgiades, who was the epitome of rigor and grace, Celeste Fraser Delgado, Juan Carlos Rodríguez, Karen Cook, Kairos Llobrera and Leonard S. Rosenbaum, whose editorial guidance was indispensable. To series editors Licia Fiol-Matta and José Quiroga and colleagues Jenny Davidson, David Lloyd, Yolanda Martínez-San Miguel, Edward Mendelson, Chon Noriega, Bruce Robbins and Charles Venator-Santiago, who were exceptionally generous with their comments and support, thanks so much. I am equally indebted to production manager Elizabeth Sabo from Palgrave and Maran Elancheran from Newgen Imaging Systems for their boundless patience. To my research assistants Katerina Seligmann and Larissa Brewer, and my gracious hosts in my long sojourns in Miami, Pipo Bonamino and Consuelo Becerra, what would I do without you? My sister Marianne Mason undertook the translation of one of the book's texts and did a phenomenal job. As usual, Maggie de la Cuesta keeps running a tab for my eternal gratitude.

In sum, if the support of friends is never more essential than when one falls into the category of "none of the above," the need to acknowledge all of the above is of the greatest importance. *Mil gracias a todos.* The conversation continues.

Note

1. For further discussion of this polemic, please see Frances Negrón-Muntaner and Ramón Grosfoguel, eds., *Puerto Rican Jam: Rethinking Colonialism and Nationalism* (Minneapolis: University of Minnesota Press, 1997).

Introduction

Frances Negrón-Muntaner

Ambiguity prevails when the formal rules do not matter.
Ira Sharkansky, Ambiguity, Coping and Governance

For over a century, the island of Puerto Rico has been considered peculiar according to standards of "normal" national development. Since 1952, this view has been explicitly tied to the fact that although Puerto Ricans imagine themselves as part of their own national community, they have also steered away from independence in favor of an ambiguous political status known as the *Estado Libre Asociado* (ELA) or commonwealth. Called the "best of both worlds" by its supporters and "colonialism" by its detractors, under the ELA, Puerto Ricans carry U.S. passports and can serve in the U.S. military, but cannot vote for president, or elect a delegation to Congress. In addition, while Puerto Ricans are presumably ruled by their own constitution, legal sovereignty over the island rests in the U.S. Congress.

Then, on December 13, 1998, Puerto Rico appeared to confirm its status as one of the world's politically queerest places—with a new twist.

Throughout the day, over 70 percent of Puerto Rican voters participated in an island-wide referendum to decide what the island's future relationship to the United States should be. To the surprise of many, the inhabitants of the "oldest colony in the modern world,"[1] as former chief justice José Trías Monge once famously put it, selected not independence, statehood, or even the current commonwealth, but a dark-horse column dubbed *ninguna de las anteriores* or none of the above. The question of status now turned into the status of the question: How could this have happened?

Legally Insane

It was all about the wording. Or so it seemed.

Frustrated by the last attempt to persuade Congress to sponsor a binding plebiscite and eager to exploit the symbolism of holding a consultation during the hundredth anniversary of the Spanish-American War, the pro-statehood governor Pedro Rosselló of the New Progressive Party (NPP) decided to once more push the issue before the end of his second term in office. The climate was literally not favorable; a hurricane had just hit, and some voters were outraged that Rosselló appeared more concerned about raising the status question than uplifting the island's destroyed infrastructure. Yet as the only pro-statehood advocate in recent history who had a fighting chance to walk out with a majority vote, Rosselló's mission was unstoppable, and nothing short of revolutionary: to end "the insufferable ambiguity" of Puerto Rico's political identity.[2]

Aware of the difficulties inherent in such an ambitious goal, the statehooders had a plan: Since for the past four decades all local referenda have favored proposals that support an "improved" version of the status quo, the pro-statehood majority in the Puerto Rican legislature opted against using the wording preferred by proponents of each traditional option. In its place, legislators decided to employ terms that were deemed constitutionally acceptable to the presumed legal arbiters of any decision—the U.S. Congress.[3] Regardless of how each political party typically defined its aspirations, on this ballot, "independence" meant the founding of a separate nation-state. "Associated republic" implied the creation of an independent nation that ceded certain sovereign powers such as national defense to the United States. "Statehood" referred to becoming a state of the federal union with equal rights and responsibilities, while the "current status" signified an unincorporated territory, subject to the sovereign powers of the United States.

As in an already scripted wrestling match, these definitions pleased all parties except one: the *Partido Popular Democrático* or the Popular Democratic Party (PDP), the entity that stands for the commonwealth. The PDP wished to define its option not as an unincorporated territory but as a bilateral pact between two sovereign countries that guarantees U.S. citizenship, a proposal also known as "enhanced commonwealth." While every congressional leader and White House representative ever granted a speaking part in status history has repeatedly dismissed this option as unconstitutional, the PDP protested its exclusion from the consultation. Refusing to give in, the party first challenged the ballot in court. Losing the case, the PDP then threatened not to participate in the plebiscite.

To avoid a boycott, the local parties reached a compromise inspired by a little known, if remarkable, 1993 Puerto Rico Supreme Court decision, *Sánchez Vilella and Colón Martínez v. Estado Libre Asociado et al.*[4] Arising out of a dispute over ballot language in a prior referendum, the ruling stated that voters have a right to select their "preferred option" in a status consultation. But if for any reason such an option is not available, the Puerto Rico State Electoral Commission has the obligation to inform the electorate about the right to a blank ballot and count these as votes that do not favor any of the listed alternatives. As a result, in addition to the already-familiar status options, and actual or desired commonwealth, the 1998 ballot included a fifth column identified as *ninguna de las anteriores* or none of the above.[5]

Even though the PDP heatedly campaigned for "none of the above," most commentators forecast the inevitable triumph of statehood. In support of their predictions, analysts cited Rosselló's *sí se puede* (yes, we can!) popularity among his constituents, the substantial growth of the statehood movement over the last decades, the possibility that the pro-autonomist vote would be split between the "free association" and status quo options, as well as the extreme ambiguity of "none of the above." Nevertheless, as it is not unusual in island politics, the pundits were wrong. Despite the NPP's best efforts, statehood obtained nearly the same percentage of votes as in 1993 (46.5 percent), independence received an all-time low of 2.5 percent, and neither the associated republic nor the territorial status alternative won even 1 percent of the vote each. *Ninguna de las anteriores*, however, garnered 50.3 percent of the total ballots cast.

Given that the entire edifice of mainstream Puerto Rican politics is founded on the status as a juridical question, the outcome implied that the electorate had gone legally insane. The impression that Puerto Rican voters had lost their minds was probably not lost on Rosselló himself, who now faced the embarrassing task of explaining the results to Congress. As one of the key leaders in the 1996–97 failed congressional status effort who also worked on ballot language, Alaska Congressman Don Young seemed particularly disturbed: In an urgent tone, he wrote to Rosselló and the other party presidents asking for an explanation.[6] Not withstanding the temptation to invoke the insanity defense, Rosselló explained what took place as a protest vote against his administration for his decision to sell the government-owned phone company La Telefónica to the American-owned GTE, and declared statehood the winner, as it was arguably the only rational alternative to receive a substantial number of votes.

Five months later, at a congressional hearing where all party presidents addressed the Senate Energy Committee, Rosselló added that since nearly 100 percent of the people opted for alternatives other than the ELA, the vote "indisputably constituted a virtually unanimous rejection of the status quo."[7] Not to be outdone in the use of unambiguous language, the PDP president Aníbal Acevedo Vilá claimed victory for the ELA and characterized the vote not as a condemnation of commonwealth but as "a clear rejection of statehood."[8] Not quite knowing what to say, although eager to feel like a winner too, pro-independence leader Rubén Berríos Martínez also declared a knockout victory over its arch enemy status, full incorporation, stating that "an absolute majority of voters once again refused to vote for statehood."[9]

Expectedly, given the United States' 100-plus-year history of ignoring Puerto Rican status claims even when they theoretically make more sense, the majority of congressional representatives asked for additional clarification and made no offers to pursue the matter any further. A few, like Senator Jeff Bingaman, a New Mexico Democrat, were perhaps more honest: Unable to resist the opportunity to make fun of the Puerto Rican vote, Bingaman mockingly described the "none of the above" outcome as the "free beer and barbecue option."[10] Yet, while clearly ridiculous in the best sense of the word, the vote's political effects were hard to miss. In the slightly exasperated words of former governor and pro-statehood advocate Carlos Romero Barceló: "the people of Puerto Rico decided not to decide"—at least not on the given terms.[11]

Ninguna De Las Anteriores

As a political performance, the "none of the above" vote should have come as no surprise. From at least the nineteenth century, Puerto Ricans have used theatrical means to convey or camouflage their political intentions to a variety of spectators on the island and beyond. During its "American" century, performance has been a particularly important feature of political life due to the limitations faced by Puerto Ricans as unrepresentable citizens in Congress, a fear of retaliation from the state if demands are considered "unreasonable," and a lack of influence over the mass media, which, as cultural critic Frances R. Aparicio comments in this volume, still tends to frame Puerto Ricans as "alien savages" who "challenge the forces of law and order" (chapter 12). Puerto Ricans—like other subordinate groups—are also constituted by what African-American sociologist W.E.B. Du Bois once called "double consciousness," a "sense of always looking at one's self through the eyes of others, of measuring one's soul by the tape of a world that looks on in amused contempt and pity."[12]

In addition to the awareness of being looked at as a spectacle, the people's skepticism, not to say cynicism, also rests in the assumption that actual decision-making processes are not accessible to the vast majority of Puerto Ricans. The fact that Puerto Ricans residing on the island are U.S. citizens who cannot vote in presidential elections or send a delegation to Congress, coupled with a history of racism and discrimination in the U.S. when Puerto Ricans have attempted to exercise their legal rights, has made the majority view politics as a spectacle and not the deliberative process other nationals, including many Americans, assume it to be. And to people's credit, what is spoken or performed in public—whether one lives in a republic, colony, or dictatorship—often bears little relation to how decisions are made and what action is taken. As political theorist Milovan Djilas once put it, "At intimate suppers, on hunts, in conversations between two or three men, matters of state of the most vital importance are decided. Meetings of party, conferences of the government assemblies, serve no purpose but to make declarations and put in an appearance."[13]

At the same time, the vote was not only, as Cuban performer La Lupe once famously put it, *puro teatro*. In local political terms, the results insinuated that the statehooders' growth might have reached a temporary plateau. If statehood could not win a referendum with an NPP-controlled government, relative prosperity, and a *simpatico* U.S. president (William Jefferson Clinton), then that option would not likely prevail for some time. The outcome further indicated that many participants were bored with the status question (a possibility consistent with surveys that rank crime, unemployment, and drug abuse as the most pressing priorities for island Puerto Ricans) and preferred to discuss other issues.[14] In fact, a minority of voters did just that: They reportedly took advantage of the consultation to protest Rosselló's belligerent style in handling personal and political matters.

That voters used the consultation for multiple purposes, however, has led scholars such as the sociologist Ramón Grosfoguel to dismiss the results as "not a good barometer" to analyze status politics.[15] From another place, legal scholar Christina Duffy Burnett (chapter 6) also questions the relevance of "none of the above," as for all political purposes it just means "more of the same." By refusing to engage with colonial power structures, she argues, voters only managed to endorse the continuation of colonialism in the current commonwealth form. And, to be sure, if as political scientist James C. Scott writes, "many radical attacks originate . . . in taking the values of the ruling elites seriously, while claiming that [the elites] do not,"[16] the ambiguity of "none of the above" can seem as downright reactionary.

Yet, although largely orchestrated by the PDP, a political entity described by cultural critic Juan Duchesne Winter here (chapter 7) as "comprising banal nationalism," in rejecting the clear-cut options of political modernity and symbolically disrupting the referendum's logic, *ninguna de las anteriores* may have inadvertently done different and more intriguing work; this is its great heuristic value.

The usefulness of "none of the above" as a heuristic or, in this context, a "usually speculative formulation serving as a guide in the investigation or solution of a problem,"[17] begins with the possibility of seeing the vote as a spatial metaphor. If one organizes the results from the option that obtained the least amount of votes to the one that garnered the most,

0.1% (Commonwealth, as defined by the United States)
0.3% (Free Association, a less familiar variation of independence)
2.5% (Independence)
46.5% (Statehood)
50.3% (None of the above),

it is evident that popular sentiment traveled from a nearly universal rejection of the legally defined ELA, an alternative explicitly linked on the ballot to the will of the U.S. Congress, to another possible status or way of conceiving the status as imagined by a majority of Puerto Ricans. In supporting *ninguna de las anteriores*, some Puerto Ricans then appeared to be actively rejecting (or at least resenting) not only specific status alternatives as Rosselló declared but also the way that the status question itself was posed, the very idea that the U.S. Congress, Constitution, and/or local political parties could conceive of a single solution to address the complexity of Puerto Rican (trans)locations.

Equally important, to the extent that *ninguna de las anteriores* received more votes than any option based on either the founding of an independent state or joining an already existing nation-state, the results further implied that for a significant number of voters, the available options were overly focused on nation-state membership as the solution to Puerto Rico's problems. In this regard, the boundary between "statehood" and "none of the above" appears as an abyss, a cut-off point between the alternative that seems closest to how people "live" the ELA—statehood—and desire, the desire to imagine other alternatives, including the possibility of ignoring the status question altogether.

An emblematic detail that exemplifies this last critique is that if for idiomatic reasons *ninguna de las anteriores* was immediately translated into English as the familiar phrase "none of the above," it is actually closer in meaning to "none of the preceding." Invoking time as well as space, *ninguna de las anteriores* consigns the options of statehood, independence, and colonialism to the past and so expresses both doubt and hope in the future.[18]

In this regard, rather than "distorting" the outcome, as *Village Voice* columnist Jarrett Murphy once wrote,[19] the presence of the "none of the above" option in the consultation actually helped to expose an often, overlooked truth about the current state of the status discussion: not only that most prefer not to resolve the matter as presently articulated but also that the majority of Puerto Ricans will continue to avoid turning their full attention to status resolution until it is perceived less as a juridical question of sovereignty than as a means to ward off a dangerous threat to a way of life.

At Home with Ambiguity

But what is this way of life that is imagined to be slightly better than that of a full-fledged U.S. citizen, with all her rights and financial perks, and miles away from independence, with its promise of dignity and self-determination? If colonial domination is pornographic, that is, if it is allegedly transparent to the naked eye, how can Puerto Ricans, as the painter Charles Juhasz-Alvarado provocatively put it, look away and "live in San Juan or New Haven as if colonialism did not exist?"[20]

As it has been noted by legal scholar Efrén Rivera-Ramos, part of the answer lies in how Puerto Ricans are imperfectly produced as colonial subjects in and through U.S legal discourse.[21] While the Supreme Court infamously declared that Puerto Rico "belongs to but is not part of the United States," and the territorial clause imperially claims full sovereignty over the island, the 1917 Jones Act also confirmed that Puerto Ricans were U.S. citizens who could freely circulate though the entire national territory and legally enjoy full rights in any of the 50 states. Whereas the U.S. citizenship of Puerto Ricans, on or off the island, has never meant full political inclusion, it is important to underscore that legal discourse does not produce Puerto Ricans as "colonial" subjects per se. Instead, Puerto Ricans are imagined as "territorial" citizens whose citizenship standing and national worth significantly shifts according to location. It should then not be surprising that under current conditions, status consultations do not produce "clear" answers in the terms associated with classic anticolonial movements but an oscillation or *vacilón* between U.S. citizen and Puerto Rican national identifications, without being completely tied down to either pole.

At the same time, whilst it is undeniable that the U.S. legal apparatus has contributed to the "none of the above" vote by impossibly placing Puerto Ricans as both in and out of the polity—"foreign to the United States in a domestic sense"[22]—it would be misleading to suggest that *boricua* ambivalence toward independence or statehood is solely the product of juridical categories. Similar to other border zones, even if the metropolitan state has aspired to control every inch of the insular territory, this has been more of an imperial fantasy than a reality. As noted historian Fernando Picó lyrically writes (chapter 1), status ambiguity arguably prevails in Puerto Rico because the authoritarian yet inefficient functioning of the state has actually bred a society that is largely weary of intervention in daily life that would obstruct people's autonomy and concept of dignity. Different from the ways that anti-colonial discourse portrays the impact of imperial law on Puerto Ricans, much of *boricua* everyday practice is constituted less by an overwhelming acceptance of colonial impositions than by an impressive capacity to circumvent or re-signify the state and its laws.

In addition, while self-determination activists point out that 60 percent of the island's population reportedly lives under the federal poverty line and residents endure deteriorated infrastructure, inferior government services, high unemployment, street violence, and significantly lower wages than in the United States as a symptom of classic colonialism, economist Jaime Benson Arias observes that the island represents a "paradox" in its political-economic configuration that sets it apart from most other colonial experiences (chapter 2). Although from the 1900s to the 1940s the United States relied on conventional colonial models of extreme exploitation of local labor, the post–World War II "Operation Bootstrap" period witnessed the transformation of the island's economy from an agricultural enclave to an industrialized region of the U.S. In order to produce a "modern" labor force and expand the market for U.S. goods, the state extended labor protection laws and a range of federal programs to the island. This created an unexpected irony: A colonial move to maximize profits for specific U.S. industries in a fiercely competitive global economy also ended up providing Puerto Ricans with significantly higher standards of living and protecting workers against the more extreme dislocations produced by globalization in vulnerable nation-states.

The trade-off between U.S. capital and Puerto Rican labor in an expanding global economy was to have long-lasting consequences. With access to higher incomes, federal programs, and flexible credit came a previously unimaginable ability to consume. Just to put this life-altering change in perspective: Whereas in the 1930s two-thirds of Puerto Ricans simply did not have enough to eat, by 2003, island residents were credited with a consumer purchasing power of over $40 billion a year.[23] The fact that Puerto Rican consumption is fueled not by a "healthy" local economy but rather by, in addition to federal transfers and generous credit terms, massive (if currently waning) local government employment, high public debt, tax evasion, a substantial informal economy, and a sizable narco-trade, makes this transformation no less important. Many Puerto Ricans on the island may not be able to compete in the global economy as "legit" high wage earners, yet they still live in what a San Juan ice cream vendor I once interviewed termed "luxurious poverty," a mode of consumption based on the articulation of legal, illegal and informal sectors of the economy.[24]

If for decades consumption has been viewed by intellectuals and politicians as vulgar *consumismo*, the fact that Puerto Ricans can claim a fragile share in U.S. consumption norms and access globally produced goods has been politically transformative in another, and arguably more important, way. As anthropologist Laura Ortiz-Negrón compellingly argues (chapter 3), not only is consumption currently the main form of "social activity" for many Puerto Ricans, it is largely through, and in, consumption that people live out their fantasies of self and make sense of the social order. In contrast to political projects such as independence that pitches austerity as a means to reach a dignified collective identity in an unspecified future, or statehood that ask for further submission to federal authority, consumption promises an "open-ended possibility of satisfaction"[25] that allows people to claim their desires in the present tense as consumers. This development poses one of the most productive entanglements of Puerto Ricans in the global era: Whereas capital organizes space for its own ends and transforms citizens into consumers, it also produces the conditions for "colonial" identity to be only one of several subject positions available to *boricuas* in any given context.

The disenchantment toward official politics, as Silvia Alvarez-Curbelo further elaborates (chapter 8), also results in the pursuit of private desires by and through the latest technology and global mass media. The process through which Puerto Ricans lose themselves daily to their desires to be beautiful, powerful, or larger than life is strikingly evident in the work of both anthropologist María Isabel Quiñones Arocho on women's relationship to beauty parlors (chapter 9) and writer Félix Jiménez (chapter 18) about the little known story of Luis Omar, a gay salsa crooner who perpetrated credit-card fraud on Mexican immigrants to finance his singing career. If for the women at *el biuti*, consumption constitutes a contingent space of community in which they are simultaneously the objects of commodified culture and the subjects of their own desires, in embodying the intimate relationship between consumption, mass media, and migration, Luis Omar's story constitutes the very essence of subject production in the global era: "Me, everywhere, at all times."[26]

As Luis Omar's story reminds us, with Operation Bootstrap came not only the possibility of consuming the self in desire but also the onset of Puerto Rican migration at a grand scale. Thanks to the globalization of capital, hopes for upward mobility, and more sophisticated air travel technology, Puerto Ricans became the first mass airborne labor migration in world history.[27] From the 1940s to the 1960s alone, nearly a million Puerto Ricans left for New York and other cities to relieve the island's economy and serve as an expendable source of labor to the mainland's manufacturing sector.[28] After five decades of migration flows, there are currently more Puerto Ricans—4 million according to the 2000 census—living in the United States than in Puerto Rico.[29]

Although, at times resented by intellectuals and migrants alike, the sheer diversity and scale of migration has dramatically reshaped how *boricuas* define the relationship between nationhood and territory. In the words of Philadelphia-based artist Pepón Osorio: "We view Puerto Rico not so much as an island in the Caribbean but as [what] it is: a place that migration has stretched."[30] The constant movement of bodies, ideas, and commodities across physical and virtual spaces has also facilitated a critique of normative assumptions of nationhood. Furthermore, in constantly being "on the move," as anthropologist Jorge Duany has written (chapter 4), migration has arguably contributed to imagining Puerto Ricans as a "translocal phenomenon of a new kind."

For instance, starting with ground zero of cultural production—language—Gloria D. Prosper-Sánchez (chapter 13) makes a startling observation: Even if many insist that Puerto Rican identity is fundamentally a question of speaking standard Spanish, this definition actually excludes the majority of *boricuas* who instead are "monolingual users of non-Standard varieties, code-switchers, non-native speakers, 'Spanglish' users and bilinguals." The unreliability of Spanish as a sign of national identity goes even beyond the constant contact between Spanish and English that produces much of the vibrancy of contemporary Puerto Rican speech. As literary scholar Yolanda Martínez-San Miguel has noted (chapter 14), some Puerto Rican diasporic literature is not only linguistically "hybrid"; it is also possibly untranslatable.

Equally important, the migratory context has produced more complex notions of citizenship than those offered by mainstream national legal discourses, either in Puerto Rico or in the United States. In his take on my 1994 film *Brincando el charco: Portrait of a Puerto Rican*, Alberto Sandoval-Sánchez poetically proposes that if everyday practice, legal discourse, and mass media deny Puerto Rican gays and lesbians "national" citizenship rights, the mobile visual products of the diaspora may serve as sites in which these groups can imagine alternative forms of belonging and solidarity besides the ethnonational. Complementarily, if island legislators attempt to uphold sodomy laws in part to underscore the "national" cultural differences between Puerto Rico and the United States, queer theorist Juana María Rodríguez compellingly argues (chapter 10) that lesbian activists can skillfully use the local state's own rhetoric and the support of organizations such as the American Civil Liberties Union to force the government and its homophobic representatives to, quite literally, make a spectacle of themselves.

Likewise, as sociologist Raquel Z. Rivera (chapter 16) has observed, since dominant nationalist narratives of belonging downplay racial tensions and exclude other ethnic groups from its narrative seams, the diaspora "strikes back," in cultural critic Juan Flores's terms (chapter 15), with more inclusive conceptions of community in which being *boricua* and identifying with Dominicans and African Americans, among other possibilities, is not a contradiction in terms. The majority articulation of U.S. citizenship as a nonnegotiable right can then be understood not only as a claim on the U.S. state by colonial subjects but also as the basis of a more radical demand for citizenship in excess of national, racial, cultural, and sexual categories.

The multiple ways that national, colonial, and global discourses intersect to produce a wide range of subject positions and practices makes clear why Puerto Ricans have proven so resistant to the classical narratives of self and nation implied by all traditional status choices. Given that Puerto Ricans can presently cope with—although certainly not resolve—racial discrimination, economic precariousness, and citizen exclusion by moving resources and bodies across space, the perceived costs of becoming a state, such as loss of cultural specificity, foreclosure of other political alternatives, or greater state surveillance, appear as unnecessary risks under existing conditions. Ultimately, the status quo endures not because people are indifferent to its limitations, but because it allows a wide range of individual and group identifications to coexist without completely spoiling each other. Within this ambiguous space, there are undoubtedly tremendous conflicts, inequities, and frustrations. Yet there is a place for many contradictory versions of community and self. Voters who chose "none of the above" or are unconcerned with the status debate altogether may have then opted to live with unsettled questions, instead of choosing solutions that may create greater difficulties or divisions in the future.[31]

We Are the World

In rejecting the clear-cut alternative of a separate nation-state as a way out of colonialism, Puerto Ricans have also relied on their indirect and direct contact with postcolonial Caribbean states and their diasporas. Through these encounters, besides finding Caribbean national life unappealing, some Puerto Ricans could not help but notice the lack of enthusiasm of other national subjects for nations of their own making. As Nadi Edwards writes in a classic study on Jamaican reggae, "the subject is presented as an exile living as a permanent outsider on the postcolonial/neocolonial plantation that calls itself a nation."[32] This context has prompted Carlos Pabón to argue (chapter 5) that the centrality of global capital and the erosion of the nation-state's ability to act as a sovereign power, particularly for peripheral nations, have made the debate around solving the island's status virtually irrelevant to contemporary Puerto Rican politics.

Just as significant, although under the ELA Puerto Ricans remain the object of racism, political exclusion, and stigma as an inferior other, *boricuas* are also aware that they face many of the same difficulties as those who live in a nation-state, sometimes with more resources available to address these. Even if one accepts that Puerto Rico remains a colony, the cultural hybridity, citizenship multiplicity, and economic disjuncture experienced by Puerto Ricans over the last century is increasingly acknowledged as part and parcel of contemporary life throughout the world, including in the United States.[33] Call it postmodernity, globalization, the era of transnational capital, or none of the above, this state of affairs has significantly generalized what were often thought of as exclusively Puerto Rican peculiarities. Indeed, many aspects deemed specific to the Puerto Rican twentieth-century experience are no longer considered so.

The "none of the above" vote itself is a good way to register this convergence. Despite the fact that many people still view the vote as something that only Puerto Ricans in their political "bizarreness" would do, a glance around the globe shows that this is hardly the case.[34] In the past ten years alone, blank ballots, write-ins, absenteeism, and "none of the above"-style campaigns have been organized in several nation-states where a plurality of voters insists on conveying dissatisfaction with limited political options, the incapacity of national governments to challenge global political or economic relations, and the survival of colonial hierarchies in postcolonial life.

During the 1996 Israeli elections, for instance, approximately 80,000 nonparliamentary left and independent voters opted for blank ballots rather than cede their votes to Labor candidate Simon Peres, who was running against the conservative Likud Party's Benjamin Netanyahu. The blank votes protested the fact that despite their rhetorical differences, all Israeli candidates, including those from the leftist Labor Party, tend to enact similar policies regarding their Palestinian neighbors. Similar to voters in Puerto Rico, the Israelis who chose "blank" were participating in the democratic process to underscore that there is "an unrepresented body of voters, which is nevertheless powerful enough to damage those who do not take it into account."[35]

In Argentina, when in 2001 the economy bottomed out and the country had four presidents in two weeks, protesters hit the streets to the beat of *que se vayan todos* (everybody out). Not surprisingly, the 2002 congressional elections that followed achieved the lowest voter turnout since voting was made mandatory in 1912.[36] Holding politicians directly accountable for the nation's economic disaster and their alliance to major global financial players like the International Monetary Fund, a "record" 42 percent or 9.5 million people voted blank, abstained, or spoiled their ballots.[37] As in Israel, some voters accentuated their distaste by decorating and writing messages on their ballots; a significant number even voted for the American cartoon character Mickey Mouse.[38]

Despite the fact that a 2004 World Value Survey indicated that *boricuas* are the happiest and most satisfied people on earth, as opposed to the Russians who are the least so, one of the antivotes that most closely resembles Puerto Rico's took place in the postindustrial city of Ulyanovsk, Russia, between December 2003 and March 2004.[39] In the city's parliamentary election, an option dubbed "against all" received "nearly 20 percent of the votes, more than double what any of the 14 actual candidates won."[40] Because the majority supported "against all," the Constitution called for a second round of voting. Surprisingly, the protest vote actually increased—to 21.5 percent. Unlike Puerto Rico, the concerns here were narrowly economic; residents resented the transition to a market economy that prompted a sharp rise in unemployment, low wages, and widespread poverty. Like Puerto Ricans, however, the objective of the Russian "against all" vote was to communicate the population's discontent to the country's elites while affirming their determination to effect change and have a say.

Lastly, since 2002, there is a campaign in Ireland explicitly called "noneoftheabove.com," where a group is urging the Irish government to include the option of a "none of the above" vote in all election ballots, whether paper or electronic. The main rationale for this petition is strikingly similar to that of the 1993 Puerto Rico Supreme Court decision: that voters have a democratic right "to express their will that none of the candidates on the ballot should be their political representatives."[41] Furthermore, the organizers argue that having the none of the above column may serve to increase turnout as everyone will have an option, may improve the quality of candidates in the second round, and "at the very least, acts as a catalyst for change."[42]

The "none of the above" vote and other similar practices are then not a symptom of colonial exceptionality. Rather, if differently accented, these performances of discontent are a global response to the lack of adequate policies and political imagination. And, to the extent that these practices constitute a creative response to enduring problems, one could argue that they are a symptom, if not a solution, to what can be referred to as "political burnout."

In the Third Degree

The psychoanalytic literature defines burnout as "the inability to think creatively." In individuals and groups, burnout can result from gradual exhaustion, overinvestment in an identity or process that promises to "conquer their daily misery,"[43] and constant inhibition of one of two contradictory impulses. Unarguably, all of these symptoms are evident in the Puerto Rican case.

Gradual exhaustion, for instance, is apparent, in that over the course of 106 years, Puerto Ricans have devoted enormous amounts of energy to the status question in the hope of achieving political autonomy, economic advantage, and/or freedom from humiliation. Despite these efforts, however, contemporary Puerto Ricans are not any closer to a status resolution today than their political ancestors were in 1898. Importantly, the exhaustion stems not only by the length of time occupied by the question, but also by the fact that since all involved largely accept the idea that Congress has plenary powers over the island, Puerto Ricans can only "wait" for Washington to provide them with a solution.

The overinvestment in specific ideologies, such as the "best of both worlds" or the American Dream, has also resulted in political burnout. Whereas in the two decades following the 1952 founding of the commonwealth, many Puerto Ricans shared a belief in the project of modernity; this is less prevalent today. Puerto Ricans have witnessed the difficulties of nation-building projects in the Caribbean, the rise and evaporation of industrialization, and the failed promise of the city full of opportunity, whether San Juan, New York, or Chicago. Puerto Ricans in the United States found out the hard way that even after being born and bred in the metropolis, they would never be considered full-fledged Americans nor would they necessarily follow the mythic path of upward mobility of turn-of-the-century and early-twentieth-century European immigrants. Although these experiences have not meant the end of all hope and aspirations, they have contributed to the articulation of a critical stance regarding any political project that offers utopian release from present conditions.

The last instance, the repression of one of two contradictory impulses, partly emerges from the ELA's strategy of constituting Puerto Ricans as national subjects through culture but in "association" with the United States. Given that the local state and media industry work arduously to successfully reproduce Puerto Ricans as national subjects, yet most believe that their economic well-being and political stability comes from their ties to the United States, in being constantly asked to choose between independence or statehood, Puerto Ricans must repress either the yearning to retain an autonomous sense of nationhood or the desire to maintain U.S. citizenship and access to metropolitan wealth. While people will undoubtedly opt for traditional alternatives if circumstances make currently tired ideologies the repository of new dreams, or, if they feel forced to, asking the status question in the same terms as all prior referendums will likely continue to yield the same answers for the foreseeable future.

As a gesture of refusal, "none of the above" can then open the door to alternative ways of thinking about cultural and political practices, to ask, with Picó, "whether all along we have been asking the right questions" (chapter 1). It suggests that rather than invest such energy in constantly inhibiting contradictory impulses, limiting political agency to submissive/rebellious identities, or reading into every instance a re-inscription of an essential subordination, these may be better spent in asking different questions and resolving the specific "small" problems that erode our enjoyment of life—including those historically associated with "colonialism." A politics of small problems may offer an opportunity to produce more enabling narratives of self and community by seeing through the core assumption that political identities are based on national specificity or legal precedent, not relationships that can be continuously disrupted and reconfigured at multiple levels.[44]

Politics of Small Problems

By way of conclusion, I would like to explore the politics of small problems further, through a bittersweet example: the movement to evict the U.S. Navy from Vieques (a subject alluded to in chapters 4, 7, and 8). A small island municipality off the coast of Puerto Rico that was also the site of a naval bombing range, Vieques became the stage of large-scale protests when an errant bomb killed David Sanes Rodríguez, a local resident who was a security guard inside the base. A surge of activism bent on expelling the Navy from Vieques sprang up across Puerto Rican communities on the island and elsewhere to confront the legacy of five decades of contamination, disease, inadequate transportation, and the impoverishment of the local population.

Faced with an unprecedented level of mobilization across the traditional ideological spectrum, the leading Puerto Rican political sectors were quick to offer their analysis as they jockeyed for visibility and power. Pro-independence and other nationalist groups claimed that the people of Vieques had suffered because Puerto Rico was not a sovereign state and could not control a rapacious colonial military. Statehooders, on the other hand, declared that if Puerto Rico had been a state, the militarization of Vieques would have been prevented by the clout of the island's congressional delegation. Yet in pursuing their well-placed targets, many Vieques activists used and elided both arguments.

Numbering in the thousands, the *paz para Vieques* activists simultaneously behaved as nationalists, patriots, ecologists, feminists, religious devotees, and/or transnational agents at large, lobbying everyone from the Dalai Lama to New York City mayor Michael Bloomberg. In inhabiting various subject positions as American ethnics, Puerto Rican nationals, and U.S. citizens (to name only the most obvious), the Vieques movement drew financial resources from U.S. institutions, global supporters, and island party coffers proving that under current circumstances, "local and global connections are crucial for effective political interventions."[45] The nation is not enough.

In addition, even if most observers have remarked on the significant "unity" displayed by Puerto Ricans during the anti-navy mobilizations, the many different roles played out in Vieques actually underscored that there is no single Puerto Rican identity or struggle. In the Vieques *telenovela*, one could easily spot the *criollo* nationalist patriarchs who populated the daily broadcasts. But they were not alone. Next to them were Indian civil disobedience prophets a la Gandhi; civil rights heroes inspired by Martin Luther King, Jr.; and, as Duchesne Winter ironically observes (chapter 7), members of a *boricua* style Zapatista guerilla or Palestinian intifada, complete with keffiyehs, aliases, and (unnecessary) underground hiding quarters.

Although it is true that the anti-navy mobilization became a mass campaign after it was perceived as a "national" spectacle, this was not a classic anticolonial mobilization. Only a small minority of the Vieques activists demanded independence, the end of colonialism, or the total expulsion of the U.S. military from Puerto Rico. What most local activists agitated for was the immediate resolution to a series of "small problems" affecting their bodies and everyday lives, such as a stop to the bombing practices, the construction of health facilities, more investment from the big island, and a shorter route between Vieques and Fajardo, the nearest port. This is why the movement's success in removing the military from Vieques resulted not in a change in political status but in the navy's abandonment of outdated practices and the consolidation of a global context for Puerto Rican claims on the U.S. state.

In visualizing a politics of small problems, I do not mean to imply that the problems faced by Puerto Ricans are of lesser importance than those of other groups. Rather, an awareness of the "small problems" inherent in totalizing discourses offers a continuous means of critique. As cultural theorist José Quiroga astutely notes in his essay on classic salsa (chapter 17), even if scholars have tended to view this genre as a utopian site of resistance to colonialism and racism, salsa had the "small problem" of imagining the realm of freedom in masculine terms. By invoking smallness, I am ultimately parodying the still-dominant idea that only when the "big" problems of nation-building, state founding, and/or capitalist "development" are solved, will "the people" be liberated.

Furthermore, the articulation of a politics of small problems in no way excludes other ways of intervention, minimizes the complexities of globalization, or ignores the difficulties in disrupting the extreme—not to say obscene—concentration of power that animates globalized institutions such as the U.S. military. It instead suggests that engaging with so-called small problems may have far-reaching implications on all power structures as culture has become politics; politics become, economics; and economics become, culture. In this regard, a politics of small problems is the opposite of a traumatized politics based on national identity: It aims to confront the new as if it were new, seeing it with fresh eyes. This is why the volume closes with an analysis of the accused "dirty bomber" Jose Padilla a.k.a. Abdullah Al-Muhajir's (Coda), a man whose "none of the above" identity cost him all of the state's wrath.

In naming this volume *None of the Above*, I then am not interested in validating any particular status option or reducing politics to this debate. Instead, the book loosely offers *ninguna de las anteriores* as a "certain way" to explore the intricacy of Puerto Rican locations in an increasingly uncertain world.[46] At times, the gesture of refusal embedded in "none of the above" allowed contributors to challenge the categories through which Puerto Ricans continue to be produced as racially, culturally, and politically deviant from a national, racial, or linguistic norm. At others, the term's ambiguity invited alternative ways of thinking about practices that we may not yet fully apprehend. At all times, *ninguna de las anteriores* hopes to offer a space to critically engage with the totalizing impulses of colonialism, nationalism, and globalization in a "none of the above" world.

Notes

1. José Trías Monge, *Puerto Rico: The Trials of the Oldest Colony in the World* (New Haven: Yale University Press, 1999).
2. Carlos Pabón, *Nación Postmortem: ensayos sobre los tiempos de la insoportable ambigüedad* (San Juan: Ediciones Callejón, 2002).
3. Christina Duffy Burnett and Burke Marshall, "Introduction," in *Foreign in a Domestic Sense: Puerto Rico, American Expansion, and the Constitution*, ed. Christina Duffy Burnett and Burke Marshall (Durham, NC: Duke University Press, 2001), 1–36, 22.
4. Roberto Sánchez-Vilella, *Noel Colón Martínez v. Estado Libre Asociado de Puerto Rico et al.*, Jurisprudencia del Tribunal Supremo, 93 JTS 136, 134 DPR 445, 11175–93.
5. Angel R. Oquendo, "Liking to be in America: Puerto Rico's Quest for Difference in the United States," 14 *Duke Journal of Comparative and International Law*, 249 (2005): 1–58.
6. Letter from Don Young to Pedro Rosselló, April 16, 1999. Contained in *Chairman Don Young and Senior Democratic Member George Miller to*

Members, Committee on Resources, The Results of the 1998 Puerto Rico Plebiscite (Washington, DC: US Government Printing Office, 1999), I–III, 5–41, 11.

7. "Puerto Rico Leaders Demand to Know Political Status Options; Senators Reply That Some Want 'Free Lunch,' "*PRHerald.com*, May 6, 1999.
8. Ibid.
9. Ibid.
10. Ibid.
11. Robert Friedman, "Parties Asked Interpretation of the Results of Plebiscite," *The San Juan Star*, April 17, 1999, 4.
12. W.E.B. DuBois, *The Souls of Black Folk* (New York: Penguin, 1989), 5.
13. Quoted in James C. Scott, *Domination and the Arts of Resistance: Hidden Transcripts* (New Haven: Yale University Press, 1990), 12.
14. "Puerto Rico Concerned About Crime, Unemployment, Drugs," *Puerto Rico Herald*, April 29, 2002, <www.prherald.com>.
15. Ramón Grosfoguel, *Colonial Subjects: Puerto Ricans in a Global Perspective* (Berkeley: University of California Press, 2003), 44.
16. James C. Scott, *Domination and the Arts of Resistance: Hidden Transcripts* (New Haven: Yale University Press, 1990), 106.
17. http://www.answers.com/topic/heuristic
18. I would like to thank my friend and colleague Chon Noriega for pointing this out to me.
19. Jarrett Murphy, "Puerto Rico to Vote . . . on What?," March 6, 2006, <http://www.villagevoice.com/blogs/powerplays/archives/002496.php>
20. Not coincidentally, a 2004 exhibit of contemporary Puerto Rican art curated by Deborah Cullen, Silvia Karman Cubiñá, and Steven Holmes and featuring Juhasz-Alvarado, among other artists, was titled "None of the Above." The objective of the show, which symptomatically first opened in Hartford, Connecticut, and then moved to Museo de Arte de Puerto Rico in San Juan, was to propose "a new way of seeing and thinking about Puerto Rican art, reshaping the standard curatorial frameworks that have tended to privilege nationalism, identity politics and/or geography." The influences of the artists were framed as "aesthetic," "personal," and "engaged in an international artistic dialogue," where local politics such as the status was neither central nor defining.
21. Efrén Rivera-Ramos, *The Legal Construction of Identity: The Judicial and Social Legacy of American Colonialism in Puerto Rico* (Washington, DC: American Psychological Association, 2001).
22. Quoted in Duffy Burnett and Burke Marshall, "Between the Foreign and the Domestic," in Burnett and Marshall, eds., *Foreign in a Domestic Sense.*
23. Commonwealth of Puerto Rico, Office of the Governor, Planning Board, *Economic Report to the Governor 2004* (Statistical Appendix), A-1.
24. This interview was produced in relation to my film-in-progress, *Regarding Vieques*, video, 56 minutes.
25. Celeste Olalquiaga, *Megalopolis: Contemporary Cultural Sensibilities* (Minneapolis: University of Minnesota Press, 1992), xviii.
26. Jacques Attali, *Fraternidades* (Barcelona: Ediciones Paidos Iberica, 2000), 25. My translation from the Spanish: "Yo, en todas partes, enseguida."
27. Clara E. Rodríguez, *Puerto Ricans Born in the USA* (Boston: Unwin Hyman, 1989), 3.

28. María Pérez y González, *Puerto Ricans in the United States* (Westport, CT: Greenwood Press, 2000), 64.
29. Rodríguez, *Puerto Ricans*, 3.
30. Marvette Pérez and Yvonne Lasalle, "Interview with Pepón Osorio," *Radical History Review* 73 (1999): 4–21, 5.
31. Ira Sharkansky, *Ambiguity, Coping, and Governance: Israeli Experience in Politics, Religion and Policymaking* (Westport, CT: Praeger, 1999), 145.
32. Nadi Edwards, "States of Emergency," *Social and Economic Studies* 47: 1 (1998): 21–32, 28.
33. José Trías Monge, *Puerto Rico: The Trials of the Oldest Colony in the World* (New Haven, CT: Yale University Press, 1999).
34. Jarrett Murphy, "Puerto Rico to Vote . . . on What?" *The Village Voice*, March 3, 2006, <http://villagevoice.com/blogs/powerplays/archives/002496.php>
35. Tanya Reinhart, "The Blank Ballot Strategy," October 1996, 1–5, 3, <www.zmag.org/zmag/articles/oct96reinhart.htm>.
36. Andrés Oppenheimer, "Latin American elections marred by decline in voting," *The Miami Herald*, May 30, 2002, 1–3, 1, <www.miami.com/mld/miamiherald/news/world/americas/3361>.
37. Ibid.
38. Ibid.
39. "The World's Happiest and Unhappiest Peoples," *The Orlando Sentinel*, March 27, 2005, reprinted in <http://www/puertorico-herald.org/issues2/2005/vol109n13/Media3-en>.
40. Steven Lee Myers, "Only in Russia: 'None of the Above' Is on Ballot, and Wins," *New York Times*, March 23, 2004, 2–4, 2 in *Puerto Rico Herald* <www.puertorico-herald.org/issues/2004/vol8no20/OnlyRussia>.
41. "None of the Above: Campaign for a 'None of the Above' option on electronic ballots," <http://www/noneoftheabove.ie/>
42. Ibid.
43. Stijn Vanheule, "The Dynamics of Burnout: An Analysis from a Freudo-Lacanian Point of View," <http://www.ispo.org/Symposia/Paris/ 2001vanheule.htm>, 4.
44. I arrived at this formulation after entering into a dialogue with Lisa Uperesa and Adriana Garriga López regarding their essay, "Differential Colonialism and Multiple Sovereignties: Comparative Perspectives on Puerto Rico and American Samoa-or-As a Matter of Choice." This paper was delivered as part of a conference that I organized at Columbia University's Center for the Study of Ethnicity and Race titled *Sovereignty Matters: An Interdisciplinary Conference on Sovereignty in Native American, Pacific Islander, and Puerto Rican Communities* on April 15, 2005. The essay will also appear in an upcoming volume that I will edit, *Sovereign Acts* (Cambridge, MA: South End Press, 2007).
45. Grosfoguel, *Colonial Subjects*, 17.
46. Antonio Benítez Rojo, *The Repeating Island: The Caribbean and the Postmodern Perspective* (Durham, NC: Duke University Press, 1992).

PART I

The Politics of Ambiguity

CHAPTER 1

The Absent State

Fernando Picó

Since the sixteenth century, the state in Puerto Rico has been present in the island's capital, has been personified by a governor, and has had a visible seat of power: La Fortaleza (the fortress). From there, it has issued orders, arrested, imprisoned, and even executed people. The state has dealt with pirates and invaders; has issued rules concerning coinage, health, labor, education, and public welfare; and has presided over the construction of public works. As it befits its station, it has also represented power, rationality, order, and civic pride.

Although the state in Puerto Rico at some time or another has performed most of the duties it has been entitled to carry out, it has been, for many extended periods of time, absent from the everyday life of the communities and the individuals of most portions of the island. It may seem paradoxical that one of the longest-lasting political apparatus in the Western Hemisphere, extant since 1508, scarcely changing in its attributes, functions, and laws throughout the many phases and evolutions in administration, has never fully encompassed the Puerto Rican territory, only 100 miles long by 35 miles wide. It has been, in many ways, an absent state.

In the first three centuries of its existence, after the island's discovery in 1493, the Spanish state in Puerto Rico hardly reached beyond the capital city. Many were the orders issued, the restraints, prohibitions, warnings, plans, and ordinances taken by hand relay from one municipal territory (*partido*) to the next. Some historians have given into the temptation of elaborating our history with the testimony of all those edicts and circulars. More interesting is to find out what actually happened with these orders at the other end.

From the early years of the seventeenth century, for instance, the island was a smuggling haven. The goods that could not be obtained from the Spanish port of Seville, because the galleons from the fleet only rarely stopped in the capital, the only authorized port, were cheap and plentifully traded by the Dutch, the English, and the French in exchange for cattle, hides, lumber, foodstuffs, ginger, tobacco, and molasses. As the years passed, the illegal trade with the other Europeans became so extended that by the end of the seventeenth century even the governor and the bishop were accused of investing in it. This reality induced historian Arturo Morales Carrión to speak of the two Puerto Rican societies of the seventeenth century, the officially constituted and the one engaged in illegal trade with the other Europeans.[1]

Repeated orders of Spanish rulers, issued in the Council of the Indies responsible for the overseas colonies, forbade that foreigners settle on the island. Yet, it only takes a glimpse at the eighteenth-century parish registers of towns, such as Arecibo, Coamo, or Utuado, to see that the Irish, French, Italians, Portuguese, and occasional Briton and German are happily married and eventually buried in some corner of the island. When partly as a response to the Haitian revolution, the Spanish crown finally granted legal entry to non-Spaniards through the *La Real Cédula de Gracias* of 1815, hundreds of Europeans and West Indians came forth to legalize their prolonged residence on the island.[2]

Smuggling and illegal immigration (activities that continue unabated to this day) are only two of the many areas in which legal statutes were ignored or defied. The first local officials, the *tenientes a guerra* (lieutenants), were instituted in 1692 to bring some presence of the public authorities at the local level.[3] But the *tenientes a guerra* were also local landholders, subject to the pressures of their peers, and connected by ties of marriage and *compadrazgo* (spiritual kinship derived from becoming foster fathers at baptism) to the persons they were supposed to watch over. Their capacity to implement the government's edicts was always limited by the desire of the local elites to run their affairs unhampered. The *milicias urbanas*, the local "urban militias," evidenced the same attachments. They responded more to their captains (local landowners) than to the abstract authority in the island's capital.

Another compelling example of how local investments superseded metropolitan imperatives occurred when the British government attempted to take over San Juan in 1797. These militiamen, who were often slack and remiss in pursuing smugglers and slave runaways converged on the capital, were instrumental in fighting the British and forcing their retreat. Ironically, the authorities would later appeal to the pride felt by the *criollos* for their intervention against the British to seek consent when imposing fiscal and surveillance measures against the colony.[4]

Historians have debated the impact of the eighteenth-century Bourbon reforms on Puerto Rico.[5] The liberalization of trade, concession of land titles, and reorganization of the military were measures that in the long run would help shape the entry of Puerto Rico into the nineteenth-century Atlantic market and ensure the island's value for Spain after the loss of most if its American empire. The question, however, is whether these measures changed significantly the attitudes and habits of the rural inhabitants. The granting of titles to the land and the division of the *hatos* (undivided and hereditary land grants), for instance, created a land market on the coastal alluvial plains that promptly resulted in the formation of sugarcane haciendas and the displacement of the creole population from the ranks of the landholders.[6] As *agregados* or squatters in the new haciendas, or as displaced persons who drifted to the mountains, the landless would be separated from the interventions of the state by the interposition of *hacendados* on whom the landless came to depend.

In the nineteenth century, especially after 1824, when the second constitutional regime ended and Spain lost all other territories in the New World except Cuba, the Spanish state in Puerto Rico attempted to make its presence felt at the municipal level in ways in which it had not succeeded in doing before. Immigrants were named to head the municipalities. The governor made periodic visits to town governments and left detailed instructions. New regulations colored the whole realm of social relations, from cockfighting to dances, from rules for urban decorum to those enacting the proper respect for authorities. To travel from one municipality to the next, a permit was necessary. Taxes were more efficiently collected. Vagrancy was punished with forced labor in public works. Rosters were made for compulsory and unpaid (corvée) labor on highways. The government tried to force couples living together to marry. An inventory was kept up of all beasts of burden, and owners were asked from time to time to lend them for municipal business.[7]

Apathy and resistance met all these and other attempts by the state to regulate private life. Monthly lists of those fined or imprisoned for not obeying government circulars were published in *La Gaceta*, the government's paper. Thus we find that in the western town of Aguadilla in September 1840, Juan Sanabria was fined two pesos for having gone fishing without a license.[8] In April 1842, Simón de Ribera, from Aguas Buenas, was fined one peso and had to pay another "processing" peso for having serenaded without a license.[9] Jorge Colón, from Aibonito, was fined in October 1849 for allowing his son to fly a kite on a working day, but since he was insolvent he had to spend two days in prison.[10] The lists of people fined are especially long in the period between 1850 and 1854 and coincides with Governor Juan de la Pezuela's regulations for day laborers and Governor Fernando de Norzagaray's instructions for corvée labor for his highway construction program.

The contentions around the state's efforts to dictate the contours of daily life escalated after the 1866–67 recession. At that juncture, the state attempted to regenerate its finances by having taxes paid at the beginning of the fiscal year and by impounding land and cattle in lieu of back taxes. The hurricanes and earthquakes of 1867, the frustrations for the failure of the 1866 Junta de Ultramar (Overseas Council) to discuss the political aspirations of the Cuban and Puerto Rican delegates, and the fiscal pressures of 1868 led to the Grito de Lares. This revolution was the biggest anti-Spanish manifestation in the history of the island and articulated the economic frustrations of nearly ruined landowners, the political project of the creoles, the rejection of coerced labor by the *jornaleros* (day laborers), and the emancipation hopes of the enslaved population.[11]

The Spanish state entered a phase of modernization in the 1868–73 period. The Bourbons were temporarily displaced from the throne, and a constitutional convention was convened. Although the Bourbon dynasty was restored in 1875, the processes of modernization that had come alive in Spain continued to modify the old institutions. Inevitably the reforms of the 1870s and the 1880s had their echo in Puerto Rico. The most salient reforms of this period included the abolition of slavery and freedom of the press, assembly, and religion.

Some of these reforms were desired and welcomed by the growing liberal movement in Puerto Rico, but the generality of the population either resisted or was apathetic to change. It did not matter that the Spanish state's projects for Puerto Rico were changing. Traditional mistrust of the state's initiatives remained. Thus Governor Eugenio Despujols's 1880 decree on universal education for the young was met not only by the hostility and indifference of the rural population but also by the animadversion of the propertied classes, some of whose voices were heard doubting the wisdom of schooling the rural children. Regulations on public health issues, the demographic register, the property registry, urban ordinances, the implantation of the Spanish civil code, the introduction of civil weddings, religious toleration for Protestants, the widening of the electoral franchise, and other reforms also met mixed reception. The modernizing Spanish state may have been perceived as an interloper and an intruder.

Success, therefore, was not guaranteed for its successor, the American state in Puerto Rico. As it has been amply documented, U.S. troops invaded Puerto Rico through the port of Guánica on July 25, 1898 and quickly proceeded to occupy its new colony. Despite cultural, linguistic, and political differences, many of the measures that the American authorities instituted in the early years of the twentieth century were in direct continuity with those of the Spanish authorities. There were changes in emphasis, no doubt, and the economic beneficiaries of franchises and licenses changed, but the modernizing thrust was in line with metropolitan interests to maximize the rationalization of economic and social structures.

The displaced creole and Spanish elites went into a resistance mode to the new state's reforms, such as compulsory primary education. This resistance was epitomized by the proliferation of schools and tutors for girls from propertied families, who chose this course of action so that they would not have to attend public school with the children of the workers. Although the new elite associated with the booming sugar export economy and the professions readily Americanized, this Americanization was often the excuse to adopt the racial and class prejudices of the invaders, but not their pragmatism nor investment in raising the skill level of the masses.

Much has been written about the American administrators' effort to impose their language and culture on Puerto Rico,[12] but the resistance to these policies has remained in the haze of mythology and has not been an object of systematic verification. What is often forgotten is that resistance was not circumscribed to the issues dear to cultural nationalists, but that it also involved mistrust and sabotage of government directives and policies on health, labor, welfare, urban order, and social relations. When the Puerto Rican religious leaders known as Hermanos Cheos were conducting Catholic revival meetings in the early 1900s, they were not only affirming their own traditional values but also opposing religious toleration for Protestants. In another context, it was the Iowan Governor Horace Towner who practically forced the Puerto Rican legislature to extend the suffrage to women by threatening to have Congress pass it instead.[13] These would be two of the many instances in which the neo-nationalist examination of resistance to American domination has only considered the cultural side of the issues.

Some forms of popular resistance to social regulations in the 1920s bore with them ambiguities that have not been easily ironed away by those who prefer their history moral and pedagogical. Prohibition, voted in by the majority in a referendum in July 1917, soon proved nearly impossible to enforce. The constant destructions of stills (distilleries) and the prosecution of operators, bearers, and vendors of rum hardly made a dent on production and consumption. The police force was conscientious in conducting raids but a whole network of dissembling, evading, and conniving frustrated their efforts.

Although the defiance of Prohibition eventually became a folkloric theme, an examination of police records of the period shows the complexity of the situation. Who was defying whom? In Carolina, one of the principal Republican leaders had a still in his farm and supplied consumption in town, but then prominent figures both in the Socialist and in the Liberal camps were known as chronic alcoholics. Of course none of the political leaders was ever caught in a raid, although it was evident from the records that the police knew that they were breaking the law. Resistance bred corruption, but since an example had to be made from time to time, it was the small time producers and their runners who paid.

Analogous features characterized the persecution of cockfights, a popular sport on the island. The season started right on Epiphany. The police made regular raids on the known arenas but rarely made any arrests because they just failed to get there during an actual cockfight. The same Republican leader in Carolina who had a still also had a *gallera* (cockfighting arena), but so did another one of the prominent local politicians, father of a future governor. Cockfights may have been illegal, but in 1928 when a respected person in town, a doctor, went to the police station to complain that a $100 rooster had been stolen from his yard, the police duly tracked down the robber and returned the $100 rooster to his owner.[14] No questions asked, not even when the municipal judge reported that one of his roosters had been stolen.[15]

The police were efficient in recovering the stolen goods, but not in preventing the cockfights. Corruption? No, it would be an anachronistic word to describe these social dynamics. Perhaps divided loyalties as sociability was more important than law enforcement. Obviously, and despite operating under a "rule of law," the state was not able to convince its own agents of its priorities.

If one shifts the focus to the mountain town of Cayey during the same period, one finds that the manufacture of rum and cockfights were equally prevalent. The participation of the town's elite in these activities was much more discrete than in Carolina. But the effect was the same. Some rural landowners disliked the vicinity of distilleries because the stills propitiated petty thievery in their neighborhood. They offered bland assistance to the police. In one instance, when two policemen raided barrio Lapa looking for stills, one of the landowners told them that stills were not operated on Sunday.[16] In neighboring barrio Cercadillo, another landowner, who complained that he often lost chickens to thieves, "offered his protection to the police who patrolled those barrios." One wonders how someone who could not guard his own henhouse could protect the police, but the gesture was grand.

All the elements of the picaresque novel are there, but no one was fooled. The same mechanisms of resistance that were put into place to protect stills and cockfights also operated in other matters. The enforcement of public health ordinances, for instance, was met with the same evasions and subterfuges. In Carolina during the early 1920s, just before Christmas, the police searched the backyards for pigs. People were fined for keeping them behind their homes. Each following year the same searches were conducted. The fine must have been part of the cost of fattening one's pig for the Christmas roast. But if one of those pigs was stolen, the police would soon learn of it. It was not just pigs. Goats were put to pasture on the town square in 1921, cows for milking would be kept in sheds in the backyards (one of them gored a passerby in the 1920s, and another was stolen from its shed with its calf), and of course horses were still around. The public health commissioner would periodically complain of the hazards brought by this perpetuation of the countryside in the town, but people went on ignoring him.

It has been argued that the welfare and economic development policies of the state in Puerto Rico in the last two-thirds of the twentieth century reconciled the generality of Puerto Ricans to a heightened presence of the state in their lives. True, people tend to accept social security, food stamps, land allotments, health benefits, and educational opportunities, but it is also true that many resist every effort to exact accountability for these benefits. Most people lack the necessary documents and licenses to validate the legality of their daily routines. According to economist Elías Gutierrez, the parallel economy, which is not restricted to the drug traffic and includes informal and underground economic activities, may account for half of the worth of the Puerto Rican economy. The weakness of the state is further attested by the frequency of corruption charges. The high homicide rates bear out people's distrust of the judicial capacity of the state; private vengeance rather than public prosecution claims the redress of murders.

With these realities in mind, one may truly question whether the reluctance to endorse decisively any political status option for Puerto Rico comes from indecision—an inability to choose between becoming an independent republic or a state of the union—or from people's lack of inclination to enhance the powers of the state with a well-defined resolution of status that may bring about a greater state presence in people's daily lives. Most commentators wonder whether Puerto Ricans want independence, statehood, or an enhanced commonwealth. Perhaps they should ask whether they want more government or less, more state powers, and more accountability to the state.

The only way in which people may accept the development of the state in any of its conventional versions is by allowing communities and grassroots organizations to intervene more decisively in the local public issues. Under contemporary democracy, people in Puerto Rico do not even elect district assemblymen for the municipal government; they are all elected in a general slate. Would not the direct election of assemblymen, directly responsible to their neighbors, be a first step in the strengthening of municipal governments? And would not municipal governments that are more responsive to people's needs gain more of the public's trust? I do not know the answers, but I wonder whether all along we have been asking the right questions.

Notes

1. Arturo Morales Carrión, *Puerto Rico and the Non Hispanic Caribbean: A Study of the Decline of Spanish Exclusivism* (Río Piedras: Universidad de Puerto Rico, 1971). See also Angel López Cantos, *Historia de Puerto Rico 1650–1700* (Sevilla: Escuela de Estudios Hispanoamericanos, 1978); Luis González Vales, *Gabriel Gutiérrez de Riva "El Terrible"* (San Juan: Centro de Estudios Avanzados de Puerto Rico y el Caribe, 1990), 106–11; Héctor Feliciano Ramos, *El contrabando inglés en el Caribe y el Golfo de México (1748–1778)* (Sevilla: Diputación Provincial, 1990).
2. Estela Cifre de Loubriel, *La inmigración a Puerto Rico en el siglo 19* (San Juan: Instituto de Cultura Puertorriqueña, 1964); Pedro J. Hernández, "Los inmigrantes italianos de Puerto Rico durante el siglo XIX," *Anales de Investigación Histórica* III, no. 2 (1976); Ursula Acosta and David E. Cuesta Camacho, *Familias de Cabo Rojo* (Hormigueros: the authors, 1983).
3. Cf. Walter Cardona, *Aguada: notas para su historia* (San Juan: Comité de Historia de los Pueblos, 1985), 46.
4. Cf. Gilberto Aponte, *San Mateo de Cangrejos (Comunidad cimarrona en Puerto Rico): notas para su historia* (San Juan: Comité de Historia de los Pueblos, 1985).
5. Cf. Francisco Scarano, "Puerto Rico y el reformismo borbónico, 1750–1791," *Puerto Rico: cinco Siglos de Historia* (San Juan: McGraw-Hill, 1993); Altagracia Ortiz, *Eighteenth-Century Reforms in the Caribbean: Miguel de Muesas, Governor of Puerto Rico 1769–1776* (Rutherford: Farleigh Dickinson University Press, 1983); Bibiano Torres Ramírez, *La Compañía Gaditana de Negros* (Sevilla: Escuela de Estudios Hispano-Americanos, 1973).
6. Francisco Scarano, *Sugar and Slavery in Puerto Rico: The Plantation Economy of Ponce, 1800–1850* (Madison: University of Wisconsin Press, 1984); Pedro San Miguel, *El mundo que creó el azúcar: las haciendas en Vega Baja, 1800–1873* (Río Piedras: Ediciones Huracán, 1989).
7. Cf. Lidio Cruz Monclova, *Historia de Puerto Rico (siglo XIX)*, vol. I (Río Piedras: Editorial Universitaria, 1970).

8. *Gaceta*, October 27, 1840, 4.
9. Ibid., May 28, 1842, 3.
10. Ibid., December 6, 1849, 4.
11. Cf. Olga Jiménez de Wagenheim, *El grito de Lares: sus causas y sus hombres* (Río Piedras: Ediciones Huracán, 1984); Laird W. Bergad, "Toward Puerto Rico's Grito de Lares: Coffee, Social Stratification and Class Conflicts, 1828–1868," *Hispanic American Historical Review* 60 (1980): 617–42.
12. Cf. Aida Negrón de Montilla, *Americanization in Puerto Rico and the Public School System, 1900–1930* (Río Piedras: Editorial Edil, 1971).
13. Cf. Truman R. Clark, *Puerto Rico and the United States, 1917–1933* (Pittsburgh: University of Pittsburgh Press, 1975).
14. *Libro de Novedades de la Policía de Carolina*, IX, 142.
15. *Libro de Novedades de la Policía de Carolina*, VII, 58.
16. *Libro de Novedades de la Policía de Cayey*, July 18, 1925.

CHAPTER 2

Sailing on the USS *Titanic*: Puerto Rico's Unique Insertion to Global Economic Trends

Jaime Benson Arias

The fact that since the United States claimed sovereignty over Puerto Rico in 1898, the island has become increasingly integrated into the metropolitan economy, with important social, cultural, and political consequences, has brought to the forefront the question of whether Puerto Rico is a national economy on its own ground or whether it is an economic region of the United States. In this chapter, I argue the latter premise to sketch out Puerto Rico's paradoxical participation into current global economic trends.

From 1900 to 1935, for instance, the island was a sugar and tobacco enclave of U.S. free market capitalism, characterized by high structural and seasonal unemployment, low stagnant flexible wages, weak labor protection laws, a lack of a social safety net, and widespread poverty. From 1947 to 1970, as part of Operation Bootstrap industrialization program, Puerto Rico became a differentiated region of U.S. mass consumer manufacturers, and most of the mainland's labor protection laws and the social safety net were partially extended to the island. As a result, the island became a modern U.S. industrial enclave providing its residents with one of the highest standards of living in Latin America and the Caribbean.

As a very particular participant of the U.S. post-Fordist model of capitalist development, Puerto Rico has since 1980 been part of the new global trends in production, trade, finance, and communications that characterizes contemporary world capitalism.[1] Specifically, Puerto Rico has become an enclave of U.S. pharmaceutical and computer hardware production and assembly operations global networks and its array of derived trade, financial, and informational flows. As a regional armature of the United States, that is, a region with limited local government under a central authority that makes possible capitalist accumulation in the greater political entity of which the region is a differentiated part, Puerto Rico has been simultaneously insulated and exposed to some of the most severe and perverse effects of current global capitalist trends.[2]

The island's particular insertion into current global economic trends constitutes an interesting paradox. On the one hand, the island's particular insertion into the mainland's increasingly neoliberal capitalist mode of regulation with its greater exposure to global trends has accentuated forms of labor exploitation, contingent employment, environmental destruction, social destitution, and financial speculation. On the other hand, the fact that Puerto Rico is a distinct part of three crucial components of the mainland economy (the U.S. dollar, the U.S. market or customs system, and U.S. citizenship), has safeguarded islanders from undue exposure to the dire consequences of financial disturbances that result from speculative movements on domestic currencies and banks. It has also provided its residents with minimum labor, environmental and social guarantees against current global labor super-exploitation, extreme poverty, and acute forms of environmental destruction. The paradoxical insertion of the island into global production, trade, financial, informational, and political networks is critical in understanding insular economic, social, and political dynamics.

Inside the Monster: Puerto Rico's Insertion into the Global Economy

From the early 1980s, the U.S. economy has increased its participation in the globalization of production, trade, and finances. A response to the decrease in profitability that took place in the context of the decline and subsequent demise of the U.S. self-centered Fordist model of capitalist development, from the mid-1960s to the late 1970s,[3] spurred by the increased use and cost of capital equipment, stagnant labor productivity, and skyrocketing oil prices. The globalization of production and trade has contributed to restore long-run profitability. It has accomplished this goal by liberalization of internal labor markets and access to global unskilled, semiskilled, and skilled low-waged labor, as well as greater access to foreign consumer markets and low-cost foreign intermediate industrial goods and services.

Economic globalization and the increasingly hegemonical role assumed by financial capital configured a new neoliberal mode of regulation that, combined with a new flexible regime of capitalist accumulation, restored profitability and growth to the United States. The latter was achieved by reductions in the social wage, regressive tax cuts, expansionary fiscal policy in the form of sharp increases in military spending, a monetarist approach to monetary policy, deregulation of industry, finances, and labor markets. The emergence of new computerized manufacturing, distribution, and telecommunications technologies partially compensated for stagnant growth in labor productivity, enhanced productive versatility by means of economies of scoop,[4] and reduced the transaction costs related to time and distance factors, of global production, trade, and financial networks.

Globalization of production and trade provided transnational capital with three pools of labor in one global network of production, namely (1) the unskilled low-wage labor with a large contingent of women and also children in some late industrial countries such as Malaysia, Indonesia, the Philippines, Thailand, Pakistan, and recently Vietnam; (2) the semi-skilled low-wage labor of these countries as well as those of the new industrialized ones or "nics" such as South Korea, Singapore, Taiwan, India, China, Brazil, and Mexico; (3) the high-skill, low-wage labor of the nics plus the high-skill, higher-wage labor of the industrialized countries such as the United States, Japan, and the main players of the European Economic Community.

The greater competition and exposure of the U.S. labor market to the labor markets of countries with weak or no social safety nets, little if any labor rights, and authoritarian regimes have contributed to keep in check real wages in the United States[5] while putting a cap on the wage growth in the nics and industrial latecomers. The various GATT agreements since the mid-1960s that culminated in the constitution of the World Trade Organization in 1995 as well as the coming into effect of NAFTA in 1994 has contributed to the simultaneous opening of the U.S. market to different types of foreign imports and opening of foreign markets to all kind of U.S. exports. Imports to the United States as a proportion of GDP have risen from 4.2 percent in 1960 to 14.6 percent in the year 2000.[6] U.S. exports to the rest of the world as a proportion of GDP have risen from 4.8 percent in 1960 to 12 percent in 1999.[7]

During the same period, U.S. corporations expanded the relative presence of their production networks or foreign affiliates throughout the world, and foreign corporations expanded the relative presence of their production networks in the United States as reflected by the increase in the relative shares of Foreign Direct Investment (FDI) of the United States abroad and Foreign Direct Investment in the United States of Gross Private Domestic Investment (GPDI). The share of U.S. FDI abroad of GPDI increased from 3.7 percent in 1960 to 8.6 percent in the year 2000, while the share of FDI in the United States of GPDI rose from 0.4 percent in 1960 to 16.3 percent in 2000.[8]

The subordinate, auxiliary, and facilitating role to industrial capital accumulation that financial capital assumed in the industrialized world during the Golden Age of Fordism, from 1950 to 1980, gave way to a new hegemonic position for financial capital in the post-Fordist era. This new hegemony of financial capital assumed multiple expressions since the early 1980s: rapid and profound financial deregulation, a monetarist approach to monetary policy that pursues as its main macroeconomic goal the achievement of price stability, the diffusion of financial speculation with corporate industrial assets for short-term gains and the subsequent rise in hostile corporate takeovers, the process of financial deepening of industrial firms, greater industrial concentration in all sectors by means of the rapid growth in corporate mega-merges, the mass diffusion of stock market activity, the creation of the high-risk junk bond market, the growth of high-risk investment funds, the fast and continuous creation of all types of new financial and monetary instruments, the vigorous growth in financial brokerage, and insurance and real state activities, among others.

In the context of the demise of U.S. Fordism in the early 1980s, Puerto Rico experienced a transformation from an enclave of labor-intensive apparel, textile, food products, and consumer durables manufacturing, with a growing capital intensive oil refining and petrochemical complex, into a financial tax haven for U.S. transnational technologically intensive pharmaceutical and computer hardware intermediate and final assembly operations. From 1950 to 1970, Puerto Rico was a differentiated part of the articulation of mass production with mass consumption that constituted the U.S. Fordist regime of capitalist accumulation. It was the world's leading supplier of clothing and textile goods to the U.S. market, while also hosting the subsidiary mass production operations of some of the main U.S. manufacturing corporations, such as RCA, Westinghouse, General Electric, Ford Motor Company, Coca Cola, Goya, Sun Oil, Union Carbide, and others. The island was also the sixth most important consumer market in the world for U.S. final goods.

The uneven incorporation of islanders to U.S. norms of mass consumption during the Golden Age of Fordism was achieved through the extension to Puerto Rico of the main institutional mechanisms of the U.S. Keynesian mode of regulation: collective bargaining (20 percent of the total labor force and 36 percent of the mainly feminine labor force in the apparel industry was unionized); state unemployment insurance; gradual enforcement of federal minimum wages; federal and local welfare transfer payments, federal and local public housing; the federal social security program; the massive concession by banks of residential mortgage and personal loans; the substantial emission of consumer credit cards (American Express, Visa, Master Card); the establishment throughout the island of the main U.S. retail stores such as Sears, JC Penney's, Woolworth's, K-Mart, and their consumer credit network; among others. In the midst of the crisis of Fordism in the mid-1970s, the Federal Food Stamp Program was also fully extended to the island.

As a differentiated region of the U.S. self-centered accumulation regime, Puerto Rico imported almost all of what it consumed and exported most of what it produced from and to the United States. Its openness to the rest of the world in terms of trade and financial flows as well as production networks was meager. With the exception of considerable oil imports and soap operas from Venezuela, some exposure to Cuban radio and TV shows until the early 1960s, and Mexican movies and soap operas up to the late 1960s, the island's economic and cultural relationship with countries other than the United States was very weak.

The greater openness of the U.S. market to the apparel and textile products from low-wage countries in Central America, Asia, and the Caribbean in the early 1970s, as an effect of the Kennedy Rounds GATT negotiations in Montevideo, Uruguay of 1965, resulted in the displacement of the island's apparel and textile industry as the main supplier of the U.S. market. In the context of rising wages and stagnant growth in labor productivity, Puerto Rico's garment industry was seriously wounded and lost over 13,000 jobs in the next decade.

The crisis of U.S. Fordism entailed the complete breakdown of the Puerto Rican model of industrial development by the mid-1970s. Falling profitability and rising wages undermined the two main pillars of Operation Bootstrap: tax exemption on U.S. manufacturing direct investment and low wages. The approval by Congress of Section 936 of the Internal Revenue Code in 1976 marked the incorporation of the island into the new patterns of U.S. extensive capitalist accumulation and increasingly neoliberal regulation. Section 936 transformed Puerto Rico into a tax haven for U.S. transnational pharmaceutical and electronic corporation's global trade, financial, and production circuits.

Feeling Global: Puerto Rico and Globalization

The downfall of the oil refining and petrochemical complex of Puerto Rico in the early 1980s entailed the loss of about 6,000 direct jobs in the only industry left with a relative high rate of unionization. If the cumulative effect of job losses in the apparel and textile industry since the early 1970s, the anti-organized labor policies of the Reagan and Bush administrations, the increasing exposure to the competition of low-wage countries, and the growth of the pharmaceutical and electronic industries are also taken into account, sense could be made of the reproduction in the island's labor market of the looser and more flexible patterns prevailing in the mainland. The island's labor unionization rate dropped from 20 percent in 1970 to 7 percent in 1994.

The combination of Section 936 industrial development strategy with Reaganomics inserted the island economy into the new extensive capital accumulation patterns and neoliberal regulation mode of the United States. In the pharmaceutical and electronic industries, collective bargaining was substituted by efficiency wages, where higher-than-average wages and marginal benefits dissuaded unionization and facilitated work speedups and overtime work by increasing the cost of job loss to the wage earners. Career full-time jobs are increasingly substituted by part-time and temporary employment. Greater overall local and federal deregulation entailed fewer resources to the EPA Caribbean division and to the local Environmental Quality Board, plus more lax environmental protection legislation resulting in higher rates of chemical environmental contamination by the pharmaceutical industry.

Cuts in the Food Stamp funds allocation and of other federal transfer payment social programs to the island in the early 1980s and the recent Welfare Reform have constrained average wage growth and dramatically increased homelessness and social destitution. Real wages for nonmanagement personal increased at an annual average rate of 2.9 percent between 1973 and 1996, as compared to an annual average growth rate of 6.1 percent between 1950 and 1973.[9] According to the Coalition for Human Rights of Homeless

People, by 1997 there were close to 29,000 homeless individuals in Puerto Rico.[10]

The sharp expansion of service sector employment, with fast food restaurants and employment service firms accounting for a substantial share of the job creation, as well as the rapid growth in government and retailing employment in the 1980s and 1990s, has accentuated the liberalization of the insular labor market by contributing to increase the shares of minimum wage and contingent jobs out of total employment. Contingent (part-time and temporary) jobs' relative presence has significantly increased in the local economy from 18.6 percent in 1970 to 33 percent in 1995.[11]

The expansion of the pharmaceutical and electronic industries as effect of section 936 incentives since the mid-1970s has inserted the island into the global production and trade networks of these transnational corporations. Though the bulk of Puerto Rico's external trade is with the United States, since the mid-1970s its relative commercial relationship with countries other than the United States has somewhat expanded through intracorporate trade, specially with respect to the importation of semi-processed drugs, refined and crude oil, and food products. The share of imports from countries other than the United States out of total imports rose from 35 percent in 1987 to 44.2 percent in the year 2000. Puerto Rico's main trade partners outside of the United States are, in order of importance, the Dominican Republic, Ireland, the Netherlands, Japan, and Venezuela. The island's main exports to foreign countries are, in order of importance, pharmaceutical products, computer hardware components, and food products.

As part of the U.S. customs system and its consequent trade orientation to the mainland market, in the year 2000, exports from Puerto Rico to the United States represented 87.8 percent of total local exports and 53.5 percent of the island's Gross Domestic Product. Puerto Rico's economic competition with countries outside of the United States has been and continues to be for a share of the U.S. market. The increasing openness of the U.S. economy to the industrial imports from low-wage countries as an effect of the GATT agreements, the Caribbean Basin Initiative, and NAFTA have taken their toll in the local labor-intensive manufacturing industries, especially the apparel and food products sectors, which have experienced a reduction of about 12,000 jobs since 1995. The Section 936 phase out since 1996 and the recent world economic slowdown have also contributed to the contraction of the local manufacturing sector.

During the same period the pharmaceutical and electronic industries have continued to grow, becoming the main employers of the local manufacturing sector. The recent admission of China to the World Trade Organization and the concession of favorite nation status by the United States, as well as the creation of Hemispheric Free Trade Market of the Americas in 2005, are events that will undoubtedly have profound effects on the local manufacturing sector, especially on the labor intensive industries.

As a differentiated part of the U.S. economy, Puerto Rico has also taken part in the globalization of production by experiencing a sharp increase in direct foreign investment from countries other than the United States during the 1990s. Since there is no data on external direct investment for Puerto Rico, I used as proxy the data on total direct investment commitments made by local, U.S., and foreign firms recorded by Fomento or the local Economic Development Administration. The share of foreign direct investment commitments out of total commitments rose from 10 percent in the 1980s to 20 percent in the 1990s. Most of these investments have been in the pharmaceutical and chemical industries by mainly British, Dutch and German transnational corporations.

Financing the Local

Section 936 loopholes gave way to the laundering of U.S. corporate global profits through the local banking system by means of the mechanism of transfer pricing. A hypothetical example of how the transfer pricing mechanism works is the following: A contraceptive pill production plant of Eli Lilly in Carolina, Puerto Rico, buys estrogen from its laboratory in Paris, France, at a lower price (below its cost of production); the Eli Lilly laboratory reports losses in France and does not have to pay taxes there, the local plant produces the pills and sells them to a Eli Lilly packing plant in Rochester, New York, at an overprice; and the Rochester plant also reports losses and does not pay taxes. The net outcome is that disguised profits from Paris and Rochester have been transferred to tax-free Puerto Rico where they could be repatriated to the U.S. along with profits corresponding to the local operation free of federal corporate taxes. Fifty percent of income from intangibles, such as trademarks, patents, and licenses incorporated by the parent corporation in the mainland, could be attributed to the local corporate branch where it is tax-exempt.

In order to reduce the *local tollgate tax* (from 11 to 4 percent) on repatriated profits, 936 corporations placed half of the funds in what were called *eligible activities* such as commercial bank CDs; loans to investment banks and brokerage firms; government bonds, personal, industrial, commercial, and mortgage loans where the income generated from interests; capital gains and financial fees is exempt from local and federal taxes. The creation of the financial market of 936 funds fed and expanded the local financial sector that comprised commercial, investment, mortgage banks, brokerage firms, insurance companies, and personal loans firms by providing substantial funds at preferential low interest to banks and other financial intermediaries, thereby fueling short-term financial and real estate speculation.

The groundwork for the local hegemony of financial capital was set through the creation of the local 936 funds' financial market in the mid-1970s. Financial deregulation and the monetarist orientation of U.S. monetary policy in the 1980s and 1990s finished the job consolidating financial capital's domination of the local scene.

Though Congress approved a ten-year phase out of Section 936 in 1996, which eliminated immediately the 936 funds financial market, the financial sector has continued its spectacular growth by substituting 936 funds for higher cost funds from U.S. and European banks, while continuing to feed—though to a lesser extent—from the global profits of U.S. and increasingly foreign transnational pharmaceutical and electronic corporations in the late 1990s. Laundering of global profits through the local financial sector continues to be done, given that though the federal tax exemption on corporate profits has been reduced to around 40 percent of total profits, it is still a preferable scenario than paying taxes on all profits.

The main U.S. brokerage firms and investment banks have local branches in Puerto Rico. A local stock index of mainly mortgage and commercial banks stocks, the Puerto Rico Stock Index (PRSI), was initiated in the mid-1990s. Several local capital investment funds have been established, including several high-risk venture funds. The finance, insurance, and real state sectors comprised 13.3 percent of total local internal net income in the year 2000, second only to the 46.2 percent contribution of the manufacturing sector (a contribution that is artificially enhanced by the disguised inflow of profits that result from the mechanism of transfer pricing).[12]

Globalization of the local financial sector in the 1980s and 1990s has been considerable. The ratio of mortgage loans to total external financial private long-term investment in Puerto Rico rose from 58.4 percent in 1991 to 63.5 percent in 2000, while the proportion of bank debts out of total external financial private short-term investment rose from 13 percent in 1991 to 83.4 percent in 2000.[13]

Though without doubt the money laundering of global corporate profits via banks and brokerage firms by the pharmaceutical and electronic industrial sectors has played a major role (at its peak this entailed that 936 funds in commercial banks and brokerage firms amounted to around $12 billion), several other factors have also contributed to this globalization of Puerto Rican finances. Among them are the following: the incursion in the local scene of two important Spanish banks (Santander Central Hispano and Banco Bilbao Viscaya-Argentaria) and other European banks (Eurobank and Scotiabank), the establishment since 1989 of 35 international banking entities that offer services only to foreign customers with the exception of the financing of local infrastructure projects, and the laundering of illegal drug money through local and international banks (Puerto Rico is an important transit route and consumer market to illegal drugs from South America).[14]

The globalization of local finances has contributed significantly to finance and fuel construction and consumption activities as the main motors of local economic growth since the early 1990s. The spectacular growth in the construction of highways, water aqueducts, a new urban subway system of transportation, housing, fast-food restaurants, shopping malls, and outlets has spurred the growth of local income and employment in the past decade at the expense of severe environmental destruction in light of increased federal and local deregulation trends.

On the other hand, the globalization of local financial flows has also contributed to finance the solid growth in local consumption expenditures during the last two decades. In conjunction with the high income effect that the illegal drug trade has over the local economy (some analysts have estimated that its contribution to local net income is similar to that of the pharmaceutical industry), legal and illegal financial inflows have helped enhance significantly local consumption. Consumer debt as a proportion of personal disposable income rose from 43.6 percent in 1992 to 48.3 percent in 2000.

Puerto Rico is also the most important consumer market in the Caribbean and one of the main consumer markets in Latin America. Some of the biggest world consumer good retailers have significantly expanded their presence in Puerto Rico lately. JC Penny's recently opened its biggest store in the world in the Plaza Las Americas shopping mall in San Juan. The biggest outlet mall in the world recently opened in Canóvanas, in the eastern coast of the island.

Conclusion

In sum, Puerto Rico's particular insertion into the global economy during the most recent decades has been at least paradoxical. As a differentiated region of the U.S. economy, it has experienced a greater level of exposure to the global corporate trade, production, and financial circuits of U.S. pharmaceutical and electronic corporations. Similar to the rest of the U.S. economy, its labor intensive industries have suffered significant employment reduction as effect of increase in U.S. trade openness to clothing and food imports from countries with lower wages, weaker environmental labor protection, and relatively more authoritarian political regimes.

At the same time islanders have been insulated from the most wild and perverse forms of financial speculation, labor exploitation, environmental depredation, and social destitution that has characterized current economic globalization trends, by being an unequal part of the U.S. economy and political system. The stability of the U.S. dollar, the application of federal minimum wages, labor and environmental protection laws, as well as the participation in several social transfer payment programs, have afforded a minimum level of protection to island residents from the most savage forms of global capitalism.

As a result of the increasing neoliberal regulation mode of the United States, Puerto Ricans have also suffered from real wage stagnation, greater employment insecurity, higher relative joblessness and inflation rates, greater poverty levels, as well as rapid environmental destruction. Cuts in the social wage, overall deregulation of labor and environmental protection, and financial and industrial markets have been the key components of U.S. and local neoliberalism. These contradictory processes are hence constitutive of the Puerto Rican *vacilón*, understood as an enjoyable vacillation in the "best of two worlds."

Notes

1. In contrast with the Fordist model of capitalist development, which entailed the articulation of mass production with mass consumption, by means of the generalization in manufacturing of the automated assembly line, as well as the

institutionalization of collective bargaining and a welfare state, the post-Fordist model of capitalist development is characterized by flexible production systems made possible by the digital informational technologies revolution, in combination with deregulated labor, product, and financial markets.

2. Lack of or weak labor laws (minimum wage, six-to-eight-hour work days, collective bargaining, the right to strike, child labor laws), environmental protection laws, as well as welfare and public health programs for the poor and unemployed.
3. The Fordist capitalist model of development was self-centered in the sense that over 90 percent of domestic mass production was geared and absorbed by domestic consumer demand.
4. Economies of scoop refers to the significant reduction in the time taken to reconfigure production equipment from one product line to another and the consequent gains in sales and income for the firm when it is able to respond more effectively to the fluctuations in market demand.
5. Real hourly wages in the United States fell at an annual rate of 0.4 percent from 1973 to 1996, grew at an annual rate of 2 percent between 1997 and 2000, and stalled at a annual rate of 1.2 percent from 2001 to 2004.
6. "Current-Dollar and Real Gross Domestic Product (Seasonally adjusted annual rates) & U.S. International Transaction Accounts Data," Bureau of Economic Analysis, U.S. Department of Commerce, March 16, 2002.
7. Bureau of Economic Analysis, U.S. Department of Commerce, *US International Transactions Accounts*, March 16, 2002.
8. Ibid.
9. Commonwealth of Puerto Rico, Office of the Governor, Planning Board, *Economic Report to the Governor 1981 & 2000* (Statistical Appendix).
10. *El Nuevo Día*, April 14, 2002, 4.
11. Elías Gutiérrez, *El Nuevo Día*, March 21, 1997, 27–28.
12. Commonwealth of Puerto Rico, Office of the Governor, Planning Board, *Economic Report to the Governor 2000* (Statistical Appendix).
13. Commonwealth of Puerto Rico, Office of the Governor, Planning Board, *Balance of Payments: Puerto Rico 2001.*
14. Alfredo Padilla, Commissioner of Financial Institutions of Puerto Rico, declared, at a hearing held by the Commission of Bank and Consumer Affairs of the insular Senate, that local laws to fight against money laundering activities are "dead letter" and that nobody has been prosecuted for money laundering under the 1992 local Law 33 against Organized Crime and Money Laundering (Miguel Díaz Román, *El Nuevo Día*, May 21, 2003, 95). Testifying to the same Commission, José Ramón González, president of Bank Association of Puerto Rico, stated that local law enforcement agencies in charge of investigating and prosecuting money laundering activities have not filed charges against anybody or realized any investigation on *suspicious* transactions. He also declared that local banks regularly send Suspicious Activity Reports (SARs) to local law enforcement agencies on transactions realized by their customers and foreign banks, transactions that are not investigated or followed up on. In the hearing it was reported that between the years 1999 and 2000, SARs submitted on potential money laundering activity increased from 316 to 1,063 (Miguel Díaz Román, *El Nuevo Día*, May 23, 2003, 95).

CHAPTER 3

Space out of Place: Consumer Culture in Puerto Rico

Laura L. Ortiz-Negrón

In Puerto Rico, it is said that going shopping is a national pastime. And this is not only because the island, which is only 100 by 35 square miles with a population of nearly 4 million, is plastered with malls, megastores, cars, suburbs, highways, and cell phones, but also because these shopping malls are always full in a country where salaries are relatively low, unofficial unemployment rate is close to 30 percent, and 60 percent of the population receives federal nutritional assistance through the program known as PAN (not coincidentally an acronym that means "bread").

Despite the centrality of consumption in Puerto Rico, discourses emanating from the state and the church—those from the state in an even more hypocritical manner—incite people to save money, although this practice is nearly impossible. People are told that they should not shop so much, although everything around them incites them to do so. Newscasters report that the cities are being revitalized, but most large-scale construction is aimed at building even more malls and superstores.[1] Religious figures call to the citizenry to attend church on Sundays, but even devout Puerto Ricans prefer to go to Plaza Las Américas, the Island's largest mall. Perhaps already convinced of their failure to attract parishioners and followers, the local religious organization known as "mitas" has opted to go to Plaza to disseminate their teachings and services, and, in similar fashion, political pundits broadcast their radio shows from the Montehiedra Mall.

In this chapter, I argue that the centrality of shopping in public discourse and as an everyday practice can serve as a heuristic device to question the limitations of certain structures, social categories, and discourses that attempt to explain contemporary Puerto Rican society. Relying on extensive fieldwork in Puerto Rican shopping malls and stores, and engaging in theoretical practice on consumer culture as a phenomenon, I suggest that not only is shopping the primary social activity that Puerto Ricans engage in as a group, but also that any attempt to morally judge this practice critically misunderstands the "social" in Puerto Rico.

Shopping in Theory

The concept of "consumer culture" is deceptive since it is polysemic and contentious. In some ways, it is easier to start by defining what consumption is not. Consumer culture, for instance, is not sustained by binary categories such as those who shop and those who do not, nothing more outrageous. Nor is it about buying or literally using things. Rather, consumption tells us about the social structure and about ourselves as subjects, a way of seeing and experiencing the world. As one consumer told another in a shopping mall where I was interviewing people, "Come so you can see this, you have to see this, wow, what beautiful things!" to which the other consumer responds, "I don't want to see it. I don't want to see any more ornaments. God! Shopping is the only way that I enjoy myself." Consumer culture is then nothing short of our historical era's experience of enjoyment and frustration from and through capital.

The extent to which there is no "exterior" to shopping can be gleaned from its widespread enjoyment. According to John Goss, consumption is so significant in contemporary life that "[s]hopping is the second most important leisure activity in North America and although watching television is indisputably the first, much of its programming actually promotes shopping."[2] Despite much public discourse about the national differences between Puerto Ricans and Americans, I have found that consumer culture in both contexts is quite similar. In each case, the objective is to be in tune (eye, audio, touch) with and through an incessant flux of consumption signs. In our ability to inhabit these spaces without territorial, symbolic, or functional limits, we encounter a new form of the social.[3]

From a sociological point of view, being in tune is also to partake in mobile cultural spaces, transferable and self-referential. If in the first half of the twentieth century, advertising was a complementary practice to the business of selling, now it has its own sphere of power. As French sociologist J. Baudrillard observes, in this historical juncture, desire is a productive force of capital.[4] If seduction used to be part of the personal and the private sphere, it is now a form of mass-mediated regulation.

Although it is true that consumer culture presupposes the production of jobs, income, and consumer subjectivities, it also brings forth new articulations and sociocultural processes that privilege desire. Consumer culture is a system that brings together all that was previously dispersed and excluded from social space: food, auto, clothes, jewelry, images, the mall, credit, desire, technology, images, and television, just to name a few items. In addition, we consume through television, Internet, films, cell phones, catalogues, or shopping centers all stages for the production of new social meanings and practices.

In this sense, consumer culture has developed a mass-media infrastructure designed to undermine class ideologies in their crudest form as well as the ideas of necessity, recreation, entertainment, and leisure. It also underscores how consumption has displaced the traditional socializing structures of the school, church, and family. This process conforms to the production of consumer subjectivities and diverse consumption locations. It is through the proliferation of diverse media and intensive advertising that multiple discourses are produced enunciating access to commodities (signified objects) for all consumers; hence the media is simultaneously our most illustrative register of the social. Advertising, as writer Michel Houellebecq has commented, is a new way of promising a sense of being to people, as it "produces a hard and terrorist superego . . . and tells the individual that he has to desire . . . if you fall behind you are dead."[5]

Consumers hence signify and re-signify their social relations and identities through objects, spaces, images, and services produced by the mass media.[6] For instance, the Marshalls store located in the Puerto Rican neighborhood of Caparra is a social space that comprises many different women and men as clients. These consumers have diverse tastes, formations, and social origins. In this store, you can indistinctly run into an ex-Miss Universe, a bourgeois wife from Guaynabo, a TV journalism personality, a waitress, or the ex-president of the Supreme Court of Puerto Rico. As this is one of the few and arguably the most relevant spaces in which different sectors may interact in contemporary Puerto Rico, the social order becomes meaningful only in and through consumption.[7]

Due to consumption and the centrality of mass media, the most powerful forces of postmodern capital, the relationships between production and values become semantically unstable. Under these circumstances, is it possible to speak about production solely in terms of the workplace? Is it possible to speak about work as a process through which I progress and liberate myself from poverty as the dominant "Operation Bootstrap" ideology disseminated, or as the site only of exploitation and discipline that some intellectuals claim? Is it reasonable to speak about leisure as private and intimate space where capital is absent? Does it still make sense to speak about ideology as the (mis)representation of reality when faced with the simulation and frenzy of signs as a *Wag the Dog* effect? Is it still possible to talk about an auto solely in terms of its function as a means of transportation?

I would argue that this framing is obsolete. Consumption has substantially re-signified our social relations in at least three key ways. First, if consumption is an accumulation regime that takes what you do not have or the little that you recuperate as labor through credit, it is through consumption that one recuperates and re-signifies the imposed negation as symbolic compensation. In other words, consumer culture not only sucks you dry but also opens up spaces of enjoyment absent from other everyday contexts. It is through consumer culture, for instance, that one escapes from the utilitarian character and precariousness of modern and postmodern life.

Second, to the extent that several forms of appropriating the external world represent a democratic experience through high-tech cyberspace and objects of consumption, the majority of us now have access to that world, and can see it and enjoy it as our own. Last, once the market of commodities becomes democratic and these become organic to desire (seduction and experience), old ideas about the need and function of objects become completely outdated. And to the extent that such diverse matters as "progress," "the ego," "social morality," "profit," "social status," and "aesthetics" are condensed in the object formerly known as "commodity," consumption is inescapable.

The processes outlined above underscore not only how capital appropriates the private sphere and intimate space, as well as the impact of virtual culture as a referent for the real, but also explains why people cannot do without a television set and cell phone, when in other historical periods these objects were perceived as accessories. To put it another way, the idea of going shopping for a dress, a piece of jewelry, or go to a mall no longer serves a utilitarian purpose in the modern sense. For many of the people involved in my study, the seduction of the object is reason enough to purchase it. For others, the purchase of certain objects is perceived as a skill in the accumulation of cultural capital and social standing, an important part of being a member of the community.

Not only is consumption a signifying relationship, the object itself stands beyond its exchange value and its function as it was defined in modernity. In the lives of consumers, there are so many objects and spaces that can be used for so many reasons other than those originally intended. For instance, as part of my study, I went to a furniture store that had been established two years prior and was amply publicized. I stayed in the store for three hours observing how consumers—mostly families, women, and couples—interacted with the goods. Significantly, the many attempts of the salespeople to sell them something was largely unsuccessful. Many of the people moved from piece to piece, from bed to bed, feeling the texture and the comfort of these or those objects that will never be found in their real bedrooms—or that perhaps could be. I observed a young woman, for instance, speaking with her boyfriend in a seductive tone: "Come and try this out, you will not regret it. Lie here with me." It was a moment of enchantment: the Disney World game between object and space. None of the consumers who entered the store during those three hours asked a salesperson for the price of an item or to point out the advantages and disadvantages of, say, the waterbed, the table with six chairs, the zero percent interest financing, or how to apply for the store's credit card.

The consumption taking place here recalls the etymological meaning of the word "consumere" in Latin: destruction, consumption, everything. Consumption also is to consume oneself and with summa, the realization and completion of an act of relation, what in French is referred to as "consommation." And here lies the dual, paradoxical, and ambivalent semantic implication of consumption. As consumers, we spend (become indebted) and gain enjoyment in this double game of consumption. Simultaneously, the consumer as a subject with agency assumes consumption as a space to articulate demands and, sometimes, a site of struggle. In this context, the consumer continuously searches for the experiences and demands offered by the objects through consumption to the extent that these produce themselves as relation-signs of comfort, leisure, aesthetic, pleasure, freedom, and affection, among other meanings.

Consumer culture offers the subject the gratification of the present in an indeterminate world that no longer believes in utopias. In the specific case of Puerto Rico, this is a world without political options where everyday life has collapsed in the wake of the project of "modernity."[8] An example of this phenomenon took place in October 2000 when the island witnessed the grand opening of Macy's department store in Puerto Rico. According to the island's main newspaper, whose reporters interviewed various visitors to the event, the response was overwhelmingly positive. One woman is quoted as commenting, "Thank God that Macy's arrived in Puerto Rico." This comment is posted on a professor's door with the added commentary: "No further questions to the witness." To this exchange, what can the anthropologist say? To call on God to underscore an activity that many consider mundane, and to see how signs speak to each other, leaves us to conclude that the ethnographer has nothing left to represent, report, or interpret.

If you take these transformations of capital and of consumer subjects into account, consumer culture is neither a fracture nor a crisis, but an implosion of hegemonic social science categories such as production, necessity, reality, alienation, and false ideology, among others. This prompts the following question: Can we hold a mirror to consumer culture? What representational relations do classic notions of production, function, class, reality, necessity, alienation, and false ideology, amongst others, have with consumer culture. As a gesture intended to provoke critical thought, I would affirm that most of the traditional sociological categories that French sociologist Baudrillard has called the "metalanguage of reality" are outmoded.[9] In an attempt to grasp the phenomenon, consumer culture has been reformulated by several scholars as the contemporary hegemonic phase of capital.[10] However, from sociology and anthropology, as from cultural studies and poststructuralist theory, consumer culture is no longer conceptualized through functionalist or classical Marxist perspectives on the social, but from other theoretical coordinates.[11] In revisualizing consumer culture, categories such as kinship, family, community, solidarity, and support have been redeployed to describe shopping as a social and affective technology.[12] For instance, when I asked a 42-year-old woman, who is a teacher and lives in the southern part of the island, what she accomplished by going shopping, she responded, "If I don't go shopping, then I have problems. I am very Catholic and I help my church, but going shopping on Friday is a very important ritual for my daughter and me. When we go out on Fridays, I can talk to my daughter and share with her. It's our time to talk about our things, without my husband and two sons. We really enjoy it a lot."

This type of consumption, however, is also a struggle, as consumption constitutes an obligation that has significant economic impact on the subject. In this sense, consumer culture is a social space akin to the traditional duel.

For instance, as I am talking to a middle-aged woman at a San Juan store, I remark, "To shop is marvelous, right? If it wasn't for this . . . The truth is that there are so many beautiful things," to which the woman responds, "Girl, I can't live without this and without the television set." This answer prompts me to say, "If I had more money, I would buy more." And she responds, "I buy with credit to the hilt because I will never have money. I go to the refinancing office and renew my loan and I pay it, and I get into debt again, and this is the deal. Salaries here are not enough to eat but Plaza is always full, wall-to-wall. So I'm not crazy. I look at all the specials and I see what's good for me. To shop is really an obligation; there is no way to escape it. Sometimes that bothers me. But at other times, I ask myself, why was I born poor with so many pretty jewelry selections!"

At the same time, one of the early conclusions of my work is that for many consumers going shopping is not a particularly special activity. To them, consumption is part of their daily routine, and it does not interrupt their lives or constitute a crisis. One of the people whom I interviewed, a middle-aged man who is a teacher, commented, "The mall owners are rich people and together with the major churches come to inaugurate the additions to the shopping malls. You can see them cutting the ribbons, and then they appear on television. That means that to consume is a legitimate activity." This type of characterization contrasts significantly with public discourse on the shopping that argues that consumption destroys Puerto Rican identity. An identity, of course, that never was.

Wal-Mart Versus the Nation

As a concept, consumer society represents an entire configuration between political economy and mass media, based on the assumption that consumption is the dominant social sphere.[13] This is the case because the modernization processes of the island, following Fordist and post-Fordist logics,[14] transformed consumption into the dominant social force in Puerto Rican society.[15] The island's urban design, where suburbs and highways have at their center a mall and are linked by cars, is the spatial surface of Puerto Rico. This is economically feasible due to the island's ample financing and credit infrastructure, state and federal aid, as well as the informal and narco-economies.

The central axiom of the Fordist regime presupposed the disjuncture of income and expenses. For this reason, Puerto Rico's credit infrastructure is so ample and diversified, designed to match desired levels of consumption.[16] Among the options are credit cards with different payment options, deferred payments, leasing, time-sharing to enable vacationing, flexible lines of credit, and refinancing for personal expenses, among others. Confronted with this inherent feature of the Fordist scheme, consumers cannot be expected to save and pay all their debts even if a moralistic discourse exhorts them to. People keep afloat by paying one credit card with another, pay debts in alternating months, borrow money from friends and relatives, or simply confront the anguish of nonpayment. In this context, most holidays throughout the year like Christmas, summer vacation, "back-to-school," and Mother's Day are experienced with a mixture of happiness and distress.

As I mentioned earlier, despite the centrality of consumer culture, most local discourse views it as the "problem of consumption" or "consumerism."[17] It is common to hear that consumerism is a social problem that needs to be addressed and controlled, completely ignoring its relationship as a necessary practice demanded by the logic of capital that structures and guarantees the social reproduction of Puerto Rico. In other words, to attack consumption is to attack the very motor of the economy, multinational corporations, developers, government as a provider of jobs, profits, and all those social relations that are sustained through mass consumption. Consumption is then not an aberration but the mechanism that coheres the social system.

In this sense, there is no way out of the dominant social structure through which one lives and survives as laborer/consumer and as a citizen. It is through consumption that behaviors and social relations are defined and valued. Within this context, the cynicism of an anticonsumption discourse rests on the assumption that consumerism is an individual problem, as if the average person made decisions concerning the island's "mallification," the seduction of publicity campaigns, and the diversity of shopping options. This discourse is produced from the vocal and silent voices of government, private enterprise, the church, intellectuals, and the shoppers themselves.[18]

Remarkably, even when globalization processes structure the world, a prevalent mode of criticism of consumption relies on the notion of cultural imperialism and the centrality of national identity.[19] An important example is the struggle proclaimed against the "Walmartización" of Puerto Rico, which is framed within the context of imperialism's threat to the nation. Through a discursive deployment, the store, in actuality a transnational corporation, becomes "la nación Wal-Mart" (Wal-Mart nation), a neo-imperial power. It is argued that the dominance of the Wal-Mart chain will destroy the city in its imaginative and aesthetic sense.

From this discursive strategy a question immediately arises: Why rely on the mimesis of nation/empire in opposing Wal-Mart after more than 40 years of imposing a Fordist/post-Fordist homogenizing economic model on the island? Why oppose Wal-Mart, employing a neo-nationalist discourse when most of the subordinated groups in Puerto Rico are more immediately oppressed by other Puerto Ricans? And if capital is capital wherever one is situated, and if capital requires us to be consumers, why are we not also against Banco Popular, financing entities, real-estate speculation, or the Puerto Rico Bank Association? Moreover, if Wal-Mart were to take the shape of a small store in the city, would that be acceptable? Why not recuperate a broader social, aesthetic, and ecological argument that problematizes the island's "non-cityness" or the collapse of its foundations?

At the same time, popular response to Wal-Mart and shopping in general suggests that shoppers not only experience and signify life as desire, but can also grasp the political economy of consumption itself. In other words, if

Wal-Mart sells rice and beans at a lower price than a locally-owned store like J. F. Montalvo, then most shoppers will buy at Wal-Mart. If the mall is a recreation and therapeutic space despite being part of global capital, this is not so much a contradiction as indicative of the capacity of subordinated sectors to reappropriate and transform a situation imposed by political and economic power. It is this capacity for transforming of space, where the mall constitutes a type of sphere(s) of agency and desire, that opposition/competition within the same political economy is registered.

While some may find this context politically discouraging, it also opens new questions and possibilities. For instance, would it be possible to produce a discourse that would simultaneously advocate and critique shopping and malls? From what points of view could this be accomplished? Would it be possible to denounce, at the same time that one acknowledges the radical side of consumption, the ecological-urban problems, the financing terms, and to hold those responsible accountable? Can we envision a way to constitute a consumer movement that educates, identifies, and produces strategies to reclaim rights at the same time that it defends and proposes alternative aesthetic politics?

An example of such a position already exists and can be observed in the activities of the "Caminantes de Plaza," a group of elderly people who use the mall to exercise, socialize, and offer each other support. For some of them, the mall is the most sacred place in their everyday lives. For others, the mall is the only alternative. And for yet another group, the mall has the same intensity of enchantment of the Spanish colonial public square (plaza). But instead of a recuperation of the past, the mall is the new plaza, a transformation of the former space, in which as one of the "Caminantes" observed was the place "where the male went to hunt in the forest." If the mall is what survives of the social, it is in part because it re-signifies the difficulties of living and at the same time reinvents life, not through the trope of the mask but through a relationship between objects and spaces.

In sum, consumer culture in Puerto Rico exposes the remains of modernity and the creative reimaginings of what Puerto Ricans do with those remains. It also underscores the struggle between liberation and frustration that arises from our collective consumption practices. In this sense, to think that the concepts of function and necessity help us to understand consumption and that destiny organizes our lives appears as clearly naive.

Notes

This chapter was translated by Frances Negrón-Muntaner.

1. According to the Planning Board of Puerto Rico, a shopping center is a commercial development of 100,000 square feet or more. Following this criterion, there is an official estimate of 64 shopping centers in the island. However, Dr. Carlos Guilbe, economic geographer and professor at the University of Puerto Rico, indicates that in order to avoid zoning and licensing restrictions during the 1990s, developers began to establish shopping centers of less than

100,000 square feet. Once established, developers would expand the shopping center in excess of the originally zoned limit. According to Dr. Guilbe, this led to an estimate of 90 shopping centers in Puerto Rico. This exponential growth of sites for consumption has mostly been accounted for by economists and urban planners. See Carlos Guilbe, *Historia y desarrollo de los centros comerciales en Puerto Rico* (San Juan: Administración de Fomento Comercial, 2000), and Antonio R. Gómez, "Megatiendas ven en la Isla una 'mina de oro,'" *Primera Hora*, November 24, 2003.

2. John Goss, "The 'Magic of the Mall': An Analysis of Form, Function, and Meaning in the Contemporary Retail Built Environment," in *The Economic Geography Reader*, ed. John Bryson et al. (England: Wiley, 1999), 315.
3. *The Mirror of Production* and *For the Critique of the Political Economy of the Sign* by Jean Baudrillard register this new theoretical threshold. See Jean Baudrillard, *The Mirror of Production* (St. Louis: Telos Press, 1975), and *For the Critique of the Political Economy of the Sign* (St. Louis: Telos Press, 1981). Baudrillard establishes the need for the transcendence of the categories of production, labor, value, and "Man" due to their utilitarian character and the complexity of consumption as symbolic space. For his part, Fredric Jameson explores the cultural logic of late capitalism wherein images and infinite presents are constitutive of this world. In a different register, Pierre Bourdieu elaborates the differentiations within social space, which is constituted by two forces: economic capital and cultural capital. It is in this social space that differentiation's can be comprehended—and social class only within space. According to Bourdieu, "social classes do not exist. . . . What exists is a social space, a space of differences within which classes exist in a type of virtual state, not as something given, rather as something to be accomplished." See Pierre Bourdieu, *Capital cultural, escuela y espacio social* (Mexico: Siglo XXI, 2000), 38. And from a different angle, Mike Featherstone undertakes to examine lifestyles in which patterns of consumption are no longer sustainable wedded to class identity or status. See Mike Featherstone, *Consumer Culture and Postmodernism* (London: Sage, 1991), 16–21. The production of a theoretical discourse regarding *something new is happening* is extensive and intensive, and point to what I believe mark this new threshold as effects of theory.
4. Jean Baudrillard, "The Theory of Consumption. Part II," in *The Consumer Society—Myths and Structures* (London: Sage Publications, 1998).
5. Michel Houellebecq, *El mundo como supermercado* (Barcelona: Anagrama, 2000), 68–69.
6. Within this contemporary scene, the work of Stuart Hall, "Encoding/ Decoding" initiated a different reading of the subjects' agency via the multiple meanings generated by signs, or what is referred to as "in dominance" before media culture. See Stuart Hall, "Encoding/Decoding," in *Media, Culture, Language* (London: The Centre for Contemporary Cultural Studies, University of Birmingham, 1991). Relevant here is a classic work by Daniel Bell, *Cultural Contradictions of Capitalism*, that undermined the facile correlation traditionally established between production and sociological notions such as class. See Daniel Bell, *Cultural Contradictions of Capitalism* (New York: Basic Books, 1976). The weakening of notions of class, labor, and production that has occupied us from the work of Marx is even more evident in recent theoretical examinations of the social. It is this autonomy that marks the precariousness of critical thought and simultaneously marks the

defeat of modern rationality at the hands of structuralism and post-structuralism. The crisis of legitimation, for example, manifested during the events of May 1968, signified this theoretical process at the level of the social.

7. Mary Douglas and Baron Isherwood, *The World of Goods: Towards an Anthropology of Consumption* (London: Routledge, 1996).
8. In the first place, the culture of consumption responds historically to an economic regime (consumer society, Fordism, and post-Fordism) which has been articulated in Puerto Rico from the 1960s and which is now registered in pandemic fashion. Over the past four decades in Puerto Rico, the economic process of Fordist assimilation has placed in evidence the problem of "development" in the country.
9. See Jean Baudrillard, *Revenge of the Crystal: Selected Writings on the Modern Object and Its Destiny, 1968–1983* (London: Pluto Press, 1999).
10. More contemporary treatments include the works of Jean Baudrillard: *The System of Objects* (London: Verso, 1996); *For a Critique of the Political Economy of the Sign* (St. Louis: Telos Press, 1981); *The Consumer Society: Myths and Structures* (London: Sage Publications, 1998); and *Revenge of the Crystal: Selected Writings on the Modern Object and Its Destiny, 1968–1983* (London: Pluto Press, 1999).
11. At the international level, social scientists from different fields have begun to produce research on shopping and the mall. The Spanish sociologist José Miguel Marinas has explored the sociohistorical origins of consumer culture and its social development in Spain. See J. M. Marinas ("Ciudad y consumo del barroco a los pasajes comerciales," *Cuadernos de realidades sociales* 55–56 [2000]: 111–43; *La fábula del bazaar. Orígenes de la cultura del consumo* [Madrid: Antonio Machado Libros, 2001]). In Mexico, researchers Maritza Castro-Pozo and Inés Cornejo-Portugal carried out a study on the symbolic appropriation of the mall by young people. See M. Castro-Pozo and I. Cornejo-Portugal ("La privatización afectiva de los espacios comerciales por las y los jóvenes," *Revista Ciudades—Culturas del espacio público* 27 [1995]: 24–28). One of their arguments is that an "affective privatization" of the public space takes place through social interaction in the mall. Russell Belk, a professor at the University of Utah, conducted a research project on the *Consumption Patterns of the New Elite in Zimbabwe*, concluding that old elites, as well as globalization, shape the consumption patterns of the *nouveaux riche* in developing countries (Russel Belk, "Consumption Patterns of the New Elite in Zimbabwe." Paper presented at the Social Science History Association Conference, Pittsburg, October, 2000). In England, anthropologist Daniel Miller has carried out various studies on shopping that explore the symbolic processes embedded in it. See Daniel Miller, *A Theory of Shopping* (New York: Cornell University Press, 1998). And in a different context, John Clammer explores the relation between shopping and the building of identity in Japanese society (John Clammer, *Contemporary Urban Japan: A Sociology of Consumption* [London: Blackwell, 1997]). Likewise, Don Slater, George McCracken, Mary Douglas, Mike Featherstone, and Arjun Appadurai, among others, have conceptualized going shopping and relations through merchandize as the material culture in which social significations and rationalities achieve force and become comprehensible. See Don Slater, *Consumer Culture and Modernity* (Cambridge: Polity Press, 1997); George McCracken, *Culture and Consumption: New Approaches to the Symbolic Character of Consumer Goods and Activities* (Bloomington: Indiana University Press, 1990);

Mary Douglas and Baron Isherwood, *The World of Goods: Towards an Anthropology of Consumption* (London: Routledge, 1996); Mike Featherstone, *Consumer Culture and Postmodernism* (London: Sage, 1991); and Arjun Appadurai, ed., *The Social Life of Things: Commodities in Cultural Perspective* (Cambridge: Cambridge University Press, 1986). The culture of consumption provides meaning to everyday life while simultaneously appearing as a ritualized practice wherein society is remade. Mary Douglas and Baron Isherwood view consumption as a symbolic medium of communication that constitutes part of the information system in which we live. Hence, communication links are constituted via consumption.

12. See Daniel Miller, *Material Culture and Mass Consumption* (Oxford: Blackwell, 1991).
13. From the perspective of political economy, the hegemony of the societies of consumption in many of the advanced countries and semi-peripherals have their historical basis in the configuration of *Fordism* as a regime of accumulation and reproduction of capital based on a norm of consumption. This process began in the 1920s and was consolidated in the United States by the 1950s.
14. Some references on the topic of Fordism and post-Fordism as regimes of capital accumulation include Alain Lipietz, *Mirages and Miracles: The Crises of Global Fordism* (London: Verso, 1987); David Harvey, *The Condition of Postmodernity An Enquiry into the Origins of Cultural Change* (Oxford: Blackwell, 1989); Michel Aglietta, *Regulación y crisis del capitalismo* (Spain: Siglo XXI, 1986); Krishan Kumar, *From Post-Industrial to Post-Modern Society: New Theories of the Contemporary World* (Oxford: Blackwell, 1995); and Josef Esser and Joachim Hirsch, *Post-Fordism* (Oxford: Blackwell, 1994).
15. Although there is a complex social history regarding this phenomenon and its relationship to modernization in Puerto Rico dating from the 1950s, at present there are various factors that articulate a regime of elevated consumption. Amongst these is the dominant socio-urban design, with its axis being the mall sustained by the informal economy, narco-economy, a broad and flexible financing structure, as well as a mediatic economy.
16. This credit structure does not include the informal economies and narcotics trade as two other economic connectors inside the spectrum of financial flows and consumption.
17. The notion of consumerism is defined as those ideological and discursive representations of consumption as a practice of great value within a local context or given society. On the other hand, consumerism denotes consumption as a social and moral problem that is framed in its historical trajectory. However, some scholars tend to collapse these two notions whereby consumerism refers to both phenomena.
18. See, for example, Delia Rivera, "El día después," *El Nuevo Día*, December 29, 2004; Santiago Alvarez and Luis Francisco, "La juventud y la violencia," *El Nuevo Día*, July 31, 2004; Marcia Rivera et al., "El consumo, 'problema o panacea': sus efectos sobre el individuo y la sociedad," *El Nuevo Día, Revista Domingo*, December 28, 2003, *Sección FORO*; José Molinelli Freytes, "Tres monumentos a un nuevo dios," *El Nuevo Día*, October 18, 2003.
19. As I have indicated in various conferences, the dualistic schema has been displaced in the case of Puerto Rico in its colonial relationship with the United States. The "colonial problem" is produced discursively as the root cause of an Americanization or assimilation of Puerto Ricans to the imperial culture.

Within this discourse, the native, the pre-modern or Puerto Rican not only assumes a superiority before the Empire moreover, the Empire signifies a barbaric invasion poised to annihilate the Puerto Rican people. See Silvia Alvarez-Curbelo, *La nación Wal-Mart y la ciudad de San Juan* (Ponencia presentada en al XI Reunión Anual de la Asociación Puertorriqueña de Historiadores, October 3–4, 2003. UPR-Humacao).

CHAPTER 4

Nation and Migration: Rethinking Puerto Rican Identity in a Transnational Context

Jorge Duany

As an overseas possession of the United States, Puerto Rico has been exposed to an intense penetration of American capital, commodities, laws, and customs unequal to other Latin American countries. Yet today Puerto Ricans display a stronger cultural identity than most Caribbean peoples, even those who enjoy political independence. At the beginning of the twenty-first century, Puerto Rico presents the apparent incongruity of a stateless nation that has not assimilated into American mainstream culture. Puerto Rico may well be considered a "postcolonial colony" in the sense of a people with a strong sense of national identity but little desire for a nation-state, living in a territory that legally "belongs to but is not part of the United States."[1]

In addition to its unresolved colonial dilemma, Puerto Rico is increasingly a nation on the move: a country whose porous borders are incessantly criss-crossed by migrants coming to and going away from the island. Since the 1940s, more than 1.6 million islanders have relocated abroad. According to the 2000 Census, 47.2 percent of all persons of Puerto Rican origin lived in the continental United States.[2] At the same time, the island has received hundreds of thousands of immigrants since the 1960s, primarily returnees and their descendants, and secondarily citizens of other countries, especially the Dominican Republic and Cuba. By the year 2000, 9.3 percent of the island's residents had been born abroad, including those born in the mainland of Puerto Rican parentage.[3]

This combination of a prolonged exodus, together with a large influx of returnees and foreigners, makes Puerto Rico a test case of transnationalism, broadly defined as the maintenance of social, economic, and political ties across national borders.[4] The growing diversity in the migrants' origins and destinations undermines the ideological premises of traditional discourses of the nation based on the equation among territory, birthplace, citizenship, language, culture, and identity. Above all, it is increasingly difficult to maintain that only those who were born and live on the island, and speak Spanish, can legitimately be called Puerto Rican. As the sociologist César Ayala puts it, the Puerto Rican case suggests that "the idea of the nation has to be understood not as a territorially organized nation state, but as a translocal phenomenon of a new kind."[5]

As Puerto Ricans move back and forth between the two countries, territorially grounded definitions of national identity become less relevant, while transnational identities acquire greater prominence. So far, scholarly discussions on transnationalism have tended to exclude the island and its diaspora because Puerto Ricans are U.S. citizens and therefore do not cross international frontiers when they move abroad. However, Puerto Rican migrants cross significant geographic, cultural, and linguistic borders between the island and the mainland, and this displacement helps to reconfigure their national identities. More specifically, I propose that the emergence of cultural nationalism as a dominant discourse in Puerto Rico is partly the result of a growing diaspora since the 1940s.

The objective of this chapter is to explore the impact of transnational migration on the cultural identities of Puerto Ricans on the island and in the U.S. mainland. Given the context of widespread geographic dispersion and continuing colonial status, my thesis is that cultural nationalism is better attuned than political nationalism to imagine Puerto Ricans as a community. Rather than weakening the sense of national identity, transnational migration has actually strengthened "long-distance nationalism," that is, the persistent claim to a national identity by people residing away from their homeland, even for long periods of time.[6] What has declined over the past five decades is the public support for the political nationalist position that holds that Puerto Rico should become an independent country to preserve its culture apart from the United States. The issue is not whether Puerto Ricans constitute a nation but what kind of nation they identify with.

Between the Island and the Diaspora

Two key questions guide my analysis of the relationship between nation and migration in Puerto Rico. To begin, how can most Puerto Ricans imagine themselves as a nation, even though few of them support a separate nation-state? I address this issue by making a careful distinction between political nationalism—based on the doctrine that every people should have its own sovereign state—and cultural nationalism—based on the assertion of the moral and spiritual autonomy of each people—as expressed in the protection of its historical patrimony as well as its popular and elite culture.[7]

Whereas political nationalism insists on the necessity of independent states, cultural nationalism can be reconciled with other forms of self-determination, such as free association. While political nationalists concentrate on the practical aspects of achieving and maintaining independence, cultural nationalists are primarily concerned with celebrating or reviving a cultural heritage, including the vernacular language, religion, and folklore. Cultural nationalism conceives of a nation as a creative force based on a unique history, culture, and territory, while political nationalism equates the nation with the state. This distinction between the two basic forms of nationalism is made only for analytical purposes, because they often overlap in practice.

My second question regarding the relation between nation and migration is the cultural impact of the massive exodus to the mainland over the past five decades. I argue that diasporic communities are part of the Puerto Rican nation because they continue to be linked to the island by an intense and frequent circulation of people, identities, and practices, as well as capital, technology, and commodities. Over the past decade, scholars have documented the two-way cultural flows between many sending and receiving societies through large-scale migration. Peggy Levitt has referred to such movements of ideas, customs, and social capital as "social remittances," which produce a dense transnational field that blurs the geopolitical borders between the Dominican Republic and the United States.[8]

Similarly, Puerto Ricans moving back and forth between the island and the mainland frequently carry not only bags full of gifts, electronic appliances, and personal effects, but also their cultural practices, experiences, and values, such as ideas about respect and dignity. I propose that, culturally speaking, the Puerto Rican nation can no longer be restricted to the island but is instead constituted by two distinct yet closely intertwined fragments: that of Puerto Rico itself and of the diasporic communities settled in the continental United States. The multiple implications of this profound territorial dispersion on popular expressions of nationalism have not been fully explored. More specifically, the cultural impact of return and circular migration on the island awaits systematic exploration. I therefore advocate a transnational approach to contemporary Puerto Rican culture that moves beyond territorial boundaries to analyze the continuing sociocultural ties between the diaspora and its communities of origin.[9]

Here one needs to question the fixed locations from which much of the nationalist discourse has traditionally framed the nation. To quote Benedict Anderson's famous definition, nations are not always imagined as "inherently limited and sovereign."[10] As a consequence of large-scale and sustained migration, popular images of Puerto Ricanness have been thoroughly deterritorialized and transnationalized. Still, they may influence people's everyday lives by providing powerful and evocative representations of their cultural identities. For instance, the *jíbaro's pava* (the straw hat typically worn by highland subsistence farmers on the island) is constantly displayed as a visual icon of Puerto Ricanness in the United States. The *pava* reappears in the most unlikely places, such as public schools in Brooklyn, folk festivals in Central Park, the Puerto Rican Day Parade along Fifth Avenue, and Smithsonian Institution exhibits.

Another example is the construction of *casitas*, small wooden houses reminiscent of the island's rural dwellings, in the abandoned lots of the South Bronx and the Lower East Side of Manhattan.[11] *Casitas* represent the reinvention of a preindustrial time and place, nostalgically remembered as a tightly knit community of relatives, friends, and neighbors, before the advent of urbanization and migration. In Chicago, the *Paseo Boricua* along Division Street has reclaimed the neighborhoods where Puerto Ricans used to live by erecting two enormous steel Puerto Rican flags, building a casita in honor of the nationalist leader Pedro Albizu Campos, and celebrating street festivals on such occasions as Three Kings Day, the People's Parade, and patron saints' feasts.[12] These examples suggest that symbolic expressions of Puerto Rican identity are no longer circumscribed to the island and may well have intensified in the U.S. mainland. Similarly, cultural practices and identities have often moved back from the diaspora to the island, as suggested by the cases of salsa and rap music, to mention just two examples.

The diaspora has mobilized standard concepts of the nation, culture, language, and territory. Population displacements across and within geopolitical borders have weakened political nationalism and broadened cultural identities in many countries.[13] In Puerto Rico, five decades of uninterrupted migration to the mainland have unsettled the territorial and linguistic boundaries of national culture. For instance, second-generation migrants who return to the island—often dubbed pejoratively Nuyoricans—may speak English better than Spanish and still define themselves simply as Puerto Rican.[14] While the Spanish language continues to be a basic symbol of national identity on the island, it has become a less reliable mark of Puerto Ricanness in the mainland.

Any definition of the island's political status must take into account the growing strength of cultural nationalism, as much as the increasing dispersal of people through the diaspora. Thousands of Puerto Ricans have developed mobile livelihood practices that encompass several places in the mainland as well as on the island. Most Puerto Ricans on the mainland have expressed a strong desire to participate in referenda on the island's political status. According to public polls, the status preferences of Puerto Ricans residing on the mainland are very similar to those on the island—that is, they tend to favor commonwealth status, rather than statehood or independence.[15] Those who live abroad, speak English, and participate in U.S. politics must be included in public and academic discussions on the future of Puerto Rico. They are part and parcel of a nation on the move.

El Vaivén: Moving Back and Forth

The Spanish folk term for the back-and-forth movement of people between Puerto Rico and the United States is *el vaivén* (literally meaning "coming and going," or, according to the *Appleton New Cuyás English-Spanish Dictionary*, "fluctuation"). As used in the present chapter, this culturally dense word refers to the constant comings and goings in which thousands of Puerto Ricans are involved.[16] For some, it implies that some people do not stay put in one place for a long time, but move incessantly, like the wind or the waves of the sea, in response to shifting tides. More ominously, *vaivén* also connotes unsteadiness, inconstancy, and oscillation.

I prefer to use the term in the more neutral sense of a back-and-forth movement, without implying that people who engage in such movements never set roots in particular communities. Nor do I mean that most Puerto Ricans are circular migrants in the restricted sense of relocating frequently between Puerto Rico and the United States. *La nación en vaivén*, the "nation on the move," might serve as an apt metaphor for the fluid and hybrid identities of Puerto Ricans on the island and in the mainland, suggesting that none of the traditional criteria for nationhood—a shared territory, language, economy, citizenship, or sovereignty—are fixed and immutable. All of these criteria are subject to constant fluctuation and intense debate in Puerto Rico and its diaspora, even though the sense of peoplehood has proven remarkably resilient throughout.

Over the past few decades, Puerto Rico has become a nation on the move through the relocation of almost half of its population to the United States and the continuing flow of people between the island and the mainland. Contrary to other population movements, much of the Puerto Rican exodus entails a restless movement between multiple places of origin and destination. The number of returnees to the island began to surpass those leaving for the mainland in the early 1970s, especially as a result of minimum-wage hikes on the island and the industrial restructuring of New York City, the traditional center of the Puerto Rican diaspora. But mass emigration resumed during the 1980s, at the same time that return migration continued unabated, foreign immigration increased, and circular migration emerged as a significant phenomenon.

The numbers of people engaged in the back-and-forth movement between the island and the diaspora are staggering. Between 1990 and 1999, net migration from Puerto Rico to the United States was estimated to be 325,875 persons, compared to 490,562 persons between 1980 and 1989.[17] Between 1991 and 1998, Puerto Rico received 144,528 return migrants.[18] In 1994–95 alone, 53,164 persons emigrated from the island, while 18,177 immigrated. Nearly 95 percent of those who moved to the island were return migrants and their children.[19] The 2000 Census found that 6.1 percent of Puerto Rico's entire population of 3.8 million had been born in the United States and that 3.2 percent had been living there in 1995.[20] In short, contemporary Puerto Rican migration is best visualized as a pendular or "revolving-door" movement, rather than as an irrevocable and unilateral displacement.

Although scholars disagree as to the precise terminology, magnitude, and impact of circular migration, most convene that the Puerto Rican diaspora has become a sustained bilateral movement of people. Estimates of the volume of circular migration between the island and the mainland vary widely, depending on various definitions, sources, methods, and approaches. In Carlos Vargas-Ramos's sample of return migrants in the town of Aguadilla, more than 42 percent would qualify as circulators.[21] According to the 1990 Census, 130,335 people moved back and forth between the island and the mainland—more than 23 percent of those who left Puerto Rico—during the 1980s.[22] According to a more recent survey conducted in Puerto Rico, more than 13 percent of all return migrants had moved at least twice between the island and the mainland.[23] Regardless of the exact number, back-and-forth movement has become a key feature of contemporary Puerto Rican society. Although most people move from the island to the United States, a growing proportion of the island's population are returned migrants and their offspring.

The current literature on transnationalism helps to frame Puerto Rican migration in a broader context. Transnationalism is commonly understood as the establishment of multiple social, economic, political, and cultural links between two or more countries, including but not limited to actual physical movement.[24] Applying this definition to Puerto Rico must take into account that the island is not a sovereign state, and therefore the analytical distinction between state and nation must be made carefully. For example, government authorities do not police Puerto Ricans moving between the island and the mainland, unlike those who cross international frontiers. However, the subjective experience of migration for many Puerto Ricans as a dual process of deterritorialization and reterritorialization has been well established.[25] As Puerto Ricans commonly say, moving abroad involves *irse pa' fuera*, literally "going outside" the Island-country. For some migrants, the United States is culturally as foreign as the Dominican Republic or Venezuela—although they share U.S. citizenship with residents of the mainland. Even the colonial legislature of Puerto Rico recognized this fact in 1947, when it called the United States an "ethnologically strange setting."[26]

During the past decade, the metaphor of Puerto Rico as a nation on the move has taken additional meanings. On May 4, 2000, the U.S. Navy carried out Operation Access to the east, removing more than 200 peaceful demonstrators from its training grounds in Vieques, a small island-municipality off the eastern coast of Puerto Rico.[27] Those practicing civil disobedience included a wide spectrum of political and religious leaders, university students, and community activists. The protests had been sparked by the accidental death of security guard David Sanes Rodríguez during a military exercise in Vieques on April 19, 1999. Soon thereafter, Puerto Ricans of all ideological persuasions and walks of life called for an end to live bombings, the navy's exit, and the return of military lands to the civilian residents of Vieques. Nearly 89 percent of those surveyed in a 2000 public opinion poll supported the immediate exit of the U.S. Navy from Vieques.[28] As a result of this prolonged struggle, the Puerto Rican nation was symbolically extended beyond the main island to Vieques—*la isla nena*, or the baby island, as it is affectionately known—as well as to Culebra and other smaller territories of the Puerto Rican archipelago. It is now more appropriate than ever to speak about the islands of Puerto Rico, especially if one includes Manhattan in the discussion.

A noteworthy development was the active participation of leaders of the Puerto Rican diaspora in the "peace for Vieques" movement. Two of the three mainland Puerto Rican congresspeople to the U.S. House of Representatives, Luis Gutiérrez and Nydia Velázquez, were detained during Operation Access to the east. The third, José Serrano, was arrested inside the White House grounds demanding the navy's immediate exit from Vieques.

Many other Puerto Rican leaders from New York have publicly expressed their support for the peace movement on the island. Thus, Puerto Rican national identity moved abroad in two main directions—both across a short distance to Vieques and across the "big pond" of the Atlantic Ocean to the mainland. For the moment, the public discourse on the Puerto Rican nation has broadened beyond territorial boundaries and across political differences.

From Colonialism to Transnationalism

After World War II, following a worldwide wave toward decolonization, Puerto Rico obtained a greater degree of autonomy from the United States. In 1952, 81 percent of the Puerto Rican electorate approved the constitution of the *Estado Libre Asociado*. Although commonwealth status did not alter the basic contours of the colonial situation, it permitted—perhaps even required—the adoption of cultural nationalism as a state policy on the island. Since the mid-1950s, the Institute of Puerto Rican Culture and other government agencies have promoted a distinctive nationalist iconography based on powerful symbols such as the Spanish language, the *jíbaro*, the Taíno Indian heritage, and the folk art of carving *santos*, the small wooden sculptures of Catholic saints. Like other nations, Puerto Rico has developed its own set of collective myths, memories, rituals, and images, such as the flag, anthem, and seal, as well as participation in Olympic sports and international beauty contests.

Such icons have been widely diffused on the island and in the mainland, and have strengthened the sense of being Puerto Rican as opposed to American. Their popular appeal, however, has not translated into massive support for independence or even free association with the United States. Cultural nationalism has been practically divorced from political nationalism on the island. As the sociologist Felipe Pimentel has argued, "Puerto Ricans have achieved many of the things that other colonized people only got after obtaining independence, of course, with the exception of political sovereignty."[29] Although the lack of sovereignty is still a major issue, to a large extent Puerto Rico has been able to develop its economy, preserve its culture, and expand many of the political and social rights of its citizens under commonwealth status.

Although political nationalism has waned on the island, cultural nationalism is firmly entrenched among Puerto Ricans. In a recent poll conducted on the island, more than 60 percent of the respondents chose Puerto Rico as their nation, while 17 percent considered both Puerto Rico and the United States to be their nation, and only 20 percent mentioned the United States alone.[30] Other empirical studies, conducted in the mainland, have confirmed that most Puerto Ricans see themselves as part of a distinct nation and share a specifically Puerto Rican, not American or Latino, identity.[31] Across a broad spectrum of social classes, political affiliations, and racial groups, islanders identify themselves primarily as Puerto Rican, not as Caribbean, Hispanic, or American, even as they recognize the material and symbolic benefits of

U.S. citizenship.[32] Throughout this chapter, I have argued that Puerto Ricans on and off the island assert a strong national, not just ethnic, identity, even though most of them do not support independence for their country.[33]

I think it is appropriate to call this sense of peoplehood "national" because it is grounded in a shared past, a territory considered to be the homeland, and a linguistic and cultural heritage that may not be common to all Puerto Ricans on both shores, but continues to be cherished by most. In their daily lives, many Puerto Ricans experience a profound fissure between nationhood and statehood as sources of collective identity, as manifested in having two flags, two anthems, two languages, and two sets of allegiances, sometimes conflicting, frequently overlapping. Like Quebec, Scotland, or Catalonia, Puerto Rico remains a stateless nation, rather than simply another ethnic minority within an imperial state. That is why most Puerto Ricans call Puerto Rico their nation, not the United States.

Transnational migration has eroded the exclusive territorial and linguistic boundaries of the Puerto Rican nation. Since the beginning of the twentieth century, the Puerto Rican government sponsored large-scale migration to the mainland as a safety valve for the island's overpopulation and unemployment problems. During the 1940s and 1950s, public officials and planners conceived Puerto Ricans in the United States as "migrant citizens" in need of assistance, orientation, and organization. For decades, commonwealth leaders treated the Puerto Rican community abroad as a symbolic extension of the island's culture rather than as an independent entity. In turn, migrant grassroots groups constructed their own identity primarily as Puerto Rican, but did not accept wholesale the traditional discourse of Puerto Ricanness, especially its exclusive definition of the nation on linguistic and territorial grounds. Those who move back and forth between the island and the mainland are likely to be bilingual and bicultural, as well as unbound by a fixed location in either place, yet most perceive themselves to be as Puerto Rican as those who move less frequently.

Through migration, Puerto Ricans have become members of a translocal nation "whose boundaries shift between the archipelago of Puerto Rico and its U.S. diaspora."[34] Among recent Latino immigrants in the United States (including Mexicans, Cubans, and Dominicans), only Puerto Ricans insist on calling themselves simply Puerto Ricans, rather than Puerto Rican-Americans, which speaks volumes about their persistent stress on national origin and their adamant rejection of a hyphenated ethnicity. No major Puerto Rican organization on the mainland calls itself Puerto Rican-American, contrary to many hyphenated associations among Cuban-Americans, Mexican Americans, or Dominican Americans, not to mention African Americans, Italian Americans, or Asian Americans.

Many contemporary representations of Puerto Ricanness in the mainland are thoroughly diasporic notions based on long-distance nationalism, especially of a cultural sort.[35] Unlike well-established nation-states, Puerto Rico cannot be imagined from any fixed location as a sovereign community, exclusively tied to a single territory or language, and characterized by a sense of deep, horizontal comradeship.[36] Rather, it is a geographically, politically, linguistically, and culturally-splintered country. Moreover, few Puerto Ricans can now imagine their nation apart from some form of permanent association with the United States.

Throughout the twentieth century, Puerto Rican migrants have maintained strong social and cultural ties to their homeland and developed alternate conceptions of their own identity. Voluntary associations in the United States selectively appropriated the discursive practices traditionally associated with being Puerto Rican, yet they continued to portray themselves as part of a translocal nation divided between the island and the mainland.[37] During the 1940s and 1950s, voluntary associations of the Puerto Rican community proliferated, especially in New York City, cultural practices, such as parades, folk festivals, popular music, and sports events. As a 1955 newspaper article published in New York put it,

> Thousands of *boricuas* [Puerto Ricans] are dispersed around the world and none of them, with very rare exceptions, denies his Puerto Rican homeland or race. That is the seal and the distinctive mark that we all carry with us. That mark or peculiar way of being is what distinguishes us from other races and fellow peoples of the New World.
>
> Through his presence, his way of acting or speaking, whether on purpose or unconsciously, the Puerto Rican is easy to identify wherever he may be. And this is markedly so both in the case of the *boricua* with little academic preparation and in nuclei with more education.[38]

Even in the 1960s, when second-generation immigrants began to assert their claims as a separate ethnic minority in the United States, they often deployed the rhetoric and tactics of cultural nationalism, rather than define themselves as hyphenated Puerto Rican-Americans. Thus, the Puerto Rican diaspora has nurtured what Benedict Anderson, Nina Glick Schiller and Georges Fouron have called long-distance nationalism as part of the rise of identity politics after World War II.[39]

Conclusion

No country in recent history has undergone a more prolonged and massive displacement of its people than Puerto Rico. Recalling Ireland's experience during the second half of the nineteenth century, Puerto Rico exported almost half of its current population to the United States after World War II. Unlike Ireland and other major sending countries in Europe during the heyday of emigration, the island has received a growing number of return migrants since the 1960s, as well as large influx of foreign immigrants from neighboring countries such as the Dominican Republic and Cuba. Such dizzying nomadism—a constant dislocation and relocation of peoples, practices, imaginaries, and identities—has been posited as one of the defining moments of a global, transnational, or postmodern age.[40] That may well be so. But regardless of one's theoretical or political preferences, representing nations on the move remains difficult. I have explored alternative approaches to the problem, by mobilizing the object of study—the relationship between nation, migration, and identity—through time and space, as well as by looking at it from various methodological standpoints and identifying multiple social actors and ideological positions.

Rethinking the resilience of Puerto Rican identity against all odds provides insights about the workings of colonial, nationalist, and transnational discourses. My analysis suggests that political nationalism tends to weaken with the constant transgression of national boundaries through large-scale migration and the emergence of a new (*lite*) form of colonialism. Diasporic communities often develop different representations of identity from the dominant nationalist canon by stressing their broad kinship, cultural, and emotional ties to an ancestral homeland, rather than its narrow linguistic and territorial boundaries. This strategy is typical of what some analysts have dubbed long-distance nationalism.[41] In the terms proposed throughout this chapter, cultural nationalism may prosper more easily than political nationalism in places where much of the population has become transnational. It can help to advance the multiple economic and political interests of various sectors of society, such as intellectuals, politicians, entrepreneurs, and even migrant workers, without necessarily establishing a sovereign state.

Given the current lack of popular support for political nationalism in Puerto Rico, the struggle for citizenship rights, democratic representation, entitlement of disenfranchised groups, and community empowerment will most likely have to be advanced within the limits of cultural rather than political nationalism. Cultural nationalism might not pose a radical challenge to the colonial status of Puerto Rico, but it may slow down the island's further assimilation into the United States. In a transnational context, cultural nationalism may well be the only viable strategy to define and promote a common identity between Puerto Ricans on the island and in the diaspora. Although much work remains to be done, it is increasingly clear that national identities flow and at the same time endure across many kinds of borders, both territorial and symbolic.

Notes

An earlier version of this chapter was presented as the Earl and Esther Johnson Lecture at the Master of Arts Program in Social Sciences at the University of Chicago, November 2, 2001, and at the Department of Sociology and Anthropology at Swarthmore College, November 30, 2001. I would like to thank Robin Derby Yarimar Bonilla, and Raquel Romberg for their kind invitations to present this paper and Suzanne Oboler, Frances Negrón-Muntaner, César Ayala, Miguel Díaz-Barriga, Braulio Muñoz, Dain Borges, Emilio Kourí, and several anonymous reviewers for their incisive comments and suggestions.

1. Since 1898, Puerto Rico has occupied a juridical limbo within the framework of the U.S. Constitution. For excellent analyses of the legal doctrine establishing

that the island "belongs to but is not part of the United States," see Christina Duffy Burnett and Burke Marshall, eds., *Foreign in a Domestic Sense: Puerto Rico, American Expansion, and the Constitution* (Durham, NC: Duke University Press, 2001), and Efrén Rivera Ramos, *The Legal Construction of Identity: The Judicial and Social Legacy of American Colonialism in Puerto Rico* (Washington, DC: American Psychological Association, 2001). Throughout this chapter, I will use the term "colony" in the classic sense of a territory under the direct political and economic control of an external power, a definition that clearly applies to Puerto Rico. Juan Flores has used the term "postcolonial colony" to refer to U.S. domination over the island after the establishment of the *Estado Libre Asociado* in 1952. See Juan Flores, *From Bomba to Hip Hop: Puerto Rican Culture and Latino Identity* (New York: Columbia University Press, 2000).

2. U.S. Department of Commerce, Bureau of the Census, *The Hispanic Population*, 2001, <http: // www.census.gov. /prod /2001pubs/c2kbr01-3.pdf.>.
3. U.S. Census Bureau, *Census 2000 Summary Files (SF3)—Sample Data. Geographic Area: Puerto Rico*, 2002, <http: //factfinder.census.gov/servlet/ QTTable?_ts=49209160130>.
4. See Linda Basch, Nina Glick Schiller, and Cristina Szanton-Blanc, *Nations Unbound: Transnational Projects, Postcolonial Predicaments, and Deterritorialized Nation-States* (New York: Gordon and Breach, 1994); Nina Glick Schiller, Linda Basch, and Cristina Blanc Szanton, eds., *Towards a Transnational Perspective on Migration: Race, Class, Ethnicity, and Nationalism Reconsidered* (New York: New York Academy of Sciences, 1992).
5. César Ayala, letter to author, March 11, 2001.
6. See Benedict Anderson, *Long-Distance Nationalism: World Capitalism and the Rise of Identity Politics* (Amsterdam: Center for Asian Studies, 1992); Nina Glick Schiller and Georges Fouron, *Georges Woke Up Laughing: Long-Distance Nationalism and the Search for Home* (Durham, NC: Duke University Press, 2001).
7. See John Hutchinson, "Cultural Nationalism and Moral Regeneration," in *Nationalism*, ed. John Hutchinson and Anthony D. Smith (Oxford: Oxford University Press, 1994), 122–31.
8. See Peggy Levitt, *The Transnational Villagers* (Berkeley: University of California Press, 2001).
9. See Basch et al., *Nations Unbound*; Schiller et al., *Towards a Transnational Perspective.*
10. See Benedict Anderson, *Imagined Communities: Reflections on the Origin and Spread of Nationalism*, 2nd ed. (London: Verso, 1991).
11. See Luis Aponte-Parés, "Pequeñas Patrias: Appropriating Place in the American City," Paper presented at the Second Conference of the Puerto Rican Studies Association, San Juan, September 26–29, 1996.
12. See Nilda Flores-González, "Paseo Boricua: Claiming a Puerto Rican Space in Chicago," *Centro: Journal of the Center for Puerto Rican Studies* 13, no. 2 (2001): 6–23.
13. See Basch et al., *Nations Unbound.*
14. See Ana Celia Zentella, "Returned Migration, Language, and Identity: Puerto Rican Bilinguals in Dos Worlds/Two Mundos," *International Journal of the Sociology of Language* 84 (1990): 81–100.
15. See Angelo Falcón, "A Divided Nation: The Puerto Rican Diaspora in the United States and the Proposed Referendum," in *Colonial Dilemma: Critical*

Perspectives on Contemporary Puerto Rico, ed. Edwin Meléndez and Edgardo Meléndez (Boston: South End Press, 1993), 173–80.

16. See Clara Rodríguez, "Puerto Rican Circular Migration Revisited," *Latino Studies Journal* 4, no. 2 (1993): 93–113.
17. The estimate is based on the difference between outbound and inbound passengers between the island and the mainland, as reported by Puerto Rico's Planning Board. Many scholars have noted the unreliability of this method of calculating the volume of population movements between Puerto Rico and the continental United States. The U.S. Census Bureau recently released much more conservative estimates of net migration between the island the mainland: 126,465 persons for the 1980s and 111,336 for the 1990s. See Matthew Christenson, *Evaluating Components of International Migration: Migration Between Puerto Rico and the United States. Population Division, Working Paper Series No. 64* (Washington, DC: U.S. Bureau of the Census, 2001). However, to ensure the consistency of the data, I prefer to use the historical series based on the Junta de Planificación. See Junta de Planificación de Puerto Rico, *Movimiento de pasajeros entre Puerto Rico y el exterior. Años fiscales* (Unpublished document) (San Juan: Junta de Planificación, Programa de Planificación Económica y Social, Subprograma de Análisis Económico, 2001).
18. Junta de Planificación de Puerto Rico, "Migración de retorno en Puerto Rico," in *Informe económico al Gobernador, 1999* (San Juan: Junta de Planificación de Puerto Rico, 2000), 1–16.
19. See Luz Olmeda, "Aspectos socioeconómicos de la migración en el 1994–95," in Junta de Planificación, *Informe económico al Gobernador, 1997* (San Juan: Junta de Planificación de Puerto Rico, 1998), 6–12.
20. U.S. Census Bureau, *Profile of Selected Social Characteristics: 2000. Geographic Area: Puerto Rico*, 2002, <http: // censtats.census.gov /data /PR/0472.pdf>.
21. See Carlos Vargas-Ramos, "The Effect of Return Migration on Political Participation in Puerto Rico" (Ph.D. dissertation, Columbia University, 2000).
22. See Francisco Rivera-Batiz and Carlos E. Santiago, *Island Paradox: Puerto Rico in the 1990s* (New York: Russell Sage Foundation, 1996).
23. Jorge Duany, *The Puerto Rican Nation on the Move: Identities on the Island and in the United States* (Chapel Hill: University of North Carolina Press, 2002), 223.
24. See Schiller et al. *Towards a Transnational Perspective*; see also Sarah Mahler and Patricia R. Pessar, "Gendered Geographies of Power: Analyzing Gender Across Transnational Places," *Identities* 7, no. 4 (2001): 441–59.
25. See Agustín Laó, "Islands at the Crossroads: Puerto Ricanness Traveling between the Translocal Nation and the Global City," in *Puerto Rican Jam: Rethinking Colonialism and Nationalism*, ed. Frances Negrón-Muntaner and Ramón Grosfoguel (Minneapolis: University of Minnesota Press, 1997), 169–88; Gina M. Pérez, *The Near Northwest Side Story: Migration, Displacement, and Puerto Rican Families* (Berkeley: University of California Press, 2004); Ana Yolanda Ramos-Zayas, *National Performances: The Politics of Class, Race, and Space in Puerto Rican Chicago* (Chicago: University of Chicago Press, 2003); Carmen Teresa Whalen, *From Puerto Rico to Philadelphia: Puerto Rican Workers and Postwar Economies* (Philadelphia: Temple University Press, 2001).

26. Duany, *Puerto Rican Nation on the Move*, 171.
27. For an excellent anthropological analysis of how the Vieques peace movement galvanized cultural nationalism and other grassroots movements in Puerto Rico, see Katherine T. McCaffrey, *Military Power and Popular Protest: The U.S. Navy in Vieques, Puerto Rico* (New Brunswick, NJ: Rutgers University Press, 2002).
28. Ibid., 172–73.
29. Felipe Pimentel, personal communication, November 14, 2002.
30. Cited by Julio Muriente Pérez, *La batalla de las banderas y la cuestión nacional: Fanon, Memmi, Césaire y el caso colonial de Puerto Rico* (San Juan: Cultural, 2002), 46.
31. See Rodolfo de la Garza et al., *Latino Voices: Mexican, Puerto Rican, and Cuban Perspectives on American Politics* (Boulder, CO: Westview, 1992).
32. See Nancy Morris, *Puerto Rico: Culture, Politics, and Identity* (Westport, CT: Praeger, 1995); Angel Israel Rivera, *Puerto Rico: Ficción y mitología en sus alternativas de status* (San Juan: Nueva Aurora, 1996).
33. Ramón Grosfoguel, Frances Negrón-Muntaner, and Chloé S. Georas have argued that Puerto Ricans imagine themselves as both a national and ethnic group, depending on the context. See Ramón Grosfoguel, Frances Negrón-Muntaner, and Chloé S. Georas, "Beyond Nationalist and Colonialist Discourses: The Jaiba Politics of the Puerto Rican Ethno-Nation," in *Puerto Rican Jam: Rethinking Colonialism and Nationalism*, ed. Frances Negrón-Muntaner and Ramón Grosfoguel (Minneapolis: University of Minnesota Press, 1997), 1–38. However, I find their term "ethno-nation" confusing, insofar as it combines two different forms of identification, political mobilization, and discursive practice.
34. Laó, "Islands at the Crossroads," 171.
35. See Anderson, *Long Distance Nationalism*; Schiller and Fouron, *Georges Woke Up Laughing.*
36. See Anderson, *Imagined Communities.*
37. For an overview of the cultural practices of Puerto Rican voluntary associations in the United States, see Duany, "Chapter 8."
38. Manuel Marictta, "La celebración del Día de los Hijos Ausentes en los Pueblos de Puerto Rico," *Puerto Rico y Nueva York: Magazine Mensual Ilustrado* 2, no. 2 (1955): 32.
39. See Benedict Anderson, *Long Distance Nationalism*; Schiller and Fouron, *Georges Woke Up Laughing.*
40. See Iain Chambers, *Migrancy, Culture, Identity* (London: Routledge, 1994).
41. See Schiller and Fouron, *Georges Woke Up Laughing.*

CHAPTER 5

The Political Status of Puerto Rico: A Nonsense Dilemma

Carlos Pabón

Throughout the twentieth century, the traditional political discourse in Puerto Rico centered on the question of the island's status, that is, the juridical and political relationship between Puerto Rico and the United States. The twentieth century is over, but the political debate about the status continues unabated. This chapter locates the so-called Puerto Rican status question within the context of the crisis of the nation-state. From this critique, I will propose that the political status question in Puerto Rico is a debate that is much a do about nothing, a nonsense dilemma based on an obsolete political paradigm that stifles political imagination and blocks alternate political imaginaries.

Puerto Rico's status politics relies on three "options" defended by specific parties. Each of the three status parties—the Puerto Rican Independence Party, the Popular Democratic Party, and the New Progressive Party—insists that its preferred status option (independence, autonomy, and statehood respectively) is the only one capable of resolving the fundamental political, social, and economic problems of the island. Thus each party postulates that its political-ideological orientation is radically different from the others. According to the traditional political understanding of the Puerto Rican political culture, independence is associated with the left, the *Estado Libre Asociado* (actual commonwealth status) with moderate liberal positions, and statehood with the conservative right.

But notwithstanding the rhetoric of these parties, what actually occurs is the three status options are variants of the same discourse on national sovereignty. The political discourse of the three main political parties, despite their apparent differences, have as a central trope national sovereignty, be it as a claim for an independent or autonomous national state or as a demand to complete the island's annexation to the United States. And I ask, what do the traditional status formulas based on nineteenth century's assumptions about the nation have to offer the twenty-first century's micro-electronic revolution, cyberspace, and genetic engineering world? Is it the case that any of the status alternatives will resolve drug trafficking or the ecological crisis, just to mention two problems in which the local and the global are clearly articulated?

While in different intellectual and international political forums there is a growing debate about the crisis of the nation-state and the decline of sovereignty, and the question of what is sovereignty is argued over with great intensity, in Puerto Rico the political discussion is whether sovereignty emanates from the U.S. Congress or the Puerto Rican people. In doing so, the status paradigm ignores the paramount political implications of the crisis of the nation-state and of the principle of territorial sovereignty in the context of globalization.

After the Westphalia peace accords of 1648, the principle of territorial sovereignty became the fundamental juridical-political concept of the nation-state.[1] This principle designates the power that a nation-state has over its territory. In other words, it encodes the nation-state's prerogative to make final decisions and impose the law on a territorially bound national community. A loss of sovereignty hence implies a loss of control over the national territory's concerns. Today, the principle of territorial sovereignty is in crisis. Not only because globalization limits, but also it deeply undermines national sovereignty, and with it, its power to control and regulate the flow of commodities, people, information, and diverse cultural forms significantly declines.[2] This is why there is a generalized concern for the progressive weakening of the nation-state's maneuvering space to decide major issues. Consequently, there is the paradoxical situation that while nationalisms gain in intensity, the nation-state, as an isomorphic configuration of the territory, ethnos, and state apparatus find itself in a serious and profound crisis.

Wolfgang Hein has pointed out that the globalization process has greatly accelerated over the last few decades, creating increasing problems with the territorialized political organization of the state. This process leads the nation-state to precariousness because it creates social, economic, and ecological problems that citizens ask their national states to solve while globalization increasingly reduces the ability of nation-states to solve those very same problems. This contradiction appears to be one of the central causes of the crisis of governing that many consider as one of the main problems of the contemporary world. For Hein, if more adequate forms of transnational political coordination that transcend the frame of the nation-state are not found, social catastrophes on a global scale such as ecological crisis, regional wars, massive migrations, epidemics, and so forth will occur with a more widespread impact. That is why, for him, any perspective on globalization that is not willing to accept world catastrophes as a form of political transformation has to realize that the deepening of the process of globalization is not going to stop, and in the long run, this process will demand its equivalent on the global political sphere.[3]

As Roberto Bergalli and Eligio Resto point out, there is a growing consensus that the international community faces urgent problems that cannot be addressed within the cage of the old trope of national sovereignty.[4] The argument I am making is not that we should adopt the proposals that Hein, Bergalli and Resto, and other authors have made about the configuration of a new global political order,[5] but rather that we should recognize that it is indispensable to explore the dimensions and implications of the crisis of national/territorial sovereignty. One of these dimensions is that the globalizations of capital, financing and commerce have not gone hand in hand with a democratic control of global proportions. This global democratic control constitutes one of the most important ethical challenges to globalization. What is evident is that independently of which democratic mechanisms are created, these cannot be an amplified reproduction of the mechanisms and prerogatives that have characterized the system of nation-states.[6] To establish democratic mechanisms appropriate to the era of globalization, new social forces and actors, different from those of nation-states, will be required.

I am not proposing the imminent disappearance of the nation-state. It is obvious that nation-states exist and will continue to exist for the immediate future. I do propose that the historical period characterized by the hegemony of the nation-state system is coming to an end. In the era of globalization, the nation-state increasingly becomes more outdated, and other forms of adhesion and identification struggle to take its place. Even when nation-states will continue to exist, the erosion of the nation-states' power to monopolize loyalties will stimulate the proliferation of identities divorced from national states.[7]

One would have to ask if the principle of territorial sovereignty, in crisis today, is even desirable. Who champions national sovereignty today? What is national sovereignty good for, or better still, whom does it serve? The new right in the United States and Europe invokes it to expel immigrants from its territories; the Brazilian ranchers to destroy the Amazonian jungle; the Cuban state to proclaim its right to build a Chernobyl-style nuclear plant; the Chinese to massacre students who struggle for democracy; the Russian to legitimize the government's bombing of the Chechens; the Israeli to crush Palestinians; and the Serbian to carry out "ethnic cleansing" against Bosnians, Croatians, and Kosovars; and it is desired by oppressive ethnic minorities who want to create an ethnic state from which to oppress other ethnic minorities.

It is relevant to underscore the role that the nation-state and territorial sovereignty plays in the growing ethnic violence of our time. As Arjun Appadurai argues, in its desire to control, classify, homogenize, and watch over its subjects, the nation-state has frequently created, revitalized, or fractured ethnic identities that before were fluid and negotiable, hence contributing to generate ethnic conflicts that, even when they are legitimized by recalling past grievances, emerge from relatively recent situations. The conflicts that have sprung in the Balkans, former Soviet Union, or Basque Country do not arise from "tribalism" but from the modern phenomenon linked to the logic of the nation-state. This logic tends to fix—in an isomorphic configuration—state, territory, and ethnicity.

The spiral of ethnic violence can then be explained by considering the process of feedback between nationalism and ethnicity. Nationalism constructs ethnic categories that in turn motivate others to constitute counter-ethnicities. In times of political crisis, counter-ethnicities demand nation-states that are founded on counter-nationalisms. For every national movement that claims its "natural" destiny of becoming a state, there is another nationalism that arises from the first.[8] This reactive process, in which the nationalist desire to provide a nationalist configuration—a state—to an ethnic identity, unfolds, has contributed to the ethnic violence that has taken hold over much of the world after the cold war.

Moreover, it must not be ignored that with the modern nation-state and its sovereignty, politics has fundamentally become a biopolitics, that is, a politics founded upon the growing subjection of the natural life of human beings to the mechanisms and calculations of state power. And that is why, as Giorgio Agamben suggests, the typical spaces for modern biopolitics are the concentration camp and the totalitarian state of the twentieth century.[9] It is the following trinity that has made the worst catastrophes of the last century possible: national sovereignty, biopolitics, and totalitarianism. Which leads me to ask, how is it possible to defend national sovereignty after Auschwitz?

Finally, it is important to underscore the paradox between the definition of nation-state and the concept of human rights. This paradox, even when it has intensified with diasporic movements in the era of globalization, is not new. Hannah Arendt, in her book *The Origins of Totalitarianism*, originally published in 1951, argues how the refugee represents a paradox in relation to the concept of human rights within the system of national states. Referring to the refugees and exiles produced by the First and Second Worlds Wars, Arendt writes, "The conception of human rights, based upon the assumed existence of a human being as such, broke down at the very moment when those who professed to believe in it were for the first time confronted with people who had indeed lost all qualities and specific relationships—except that they were still human. The world found nothing sacred in the abstract nakedness of being human."[10]

The paradox consists in that the refugee, who should have embodied human rights more than any other, pointed toward its most radical inconsistency.[11] According to Arendt, "The Rights of Man, after all, had been defined as 'inalienable' because they were supposed to be independent of all governments; but it turned out that the moment human beings lacked their own government and had to fall back upon their minimum rights, no authority was left to protect them and no institution was willing to guarantee them."[12] From the start, Arendt states that the paradox implied in the concept of inalienable human rights is that it refers to an "abstract" human being that does not exist anywhere. As a result, the question of human rights was quickly and inextricably linked to the issue of national sovereignty and hence to the nation-state.

The implications of Arendt's arguments are fundamental: in the system of nation-states the supposedly inalienable human rights are revealed as lacking any protection at a time that it is no longer possible to conceive of them as the rights of national citizens. In other words, in the nation-state there is no such thing as human rights that are acquired by the mere fact of existing as a human being. Nobody has rights for being part of the human species. What exist are rights of citizens subject to a state, that is, national rights. And these are only conferred to citizens or political subjects who are recognized as such by the state. Citizenship, hence, is always conceived as belonging to a national community.

Arendt's arguments eloquently contribute to dislodge the sovereignty discourses, like the ones posited by the traditional political paradigm in Puerto Rico, that see in the founding and defense of national sovereignty a human rights issue. The refugee constitutes such a problematic trope in the context of national states precisely because in breaking the link between human and citizen, birth and national origin, it makes dramatically evident the founding crisis of national sovereignty.[13] In other words, it pushes the founding principles of the national state into a crisis. And this crisis allows for a radical rethinking of the main political categories of modernity. The implication of Arendt's crucial understanding is something that the so-called status question in Puerto Rico simply ignores.

Furthermore, the status paradigm also ignores that national sovereignty is always the sovereignty of the state, that is, of the political and economic sectors that control the state, and it is not a sovereignty of the "people." Puerto Rican self-determination is the self-determination of the political and economic elites, not that of the people. The "people" invoked by these elites does not exist. It is an empty signifier that is used by anyone, for any purpose. The status is hence a mechanism used by the Puerto Rican elites to better negotiate or advance its interests with the American elites.

Finally, it is also important to point out that the traditional paradigm of Puerto Rican politics has reduced what is "political" to the status question. As Emilio González Díaz has argued, in Puerto Rico "the political has been almost exclusively identified around the status question"[14] transforming a complex web of power, identities, imaginaries, and struggles to a merely legal question. This discursive operation has tended to render invisible any other definition of what one could understand by politics.

Consequently, it is practically impossible to refer to any issue that could be considered political outside of the framing of the status question. In other words, if it does not have to do with the status—independence, autonomy, or statehood—it is not political. And the reverse is also true, if the issues are not linked to status, they are not political until they are tied to this discourse.[15] The status discourse's logic is hence constituted as a blockade of initiatives, struggles, and forms of resistance that hinders the articulation of a more radical and expansive notion of "truly existing democracy." The status is like a black hole that swallows every political space in Puerto Rico.

Yet not only are the traditional political discourses on the island yoked to the status trap but also certain heterodoxical formulations, such as that of "radical statehood," made in 1997 by a group of intellectuals based on the island and the United States.[16] Even when I do recognize that this proposal tended to destabilize the coordinates of political identity set up by the traditional political debate demonstrating that you can both be a statehooder and a radical, I think that the proposal does not represent a break from the logic of the status paradigm. That is, the reduction of the political and politics to the status issue.

In fact, I think that that this proposal paradoxically contributes to the blockade that the status question imposes by linking a radical democratic perspective to a list of demands that are subordinated to one status in particular, and by not assuming these independently of the status that exists or may follow the current one. In addition, the document does not pose a political or theoretical rupture with the concepts of the nation-state or national sovereignty, but rather with one of its forms: neocolonial independence. This position does not cast off the aspiration to found a nation-state; it only suggests that this may not be a convenient political project for the majority of Puerto Ricans at this time. In this sense, the "Radical Statehood Manifesto" adopts a position that does not transcend the national/sovereignty trope.

In my view, what can be proposed in relation to the crisis of the nation-state and territorial sovereignty is the possibility of imagining new forms of post-national communities that are not founded upon being native to a territory or ethnic affiliation or belonging to a state. In other words, communities that break down the nation-state–territory equation that constitutes the foundation of the modern national state. I refer to extraterritorial or aterritorial communities, fluid and reciprocal,[17] communities that claim their right to be by the mere fact of being there or the desire to be there as a political subject. Is not it perhaps possible to think of a community made out of singularities that do not affirm an identity, or like Agamben points out, one in which "humans co-belong without any representable condition of belonging?"[18]

Instead, in contemporary Puerto Rico, the foundation of political agency rests upon the definition of who are Puerto Ricans, in other words, who fulfills the ethnic and cultural criteria to be able to decide the political "destiny" of the country's political status. But there are a growing number of immigrants—Dominicans, Cubans, Haitians, and so on—many of who are undocumented and refugees. What happens with them? Are they or are they not part of the political community? What rights do these groups have? For some, these diasporic groups are by definition excluded from political rights because they are not Puerto Ricans. There is also the issue of the political and cultural exclusion aimed at so-called nuyoricans, those who move back and forth between the island and the United States. Last, there is the issue of Puerto Ricans who are increasingly excluded from the category of "citizen" for being labeled "criminals" "sexual deviants," "homeless," "undesirable youth," "addicts," or "poor and black"; ultimately, for being an excessive, disposable, population.[19]

It is important to recognize that one of the main characteristics of globalization is that fewer social sectors are representable within the nation-state. This is not only the case, for instance, with the growing number of refugees or immigrants which already constitute a permanent mass of noncitizen residents or "denizens" that do not want to be naturalized or return home.[20] Among the denizens are also national subjects, who are increasingly excluded from the condition of "citizen"—youth, the unemployed, sexual minorities, racial minorities, criminalized populations, and so on. In this sense, the political order of the nation-state deprives, on the one hand, foreigners, undocumented workers, refugees, or immigrants of political rights, and, on the other, a growing group of national subjects who are ostensibly "citizens."

To reflect on the crisis of the nation-state and national sovereignty in the context of globalization implies a rethinking of new forms of democratic articulation and post-national extraterritorial or, even better, aterritorial citizenship. But this is precisely what the status paradigm does not permit. Modern societies are founded upon the premise that the nation-state will govern over its territory—it will be sovereign—while modern democratic theory provides citizens the right to deliberate on common issues within the confines of the nation-state. But, as I have argued, both spheres are deeply undermined or profoundly redefined by globalization.

It is then necessary to radically rethink both issues, that of territorial sovereignty and democracy, to respond to the challenge of new articulations between the global and the local. If not, the Puerto Rican political "debate" will remain swamped under the status issue, which is, a nonsense dilemma. Except, of course, for the politicians and others who lives off it. For here lies the irony of the status question in Puerto Rico: those who declare that their fundamental political goal is to resolve the island's status are the ones who most dread its resolution, because without the issue of the status they would cease to have the issue that justifies their political existence. Thus these sectors will continue a status debate that is much ado about nothing: nothing that really matters, that is, in today's world.

Notes

This chapter was translated by Frances Negrón-Muntaner.

1. Arjun Appadurai, "Sovereignty without Territoriality: Notes for a Postnational Geography," in *The Geography of Identity*, ed. Patricia Yaeger (Ann Arbor: University of Michigan Press, 1996), 41.
2. Ibid., 41–42.
3. Wolfgang Hein, "El fin del Estado-nación y el nuevo orden mundial," *Nueva Sociedad* 132 (1994): 94–98.
4. Roberto Bergalli and Eligio Resta, eds., *Soberanía: un principio que se derrumba. Aspectos metodológicos y jurídico-políticos* (Barcelona: Paidós, 1996), 10.
5. See David Held, *La democracia y el orden global: del Estado moderno al gobierno cosmopolita* (Barcelona: Paidós, 1997).
6. Zygmunt Bauman, *Globalization: The Human Consequences* (New York: Columbia University Press, 1998).
7. Arjun Appadurai, *Modernity at Large: Cultural Dimensions of Globalization* (Minneapolis: University of Minnesota Press, 1996), 19, 158–99.
8. Ibid., 162–63.
9. Giorgio Agabem, *Homo sacer: el poder soberano y la nuda vida*, trans. Antonio Gimeno Cuspinero (Valencia: Pre-Textos, 1998), 11–13, 152, 155–56.
10. Hannah Arendt, *The Origins of Totalitarism* (New York: Harcourt, 1976), 299.

11. See Giorgio Agamben, *Means Without Ends: Notes on Politics* (Minneapolis: University of Minnesota Press, 2000), 14–26.
12. Arendt, *Origins*, 370.
13. Agamben, *Means Without Ends*, 14–26.
14. Original Spanish: "lo político ha ido definiéndose de manera casi exclusiva en torno a la llamada cuestión del *status.*"
15. Emilio González Díaz, "El misterio de la santísima trinidad y el partido del *status*," *bordes* 1 (1995): 6–9.
16. Juan Duchesne, Chloé Georas, Ramón Grosfoguel, Agustín Lao, Francés Negrón, Pedro Ángel Rivera, Aurea María Sotomoayor, "La estadidad desde una perspectiva democrática radical: propuesta de discusión para todo el archipiélago puertorriqueño," *Diálogo* (February 1997): 30–31.
17. See Agamben, *Means Without Ends*, 23–26.
18. Giorgio Agamben, *The Coming Community* (Minneapolis: University of Minnesota Press, 1993), 86.
19. See Madeline Román and Miriam Muñiz, "Restos/arrestos/retos: The Surplus-Waste Citizenship (contrapunteo)," *bordes* 9 (2002): 14–25.
20. Tomas Hammar, *Democracy and the Nation State: Aliens, Denizens, and Citizens in a World of International Migration* (Brookfield: Grower, 1990).

CHAPTER 6

"None of the Above" Means More of the Same: Why Solving Puerto Rico's Status Problem Matters

Christina Duffy Burnett

In December of 1998, a slim majority of the Puerto Rican electorate chose "none of the above" in a plebiscite on the future of Puerto Rico's relationship to the United States. With this choice, 50.3 percent of the voters rejected several more familiar alternatives on the ballot: statehood, independence, and a continuation of Puerto Rico's current commonwealth status, along with a fourth option labeled "free association."[1] Previous plebiscites had yielded victories for an improved or "enhanced" version of commonwealth status.[2] But the absence of "enhanced" commonwealth from the 1998 ballot, along with the addition of "none of the above," changed the dynamic: supporters of enhanced commonwealth rallied to the cause of "none of the above" in order to protest the exclusion of their preferred alternative, and in their wake followed all those who wanted to take this opportunity to just say "no."

Interpretations of the inscrutable outcome of the plebiscite proliferated, but consensus on its significance proved elusive. Island political leaders proffered clashing views in a hearing before a U.S. Senate committee, while pundits and the public tried out their own ideas: that the voters who chose "none of the above" had wanted to express their opposition to the government's decision to hold the plebiscite too soon after a hurricane had devastated parts of the island; that they had wished to register a protest against the then-recent privatization of the telephone company; that they had been afraid that a victory for statehood specifically would subject them to immediate federal taxation.[3] But in the end, the only solid conclusion to be drawn was that a victory for "none of the above" offered a mandate for nothing at all.

Despite this apparently disappointing outcome, certain members of the Puerto Rican intelligentsia embraced the victory of "none of the above," or at least its null verdict on a concrete proposal for resolving what has come to be known as Puerto Rico's "status problem." While the voters' motivations proved difficult to pin down, among intellectuals the celebration of "none of the above" seemed to be largely driven by a conviction that the so-called status problem had somehow become too complex to be resolved by a simple choice on a paper ballot. As they saw it, the traditional status debate offers old and inadequate solutions for new and unprecedented problems; "none of the above," in this view, was a welcome rejection not only of the other options on the ballot but also of the status debate itself.[4]

The popularity of "none of the above" inspired the question to which this chapter responds, which was posed to me as part of an invitation to speak at The Puerto Rican Vacilón, the conference that gave rise to this volume: "whether formal decolonization represents an outdated way to address [Puerto Rico's] contemporary challenges."[5] The question, in other words, was whether "none of the above" augured a new age, and a better one; whether its victory at the polls responded to new realities that the old status options could not even begin to address. In response, I argue that formal decolonization for Puerto Rico is by no means outdated; it is, rather, long overdue.

The argument against formal decolonization—which is to say, in favor of "none of the above"—rests on questionable premises: that Puerto Rico's new challenges have somehow rendered the old ones irrelevant; that territorial sovereignty and the nation-state have somehow become more ambiguous and complicated today than they were in the past; that the status debate can somehow be settled simply by putting it aside, without ever actually solving, the problem that gave rise to it in the first place. None of these premises, I argue below, stands up to scrutiny. Moreover, defenders of the victory of "none of the above" have overlooked a crucial flaw inherent in that result: For all their rhetoric about a visionary and forward-looking challenge to an outdated and unproductive debate, the actual consequences of "none of the above" are impossible to distinguish from an emphatic reaffirmation of Puerto Rico's colonial status quo.

Between the "Premature" and the "Outdated"

Where status is concerned, the argument that Puerto Ricans should discard an old debate, devoting their energies to new challenges, has a strangely familiar ring. After all, in the not-so-distant past, political leaders who claimed to know best informed the people of the island that formal decolonization was premature. It might well be asked: how did decolonization go from "premature" to "outdated" without stopping at "timely"?

Over 50 years ago, Puerto Rico's political leaders decided to postpone a final resolution to the island's colonial status; specifically, they put aside the problem of Puerto Rico's lack of representation at the federal level and second-class status under federal law, in order to focus instead on local self-government and on the pressing economic problems that had kept many of the island's people in a state of grinding poverty.[6] During this transformative period in the 1940s and 1950s, Puerto Rico underwent economic reforms leading to a higher overall standard of living, along with significant political changes at the local level. Puerto Ricans for the first time elected their own governor in 1948 (replacing a system of presidential appointment), and, in 1952, they adopted their own constitution, acquiring in the process the official name of "Commonwealth of Puerto Rico."[7]

At the time, many saw these events as a visionary alternative to an unproductive debate. Postponing a decision among the traditional status options, political leaders instead gave the island's electorate a simple "yes or no" choice on whether to adopt a local constitution and become a "commonwealth," and the affirmative vote prevailed.

Yet despite the overwhelming popular endorsement of this transition to commonwealth status, Puerto Rico's fundamental colonial problem remained untouched: The island remained subject to most federal laws, while its people, still U.S. citizens, continued to be disfranchised at the federal level, and to be treated differently from other citizens under federal law.

Puerto Rico's persistent colonial status had—and continues to have—enormously damaging consequences, both symbolic and practical. The symbolic harms of colonial subjection are obvious; the more practical harms in this case include the fact that the island's non-voting "Resident Commissioner" in Washington has nothing but the smile on his face to offer in return for the vote of a colleague on legislation affecting Puerto Rico; that Puerto Rico must therefore spend staggering amounts of taxpayer money on lobbyists to represent the island's interests, and sometimes even merely to ensure that it is not inadvertently excluded from a given federal bill;[8] that representatives elected elsewhere in the United States (who by virtue of their voting power wield much greater influence than Puerto Rico's own non-voting delegate) act as self-appointed spokespeople for Puerto Rico, while having no accountability to Puerto Rican voters;[9] that Puerto Ricans have no voice in the selection of the president, but can be and have been drafted into military service in the U.S. armed forces.[10] And the list goes on.

Recognizing the persistence of Puerto Rico's colonial situation, the leadership of the political party that had designed commonwealth status in the first place embarked on a quest for "enhancements," petitioning Congress for the desired improvements to the commonwealth arrangement immediately after the transition to that status took effect—and for decades to come—without success. Ever since, Puerto Ricans have continued to engage in a seemingly interminable debate over how to put an end to their formally colonial relationship to the United States.

In short, new challenges inspired new approaches, but the old problem did not simply disappear as a result. The reforms of the 1940s and 1950s, important as they were, did not make Puerto Rico's status problem any less important to solve. And the debate over how to solve the problem persisted for a simple reason: The problem itself persisted. No amount of visionary and forward-looking activity could change that fact, as long as such activity failed to tackle the problem itself.

The same holds true today: New issues have arisen (they always do), but the old problem remains. Yet now, instead of trying to divert attention from the status problem by labeling a solution "premature," critics of the status debate have tried to make the issue disappear by christening it "outdated."

Historian Carlos Pabón (chapter 5), for instance, complains that the traditional status alternatives, which he argues rest on nineteenth-century premises about territorial sovereignty and the nation-state, should cease once and for all to be a topic of popular political discussion, because they have nothing to offer the twenty-first century "micro-electronic revolution, cyberspace, and genetic engineering world." The proposed status options, he insists, cannot resolve contemporary challenges such as "drug trafficking or the ecological crisis."

Indeed not! (Nor, one might add, can the current status.) All that a status option can do is solve the status problem. A solution to the status problem can, in turn, create conditions far more conducive to the resolution of other contemporary challenges, but no one should expect the traditional status options, or any *de jure* political arrangement, to solve all of Puerto Rico's contemporary challenges.

In their enthusiasm to deploy an analysis of Puerto Rico's colonial condition that captures complex twenty-first-century realities, critics of the status debate have defined Puerto Rico's contemporary challenges so broadly as to make it impossible to know even where to begin to address them. No wonder the traditional status options start to look inadequate. If one defines "decolonization" as the elimination of all forms of subjection, or if by "colonialism" one means the staggering imbalance of power between the United States and Puerto Rico, or if by "contemporary challenges" one means every imaginable contemporary challenge, then of course one can easily reach the conclusion that decolonization is unrealistic, and anyway unequal to the vicissitudes of postmodernity.

Without denying the breadth and complexity of Puerto Rico's contemporary challenges, however, I propose instead that we understand "colonialism" as one commentator has suggested: as "a simple and perfectly useful word to describe a relationship between a powerful metropolitan state and a poor overseas dependency that does not participate meaningfully in the formal lawmaking processes that shape the daily lives of its people."[11] Decolonization, in turn, refers simply to the implementation of a political status that offers meaningful participation to all citizens in the formal lawmaking processes of a credibly democratic system, not, mind you, a utopia—just meaningful participation and basic democratic legitimacy. Once such a status is in place, those other contemporary challenges will still deserve attention, but at least the harms arising directly out of a status of formal colonial subjection will have been addressed as effectively as they can be addressed; the obstacles that an illegitimate political arrangement poses to the effective resolution of other issues of public concern will have been largely swept aside.

Formal decolonization for Puerto Rico has been postponed for centuries. No one, under these circumstances, should think of formal decolonization as premature, much less outdated. The moment for formal decolonization is right now, and always has been.

Of Sovereign States and Straw Men

Those "nineteenth-century" premises that supposedly form the basis of the traditional status options loom large in current criticisms of the status debate. In our twenty-first-century world, the critics argue, there can be no room for old-fashioned ideas about nation-states exercising sole sovereignty and control over their own neatly-bounded territories. Citing the "crisis of the nation-state" and the "era of globalization," these skeptics exhort us to leave behind the "Westphalian" model of the territorially-bounded sovereign nation-state, and to come to terms with today's "post-national" realities.

These arguments, too, sound strangely familiar. Academics have been auguring the demise of territorial sovereignty and the nation-state for a very long time, and they have reliably alluded to an imaginary past when nation-states were simple, and territorial sovereignty complete. As international law scholar David Kennedy has observed, "the leading 'new' scholars of my generation . . . reaffirm some of the field's most familiar and dogmatic propositions: that sovereignty has eroded, that international law should be understood politically, that the boundary between international and municipal law is porous, that international law may not be as universal as it pretends, that the international regime is better understood as a process or multilevel game than as government by legal norms." These ideas, Kennedy goes on, "have been part of disciplinary common sense for a century." Yet for some reason, today's academics have "turned them into a fighting faith."[12]

What past do these new scholars have in mind, anyway? Certainly it cannot be Westphalia, despite the ubiquitous references to the so-called Westphalian model of the territorially-bounded sovereign nation-state in the scholarship trumpeting the decline of an old order. The treaties comprising the Peace of Westphalia in 1648—centuries, that is, before the emergence of anything approximating the modern nation-state—dealt with an immensely complicated web of interrelated sovereign-type prerogatives among an array of entities—some vaguely resembling proto-nation-states, others not at all.[13]

Perhaps these scholars have in mind the nineteenth century, when the so-called Westphalian model of the nation-state supposedly reached its culmination. Yet the nineteenth century also saw European and American imperialists (seeking to justify their colonial projects abroad) going so far in their efforts to manipulate the idea of sovereignty as to render it virtually meaningless. The Europeans who gathered at Berlin in 1884–85 to carve up Africa among themselves, for instance, reasoned that African leaders were sovereign enough to give "native consent" to the transfer of control over territory, but not sovereign enough to enter into bona fide treaties; that protectorate status preserved "internal" sovereignty while delegating "external" sovereignty, rendering the purportedly protected entity a "semi-sovereign" state; and that in the case of at least one protectorate, "the internal as well as the external sovereignty had passed to the protecting Power, but the territory [had] not been formally annexed."[14] Decades earlier, the U.S. Supreme Court had subjected Native Americans to the status of "domestic dependent nations" to justify treating them as sovereign and not sovereign at the very same time; and not long thereafter, the court would describe the territories annexed in 1898, including Puerto Rico, as both "foreign" and "domestic," by way of explaining how they could be subject to U.S. sovereignty and at the same time not be part of the United States proper.[15]

Evidently, these people did not live in a world of territorially-bounded sovereign nation-states, nor did they think they did. As they well understood, the concept has always been a fiction: a heuristic, and often a very useful one, but not now, nor ever before, a descriptive label in any precise sense.

As all of this suggests, territorial sovereignty and the nation-state have become no more ambiguous and complicated today than they were in the past. Moreover, none of the traditional status alternatives—neither statehood, independence, commonwealth, enhanced commonwealth, nor free association—assumes the existence of a world of neat and tidy nation-states, and none of them depends on it. Each of these alternatives actually embodies quite a complex set of ideas about the intersection of territory, sovereignty, democracy, legitimacy, power, and interdependence. The seemingly simple terms associated with the status debate—words such as "sovereignty," "independence," and "statehood"—should not deceive anyone, much less the savvy scholars of the post-national moment.

The argument that decolonization cannot serve twenty-first-century realities rests on the invention of an iconic age that never was: an Edenic world in which the nation-state was not in crisis and globalization had not yet begun. Such oversimplification should not be deployed in the service of an argument against formal decolonization (or at all, for that matter). Formal decolonization can serve crucial a function today, just as it did in the past. It is a mistake to conclude that formal decolonization has outlived its usefulness because the simple Westphalian world that produced it has passed. No such world ever existed.

Closing Constitutive Questions

The argument that Puerto Ricans should simply cease to engage in the status debate and move on to more important matters assumes that Puerto Ricans have deliberately chosen to waste their time on an irrelevant discussion. It is as if they suffered from a decadent addiction, as if the time had come to go cold turkey. But the persistence of the status debate does not call for a 12-step program to help Puerto Ricans kick the habit. Rather, the persistence of the debate attests to a well-founded and widespread recognition that Puerto Rico's *de jure* relationship to the United States needs resolution: that the island remains, in a formal sense that matters, a colony, and that something needs to be done about it. The argument over what should be done saps attention and energy away from other contemporary challenges, to be sure, but that argument embodies a collective effort to make a direct intervention into one of the most serious and longstanding of those contemporary challenges.

In Puerto Rico, as in any colonial situation, fundamental questions concerning how the polity should be organized—call them "constitutive" questions—have yet to be answered in a way that satisfies anyone but a few, staunch supporters of the colonial status quo (such as that resounding 0.1 percent of the electorate who voted for "territorial commonwealth" on the 1998 ballot). How should Puerto Ricans constitute themselves as a political community? Should they have a formal association with the United States and, if so, what sort of association should this be? What government (or governments) should be principally responsible for addressing their day-to-day problems? What form should such government take, and how should it be held accountable to the people it governs? Such are the questions that a fair, effective, and broadly persuasive process of self-determination should resolve, as best they can be resolved. Because the asymmetries of colonialism cannot provide satisfactory answers, those they do provide can only be temporary, and constantly contested. And so the debate continues, as well it should.

The failure to resolve constitutive questions has robbed Puerto Ricans of a viable and legitimate framework for ordinary political deliberation. Instead, high-stakes issues that should be settled as a precondition to the effective conduct of daily political life have come to dominate—and distort—public discourse.

In one of the most obvious examples of the distorting effect that the failure to resolve the status problem has had upon public life in Puerto Rico, the island's political parties do not align themselves along a spectrum having anything to do with ordinary issues of public concern, such as health, education, jobs, crime, or the environment. Instead, the parties define and distinguish themselves according to their preferred status alternatives: statehood, independence, and enhanced commonwealth.[16] As the qualifier "enhanced" indicates, none of the parties, not even the pro-commonwealth party, advocates the continuation of the status quo.[17] The intractable disagreements among the various segments of the electorate concern what to do, not whether to do something. This stalemate, combined with federal inertia, and in many cases resistance, has conspired to keep Puerto Ricans trapped in a condition of subjection—and mired in a bitter and divisive argument over how to get out.

As one former governor has written, the failure to resolve Puerto Rico's status problem

> divide[s] the people and breeds unending conflict . . . At least 75% of the voters align themselves with status options, as opposed to candidates, programs or solutions to pressing problems. It is as if breaking up the Union into 50 pieces, or redefining the states to cut their number in half, were the only dominant issues in every presidential election in the U.S.[18]

Indeed, it is not only "as if" breaking up the Union were the only dominant issue in every election. In Puerto Rico, whether to break up the union—the union between Puerto Rico and the United States, that is—is *in fact* the dominant issue in every election.

And how could it not be? If one believes that Puerto Ricans ought to be granted full and equal voting rights at the federal level, why should one support, say, a gubernatorial candidate who is willing to trade those in for a nebulously defined "enhanced" autonomy—no matter how brilliant the candidate's platform on social welfare or environmental reform? If one believes that Puerto Rico ought to be independent, why should one support a candidate who supports the irreversible step of admission into statehood—even if that candidate has outlined a compelling program of economic development or crime prevention?

It should come as no surprise that the status issue trumps other issues. Where political self-determination remains unrealized, the debate over it will interfere with, and most likely take precedence over, ordinary politics; Puerto Rico is no exception. This is because constitutive questions matter not only on their own merits—recall the symbolic and practical harms of colonialism—but also because the answers to them have implications for how a polity can most effectively address those day-to-day issues of ordinary public concern. It is therefore completely understandable and eminently justifiable that many Puerto Rican voters give priority to the resolution of the constitutive question of status and, with it, to the eradication of an illegitimate and ineffective framework for political deliberation. Their insistence on the importance of the status issue does not reflect a misguided desire to ignore other problems; on the contrary, it reflects a considered judgment on how best to set the conditions to address those other problems productively.

Some critics of the traditional status debate have suggested, striking a particularly cynical note, that Puerto Rican political elites actually have an interest in perpetuating the status problem, and the debate that goes with it; as Pabón puts it, the status issue "justifies their political existence." But this is little better than name-calling. Since the allegation rests on the imputation of secret motives, the charge can neither be proven nor refuted. Moreover, such an insinuation is particularly perverse, since it amounts to an assertion that people who give their lives to political causes are *for that very reason* to be mistrusted. Are there not political causes that merit such commitment? And is the basic structure of the polity not such a cause? In this sense, the status issue has indeed "justified the political existence" of not a small number of serious people for several generations as well it ought. In any case, the notion that a solution to the status problem would leave Puerto Rican politicians rudderless and paralyzed is simply not credible. The end of the status problem would not be the end of politics; it would be the end of the status problem. The politicians, no doubt, would find other issues.

There is no question that Puerto Ricans would be better off if they could simply stop their hand-wringing over colonialism, and get on with the project of building a healthy polity and a just society. On this much, the critics and I agree. But putting aside a debate over colonialism requires more than just saying the debate is over; it requires making sure that colonialism itself is over.

Conclusion

As I worked on the early stages of this chapter, I met a legal scholar who had spent several years at the U.S. Department of Justice. He asked me where I was from, and when I said I was from Puerto Rico, he instantly exclaimed, "Puerto Rico! You people have *got* to solve the status problem!" This reaction greatly surprised me, since I am used to hearing something having more to do with the beauty of the island's beaches. When I asked him why he had reacted that way, he replied, "When I was at the Justice Department, Puerto Rico issues came up occasionally. And no matter what the issue was, the issue was status. Everything was about status. *We could never get anything done.*"

This, I suppose, was the lawyer in him talking, not the legal scholar. Scholars, generally, do not approach problems with the aim of "getting things done." The task of a scholar is not to close questions, but to keep them open: to adopt a critical stance, to follow one question with another, and to challenge claims to certainty. This may account, at least in part, for why decolonization has lost its luster among some members of the Puerto Rican intelligentsia. The term has been overused. It sounds too linear. Too simple. Too final. It should make any good scholar suspicious.

But my aim in this chapter has been to suggest that polities have much to gain from simply closing certain questions, and that Puerto Rico specifically has a great deal to gain from closing—not evading—the status question. Postponing a resolution to this fundamental problem (or declaring a resolution outdated) in order to focus on other pressing issues gets it exactly backward. The failure to resolve basic matters of political organization, relegating them instead to perpetual limbo, may make good material for scholarly conversation, but it is a terrible way to conduct political life.

Notes

1. For a summary of the plebiscite results, see <http://eleccionespuertorico.org/1998/summary.html> (June 17, 2004); see also "The Results of the 1998 Puerto Rico Plebiscite," Report by Chairman Don Young and Senior Member George Miller to the Committee on Resources, U.S. House of Representatives, Serial No. 106-A, 106th Cong., 2nd sess. (November 19, 1999), in Appendix D. For the definitions of the status options, see *ibid.* at Appendix A (reproducing the definitions as published in *The San Juan Star*, November 22, 1998).
2. See <http://eleccionespuertorico.org/1993/summary.html> (June 17, 2004); "Results," cited note 1, in Appendix D.
3. The hearing took place before the Senate Committee on Resources, one of a number of federal entities with jurisdiction over matters related to Puerto Rico's status. For a transcript, see <http://www.puertorico-herald.org/issues/

vol3n21/ senatetranscript-en.shtml> (June 17, 2004). For a sampling of other interpretations of the plebiscite, see, for example, Carolina González and Owen Moritz, "Isle's Future Uncertain," *Daily News* (New York), December 15, 1998: ("[E]choing the sentiment of many island residents, [one voter] said he cast a protest vote for 'none of the above' because the government went ahead with the referendum 'right before Christmas and right after the hurricane.' "); William Branigin, "Puerto Rico Leader Vows to Press for Statehood," *Washington Post*, December 15, 1998, A10: (describing the outcome as "a divisive and ambiguous result, leaving politicians [in Puerto Rico] free to attach widely varying interpretations," and noting that "[p]olitical analysts said the 'none of the above' vote not only reflected those concerns [of *status quo* supporters] but served as a catch-all category for people to express dissatisfaction with [Governor] Rossell[ó] for other reasons, including his efforts to privatize the island's telephone company over the opposition of local unions"); Mireya Navarro, "Looking Beyond Vote in Puerto Rico After 'None of the Above' Is Top Choice," *The New York Times*, December 15, 1998, A16: ("[P]olitical analysts [in San Juan] say that [the "none of the above" option] also sheltered those who feared statehood as too drastic a change and those resentful of Governor Rossell[ó]'s style of governing. The governor himself said he thought voters rejected him more than the statehood option for such decisions as the sale of a majority stake of the government-owned telephone company to a private consortium this year, which led to a bitter strike by telephone workers.").

4. See, for example, Carlos Pabón's contribution to this volume: "The Political Status of Puerto Rico: A Nonsense Dilemma."
5. The Puerto Rican Vacilón: A Conference on Current Debates in Puerto Rican Culture and Politics, University of Miami, April 18–20, 2002. I do not mean to suggest that the conference organizers themselves embraced the plebiscite result, only that they recognized that others had, and thought it was worth exploring why.
6. Residents of Puerto Rico do not vote in presidential elections; they have a single, nonvoting "Resident Commissioner" who sits in the House of Representatives. On the U.S. territories' presence in Congress, see Abraham Holtzman, "Empire and Representation: The U.S. Congress," *Legislative Studies Quarterly* 11 (1986): 249.
7. For an account of this period by one of these leaders, see José Trías Monge, *Puerto Rico: The Trials of the Oldest Colony in the World* (New Haven: Yale University Press, 1997), at Chapters 9–11.
8. See Chris Mooney, "Treasure Island," *American Prospect* 11, no. 21 (September 29–October 5, 2000), <http://www.prospect.org/print/V11/21/mooney-c.html> (June 14, 2004).
9. Representative Luis Gutiérrez (D-Illinois), an ethnically Puerto Rican congressman, exemplifies this problem well. See, e.g., "U.S. Congress," *Chicago Sun-Times*, March 10, 2002, editorial: (observing that his "critics complain, with some cause, that Guti[é]rrez sometimes acts like he believes his district is in Puerto Rico").
10. For a brief overview of Puerto Ricans' service in the U.S. military, see <http://www.veteransforpr.com/history.htm> (June 17, 2004).

11. José A. Cabranes, "Some Common Ground," in *Foreign in a Domestic Sense: Puerto Rico, American Expansion, and the Constitution*, ed. Christina Duffy Burnett and Burke Marshall (Durham: Duke University Press, 2001), 40–41.
12. David Kennedy, "The Twentieth-Century Discipline of International Law in the United States," in *Looking Back at Law's Century*, ed. Austin Sarat, Bryan Garth, and Robert A. Kagan (Ithaca: Cornell University Press, 2002), 405.
13. See Andreas Osiander, "Sovereignty, International Relations, and the Westphalian Myth," *International Organization* 55, no. 2 (Spring 2001): 251.
14. Martti Koskenniemi, *The Gentle Civilizer of Nations: The Rise and Fall of International Law 1870–1960* (Cambridge: Cambridge University Press, 2001), 125 (internal quotation marks omitted); see generally ibid, Chapter 2.
15. *Cherokee Nation v. Georgia*, 30 U.S. 1, 17 (1831); the *Insular Cases*, see, e.g., *Downes v. Bidwell*, 182 U.S. 244 (1901).
16. The "free association" option has gained increasing support in recent years, but has not been formally endorsed by any political party as part of its platform. An organization called PROELA, loosely associated with the pro-commonwealth party, backed the "free association" option in 1998 and defended it before Congress. See Letter to Chairman Don Young from Luis Vega-Ramos, president, PROELA, in "Results," cited note 1, in Appendix C.
17. I have analyzed proposals to "enhance" commonwealth status elsewhere. See Christina D. Burnett, "The Case for Puerto Rican Decolonization," *Orbis: A Journal of World Affairs* 43 (Summer 1998): 433.
18. Rafael Hernández Colón, *La nación de siglo a siglo y otros ensayos* (Hato Rey, Puerto Rico: Ramallo Bros. Printing, 1998), 230.

PART II

Politics as Spectacle and the Spectacle of Politics

CHAPTER 7

Vieques: Protest as a Consensual Spectacle

Juan Duchesne Winter

For over 60 years, the U.S. Navy used the island of Vieques, a municipality of Puerto Rico, as a bombing range and munitions depot, squeezing its population in the middle and affecting every aspect of the community's everyday life. After the death of David Sanes Rodríguez, a *viequense* security guard who was killed when two errant bombs missed their target inside the range, a broad-based coalition of church, community, government, the political left and other groups joined the "peace for Vieques" drive, demanding an end to the use of Vieques as a bombing range. On May 1, 2003, the activists obtained the avowed goal when the Department of Defense transferred its land to the Department of the Interior, which in turn declared it a wildlife refuge.

Despite claims that the Vieques saga was fundamentally a victory of the "Puerto Rican people," I would argue that it exemplified the success of what can be defined as the "political activist movement" in Puerto Rico. The political activists succeed not because they threaten dominant power structures but because they are able to secure an outcome that is beneficial to the current political elite, both on the island and in the United States, and to consolidate a political horizon that encompasses the demands already agreed upon. That is, this form of activism confirms the nation-subject, which in turn generates democratic consensus as a mode of *consent* to existing power.

When discussing the existing power structure, we are not referring necessarily to the authority of a specific jurisdiction, such as that of local or federal institutions, but to the power of Empire, that is, of global capital as shaped by local and U.S. capitalist elites. Puerto Rican *neo-nationalism* embodies a mutation of historical nationalism into a "really existing" ideology that discards the anticolonial-national liberation project, and embraces the identity politics of cultural affirmation as its Northern star. Within this new horizon the nation is reduced to an identity project, in face of which sovereignty issues remain ancillary.[1]

This brand of political activism is able to project the legitimacy within the limits of the neo-national horizon by its ability to address some pressing sociopolitical maladies: ecocide; vast contamination; and unproductive, authoritarian control of the territory by the military. Ironically, the political-activist discourse that is supposed to be the platform from which to express diverse opinions that may interrogate *the power of what exists* becomes a platform from which to cement consent and from which to thwart any signs of political dissent. In making this argument, we do not contest the quota of achievements and sacrifices brandished by the leaders of the new consensual activism. They have gained their place in the battlefield that is now theirs and that we, the "contemplative theorists," have no interest in questioning. The paragraphs that follow attempt to diagnose, with the benevolent cruelty that characterizes this type of criticism, the transformation of the contemporary activist performance during one recent episode: Vieques.

Activism as a Tool to Sustain Power?

Contemporary activist performance has experienced many changes. For example, let us start by examining Vieques within the context of a prolonged and intermittent battle against the presence of the U.S. Armed Forces. The anti-Navy activists of the 1970s and 1980s who defied the law to achieve their objectives and who also maintained a pacifist strategy, had very different experiences than their twenty-first-century counterparts. They exposed themselves to harsher treatment such as being the object of gratuitous scrutiny and receiving much stiffer legal penalties. They were subjected to being humiliated and discredited by political and capitalist institutions in different venues, primarily in the media. Covert surveillance activities and U.S. government operatives also targeted them. One Vieques activist of that era, Angel Cristóbal Rodríguez, died in a U.S. federal prison under mysterious circumstances. His body was badly beaten. Prison authorities have unconvincingly explained his death as the result of a suicide attempt. They seem to imply he beat himself to death!

The activists of the 1970s and 1980s were hence either ignored, persecuted, repressed, or subject to an obliterating propaganda that turned them into invisible or marginalized subjects. The political activists of the twenty-first century, however, have at their disposal an array of attractive assurances and offers: (1) be able to have their say without any negative retributions, (2) be a part of all pertinent headlines, (3) be the object of favorable publicity, (4) be morally and politically blessed by the local religious and political institutions, and (5) be rewarded by the local political elite with sociopolitical advancement. Irrespective of their sincere motivations, it is undeniable that a cynical and hypocritical sociopolitical process is absorbing the political activists of today.

Although political activism entails risks—detentions are always abusive, and doing time is never as easy or brief as one would like—not all types of activism entail the same risks or benefits. For example, the risks and rewards are 100 percent positive for the international celebrity that makes a guest appearance in the activist scene, such as Edward James Olmos or a member of the Kennedy clan. That balance is almost 90 percent positive for the local celebrity and for an array of professionals, relatives, and friends of the local political and cultural elite who lead and organize the event. The treatment is different, however, for the "unknown" individuals who play the role of extras (as "the people of Vieques" or "the people of Puerto Rico") in the activist scenario. Still, irrespective of the risks or rewards associated with being an anti-navy activist in Puerto Rico, what is evident in this process is the "positive strength"[2] that results from participating in a legitimate movement.

It is important to note that the behavior of these activists lies in a nether zone between being victims and benefiting from the process. They may yet be really victimized when the spectacle is over. Still any possible victimization that they may endure is very different from that suffered by other contemporaries. For example, the activists in Vieques receive strong and enthusiastic coverage from no other than the biggest capitalist news venture on the island, *El Nuevo Día*. This is the result of the restructuring of capitalist institutions in the island. It is also notable how the media turns an event that would have ordinarily required direct activist participation into a highly watched and passively followed spectacle. We are contemplating the local version of a phenomenon already seen in other regions: that is, activism as a predetermined spectacle conditioned by sociopolitical strategies of the state. We are witnessing, in sum, a complex but effective collaboration between the state and the masses.[3]

The ZOPECs: The "Zonas de Protesta Espectacularizada y Consensual" or Zones of Consensual Spectacular Protest

The pro-commonwealth Popular Democratic Party (PDP)[4] has adopted, almost to perfection, the spectacular form of consensus building. This is an indication (among others) that there is PDP for a long time. The PDP is the only local political entity that has been able to incorporate the postmodern ethos, comprising banal nationalism, the marketing of values, and a painless, calculated risk ethics, such as described by Gilles Lipovetsky.[5] It is true that, as stated by the sociologist Emilio González Díaz,[6] the PDP's ability to *rally* the masses has ended. That is, the PDP is no longer a modern ideological party. The nature of its mutation can be attested by the phrase: "the PDP is dead, long live the PDP!" The PDP has renewed itself as a post-ideological party under the leadership of Sila María Calderón. That is, its command structure, since Sila María Calderón's tenure, has acquired an extraordinary capacity for spinning any opposing views, accommodating them to an *all-included* political imaginary. Still, how does this process work? Zones or foci of scene-making emerge or are designated on the margins of contestation.

These are negotiable, dispensable, and affordable; their existence does not destabilize the Empire's general hegemony (imperial power as such can allow itself a purely local and provisional instability). The "zones of consensual spectacular protest" are event oriented, that is, they correspond to temporal and spatial coordinates, to discourses and practices that describe a series of events. Let us complete this definition with the Vieques example.

This is the case of the military training camp in Vieques, a relic of a still-operating aspect of the imperialist military system whose non-digitalized infrastructural remnants have to date required military exercises not yet virtualized. It is expected that in the near future virtual technology will transform not only how the military performs its training but also the way in which war is waged. It is evident that Vieques as a military training ground had become obsolete despite the fact that the military did not want to get rid of Vieques that easily. But the military is just an instrument of capitalist institutions. The circulation and expansion of wealth are much more important for an imperialist nation than assessing the validity of keeping a military resource, in this case Vieques, which is archaic.

Therefore Empire, which includes both the local and federal political machinery, can use this zone of debate (strongly emblematic thanks to an old antagonism that virtually survives) as if it were a lure for the masses. This fulfills three objectives: having a ZOPEC that is available for activism; performing a socioeconomic restructuring of the zone in question, that is, Vieques; and disposing of any possible internal dissent within the homogenous activist movement. (This could be accomplished by packaging the obsolete sectors into a "*lost*" *missions* category). After the exit of the U.S. Navy, Vieques will become a prime target for international capitalist ventures, such as the tourist industry, and will provide an oasis for those looking for upward mobility. In sum, Vieques will no longer be the territory of one capitalist institution, that is, the navy, but rather of another capitalist institution, that of the tourist industry. The activists *act*, not always unwittingly, as political-historical *nettoyeurs* that legitimize a developmentalist narrative.

The ZOPECs give room to modes of activism that do not destabilize power institutions but rather facilitate cultural and political absorption of possible hot points of dissent, they provide for historically sanctioned eradication and reassessment of supposedly "obsolete" views, and they supply sources of release that neutralize resisting and opposing forces. Still, what are the factors that distinguish this process from other processes of opposition? Activism in the island takes shape in light of other forms of resistance that are less manageable. Thus, the consensual repression of various sources of resistance that are destabilizing to the status quo becomes necessary. This is achieved in part through the mechanisms of legitimization of the state that allow for the homogenizing effect of the ZOPEC. The institutions that generate consensus comprise entities ascribed to the state as well as corporate and "civil society" organizations. They manage public discourse around demands legitimized within the ZOPEC.

The agglutinating demands concerning the Vieques struggle boil down to the issue that Vieques residents are U.S. citizens who should not be exposed to the dangers of military activities that occupy their surroundings, limit available space, and depredate upon their environment and their health. It is a neutral, citizenship approach that leaves aside the dangers of militarism as such, as well as a wide range of problems related to the presence of imperial armies, besides the fact that regardless of whether a community is composed of citizens or noncitizens of the United States, it has a right to reject the militarization of its territory.

The effect of the ZOPEC is to silence or draw attention apart from an array of demands, many coming from the Vieques community itself, that may be loosely tied to the navy issue, such as those related to the long, historical administrative neglect of the island's population, clearly linkable to racial and social discrimination. Also excluded are a profound critique of U.S. military presence in the territory of Puerto Rico as a whole, and the militarist culture of violence it has bred. Only a marginal attention has been drawn to positive alternatives to the developmentalist project and the community's consensual manipulation that the corporate, government, and civilian discourses impose as exclusive models of political action.

But this spectacular censorship extends to the entire country, not only Vieques, and governs all aspects of academic life, culture, and politics to the extent that the population is forced to live their lives following the dogma of "you are either with me or against me." Those who do not abide by the slogans are deemed traitors and agents of the opposition. Thus once the PDP hegemonic force sets up the accepted guidelines for activism, *really existing* protest culture assumes an authoritarian slant, and the distance between the injurious rumor, the enraged attack, and coercive action, within or without its ranks, becomes narrower. Activism becomes a means for furthering the institutional and ideological views of a group, mostly the neo-nationalist elite that cohabits with the ruling PDP. Still as the imminent economic crisis puts the neo-nationalist consensus to the test, we may expect interesting turns in the repressive activity of the state. The people within this political-activist formation most compromised with a real alternative politics may be singled out and alienated from the cohabitation arrangement.

Within this process, the role of the guardians of consensus is to neutralize, dissolve, or detour any form of dissidence. Still, the success of the guardians of consensus requires the help of the media. The local corporate media, for example, which has the ability to reach a vast audience, plays an essential role in legitimizing and establishing consensus for the island's activists. This is extremely helpful for the consensus seekers who are trying to further the views of the establishment. In many ways the guardians of consensus accomplish what the establishment cannot, that is, to control or delegitimize any sources of dissent. As noted by Luis Pérez,[7] a forced and imaginary consensus results in the dissemination of a mediocre and anti-intellectual rhetoric. For example, the rhetoric that is often dished out to the local population in order to establish a sense of identity and national pride includes statements such as "how attractive we are, what a great and loving family we are," and a wealth of similar sugar-coated hypocrisies that play on a banal national narcissism, as well as other stronger statements that moralize and draw suspicion to any source of dissent that could jeopardize the established monopoly of consensus. In sum, both the public and corporate power, specifically the media, is willing and able to exclude any form of alternative discourse, even if it requires reviling or ostracizing people.

Boca-Cloaca or Mouth-Sewer Discourse

Governor Sila María Calderón and prominent members of her executive were very proficient in establishing what may be called the *boca-cloaca* or *mouth-sewer* discourse. It may seem paradoxical, but the *boca-cloaca* discourse legitimizes itself by providing consistency, from above, to the ZOPEC discourse. On the one hand, the ZOPEC discourse must be analyzed within the theatrical and consensual context in which it occurs. The *boca-cloaca* discourse, on the other hand, must be examined as a force that devours and incorporates any type of statement, all types of ideology of the contemporary political spectrum, from the Marxist and Stalinist to the pro-commonwealth, and goes through all the decontextualized corporate and neoliberal arsenals as well as religious, and even new age, conventions. Any statement (or specific discourse practice) that transcends the magnificent screen, deviates from the established consensus, or generates unsustainable contradictions, is bluntly dismissed, as if it had never been uttered. Thus, the *boca-cloaca* discourse operates very similarly to the Pac-man game where Pac-man eats everything in front of it, but with the added feature that in the *boca-cloaca* discourse any object consumed is immediately defecated.

The *boca-cloaca* discourse is, then, as efficient as it is disposable, which serves the ZOPEC well, since it is always ready to be obliterated. For example, the mediation apparatus and the institutional and governmental representatives legitimize civil disobedience by framing it in a liberal and nationalist context and by invocating genocide and apocalyptic confrontations. This spectacle, however, is followed by discourse practices that exist within the law, morality, and order and which defer all alternate forms of activism to those established by the mandated consensus.

Protest against the designated target ends up actually responding to pressures coming from state-related entities such as the media, the church, and public and corporate organizations. Ironically, *not protesting* may be seen by the entities in power as suspicious behavior. A poster placed at the University of Puerto Rico, Río Piedras, for instance, states that "the Navy in Vieques is dangerous, but even more dangerous are those that sit and watch and don't do anything." The underlying fascism in this statement is obvious.[8] Protesting against issues that lie outside those condoned by the state is, of course, excluded. The issues that can be objected to with the state's approval, however, do not always remain static and are sometimes conflicting as protesters can support neo-nationalist views with the same fervor as they can support and even adopt pro-commonwealth and pro-statehood views. Everything goes when it furthers a cause. It is in this dichotomy that the discursive practices of the island, like or as, the ZOPEC lie.

No Contradiction between Neo-Nationalism and the United States

One might assume that the consensus cementing the fusion of the local government and Puerto Rican society, as a colonial-national power, could reinforce the colonial contradictions of the Puerto Rican-U.S. relationship. It could also be assumed that neo-nationalists live up to their anti-imperialist self-image by incessantly pointing to trivial differences between the Puerto Rican state and the imperialist regime of the United States. This rhetoric might allow for spectacular visions regarding the liberation and rebirth of the Puerto Rican nation. However, the diffusion and ultimate establishment of this rhetoric could not happen without the stellar performance of Sila María Calderón as the spokesperson of the embryonic nation-state. *Banco Popular*,[9] the local elite, the so-called *melones*,[10] the corrupt syndicates, the newspaper *El Nuevo Día*, a myriad of publicity agencies, the clergy and their "people" all seem to march against the United States of America—for God's sake! What a moving, extraordinary revolutionary epic!

But their superficial talk of "contradictions" between conceptually static ideas of nationality and identity only serve as a ruse in deviating or suppressing attention from other problems that are truly pressing today, such as the globalization process that has redrawn previous nation-state dynamics, and has imposed massive privatization and alienation of natural, social, and cultural resources from communities and individuals. Such a hegemonic, spectacular set-up does not even address the profound coloniality of power, namely, the continued symbolic, economic, and political relationships between colonial powers and their former colonies, which pervades Puerto Rican society far beyond juridical issues of formal colonialism concerning state sovereignty. The neat end product of such a discourse is the continued allegiance to the colonial status quo of the "Commonwealth."[11] An allegiance that can hardly be conceived as anti-American, in the non-culturalized sense of being anti-imperialist, since it never contests Empire as such.

This kind of pro-commonwealth discourse, however, does not hold exclusive rights to the use of shallow statements and assertions. The apocalyptic warnings of the New Progressive Party (NPP) to those supposedly expressing anti-American views ("The Americans are leaving! This is the end of the world!"—claim NPP politicians) show that even though the postmodern neo-nationalist discourse might not necessarily amount to a feat of sophistication, the pro-statehood discourse is dismally disingenuous. The supposedly anti-American neo-nationalism, as expressed in the most standarized *boca-cloaca* utterances, is in essence very pro-American. Let us reminisce about the mediating power of this spectacle-driven society. The endless, banalized recreation of the identity melodrama somewhat explains the island's existential dichotomy. That is, to talk about changing *everything*, the act of *being* itself (*to be or not to be* . . . Puerto Rican) as a way to avoid changing anything.

The obvious riddle: In the dominant political imaginary of the island, what is that which means *everything* without meaning anything? The "status issue." From a broad hegemonic perspective, the status of Puerto Rico is as innocuous as it is dispensable. There are mechanisms for the reproduction and recreation of the local society that do not depend on the resolution of the island's status. Any conceivable option for the future political status of Puerto Rico (independence, autonomy, statehood) will be framed by the global geopolitics of the nation-state, which is impossible to reconcile with a narrowly conceptualized nationalism.

It is a well-known historical fact that anticolonial liberation movements mainly addressed the colonial issue in terms of an exclusive state-sovereignty frame. Though these anticolonial movements succeeded in achieving independence from their colonial masters, they did not abolish the coloniality of power as a social process. A subaltern insertion of those postcolonial countries in the world system subsists to this day.[12] They did not break away from colonialism. Such a failure has resulted in the continued existence of neocolonial societies within legally independent states. Puerto Rican neonationalism has rarely, if ever, examined this fact. It has even moved a step backward in comparison to national liberation politics of the 1960s and 1970s refusing to even prioritize the issue of colonial power, and supplanting it with a shallow identity politics.

The local neo-nationalist movement addresses the status issue in a purely negative fashion; it is not committed to independence but to the defense of the status quo as a populist bulwark against the statehood status option put forward by the NPP. Neo-nationalism has stripped anticolonialism to a bare anti-statehood stance with hardly any social content. A Puerto Rican anticolonial and anticapitalist movement needs to recognize that the slight legal and jurisdictional differences entailed in each status option will not suffice to significantly change colonial-capitalistic institutions on the island. Status change is not a sufficient condition for a profound social transformation, and it is not even clear that it might be a necessary condition. The fact that none of the status options envisioned to this day propose changing significantly how Puerto Ricans relate to the colonial and capitalistic relations that deeply structure island society, explains, to some degree, why activism on the island is driven by the routine theatrics and ambivalences of desire, rather than compelled by an authentic expectation of the new.

On Protest and Spectacle

Let us conclude with a Debordian colophon. According to Guy Debord, the *society of spectacle* not only transforms the world into a spectacle but turns the spectacle into the only world possible, in a totalizing image, exclusively defined by commodity values and their market permutations. In this sense, the situationist theorist speaks of the "false struggles of the spectacle" that turn the social actor into a spectator of his own experience as a producer of daily life. The role of spectator assumed by the subject separates her from the very conflicts of her existence that are made to enter the spectacle as the exclusive scenario of social reality. Nothing exists beyond the spectacle, claims Debord in his theoretical bid to unmake the *society of the spectacle* inside out.[13]

In lay terms: Vieques activism on the island has taken shape in front of the television cameras that provide it with the right shot, the right movement, the right stage, and the appropriate touch of realism, all of which are necessary for landing an interview on prime time television or a popular talk show. The following is a very "cute" example: A very well-known leader of the "Friends of the Sea" (Amigos del Mar) group went on prime time television, along with other members of the organization, looking like a *zapatista* guerrilla who was ready to take forth the revolution. The interview took place in a safe house where the group was organizing its illegal entry onto Navy-controlled territory in Vieques. The secrecy surrounding the event is, of course, a mere pose, since the place was very well lit and full of cameras and journalists. Furthermore, to add to the absurdity of the event, the full name of the leader of the organization, who happened to be wearing a mask, was revealed on the bottom of the TV screen for all of us to see. The leader's narcissism, coupled with not being afraid to reveal his association with the organization (in this instance he knows he will not be punished by the local police), made revealing his identity not only safe but also desirable.

In sum, the days of hard political activism, that is, the activism that takes decades of tenacious, almost anonymous work with a community to carefully give shape to a movement, such as that of the *zapatistas*, or other traditional left militants, are long gone. In those days massive public actions were a way of defying in the public's eye the status quo imposed by the establishment. Big manifestations provided a symbolic scenario that allowed the measure of forces against the state. Today the success of a certain activist movement is measured by its ability to penetrate the media and become a highly rated spectacle within corporate media standards. Thus, it is virtually impossible for other forms of activism that do not rely on a predetermined consensus or theatrics to compete with the media coverage of *El Nuevo Día* or Teleonce TV. In Europe this type of activism has been called the *McProtest mode* because it is highly processed and results can be obtained almost instantly, as when buying fast food at McDonald's. A British columnist in *The Guardian* who remarked about the phenomenon of the *McProtest* notes that the modern activist movement may need to develop a Protest Card, which activists can use to deal with all arrests, detentions, court proceedings, and legal arrangements in an efficient manner.

Here in Puerto Rico we could create the Civil Disobedience Card. It would be a big hit. Since real *viequenses* make up a very small number of the activists forces extant on the island of Vieques, there would be greater market for it on the mainland Puerto Rican population. To paraphrase Sila María Calderón's *boca-cloaca* mode of speech, "May God protect all the *beautiful people* who protest under the aura of the church, politics, and media celebrities! Let's pray for them." God forgive those party poopers who theorize without doing anything. But let's pray for them too, why not? Everything must be done to achieve the consensus and consent to the existing way of life while the beautiful souls become canonized in the images of protest *comme il faut.*

As long as the McProtesters prevail, with the backing of the church, the media, and the establishment, of course, and no one questions the status quo, their brand of "comfortable" activism will be around for a long time. Costumers will continue to crowd the malls, and the compulsive patterns of consumption of the Puerto Rican population will remain unchanged despite any signs of protest. While activism is governed by theatrics and banality, all remains the same.

Notes

This chapter was translated by Marianne Mason. Author's Note: The original Spanish version of this chapter was written in July 2000. I have supplied notes to the English translation and clarified some baroque passages. These minor revisions have preserved the satirical tone of a polemical tract written as a spontaneous reaction to immediate events. It was widely circulated on the Internet and drew some strong comments and threats from many activists. But the readers who identified with an alternative politics were very receptive.

1. For more on neo-nationalism, please see Carlos Pabón, *Nación Postmortem: ensayos sobre los tiempos de la insoportable ambigüedad* (San Juan: Ediciones Callejón, 2002).
2. This is an ironic allusion to the local candidate for Governor Sila María Calderón's main campaign slogan at the time: "fuerza positiva."
3. Here we consider the state, following Thomas Ehrlich Reifer, as a "National Security State Corporate Complex," which comprises a closely knit web of media, corporate, military, and political power relations in which the private and "public" spheres of interests are mainly indistinct. Please see Thomas Ehrlich Reifer, "Globalization and the National Security State Corporate Complex (NSSCC) in the Long Twentieth Century," in *The Modern/Colonial World-System in the Twentieth Century*, ed. Ramón Grosfoguel and Ana Margarita Cervantes-Rodríguez (Westport: Praeger, 2003).
4. The PDP, *Partido Popular Democrático* (Popular Democratic Party; PDP) was engaged, at the time of the main developments of the Vieques struggle, in a full blown electoral campaign to regain the colonial governorship of the island, which it obtained in the November elections of 2000. It is widely held by political analysts of varying political tendencies that the Vieques campaign was skillfully co-opted as a main media and political asset by the PDP's candidate for Governor Sila María Calderón.
5. See Gilles Lipovetsky, *L'ethique indolore des nouvaux temps democratiques* (Paris: Éditions Gallimard, 1992).
6. Unpublished conference.
7. Unpublished conference.
8. This observation strictly applies to the election campaign period of 1999–2000, which coincided with the PPD's electoral manipulation of the Vieques movement.

9. The *Banco Popular of Puerto Rico* (BPPR), in whose board of directors Sila María Calderón sits, is the largest banking institution in Puerto Rico purported to retain "national ownership," whatever that means, in a multiple stock-owned global firm. The *BPPR* is a main contributor to *nation-building* cultural enterprises that remain within banal identity politics.
10. The *melones*: Spanish for watermelons, which are green on the outside and red inside. It is a popular metaphor that points to people who outwardly claim to be pro-independence while owing exclusive allegiance to the PDP and voting for its main candidates. Green is the traditional color of the *Partido Independentista Puertorriqueño* (PIP, or the Puerto Rican Independence Party. Red is the color of the PDP, a party that has removed Independence claims from its platform since the late 1940s. The *melones* constitute a considerable political fraction without whose support the PDP cannot expect to win a general election.
11. "The Commonwealth of Puerto Rico" is the English title given to the existing colonial status decreed by U.S. Congress in 1952 (Law of Federal Relations No. 600), which bears the ironic Spanish title of "Estado Libre Asociado de Puerto Rico" (Free Associated State of Puerto Rico).
12. See Aníbal Quijano, "Colonialidad del poder, eurocentrismo y América Latina," in *La colonialidad del saber: eurocentrismo y ciencias sociales*, ed. Edgardo Lander (Caracas: UNESCO, 2000).
13. Guy Debord, *La societé du spectacle* (Paris: Éditions Buchet-Chastel, 1967).

CHAPTER 8

Entertainment Tonight! Puerto Rican Media and the Privatization of Politics

Silvia Alvarez-Curbelo

Mainstream journalists purport to give citizens true information they need to make informed choices to make the democracy work. They also claim that they are different from tabloid journalists who merely give people interesting but unimportant stuff.

Samuel P. Winch, Mapping the Cultural Space of Journalism

Scandal is gossip made tedious by morality.

Oscar Wilde, Lady Windemere's Fan

Life is a soap opera / in which we all want to act.
Tito Rojas, "El gallo salsero" (With a Shakespearian twist), "Porque este amor"

Some time ago an assistant producer for one of Puerto Rico's television evening news programs asked for my comments regarding the use of naked women doing news in the Internet. I declined because I had not entered the sites, but, nevertheless, I asked her why were they spending precious TV minutes on that subject (they had scheduled a three-day series). Her reply was most illuminating: "Don't you think that it is necessary to fix the boundaries between journalists (a legitimate profession) and these impersonators?" I pointed out that her contention was rather paradoxical because in order to reinforce the boundaries between "serious" journalism and racy entertainment, the TV station was engaging in a "soft-porn selling approach" advertising the *exposé*. She told me that I had an interesting point and would call me later after consulting with the reporter doing the assignment. Of course she never did.

The setting, fixing, redefinition, and effacement of boundaries is an ongoing theme in contemporary communications studies.[1] The English language, which has such a wonderful ability to create neologisms, has produced such denominations as infotainment, informational, docudrama, reality show, and e-commerce to keep pace with the multiplicity of products that are generated by the media and the Internet. But the question of boundaries does not relate only to the emergence of new and hybrid communication genre. It has to deal also with the genealogy and fate of a cultural cartography of modernity that still brandishes a discourse of jurisdictions, of frontiers between public, social and private spaces, between political processes and entertainment dynamics, between citizens and consumers.

In a provocative article published by the Chilean *Revista de Crítica Cultural*, Leonor Arfurch proposes a revising of the widely held notion of modernity's original boundary disposition. Arfurch sees the opposition between a private sphere and the public and social realms not as a constitutive feature of the modern experience but as a discursive effect, a product of rules, constrictions, power operations that pursue the control of reactions, desires, and emotions. She argues that the contemporary escalade of the private can be interpreted as a response to the disenchantment toward politics, to the desertion of the public scene, to the failures of the equality ideal, to the monotony of "real" lives.

It is perhaps this divorce between social aspirations and the concrete possibilities of success that explains the intensity of the struggle for the singularity of the self in a society that abhors difference.[2] However, much of the bibliography on the boundaries issue in the field of communications partakes of the assumption of distinct and regulated spheres: the private, the social, and the public. The last sphere, defined by many as a field of responses to macro-social expectancies, suffers today, according to José Luis Dader, from *elephantiasis*, that is, from the rampart conversion of private events and social events into public ones.

Furthermore, Dader affirms that the uncontrolled expansion of public space has become the most acute sociopolitical problem of today's society.[3] The contention that private space categories and practices in the form of market and entertainment exchanges have displaced the rationality-based categories, such as public sphere, public opinion, and citizenship, usually follows the disclosure of figures such as the following: In 1995, ABC, NBC, and CBS spent 1,592 minutes on the O.J. Simpson murder trial, 418 minutes on the Oklahoma City bombing, and 318 minutes on the war in Bosnia.[4] The encroachment and trespassing theory in all its variations is still the most popular platform in boundary research.[5]

Although many island commentators tend to frame Puerto Rican politics in terms of the metanarrative of decolonization, which is in turn located within "serious" legal discourse, I wish to address the 2000 Puerto Rican gubernatorial race and the apparent blurring of boundaries between public and private realms and between political communication and entertainment that characterized the bitter campaign and contemporary island politics in general. To explore these questions, I will limit this chapter to a brief characterization of the complex boundary scenario that was highlighted during one day: October 18, 2000.

In pursuing my hypothesis, namely, that the "political" has undergone a series of transformations in contemporary Puerto Rico that cannot be understood through traditional critiques of colonialism, I am relying on a series of assumptions. First, I propose that boundaries are political, cultural, and intellectual power exercises. Second, although for many years the government and the political parties (and its bureaucratic and institutionalization practices) have organized and hegemonized public space in Puerto Rico, this function has been gradually transferred to mass media under the form of entertainment but with the consent and acquiescence of the political institutions and actors.

In addition, I propose that the intensified use by the mass media of entertainment codes such as voyeurism and entertainment formulae such as soap opera, reality shows, and gossip programs during the recent electoral contest can also shift in intensity and emphasis when the actors are not hegemonic subjects on the axes of race, gender, or sexuality. In the 2000 contest, the entertainment "value" of the elections, for instance, was invigorated by the fact that a woman was the candidate for one of the major parties. At the same time, I will argue that a series of pseudo-events and pseudo-scandals emerged as a sideshow to the articulation of a plural, alternative, and deliberative public space sparked by the Vieques crisis at the start of 2000, which neither the mainstream media nor the political parties could control. By the "Vieques crisis," I am alluding to the demand of religious, community, government, Leftist, and other groups upon the state to achieve the exit of the U.S. Navy from its bombing range in the municipality of Vieques.

The Pseudo-Event

To further explore the place of pseudo-events as a form of politics in the Puerto Rican context, I would like to first define the term. In 1964, Daniel Boorstin published *The Image: A Guide to Pseudo-Events in America* (Harper Colphon Books, 1964), a path-breaking book that has retained its value for more than three decades. A pseudo-event, Boorstin declares, is a synthetic novelty that possesses the following characteristics:

1. It is not spontaneous, but comes about because someone has planned, planted, or incited it. Typically, it is not a train wreck or an earthquake, but an interview.

2. It is planted primarily (although not exclusively) for the immediate purpose of being reported or reproduced. Therefore, its occurrence is arranged for the convenience of the reporting or the reproducing media.
3. Its relation to the underlying reality of the situation is ambiguous. Its interest arises largely from this very ambiguity. Concerning a pseudo-event the question, "What does it mean?" has a new dimension. Whereas the news interest in a train wreck is in what happened and in the real consequences, the interest in an interview is always, in a sense, in whether it really happened and in what might have been the motives. Did the statement really mean what it said? Without some of this ambiguity, a pseudo-event cannot be very interesting.
4. Usually it is intended to be a self-fulfilling prophecy.

One important corollary or implication is that in a pseudo-event, the specific medium or media involved no longer merely reflect the social and/or political forces around them; instead, they actively work to shape political discourse to their own purposes.[6] Sean Wilentz, Dayton-Stockton Professor of History at Princeton University, refers to pseudo-scandals as "the latest metamorphosis of Boorstin's pseudo-event."[7] The growth of antipolitical sensationalism, the criminalization of political differences, the widening of opportunities for corruption and technological innovations such as talk radio and the Internet are some of the factors that account for the proliferation of pseudo-scandals, according to Wilentz.

During the Puerto Rican 2000 electoral campaign, a particular press medium schemed a pseudo-event/pseudo-scandal and tried to provoke a populist uprising to derail Popular Democratic Party Sila María Calderón's candidacy and, by association, the still-untamed Vieques protest movement. For this occasion, I will only deal with the first aspect: the making of a populist uprising that I would argue turned sour.

As a textbook boundary issue, what happened in Puerto Rico during the whole electoral campaign could be seen as the most dramatic exhibit of the gradual encroachment of public space by an entertainment-coded private space. I propose that the campaign intensified the entertainment wiring of an already consenting public space made up by the political parties and mass media establishment. This intensification also included the renegade action by one of Puerto Rico's main newspaper that broke the boundaries of the general pact that constituted the hegemonic public space. The newspaper in question is *El Vocero*, a tabloid known for its coverage of violent crime and sensationalism.

Moved by political and possibly economic reasons (The paper's dwindling numbers are *vox populi*), *El Vocero's* action was not really a departure from the privatization dynamics affecting all newspapers. Yet, for many months since David Sanes's Rodríguez death, the Vieques crisis was able to make a critical dent in its configuration and fostered an alternative public space. As the campaign progressed, the media relegitimized the parties' political monopoly by granting prime time and high visibility only to mainstream political actors.

When *El Vocero's* "disclosures" regarding candidate Sila María Calderón came about, mass media entertainment coding was fully reactivated once again.

The Soap Opera

Every four years, Puerto Rican gubernatorial candidates participate in televised debates. Over the last two decades, the candidates have represented the three main political parties, namely, the pro-statehood New Progressive Party (NPP), the pro-commonwealth Popular Democratic Party (PDP), and the Puerto Rican Independence Party (PIP). Two days before the first debate between the three gubernatorial candidates scheduled for October 18, 2000, *El Vocero* revealed its latest poll figures.[8] According to Precision Research, pro-statehood candidate Carlos Pesquera held a 3.1 percent lead over PDP Calderón (46.2 percent to 43.1 percent) as the pro-independence Rubén Berríos Martínez, notwithstanding his substantial involvement in the Vieques standoff, remained in the 5–6 percent vicinity. The pollster added that gender was not a factor; both women and men preferred Pesquera. The "watermelon" factor, that is voters who were *independentistas* on the outside (green) but *populares* on the inside (red) appeared to be on the down side. Expectations regarding the debate increased as journalists from CNN, BBC, Univisión, the Spanish press, and the *Orlando Sentinel*, among others, began to arrive on the island.

The day before the debate, the political camps ironed out last-minute details: No Puerto Rican bottled water for Pesquera and Berríos Martínez, and the set backdrop had to be repainted bronze, as the original gold resembled Calderón's campaign color. Meanwhile, journalists were criticizing the straightjacket rules established by the parties that precluded any real debate.[9] On the morning of October 18, the proverbial "anarchist bomb in the theater" was thrown by Jorge Luis Medina. The former "Video Psycho," whose movie reviews in *El San Juan Star* written in a wry and mordant New York style had enjoyed a huge cult following for many years, was the author of a big-time accusation against Sila María Calderón.

It helped that the contender was a woman, a very rich person and the protagonist of a memorable and criticized first wedding. For starters, this is the stuff villains are made of. But you need more than a viable TV character; the appropriate structure that can organize and communicate your narrative is required. This would be the soap opera, a genre very popular in Puerto Rico and whose codes could provide an effective emotional appropriation and quick political translation in wide audiences. After all, the television medium is the one that fashions the production and transmission of news, and one of television's secrets is the adoption of melodramatic commodifiable codes.[10]

Every Latin American soap opera, in its classical mode, is first and foremost a love story, but as a form of melodrama it is also a drama of recognition, as Nora Mazziotti points out. The main questions always are the following: Who is my father? Who is my mother? The symbolic or real orphanage is resolved at the end by going from unawareness to awareness (*del des-conocimiento al re-conocimiento*). At the soap opera ending, Mazziotti adds, the revelation of the true identity has the aspect of moral reparation. Those who did wrong will be punished; a restitution of order and justice is accomplished.[11] The front page of *El Vocero* on October 18 read, "La Amenaza con Inmigración" (She threatened her with U.S. Immigration). The story accused Calderón of employing a 13 year-old illegal alien Dominican as her maid during the 1980s and revealed a tale of horrors that had lasted for three years.[12] The traditional first episode of the soap opera, in which the orphanage situation with its hidden identities and moral dilemmas is presented, started with a bang.

Although Medina tried to compare the case with Clinton's nominations of Kimba Wood and Zoe Baird, it was apparent from a perfunctory reading that this was not a case of unpaid Social Security or unclear migrant status. The perverse lines of prejudice, injustice, and exploitation that made up Jennifer Colón Rivera's story constituted a compendium of a Caribbean tragedy. In order to absolutely disqualify the contender, Jennifer's testimony traveled from slavery to post-abolitionist racism, from forced migration to child labor, from sexual abuse to a string of violations of human, economic, and civil rights. Throughout all the stations of Jennifer's fall into hell, as she described her life with Calderón, the contender stood as the incarnation of evil.[13]

Jennifer's story was constructed as a web of moral depravation and hypocrisy woven by three archetypical figures in the soap opera inventory and in other melodramatic products: The contender was the cruel stepmother of Cinderella, as she mistreated the children from her husband's previous marriages. She was the capricious queen, a kind of Marie Antoinette, scornful of the poor, which would clean thoroughly her hands with moistened wipes after contact with the "undesirable" people of the "residenciales."[14] The contender was also portrayed as a headstrong *hacendada* that insisted in starchy and crisp maid uniforms that could clearly distinguish servants from mistresses. Perhaps, unable to find a local stereotype, Medina had to use a facsimile: the antebellum mistress, "the one that you see in *Gone with the Wind*" with despised Dominicans as a modern day version of slaves.[15]

Although dramatically flawed as evidenced by the need to borrow cultural references and the inconsistencies of the testimony itself, Jennifer's story, as developed by Jorge Luis Medina, described a credible system of differences, landscapes, biographies, and itineraries. As a 13 year old, Jennifer left the Dominican Republic in a *yola* (small boat). She found work at a rich family house, although her mistress despised migrants and frequently showed contempt for the increasing number of illegal Dominicans in Puerto Rico. The household was completely dysfunctional: The children were an arrogant bunch; her mistress mistreated her husband's children who conspired against her; and Jennifer was the weakest link: She could not look to anyone in the eyes; she had to keep her eyes down. Jennifer's refuge was to cry in response to her employer's insensitivity: "*Why are you crying? Nobody is dead.*"

With no medical insurance or educational opportunities, Jennifer—with only an elementary education—dreamed of getting married to her boyfriend, another Dominican who also arrived in a *yola*. She would become a ghost.

Her mistress was adamant: *I do not want to see you; you should stay behind doors.* But when she was to be seen, she had to be in uniform, a theatrical one that left no doubt as to who had power. Hatred for the poor, migrants, and *caserío* (slum) dwellers, was constant. Her mistress would not admit any proximity with poverty. She would dispense with clothing that had been touched by the "unclean"; she would burn newly acquired clothing before giving it for charity. The abhorrence of difference would culminate in the mistress's demand for Jennifer to have an abortion when she got pregnant by her boyfriend. No alien reproduction.

But being the contender, a political figure that aspired to be the governor, the story of Calderón and her Dominican maid acted also as a prophetical warning of the evils that awaited "la gran familia," the extended household of Puerto Rico, if she was elected. There was more than one political lesson: In all three narratives, women appeared as whimsical, hysterical, frivolous, cruel and insensitive, unsuitable for politics, as their domain is the domestic territory, the classical *oikos* instead of the *polis*—the political, public, and masculine realm. In the second place, the rich and famous could be punished at any time by the power of a neo-populist mass media, which championed the people. This excess, this baroque overflow was perhaps the deepest weakness of the plot.

Judge Silvia

The narrative structure was there; the *dramatis personae* were there, a receptive audience familiar with the melodramatic soap opera code was apparently awaiting. What went wrong? I could say the pseudo-event backfired because the schemers forgot an old trade practice: "One standard that journalists must apply to their reporting on the private lives of political leaders is that every charge printed or aired should be proven or accompanied by a substantial body of evidence. Sorting fact from fiction, evidence from innuendo, is a vital journalistic function at a time when increased competition among different media sources is giving campaign gossip and rumor broader circulation than in the past."[16] Or, I could say that it backfired because it was ineptly and clumsily concocted, especially when the schemers did not have a strong supporting ensemble.

Edwin Mundo, a legislator representing San Juan that had consistently criticized Calderón's performance as mayor of San Juan, suddenly appeared as Jennifer's last employer.[17] One of Puerto Rico's most popular TV programs—"Super-Xclusivo"—followed up on the Mundo connection by showing pictures of Jennifer posing for some pictures in Mundo's living room sofa. Perhaps, the paper's operative underplayed the political acumen even of its natural and loyal readers and did not anticipate a backlash from women infuriated with its gross misogyny. But I could also propose that it backfired because of an ironic, although logical twist: A better-designed and effective entertainment product answered it. The soap opera exploded the same day of the first TV debate between the gubernatorial candidates.

When I arrived at Channel 11, located near Parque Muñoz Rivera in Puerta de Tierra, the police had already established physical boundaries for the three parties. Each one of them had erected sound systems and stages; merengue and salsa bands and popular singers were available. I recalled hearing the *merenguera* Ashley from the Popular Democratic Party platform dedicating her newest hit "El poder de las mujeres" (The Power of Women) to Sila María Calderón because she was a woman, and she was staying in business notwithstanding. In the TV station lobby, the receptionist was lip-syncing Ashley as we waited for the candidates to arrive.

That evening, as I watched the debate together with a hastily assembled crowd of "experts" called by Channel 11, a poised, articulate, well-groomed Sila María Calderón stood in front of the cameras accompanied by her extended family to uphold her right to intimacy and her right to a family life and, not the least, to ratify the public space configuration that had been violated by *El Vocero*'s allegations. In the streets adjacent to the TV station, throngs of supporters from the three main Puerto Rican parties followed the debate in giant screens and cheered and booed as the candidates answered questions from editorializing journalists, many of the exchanges in the best tradition of the melodramatic code. When I left the station, the pro-statehood NPP party was over, their tents folded but the *populares* were waving their *pava* flags in streets and highways, a clear sign of who had carried the night.

Sila María Calderón won the debate not only because a boundary restitution between private and public spheres was effected or because she handled the political and discursive economy of the debate much better than the other two candidates, but, because all things being equal, in the melodramatic appropriation, the viewer always prefers the original *hacendada*, a nuanced and elusive figure whose failures are intertwined with her seductions, rather than the predictable and monolithic villain devised by third-rate script writers.

Notes

The author wants to acknowledge the valuable research assistance of Mayra Rivera, a graduate student at the School of Public Communication, University of Puerto Rico.

1. For an interesting discussion on the subject, see Samuel P. Winch, *Mapping the Cultural Space of Journalism: How Journalists Distinguish News from Entertainment* (Westport, CT: Praeger, 1997).
2. Leonor Arfuch, "Lo público y lo privado en la escena contemporánea: política y subjetividad," *Revista de Crítica Cultural* 21 (November 2000): 8–15.
3. José Luis Dader, *El periodista en el espacio público* (Barcelona: Bosch, 1992), 145–46.
4. Quoted in Susan D. Moeller, *Compassion Fatigue: How the Media Sell Disease, Famine, War and Death* (London: Routledge, 1999), 29.
5. The boundaries issue is neuralgic to the legitimating of a communication studies field in Puerto Rico. For example, although the constitution of publicity as a discourse of objects can be traced to the epistemological propositions of David Hume and the aesthetics of Schilling, as Eliseo Colón has very aptly described, many intellectuals persist in the vilification of publicity and other

discourses and mass media products. See Eliseo Colón, *Modernidad, Publicidad, Hegemonía* (San Juan: Editorial de la Universidad de Puerto Rico, 1996). Exclusionary categories such as yellow press, vaudeville, sensationalism, and so on, with populist and negative undertones, are used to distinguish communication industry products from high culture products. Even in the field of cultural studies, advertising and media analysis are in many occasions organized by conspiracy theories and by the ever-recurring theme of mass manipulation by the market. Is there a possibility of critique practices that stand equally apart from the exclusionary view of mass media discourses, practices, and products as minor and contaminated texts and from the neoliberal and neo-populist assertion of the omnipotent and defining role of the market and its sidekick, entertainment? Philosopher Irma Rivera Nieves in a soon-to be-released work on the rhetoric and erotica of the gubernatorial election campaign in Puerto Rico, based on the narratives of Derrida, Legendre, and Wittgenstein, decries the prevalent boundary between political advertising ("low") and political communication ("high") narratives. The adoption of a standardizing and lowest-common-denominator approach by media enterprises contribute, ironically, to perpetuate claims of a divorce between the two realms. In the name of erasing the difference between high and low, media enterprises frequently champion a populist subjectivity that is best described by the practice of "giving people what the people want."

6. Benjamin I. Page, *Who Deliberates? Mass Media in Modern Democracy* (Chicago: University of Chicago Press, 1996), 116.
7. Sean Wilentz, "Will Pseudo-Scandals Decide the Election?," *The American Prospect* 11, no. 21 (September 24–October 2, 2000).
8. "Gana Terreno Carlos Pesquera," *El Vocero*, October 16, 2000, 16.
9. M. Figueroa, "Con objeciones los periodistas," *Primera Hora*, October 17, 2000, 4.
10. Ignacio Ramonet, *La tiranía de la comunicación* (Barcelona: Debate, 1998).
11. Nora Mazziotti, *La industria de la telenovela* (Buenos Aires: Paidós, 1996), 14–15.
12. Jorge Luis Medina, "Los Krans-Calderón emplean indocumentada," *El Vocero*, October 18, 2000, 3.
13. Jorge Luis Medina, "Sirvienta de Sila narra tres años de infierno," *El Vocero*, October 18, 2000, 3.
14. Jorge Luis Medina, "Revela Jennifer Colón Rivera: Sila tiene asco a gente de los caseríos," *El Vocero*, October 19, 2000, 2.
15. Jorge Luis Medina, "Sila niega trabajara en su casa," *El Vocero*, October 19, 2000, 3.
16. Larry Sabato, Mark Stencel, and S. Robert Lichter, *Peep Show: Media and Politics in an Age of Scandal* (Lanham, MD: Rowman & Littlefield, 2000), 30.
17. B. Ramírez and A. Virella, "Mundo asegura contrató la empleada doméstica," *El Vocero*, October 19, 2000, 6.

CHAPTER 9

Beauty Salons: Consumption and the Production of the Self

María Isabel Quiñones Arocho

What do you want Milagros?, you ask almost in a whisper, unable to face her but looking at her reflection in the mirror. She then walks towards you and out of her trouser pocket she finds a twenty dollar bill and with an attitude, she shows it to you, and then in a soft but firm voice, she asks for a service: "Give me shocking red make-up, Marina, and cut my hair as you see fit." You feel your body trembling and your knees are about to give up, but your eyes are fixed in the mirror where Milagros grows even bigger and walks towards you expecting an answer, an answer that you will have to utter, no more excuses, Marina, look at yourself, look at her, Marina, What will you say?

Carmen Lugo-Filippi and Ana L. Vega, Vírgenes y Mártires[1]

Most women who came to the beauty salon were old and beaten up by life. Under their wasted skins, however, you could see how their agony dressed up like hope in every visit.

Mario Bellatin, Salón de Belleza[2]

Social theory has frequently linked makeup and adornment with the objectification of the female body and its construction as a passive object of the male gaze. Likewise, many feminist theorists associate beauty rituals with the sexual exploitation of women. In their view, any consumption that is organized around the beauty industry contributes to the reproduction of a male dominated society and perpetuates the alienation of women.[3] Women who succumb to the aesthetic industry are said to lose their ability to take a political stance in a patriarchal society and instead end up fighting and competing among themselves, eliminating the possibility of solidarity. In framing the debate in these terms, all these authors ignore that the human relationship to adornment in general and objects in particular have a long and complex history.[4] They also neglect the analysis of cultural practices that are shaping the construction and representation of the feminine and masculine in contemporary society.

This point of view also presupposes that there is a logical order of needs, and tacitly condemns women's fashion consumption as superfluous. In his first writings on consumer culture, however, Jean Baudrillard (1976) formulated a critique of the assumed "spontaneous" relationship between objects and needs that serves as a starting point to elaborate an alternative paradigm.[5] He proposed that need is not an origin but an alibi that creates a system or code of signs that differentiate some consumers from others. In this sense, commodities no longer designate the world itself but the identity and the status of the owner. Because they are part of a communication structure where the relationship between word, image, and referent is arbitrary, they are signs that never exhaust the possibility of signification. Above all, as consumption alludes to a process of social reproduction that is part of a human project, it is a way of producing human subjects and social orders of a certain kind. In other words, what happens at the level of consumption is a representation of what is at stake in culture. The semiotic dimensions of social life cannot be distinguished from the practical process of production/consumption. Free from the realm of necessity, our task is to examine how consumption exceeds the supposedly blind obedience to the rules of its realization in the marketplace.[6]

Recent work about consumption further suggests its importance not so much as a system that actualizes needs in terms of options and calculations but as a practice that transgresses the uses of products imposed by an economic order.[7] Rather than accepting the idea of a fully sovereign individual who confronts his needs, cultural theory proposes a subject that chooses not in function of the object's utility but as a way to participate in a social system.[8] Modern consumption represents a revolution in the parameters of social existence and is a key aspect of the relationship among people of different cultures who may find common ground in their desire for certain goods.[9] In recent years its effects are intensified by an information and mass media culture that invades all spheres of everyday life.[10] Consumption of images and texts may even have the effect of erasing the distinction between the sacred and the profane.[11] Commodities may indeed become sacred for those who believe in their power to transform lives.

The acquisition of commodities and services that takes place in beauty salons, spas, gyms, and the offices of plastic surgeons reveal a complex relationship between the construction of "femininity" and "masculinity" and the dominant aesthetic. In the specific case of women, beauty consumption appears as a form of emancipation from the constraints of daily life. Today, new technologies even offer the possibility of defying the "realm of the natural." The third woman or the indeterminate woman, as Lipovetsky calls her, "is a feminine self creation."[12] Although one must not overlook the fact that the beauty industry validates a way of life that depends on the movements of capital, it is still possible to study women's consumption strategies and tactics in order to understand how cultures intervene in the production of the social imaginary. Perhaps we may even unveil certain practices that have the effect of unsettling tendencies toward homogeneity—of people and cultures—by capital.[13]

In this chapter, I offer an analysis of consumption strategies of women in Puerto Rico's beauty salons and stylist centers. The women I have studied often complain about their lives and their fading beauty; they openly discuss their sexuality and their plans to seduce the other. They also contemplate themselves in the mirror, again and again. The mirror returns a reflection not only of their struggles and achievements, but also of their failures. For these women the construction of a desired image, through a haircut, makeup, or surgery, is a moral imperative. As they often argue, a good life is a life that is consumed by aesthetic considerations. Yet I will argue that although consumption ties people to a certain beauty ideal, it also encourages women to take responsibility concerning their own fate. In my analysis I rely on Michel Foucault's concept of the production of the self and the notion of the individual as a force of consumption elaborated by Gilles Lipovetsky.[14]

The Magic of a Mirror

"The mirror never lies," my mother used to whisper every morning when she freshened her lipstick and put on her nylons. My mother was never satisfied with her image in the mirror; she would complain that the dress did not fit right, that her legs were too fat, that she desperately needed a haircut, and so on. To me, however, she was the most beautiful *mami* in the block where we used to live. She would always leave home with her painted lips, her hair done, and polished shoes. She never failed to visit a beauty parlor, and at least once a month she would buy a new piece of clothing in doña Chenchita's boutique—without my dad finding out, of course. During the day, my mother was a teacher; in the afternoon, she cooked and did the dishes, and at night she prepared the next day's classes and supervised my homework and that of my brother. But since this was the time when gyms started to become fashionable, my mother also figured out how to squeeze visits two times a week into her tight schedule.

When my mother became ill, she decided that she would never look at herself in the mirror again. One afternoon, she went through her collection of imitation necklaces and earrings that she kept in several chests and gave them to me. "My child, take what you like the most and give the rest to your aunt." That day, I knew that my mother would die. Anguished, I took her collection of necklaces and with tears in my eyes I locked myself in my bedroom. I had never shared the rituals of beauty with my mother; I neither liked makeup nor jewelry. To leave the house disheveled was my battle cry, my gesture of adolescent rebellion. That night, however, I tried all those necklaces and earrings sitting in front of the mirror, I brushed my hair in a thousand ways, colored my eyes with green and blue shadows and my mouth red, a very intense red. The mirror offered me back an image of myself that I did not recognize. I deeply believe that it was right there, and at that moment, that my interest in the construction of a feminine ideal defined by makeup, adornment, and the possession of a voluptuous body began.

Like my mother, the women who visit beauty salons spend hours in front of a mirror. Never completely satisfied, they pursue a beauty ideal that eludes them. But they do so with such conviction that they end up believing that a visit to a beauty salon, a spa, or the office of a surgeon might indeed change their lives. Previous misunderstandings with neighbors, run-ins with demanding bosses, and kids' tantrums are left behind. After all, thick makeup not only covers the signs of age but also protects from any criticism. All complaining with friends and personnel at the beauty salon has a relaxing effect. But inside the beauty parlor, one can overhear Mariela congratulating Luz for "making miracles." "If it wasn't for my dear stylist Angela's advice, what would become of me," Yanira murmurs out loud while fixing her gaze in another woman's shoes as she crosses the street. It is no surprise that some clients may argue that "a stylist is the best friend a woman can have." Of course, it is a figure of speech. Beyond the hugs and the confessions, most clients would not have anything to do with their stylists. It is as if time and other social constraints are put on hold in beauty salons, yet clients and stylists appear to belong to different worlds.

"Everybody knows that," comments Janice, who anxiously waits for her stylist. "I do not feel a friend makes you wait that long, in fact one should not forget that this is a business." Perhaps other women feel a bit different. At the other end of the salon one can overhear Mariela congratulating Luz for "making miracles." With a big smile Luz comments, "See, how beautiful you are. You look like someone who could pose in a fashion magazine." They walk side by side until they reach the main entrance and Mariela gives Luz a five-dollar tip. Luz takes it immediately and puts it away inside one of her blouses' pockets. Tips are a very important source of income for Luz, since the salon's salary is not enough to meet all of her family's expenses. Only the owners of beauty salons make money. Mariela says goodbye with a kiss, and when the door shuts, a bell announces the stylist's return to her post. Luz turns around to the clients and asks, "Who's next?" This time, a woman named Nilsa approaches with a quiet step and comments, "I want you to do something to change this face. With all the work in the office, I have let my self go too far."

Betzaida sits in a nearby chair skimming through the pages of the last edition of *Fashion Bazaar*. The stylist vigorously brushes Betzaida's hair and cautions her that she must dye her hair to hide the gray that has sprouted since the last visit. "It's impossible for me to have gray hairs, Maria, I came barely two weeks ago. But do whatever you want because today I feel naughty. Dye my hair, cut it . . . do whatever it takes for me to seduce whoever comes close to me." At the other end of the salon, Yanira slyly looks at herself in the mirror. Sofía, another stylist, grabs a chunk of wet hair and brings it to one side of Yanira's face and winks at her. "I think that if you get a haircut, you will look sexy but with a youthful air," says Sofía with a tone of complicity. It's been a long day but Sofía does not complain. In this place, she can have the luxury of calling herself a stylist and not simply a beautician. It's the best job that she has had in the last ten years. Mariela, Nilsa, Betzaida, and Yanira visit the beauty salon with the hope that it will change their lives. Like other women clients, they wish to create an image of themselves that is in tune with the fashion trends and that, at the same time, makes them feel competent in their jobs, seductive with their boyfriends or husbands, and sure of themselves in their relations with other women. This transformation requires a certain amount of work on "the body": a new haircut, new hair color, toning massages, facials, pedicure, and manicure. But there is also a sociability that emerges between stylists and clients. Overwhelmed by infidelity, by the behavior of their children or the attitude of coworkers, many clients open themselves to the useful advice of their stylists.

In the beauty salon, women reveal their most intimate desires while negotiating with a beauty ideal that sometimes is at odds with their cultural imaginary of the feminine. The exclusiveness of the clientele that characterized the beauty salons in earlier decades, along with the fact that those who provided services either took into account their client's class origins and social status or took care of only a select group of the rich and beautiful, has given way to a more inclusive space that has a star stylist as its protagonist. He or she offers his or her talent as much to the secretary of a bank as to the wife of a prominent executive, but more often to young women who aspire to win a beauty contest crown.

A Stylist for the Masses

> I am a stylist for the masses. I could have stayed in a small salon and charged really high prices. Yet I rather work in a place where everybody can come and see me. It's true that I work a lot but I feel more comfortable.[15]

Puerto Rican stylist Magali Febles has an impressive resumé: She was responsible for taming singer Lucesita Benítez's afro, transforming actress Johanna Rosaly for her role in the famous soap opera of the 1970s, *Cristina Bazán*, and dyeing the hair of Puerto Rico's third Miss Universe winner, Dayanara Torres, from brown to black. She has also worked with other Miss Puerto Rico candidates, including Desiré Lowry and Denise Quiñones, eventually Miss Universe 2000, brushed up businessmen like Atilano Cordero Badillo and retouched many Puerto Rican politicians whose names she will not reveal. In the interview that she granted a reporter of *El Nuevo Día*, one of Puerto Rico's main dailies, she tells of her rise as beautician in a beauty salon located in the humble neighborhood of Amelia in the town of Cataño to being the owner of her own business, Magali Febles Salon and Day Spa, in San Patricio Plaza of Guaynabo, Puerto Rico. Although Magali wanted to be a lawyer and work for human rights, the fact that she was poor forced her to study cosmetology and finish high school by attending classes at night instead. That is how Magali came to work in Ileana Irving Salon where she rubbed elbows with celebrities from the entertainment business, relationships that have served her very well in her professional career.

Despite her many achievements, including the acquisition of the Miss Universe of Puerto Rico franchise (valued at $250,000), Febles does not want to just be the stylist of the chosen ones and instead declares her allegiance to the masses. Her mission is to offer others what she has attained with much effort, a wisdom that is founded in the recognition of her own history and of a body that carries the traces of blackness: ample lips, flat nose, short and voluptuous body—forms that she learned to camouflage with makeup, intense exercise routines, and, most recently, with the scalpel. Magali Febles's success reflects the impact of newly developed techniques that are now associated with people's will to succeed and their ability to submit to a discipline of self-control and sacrifice. This new ethic defines people's perceptions of self and others as well as offers a parameter for "the good life." The mass stylist is, then, a central social mediator in a world that emphasizes beauty as a moral, not economic, imperative.

To the extent that beauty products are accessible to most and diet and exercise plans become more easily accommodated to busy schedules, the new moral imperative becomes clearer. In this "new world," being out of shape is increasingly inexcusable as surgeries, liposuction, and liposculpture guarantee "a good life." A woman who goes to the gym or practices yoga exercises must include in her schedule a routine of deep skin treatments, hydration, and microdermabrasion. Whereas before women may have tried to hide the extra pounds with clothes that created the illusion of a slim body, new patterns of consumption transform the relationship between people and their bodies. Fat is out; muscle is in. It is sufficient to skim through magazines and watch local news or cable programs that report on the lives of movie stars, political leaders, and perfect husbands, to discover that "men's bodies" are also subject to beauty ideals. With increasing frequency, adolescent boys and mature men visit beauty salons and spas to remove their body hair, dye their hair, get a manicure, and pluck their eyebrows. Men also dally in front of the mirror and submit themselves to artifice. These observations lead us to the beauty salon as an important site in the production of femininity and a key space in which new Puerto Rican masculinities are imagined and lived.

The Making of the Feminine: The Powers of Seduction

In the beauty salon, the active pursuit of a certain image is not only linked to women's objectives as consumers but also to the constructions of femininity in Puerto Rican culture. The valorization of beauty reinforces a vision of femininity that seeks success in relationships with men but also articulates the desire of a traditional family, including a few children. Although eager to be recognized for their merits, women refuse to openly compete with men and continue to attribute significant value to their powers of seduction. The following conversation between a stylist and several clients serves to illustrate this point:

> PRISCILLA: Girl, I went all out and when he saw me, his eyes wanted to pop out. I was cool, you know, like I wasn't that interested. But he couldn't take it anymore and he said—baby, you look so hot.
>
> LUZ: I told you, with that makeup and haircut I knew that you were going to drive him crazy. Then, what happened?
>
> PRISCILLA: Nothing, nothing . . . with that guy you have to take it slow. You know how men are. If you give them too much, they get overwhelmed, and if you don't give them enough, they'll get tired of you. I want to keep that one for good. But I want him like crazy.
>
> SOFÍA: I think that you are doing the right thing. I know that young people today are different but there are certain things that stay the same. And there is where we women are, things haven't changed much. Make him suffer.
>
> LUZ: Well I think that if he is driving you crazy with desire, you should have sex. Tomorrow is another day.

The double game between insinuation and modesty defines the feminine in relation to seduction. Never open nor evident, seduction is subtle and demands the complete submission of the "victim." A body submitted to beauty practices mobilizes passions and anticipates the liberation of the senses. But another element enters the game of seduction: the possibility of opening oneself to an immediate pleasure sanctioned by culture. While Sofía, her stylist, advises Priscilla to play hard to get as she assumes the male inclination for "difficult" women, Luz intervenes to suggest that she let her desire run free. Priscilla now treads the slippery terrain of the multiple significations of the feminine, not so much as a passive object but as a subject who takes responsibility for her relationships with men. Her ambiguity exposes a tension between the cultural knowledge that produces her as an object for the other's gaze and her own complicity in the construction of this gaze.

The women who visit the beauty salon demonstrate a similar degree of ambiguity in their characterization of their roles as mothers and wives. Women frequently affirm that their participation in the labor market does not affect their ability to balance a partner or bring up children. But at times, they do condemn the sexual division of labor and the asymmetry of gendered expectations. Although some associate family happiness with their personal "sacrifice," many renege of the responsibilities imposed on them because of their gender. There are many complaints about how husbands do not value their domestic work, neglect to demonstrate their affection, and even abandon sexual intimacy after only a few years of marriage. In this regard, the visit to the beauty salon is a way of escaping the constraints of family life.

To this end, let's hear a conversation among a group of clients:

NORMA: Sometimes I wonder why I fix myself up so much since my husband doesn't even notice. He's one of those dreary men. But he's very affectionate with the kids.

ELIZA: It's good that he pays attention to the kids. Mine does not even do that. But, girl, women also need affection . . . you know . . . seexx. (*She roars with laughter.*)

INÉS: Look, I have to cook everyday. I like to make up unusual recipes but my husband has fixed tastes. And, of course, he never compliments my cooking. And on top of that, I have to be available when he wants to have sex . . . oh, no, sometimes I say no.

NORMA: The only thing that I know is that a woman that does not give it to him drives him to the street.

INÉS: Oh, honey, when they are going to cheat, they will! I have it all figured out. I go to the gym in the morning. After that, I do some shopping in Marshalls and then I grab a light lunch. In the afternoon, I take my two boys to football practice and then to Pollo Tropical. Nobody helps me out and my three machos don't even pick up the plate from the table. I'm not going out to work in an office so I can be a "liberated woman." Let him work to support me. No sacrifices on my end. When he gets home, he eats his Pollo Tropical dinner without complaining.

ELIZA: I can't imagine being lazy like you, not having a job. The thing is that when there is a problem, I'm always the one who has to deal with it. Taking care of our daughter, her doctor's appointments, the teachers, homework, they are all my duties. In addition to having carried her for nine months, I have to be with her all the time. My husband plays with her but rarely stays home to take care of her when I want to go out to a movie or to go shopping with some friends.

NORMA: Well, well but there is no reason to lose hope. That's why I come here, to fix myself up and forget my troubles in life. If it wasn't for these moments . . . (*All the women laugh.*)

These women view the acquisition of new skin lotions, the latest in eye shadows or hair treatments as a way out of an overwhelming everyday life. Self-gratification is the preferred strategy when dealing with an objectified world that resists women's desires. Commodities are weapons in their struggle to define not what women are but what they would like to be. Women work in the construction of a new image combining elements from available styles and fashions: seductress, ingénue, sporty, intellectual, sexy, and entrepreneurial, among others. Thus, every little transformation will require a new outfit, dress or pair of sunglasses. Suddenly, a divorced mother of three discovers that with a new haircut she feels more self-assured. A 40-year-old woman will care a good deal less about what people say when she looks at herself in the mirror and sees a much younger woman "all thanks to the toning treatment that the beauty salon offers." The businesswoman, on the other end, will imagine a perfect future when she indulges in an anticellulite treatment.

The beauty salon clients struggle to liberate themselves from a social order that appears to be fixed, even if in their attempts they may end up buying into the idea that there is only one model of feminine beauty. They will, for instance, accept to dress with pant suits but they will also avoid any gestures that denote a "loss of femininity." The firmness of this judgment may surprise those theorists who celebrate the erosion between feminine and masculine aesthetics or the so-called *gender bending*. It will also make women who struggle to be recognized by their merit and not their appearance uncomfortable. But the truth is that in many Puerto Rican beauty salons, the gauge to measure women's advancement is the possibility to adopt fashions without the restrictions of the past, and not the possibility of "crossing the divide between men and women." For some of the clients, the "essence of the feminine" is denied when women fight too openly with men or assume a demeanor associated with a masculine ideal. In this sense, clients celebrate their minimalist and soft underwear as compared with the rigid girdles of yesteryear, and also the fact that a haircut and blower do not require the old-fashioned rollers. But they are not willing to abandon lipstick, that mortal weapon in any close quarter combat.

Freed from standardized norms regarding consumption, women feel that they can buy whatever they want to buy, be it hydration products for the skin or laser rays to remove unwanted hair. One day a woman will opt for blonde locks, and next week she will prefer a deep-red dye. The demand for products that straighten hair or whiten skin appears to be immune to the proliferation of black beauty queens and actors who display their exoticism as a sign of identity. Overall, clients adhere to a beauty ideal that appears to ignore people's physical characteristics and their financial limits, while simultaneously negating certain constructions of the feminine that are now available in the market. These incongruities also have implications in the construction of the masculine, as the reader may soon find out.

Yet, while individuals play at constructing new selves, they appear to be unaware of the new microphysics of power. To the extent that new technologies open up the way for the infinite manipulation and transformation of "the body," a new subject emerges: the clone ideal. Whether emancipatory or not, we are witnessing a phenomenon that Baudrillard defined as "the hell of the Same," a seeming compulsion to create an image of oneself that erodes the distinction between self and other.[16] How does this new microphysics of power plays out in beauty salons? One image may be sufficient: a woman looking at the reflection of another woman in a mirror who exclaims, "Oh, I just want to look like her."

The Production of the Self: The Body's Discipline and the Masculine Revolution

> Why is it still considered more legitimate and theoretically more "real" to talk about the factory, hospital or office as spaces of contestation and not of the beauty parlor? It is politically urgent to revise the tactics and strategies that we have classified as worthy in the process of social transformation as well as the forms of resistance that we validate.[17]

In a heated discussion about aesthetics, Sonia and Maribel argue that regardless of how many explanations they give their clients, the majority insist in wearing bangs even if this style does not suit them or dye their hair blonde when multicolored tips are fashionable and would look better on them. "For me, a woman who fixes herself up, who has good taste and does not let herself go, never gets old and always calls attention," says Sonia concluding the debate. But one may wonder what "good taste" is. What does it mean to "look good"? What kind of manipulation is necessary to achieve the desired image?

In the context of the beauty salon, discourse about what is unpleasant and ugly is more revealing than anything that is said about beauty. For example, the stylists criticize their clients "for letting themselves get fat," for not making an effort to diffuse "skin defects," and for rarely experimenting with new techniques such as laser rays, microdemabrasion, botox, restylane, or plastic surgery. Neglected hair, unmade faces, and flaccid skin remain "women's mortal enemies." The beauty ideal celebrates "fleshy lips" and simultaneously rejects a "flat nose" and "bad hair." And for every one of these "ills," a solution is offered: A soft wave for curly and dry hair, thick layers of makeup for facial traits that need hiding, and exfoliation and toning treatments for blemishes and wrinkles. Droopy eyelids and bags under the eyes no longer overwhelm women over 50 at a popular surgeon's office.

The beauty salon, the spa, and the surgeon's office offer the techniques that will make the desired transformation possible. Here, the body is an imagined surface over which an aesthetic discourse is imposed. This dominant discourse requires that women eat less, sweat excess pounds, and remain young. The struggle against cellulite and the inevitability of aging is made evident not only in the rigorous discipline of exercise routines, the popularity of personal trainers, and the anticellulite body massages but, above all, in the matter-of-factness of women's decisions to undergo breast surgery or a liposuction procedure. This discipline of the body functions as a control device. Bringing oneself to this task and accepting one's guilt for a breach of discipline are the tools of the trade. Not surprisingly, women will frequently confess their misdemeanors way before their stylists notice them: "I got so distraught with the gray hair that I dyed it myself. And look what I've done; I've ruined it. I won't do it again," exclaims a woman at a well-known stylist center.

Women of all ages are encouraged to scrutinize themselves as a way to belong to a social body that values personal success and a steely will: "If you keep sunning yourself so much your face is going to turn into a raisin," José lectures Maritza. "Then don't come crying back to me because I don't do miracles." Although the clients almost always doubt a male stylist's "masculinity," they take their advice very seriously: "Oh, dear, you have to do something fast. Puerto Rican men are no longer into plump women," comments Antonio with complete authority to a client who has put on extra pounds. According to José and Antonio, men now prefer slim women with developed biceps who they think make perfect spouses. These are men who compete with their girlfriends and wives for body perfection and who show off their hairless faces and chests as trophies. The new male image—the metrosexual—is an essential part of this aesthetic revolution: men who pluck their eyebrows, get manicures, shave their legs, and dye their hair. Yet, as Luis Rafael Sánchez suggests in his essay "Cejas sacadas, piernas afeitadas y tips," this revolution is not necessarily linked to sexual ambiguity or homosexuality.[18]

> Policemen, cyclists, and adolescents, most of which have a very high heterosexual cholesterol level, even above normal, are not the only ones that have joined the revolutionary cause. Many men about to leave their twenties behind laugh at what people may think of them and take a little time here and there to pluck their eyebrows and shave their legs. Men in their thirties, already on the steady path of a profession or trade, also run to pierce their ears or highlight their hair in open defiance of conventionalisms.[19]

Artifice is not solely a woman's issue any more. Men also enjoy being desired. It is surprising, however, how much artifice is used to underscore masculinity. The young adolescent who dyes his hair and plucks his eyebrows is also the man who will validate his maleness by having a wife *and* a lover. If he is gay, he will seek to distance himself from the stereotype of the effeminate homosexual when exercising for hours in the gym. Even if women are as capable as men of engaging in sexual feats not imagined by our grandmothers, they do not emerge completely victorious from this gender experimentation. Although it is true that women struggle to liberate themselves, they do not escape the microscopic regulation of the other; they must project sensuality without real experience. Indeed, femininity is mostly conceived as a terrain where seduction is a better strategy than the appearance of muscles. To this cultural expectation, one must add the force of an aesthetic that proposes the anorexic model and bulimic actress as ideals. Where no other horizon seems possible, there emerges a set of tactics that distorts this aesthetic project. The control device does not act upon an imaginary of the body in the same way, and therefore, cannot produce the same effects.

. . . Resisting . . .

In many Puerto Rico beauty salons, fashions and tastes that cannot be accounted for in terms of the marketplace make their appearance. This causes much dissatisfaction on the part of the stylists when it comes to entertaining their clients' demands:

> ROBERTO: No matter what I say, Lucía always insists that I give her a haircut and style her hair as if she was going out for the evening. Imagine, she even asks me to place colorful pins [barrettes] in her hair when this is not appropriate for a woman who works in a government office!
>
> JACKIE: Nidia is worst, that one would really like me to leave her hair so blond, almost white. To top it off, there is the overly done eye shadow . . . but what can we do?
>
> MARÍA: If this is about a competition, check Wanda out. She uses clothes that are two sizes too small. I try to suggest that she wear a hairstyle and hair color that is not scandalous but she rebels.
>
> JACKIE: And what do you think about Nidia?

MARÍA: No, it's not the same. That girl has a few extra pounds but she has this attitude, "Here, I am, a little chunky but delicious." I am convinced that not all Puerto Rican men like those emaciated models.

ROBERTO: What's really ugly is when women let their flesh ooze out everywhere. It's like they don't really see themselves when they look at the mirror.

Fashion bids women to visit the beauty salon but not all women respond as expected or in the same way. Far from simply following the imposition of a beauty ideal, women make use of this distinctive and imperative repertoire in the same way that they use a moral code. They interpret it their own way and speak to it in their own class dialect. The issue is not then the workings over a "real" body but of a practice of the self shaped by multiple constraints. Culture here plays a major role. As the conversation between the stylists demonstrates, many clients value flashy fashions and over-the-counter colorful makeup and hair colors even when these choices constitute an open defiance of an aesthetic discourse that promotes harmony and subtlety. Equally disturbing, at least to some experts in the field, is Puerto Rican women's fascination with long nails painted in bright colors or their need to reveal so much flesh, even when going to church or going to pay respect to the dead.

The woman who dresses in such a way that her "flesh oozes all over the place" constructs an image of herself that is at odds with both the celebrated cultural construct of the woman who is "a bit chunky" and the globalized model whose sick demeanor is obtained by adding dark circles under her or his eyes. More than a problem of bad taste, the combination of elements found in the beauty salon adheres to an ironic and perverse logic. The desire to project a personal, unique, and incomparable identity collides with the need to be fashionable. The illusion of personal autonomy through the playfulness and exploration that consumption promotes also supposes a system of differences. As Clara Obligado suggests, consumption produces a social order that makes possible the coexistence of a pluralism that nurtures differences but works as a strict code that distinguish some consumers from others.[20]

> Today, appearances are important. If fashion offers to liberate citizens from the local and everyday, if in fashion there is a space in which we are free to choose, the choice of clothes also serves to produce uniformity, to clarify which group one belongs to while it allows the illusion of personal self-determination.[21]

People are forced to engage in a continuous renovation, a change of mask. That struggle confronts women with their most formidable competitors: other women.

Fashion Is War

> . . . lo que se luce entre ollas, no se luce entre otras.
>
> [. . . what is seen among pots, is not seen by other women.]

Flora sits anxiously near a window and at times looks out to the street. She tends to come to the beauty salon on Saturday at noon, after cleaning the house, washing clothes, and preparing lunch. Although people still admire her blue eyes, she has to also endure negative comments about her weight. As her friend Vivian could not come today Flora is feeling a bit out of place. With Vivian there, as overweight as she is, Flora can dismiss other women's looks. Both wear large sizes and their ability to wear the latest fashion trends is limited. "It was a mistake to wear this flowered blouse with this skirt," murmurs Flora as she follows with her eyes a middle-aged woman with a two piece Liz Clairbone suit with her eyes. The brand is obvious; the shirt shows off the famous designer's logo. The woman in question, Yolanda, avoids Flora. Regardless of how many times she walks by, Yolanda appears to never notice her. Although their visits to the salon always coincide on Saturdays, they have never spoken.

On her visits to the beauty salon Yolanda rarely awaits for her turn to come. She knows all the stylists very well and feels entitled to move around as she pleases. Usually she goes directly to the manicure room where her other friends, who also wear designer clothes, bags, and shoes, hang out. Today she is seated next to Berta and carefully observes the latter's manicure. Berta likes the moon and stars design on a turquoise background painted on her long and fake nails. For some reason, an incontrollable urge takes over Berta and she asks for Yolanda's opinion. Yolanda looks at her with great surprise and immediately approves the manicurist's work. The minute Berta walks away, however, Yolanda makes a gesture of repulsion, and her other friends laugh.

Through their consumption rituals, women imaginatively construct the place that they want to occupy in the social order. The clothes' tone, accessories, haircut, and makeup are elements of a complex system of inclusion and exclusion that is not based on "blood" or the display of wealth but in the capacity to spend money with a certain degree of imagination. This system works as a regulating mechanism. Women adopt the new styles and fashions as a sign of belonging to a given group and as a means to distinguish themselves from others. Yet the line that divides good and bad taste is ever changing. So is a culture that until recently dictated the allocation of different public spaces for people of different classes and skin colors. Thus, it is no surprise that local politicians exhibit "their love for the country" dancing rap tunes or attending radio interviews where their sex lives is the main topic. The sacred is not anymore so. "Way back people spoke of family values, now of money," says Yolanda with a degree of annoyance. Her comment alludes to the fact that at the beauty salon the rituals of exclusion based on perceptions of the individual's worth have given way to a social order where what constitutes success is constantly redefined. Her displeasure with Berta's familiarity and closeness was caused by her inability to grasp this new code.

In contrast to the law of conspicuous consumption of the leisure class developed by Weblen, the spectacle of displaying what one has does not require a withdrawal from all productive work.[22] Many women work and feel proud of their consumption capacity; the important thing here is attitude. While a compact mass of consumers may heap together and arrive early at a shopping mall when there is a special sale, the cool and relaxed consumer does not have to compete for what he or she desires. Money is not a problem, for there is a new generation of Puerto Ricans who flaunt their acquisitive power day and night. They prefer designer articles such as Puma walking shoes, Chanel beauty products, Rolex watches, and Louis Vuitton travel bags. For the less fortunate, as they are often referred to, there is always the fake Coach bag at the Sunday flea market or a pair shoes at Bakers or Sears that resembles "the real thing." At both ends of the social hierarchy, however, consumption is a moral duty. "If one is to be taken seriously, one must wear the latest in fashion," is the motto of a friend's eight-year-old daughter.

At the same time, the beauty and fashion industries have a strong democratizing tendency. If in the past imitation was the rule for groups that aspired to be upwardly mobile, now it is the constant renovation of accessories that determine social recognition.[23] Paradoxically, brands are one of the most important indicators of fashion's democratizing function. Even if some clients resist socially accepting certain other women who expose their purchasing power through famous designer wear, they cannot ignore them. Let us return one more time to the group led by Yolanda.

YOLANDA: Did you notice Aida's dress? A Jones of New York dress that does not go with her cheap shoes at all.

DOLORES: If you don't look at her shoes you would say that she has good taste.

YOLANDA: What do you mean? She can dress well but when she opens her mouth, you know where she comes from. I can tell the difference.

DOLORES: Well, it's not so evident to me. There are no differences any more, that's for our generation. Also, the one with the dress is her not me.

MARTA: But don't you know that Marshalls sells those famous brands and anyone can buy them?

The tension between a production/consumption system that promotes the canceling of differences and a cultural norm that still rests on the idea that "it is the person that makes the dress" and not vice versa is evident in the beauty salon. Yet in this confrontation between high fashion and clothes sold at accessible prices—ready to wear—the latter overcomes the former. Resistance to change, however, prevails among many clients. It is based on the notion that the subject has a history, whose conduct in public space guarantees his or her acceptance in certain social circles, and whose moral fiber is always under scrutiny. This contrasts with the view of a "mass" individual, pricked by his or her needs and immediate gratification. Regardless, the democratization of tastes has become the rule. Even high-fashion designers have created new lines to be sold in stores such as Target and H&M. Perhaps we owe this trend to the infamous Martha Stewart, who helped K-Mart out from bankruptcy with her "tasteful" but less expensive household items. In Puerto Rico, the outlet markets and chains like Marshalls sell "famous brands for much less," and people avidly respond to this call.

A "light" socialization promotes an upward mobility that is actively reconstituting social and cultural maps. The individual now recognizes himself or herself in the commodities that he or she possesses. As Marcuse once suggested, people "find their souls" in their cars, their music, their houses, and their kitchen gadgets.[24] Need is not the origin, argues Bauman, for commodities invade the marketplace before our possessions turn old or break down.[25] This is especially true in the technology industry. Indeed, biological technology offers a new commodity: eternal youth. At beauty salons, women boast of their breast lift surgery and the liposuction processes that restore their waists to pre-maternity proportions. These interventions are not always motivated by the eagerness to look young. Sometimes, women are just playing at being other women. Just as commodities that can be easily replaced, women face the terror of obsolescence.[26] In this brutal battle, those women who cannot pay for surgery costs will emerge defeated.

The inventory of products and services that are consumed provide a sense of a new libidinal economy. For Jameson, it is about desires that are emptied of their subversive content, of the individual's re-socialization by the logic of needs and information that has little to do with the politicized hedonism of the 1960s.[27] It could be argued, however, that consumption provides an incomparable diversification of human existence. Denied economic equality or even political power, women celebrate the techniques and products that offer them control of their lives. The powers of magic, attributed in the past to few individuals within the group, are now in the hands of common people, who possess the magic to invent themselves and construct a rather indeterminate future.[28] Even if authors like Baudrillard link the destruction of the social and the disappearance of the particular to the capacity of neutralization—of events and meanings—of the information industry, we could also argue that the intensification of affects that is at stake in the act of consumption redefines rather than annuls subjectivity.

Media images are played out in people's fantasies to produce a communication system that unlocks diverse social languages. It is a system that acts on behalf of imagination and not of the material that represents it—propaganda's impetus. Perhaps this may explain the variety of tastes and choices of clients and stylists alike. In a society that increasingly functions as a polymorphous information system, the boundary that separates the "organic" from the "inorganic" becomes porous.[29] We are living times of overstimulation; the "real" has disappeared in a hyperreality of mechanical reproductions and digital representations that have little to do with reality.[30] This hybridity produces the sense that everything or almost everything is provisional and subject to manipulation, as if people were proclaiming their rebellion against what is given. Beauty salons emerge as sites for the production of feminine and masculine ideals that are played out against cultural constraints. Social practices acquire new meanings but some cultural codes remain the same, as it is the insistence of clients on loud fashions and the value of a voluptuous body.

The politics of postmodern consumption relies on our desire to live in a world where we can freely express ourselves and circulate in function of a flexible life.[31] But this freedom is relative: Women and men always risk becoming obsolete if they do not follow the rules of the game. The promise of a flexible life imposes a new discipline of the body that provokes feelings of inadequacy and comprises great suffering. And of course, we cannot forget that the power of consumption in developed countries underscores the disparity between production and consumption in the rest of the world. Even so, the consumption that takes place in the beauty salons is one of the most important indicators of the social logic in which we all live.

The Culture of the Beautiful Sex: A New Religion?

In her book *The Beauty Myth*, Naomi Wolf argues that the culture of the "beautiful sex" is the "Church of our times."[32] The "gospel of beauty" reconstitutes archaic rituals associated with the mortification of the body and the refusal of pleasures such as good food. Women blame themselves for the sin of being fat and indulge in diets that conspire against their health and life. Obsessed with an aesthetic that functions as a police force, women are transferred from the domestic prison to the aesthetic prison. In the United States alone, 75 percent of women are considered to be overweight, and between 80 percent and 95 percent have had the experience of regaining lost weight after submitting themselves to various diet regiments.[33]

For some feminists, the new aesthetic industry re-articulates gender hierarchies by proposing that women are worth more for their appearance than their social contributions. At the precise moment in which men lost their ability to socially control women, there is an "aesthetic backlash," one that opposes women's march toward progress and equality.[34] With equal vehemence, other women propose to return to the old forms of femininity.[35] Although they are not willing to abandon their workplaces, these women condemn bra-burning feminisms and cherish the oblique powers of feminine seduction. Some postmodern theorists also echo these criticisms and proclaim the end of all feminisms. They contend that young women are currently more interested in receiving the best possible pay to exhibit themselves in the runways—as is the case with the top models and Hollywood stars—than for equal rights. It is further argued that feminism lost its power at the moment it conceptualized this type of practice as exploitation and tried to control women's sexual behavior.[36]

The passage from an activist feminist to an indeterminate individualism, as represented by the television character *Ally McBeal* or the stars of *Sex and the City*, cannot be understood if we do not take into account how commodities have found an ally in the bodies of men and women alike. The dominance of an aesthetic that privileges a narcissistic exhibitionism cannot be separated from a culture that since the end of the twentieth century has valued bodies that are slim and nimble. The victory of flat abs and tight arms is also related to the rise of a mass culture of leisure, sports, and entertainment. Although women still spend more time and money in beauty products and services, the number of men who are falling for the demands of the beauty industry is increasing exponentially. Young men who aspire to be models, television actors, or talent show participants also visit beauty salons, gyms, and plastic surgeons with the hope that any given trick—a new haircut or dye, exercise routine, or nose surgery—will do the job.[37]

It is undeniable that contemporary capitalism has made a greater exploitation of the worker by devaluing its workforce and regulating free time. But this view has neglected the analysis of the relationship between mode of production and the way we live.[38] It is necessary to transcend approaches that insist in defining consumption as irrational behavior that only contributes to enhance male domination. While it is true that women consume available texts and images, they also do not lose their agency. Through their strategies of consumption, women create their own codes, often in contradictory ways. Faced with a discourse that proposes an anorexic model that never ages as a beauty ideal, many women will submit themselves to rigorous diets and the scalpel while others will cheat. An example of this last option is a woman who values her exuberant behind and at the same time will wear a dress that is two sizes smaller. Or the woman who disregards the popularity of ethnic models and insists in making her nose smaller but inserts silicon to have fuller lips. The same thing happens with fashion. On the one hand, the persistence of a cultural norm that suggests that the person makes the dress, and on the other hand, the omnipresence of a cool consumer who secures his or her social position by wearing famous designer brands.

Consumption is also a way of dealing with a changing social order. Commodities are weapons in people's struggle to make sense of the particular in an increasing globalized world. Women buy makeup, show off a new haircut, and offer their bodies to massage therapists in order to lessen the stress of everyday life. The complicity between stylists and clients is the best antidote against the isolation imposed by domestic life or the lack of recognition in the professional context. Women move within an imaginary space made up of different styles and fashions that offer the possibility of reinventing their lives. But while this pluralism assumes the tyranny of a beauty ideal—one has to suffer to be beautiful—women also take responsibility for their own destiny even if they ignore that it is already set. Since the satisfaction of desires is impossible, an anomic logic imposes itself and becomes evident in how women lose and gain weight, exhibit faces that look like masks as a result of plastic surgery, and develop health problems associated with liposuction.

The promise of gratification prompts women to consume, revealing both its dark side and its liberation potential. By embracing an aesthetic that proposes that the body is a porous surface upon which women draw their desires, women also reject the imaginary of curvy and soft bodies associated with maternity. Men, on their part, get rid of body hair, pluck their eyebrows, and dye their hair. This phenomenon makes the slogan of "biology is not destiny" even more evident. The rules of gender are now more than ever a game of performativity.[39] Through its rituals and magic, the new religion of the aesthetic offers the possibility of defying the realm of evil, "evil" being what is perceived as "natural."[40] The question remains: Is it possible to accept the church's sacrament without believing in religion?

Notes

This chapter was translated by Frances Negrón-Muntaner.

1. Carmen Lugo-Filippi and Ana Lydia Vega, *Vírgenes y mártires* (Río Piedras, Puerto Rico: Editorial Antillana, 1981), 38. Original Spanish: "¿Qué deseas Milagros?, casi susurras, incapaz de mirarla de frente aunque siempre observando el espejo. Ella entonces da un paso decidido y saca del bolsillo derecho de su pantalón un billete de veinte, billete que blande, airosa, y con tono suave, pero firme, hace su reclamo: 'Maquíllame en shocking-red, Marina, y córtame como te dé la gana.' Un temblequeo, apenas perceptible comienza a apoderarse de tus rodillas, pero aún así no logras apartar los ojos del espejo donde la Milagros se agranda, asume dimensiones colosales, viene hacia tí en busca de una respuesta, de esa respuesta que ella urge y que tendrás que dar, no puedes aplazarla, Marina, mírate y mírala, Marina ¿Qué responderás?"
2. Mario Bellatin, *Salón de belleza* (México: Tusquests Editores, 1999), 30. Original Spanish: "La mayoría de las mujeres que acudían al salón de belleza eran mujeres viejas o acabadas por la vida. Sin embargo, debajo de aquel cutis gastado era visible una larga agonía que se vestía de esperanza en cada una de las visitas."
3. See A. Catherine Mackinnon, *Feminism Unmodified: Discourses of Life and Law* (Cambridge: Harvard University Press, 1987); Naomi Wolf, *The Beauty Myth* (London: Vintage Books, 1990); Susan Bordo, *Unbearable Weight* (Berkeley: University of California Press, 1993).
4. Arthur Marwick, *Beauty in History* (London: Thames and Hudson, 1988).
5. Jean Baudrillard, *La génesis ideológica de las necesidades* (Barcelona: Editorial Anagrama, 1976).
6. Michel De Certeau, *The Practice of Everyday Life*, trans. Steven Randall (Berkeley: University of California Press, 1988).
7. See Rob Shields, ed., *Lifestyle Shopping: The Subject of Consumption* (New York: Routledge, 1992); Arjun Appadurai, *Modernity at Large: Cultural Dimensions of Globalization* (Minneapolis: University of Minnesota Press, 1996).
8. See Pierre Bourdieu, *Distinction: A Social Critique of the Judgement of Taste*, trans. Richard Nice (Cambridge: Harvard University Press, 1984); Mary Douglas, *El mundo de los bienes: hacia una antropología del consumo* (Mexico: Grijalbo, 1990); Zygmunt Baumman, *La globalización: consecuencias humanas* (Mexico: Fondo de Cultura Económica, 1999).
9. See Jesús Martín-Barbero, *De los medios a las mediaciones* (Barcelona: Ediciones G. Gili. S.A. de C.V., 1987); Néstor García Canclini, *La globalización imaginada* (Buenos Aires: Paidós, 2000); Gilles Lipovetsky and Elyette Roux, *El lujo eterno: de la era de lo sagrado al tiempo de las marcas* (Barcelona: Editorial Anagrama, 2004).
10. Guy Debord, *La sociedad del espectáculo*, Prologue, notes and trans. José Luis Pardo (Valencia: Pre-textos, 1996).
11. See Richard Williams, *Cultura: sociología de la comunicación y el arte* (Barcelona: Paidós, 1982); Marc Augé, *Non-Places: Introduction to an Anthropology of Supermodernity* (New York: Verso, 1995); Mike Featherstone, *Cultura de consumo y posmodernismo* (Buenos Aires: Amorrortu editors, 1999); Marc Augé, *El tiempo en ruinas* (Barcelona: Gedisa, 2003).
12. Gilles Lipovetsky, *La tercera mujer* (Barcelona: Editorial Anagrama, 1999), 219.

13. Stuart Hall, "The Local and the Global: Globalization and Ethnicity," in *Culture, Globalization and the World-System*, ed. Anthony D. King (Minneapolis: University of Minnesota Press, 1998), 20–39.
14. According to Foucault, "awareness of one's body can be acquired only through the effects of an investment of power in the body: gymnastics, exercises, muscle-building, nudism, glorification of the body beautiful. All of this belongs to the pathway leading to the desire of one's body, by way of insistent, persistent, meticulous work of power on the bodies of children or soldiers, the healthy bodies." One may say that today power is invested in all bodies. For more on this topic, see Michel Foucault, *Power/Knowledge: Selected Interviews and Other Writings, 1972–77*, ed. Colin Gordon (New York: Pantheon Books, 1980), 56.
15. Magali Febles, *El Nuevo Día*, February 10, 2002, 73. Original Spanish: "Soy una estilista de masas. Pude quedarme en un salón pequeño y cobrar precios bien altos. Prefiero trabjar donde todas las personas puedan venir donde mí. Es verdad que trabajo más pero me siento más cómoda."
16. Jean Baudrillard, *La transparencia del mal* (Barcelona: Editorial Anagrama, 1991), 132.
17. María del Mar Chaluisán, "Cuerpos firmes y peleítas mongas; notas para bajar de peso," *bordes* 2 (1995): 69. Original Spanish: "¿Por qué sigue siendo más legítimo y teóricamente "real" hablar de la fábrica, el hospital o la oficina como espacios de reinvindicación y no del *beauty parlor*? Políticamente es urgentemente necesario revisar las tácticas y estrategias que hemos clasificado como dignas para la transformación y las maneras de resistencia que validamos."
18. Please see Luis Rafael Sánchez, "Cejas sacadas, piernas afeitadas y tips," *El Nuevo Día, Revista Domingo*, June 25, 2000.
19. Ibid., 13. Original Spanish: "Los policías, ciclistas y los adolescentes, en su inmensa mayoría con el colesterol heterosexual alto, incluso por encima de lo saludable, no son los únicos que militan en la empresa revolucionaria. Muchos hombres a punto de abandonar los veinte años se ríen del qué dirán y sacan un ratito para sacarse las cejas y afeitarse las piernas. Igualmente, muchos hombres trientañales, ya encarrilados en la profesión o en el oficio, corren a abrirse las orejas e iluminarse los cabellos, en abierto desafío a los convencionalismos."
20. See Clara Obligado, *Qué me pongo: mujeres ante la moda* (Barcelona: Plaza Janés, 2000).
21. Ibid., 84–85. Original Spanish: "Hoy por hoy, las apariencias son importantes, y, si bien la moda promete emancipar a los ciudadanos de lo tópico y rutinario, si bien en ella hay un espacio en el que somos libres de elegir, también la elección de la indumentaria sirve para uniformar, para aclarar a qué grupo se pertenece mientras permite la ilusión de autodeterminación personal."
22. See Thorstein Weblen, *The Theory of a Leisure Class* (New York: Viking Penguin, 1967).
23. George Simmel, *Sobre la naturaleza humana* (Barcelona: Península, 1988).
24. Herbert Marcuse, *Un hombre unidimensional*, trans. Antonio Elorza (Barcelona: Editorial Ariel S.A., 1987), 39.
25. See Bauman, *La globalización*.
26. Obligado, *Qué me pongo: mujeres ante la moda* 135.
27. See Frederic Jameson, *Postmodernism or The Cultural Logic of Late Capitalism* (Durham, NC: Duke University Press, 1993).

28. Lipovetsky, *La tercera mujer*, 219.
29. See Mark Dery, *Velocidad de escape*, trans. Ramón Montoya (Madrid: Ediciones Siruela, 1995).
30. Please see Celeste Olalguiaga, *Megalopolis: Contemporary Cultural Sensibilities* (Minneapolis: University of Minnesota Press, 1992); Jean Baudrillard, *Simulacra and Simulation*, trans. Sheila Faria Glaser (Ann Arbor: University of Michigan Press, 1995).
31. See Gilles Lipovetsky, *La era del vacío* (Barcelona: Editorial Anagrama, 1998); see also Bauman, *La globalización.*
32. See Naomi Wolf, *The Beauty Myth* (London: Vintage Books, 1990).
33. Kim Chernin, *The Obsession: Reflections on the Tyranny of Slenderness* (New York: Harper Perennial, 1991).
34. See Susan Bordo, *Unbearable Weight* (Berkeley: University of California Press, 1993); see also Susan Faludi, *Backlash* (Paris: Des femmes, 1993).
35. Elizabeth Fox-Genovese, *Feminism is Not the Story of My Life* (New York: Anchor Books, 1996).
36. Elizabeth Wurtzel, *Bitch: In Praise of Difficult Women* (New York: Doubleday, 1998).
37. Some people may argue that obsession with the body and appearance is more common among homosexuals. Likewise, others suspect lesbianism among women who work their muscles, practice sports, and wear no make-up. The comment of a man in his twenties is revealing: "I know that all women who wear short hair are not lesbians, but is the first idea that comes to my mind when I see a woman with very short hair."
38. Arturo Torrecilla, *El espectro posmoderno: ecología, neoproletario, intelligentsia* (San Juan: Publicaciones Puertorriqueñas, 1995).
39. Judith Butler, *Bodies that Matter: On the Discursive Limits of "Sex"* (New York: Routledge, 1993).
40. Margarita Rivière, *Crónicas virtuales: la muerte de la moda en la era de los mutantes* (Barcelona: Anagrama, 1998).

CHAPTER 10

Getting F****d in Puerto Rico: Metaphoric Provocations and Queer Activist Interventions

Juana María Rodríguez

Allow me to start with a joke:

> Four Puerto Ricans are sitting in a bar discussing the political landscape of the island and an upcoming plebiscite. The first states, "I'm voting for statehood, we might as well become a state and get all the benefits that come with it." Another responds, emphatically, "No, we should vote to keep the status quo, *Estado Libre y Asociado*. I don't to want to be a gringo and speak English." The third stands up and says, "I'm voting for the *Independentistas*. We may starve to death, but we will starve with dignity." Finally the fourth reveler stands up and says, "I'm voting for the Homosexual Party. If I'm going to be fucked up the ass, I want it to be done by professionals."[1]

While this joke may capture the raucous spirit of "none of the above" as the inescapable impossibility that defines contemporary Puerto Rican electoral politics, it also reflects the uneasy relationship between the nation and its homosexuals. Embedded in the humor are epistemologies that define sodomy as abject, functioning symbolically to subjugate those who spread their ass cheeks for politics as usual, and a queer alternative as inherently absurd, a Homosexual Party serving as the ultimate in ludicrous political possibilities. Recently debates on both the island and the mainland on the constitutionality of "sodomy laws" have triangulated issues of Puerto Rican electoral politics, sexual and colonial penetrations, and queer activism to create new opportunities for activist and metaphoric interventions into the meaning of "getting fucked" in Puerto Rico.[2]

In their introduction to *Puerto Rican Jam*, subtitled "Beyond Nationalist and Colonialist Discourses: The *Jaiba* Politics of the Puerto Rican Ethno-Nation," coauthors Ramón Grosfoguel, Frances Negrón-Muntaner, and

Chloé Georas challenge traditional discourses that uphold the "binary opposition of colonial subjects/feminine versus imperial power/masculine."[3] Instead, they redefine what a feminization of political maneuvering might entail though what they term *jaiba* politics. They write,

> In the Caribbean context, a patriarchal imaginary of virility and confrontational politics has mediated left-wing political strategies whose outcomes have normally been political defeat and economic disaster. Thus a "feminization" of political practices refers to a positive resignification, generalization, and extension of political strategies such as seduction, ambiguity, and negotiation, associated historically with women in patriarchal discourses, to a wide range of political struggles. It is the strategy of those forced to struggle in the terrain of the adversary.[4]

An examination of the events surrounding efforts to repeal sodomy laws in Puerto Rico, and an analysis of the rousing public debate it inspired, serve as an edifying study in the practice of *jaiba* politics in action. Furthermore, following their lead, a re-signification of the feminized sexual position of "getting fucked" allows a range of inviting political strategies and vexed metaphoric provocations to emerge in our understanding of how power and pleasure circulate in the sexual dynamic between citizens and the state.

In his essay, "Discrimen por orientación sexual: El denominado estatuto de sodomía de Puerto Rico" (Sexual Orientation Discrimination: The So-Called Sodomy Statute in Puerto Rico), José Dávila-Caballero compiles an extensive legal history of sodomy laws in Puerto Rico in which he chronicles case after case where residents of the island are brought before the court to face charges against this *crimen contra natura*—a crime that is punished, without ever being fully defined. Dávila-Caballero recounts a series of court decisions wherein it was determined to have something to do with penetration, but not necessarily with ejaculation, and something to do with carnal contact, although the exact body parts in contact remain unnamed. In *Pueblo v. León* (1947), a woman was raped, and it was established that the carnal contact had taken place "por la parte sucia" (through the dirty part); therefore it was found that the carnal act had not taken place in an ordinary manner, but in a manner "against nature."[5] Leaving one to wonder if vaginal rape—that is, if the vagina is not deemed *sucia*—would have qualified as "ordinary" and "natural."

In 1967 in the case of *Pueblo v. Santiago Vázquez*, this ambiguity led the court to consider whether the term "crime against nature" was perhaps too vague. Once again the court acted not to accept an appeal on these grounds because "dada su naturaleza vil y aborrecible no es necesario precisar los hechos imputados en la acusación"[6] (given the vile and abhorrent nature, it is not necessary to specify the ascribed acts in the accusation). In 1974 during a process of penal reform, Puerto Rican legislators worded the statute that has been in effect until very recently, known as *Artículo 103,* and it states,

> All persons who sustain sexual relations with a person of the same sex or commit the crime against nature with another human being shall be penalized with

> imprisonment for a period of 10 years. Under aggravated circumstances, the sentence can be increased to a maximum of twelve years, under attenuating circumstances it can be reduced to a minimum of six years.[7]

Although the code stated quite clearly that same-sex sexual relations fall squarely under the category of prohibited acts, it once again left the terms "sexual relations," and "crime against nature" undefined. In his astute reading of the law and its history, Dávila-Caballero unequivocally concludes that the statute did not prohibit only same-sex sexual relations and sodomy, but an indeterminate variety of acts without distinguishing the gender of the participants involved, acts that could include mutual masturbation, fellatio, and telephone sex.[8]

On October 15, 1997, into this murky sea of legal and linguistic vagueness enters Reverend Margarita Sánchez de León, co-pastor of the ecumenical church *Iglesia Comunidad Metropolitana Cristo Sanador*.[9] She and several other activists presented themselves before a commission of the Puerto Rican House of Representatives to give public testimony against a bill prohibiting same-sex marriage. During Sánchez de León's testimony, she was interrupted and asked if she was a lesbian. Representative Edwin Mundo claimed that the commission had been quite tolerant in not having her and the other activists present arrested because by virtue of their sexual orientation they had all broken the sodomy laws of the island.[10]

A few days later, the reverend turned herself in to the Sexual Crimes Division of the Justice Department after confessing to having committed the crime of sodomy just the night before. The San Juan District Attorney refused to formally charge her after informing her that lesbians could not commit such a crime because they had no "*miembro viril*" (virile member). He also refused to arrest two men who also presented themselves, stating that he would not arrest them because there was no "victim" in the case. That same day he issued a press release refusing to press formal charges in the case, and implying that Reverend Sánchez de León had personal interests in presenting her confession.[11]

Several competing definitions of the law seem to be functioning here. On the one hand, the legislator who threatened to have Sánchez de León and the other activists arrested interpreted *Artículo 103* through the declared identifications of the gay and lesbian activists—who in his mind are defined through their same-sex sexual acts. In contrast, the District Attorney seemed to require not only a penetrating penis, but also a victim of a penetrating penis. Under his interpretation of the law it seems willing participants of anal sex, for example, are not committing a crime, and can only exist in the sexualized rubric of the law if they present themselves as victims. Sánchez de León admitted to having engaged in sodomy the night before, but her confession left undefined exactly the sexual acts she purported to have committed. Did she penetrate her partner anally or was she the recipient of the said act? Under the definition of the law, did she perpetrate some other "unnatural act"—cyber sex for example? Or was the same-sex sexual act that she was guilty of a good night fondling of her partner's body?

In 1998 the American Civil Liberties Union office in Puerto Rico, with Lambda Legal Defense as co-counsel, filed suit on behalf of Reverend Sánchez de León and five other lesbian and gay Puerto Ricans. In an article, originally published in the pro-independence weekly *Claridad*, Sánchez de León wrote, "We are all aware that eliminating prejudice goes beyond repealing a particular law. At the same time, however, we must realize that this law is the institutional framework that legitimizes prejudice. . . . Through these actions, we call attention to our situation as homosexual, lesbian and transgendered people, and we expose the injustices sanctioned by the state."[12] In effect, these activists seized on their status as sexual outlaws to foment a public debate on the island on the meaning of sex, justice and national interests.

Queer Puerto Rican activists, like Sánchez de León and her cohorts, struggling for civil rights on the island, have historically had to contend with the prickly double bind of colonialism.[13] As a small disenfranchised and criminalized minority, with limited access to the power structures of government, media, and educational institutions controlled by the colonial administration, they face the daunting challenge of getting their political message across to other island residents. Aligning themselves with progressive forces in the United States, like the ACLU or Lambda Legal Defense, they risk being accused of "importing" ideas, values, and morality "foreign" to a nationalist Puerto Rican sexual economy.[14] A political hazard that La Fountain-Stokes investigates in his essay "1898 and the History of a Queer Puerto Rican Century: Gay Lives, Island Debates, and Diasporic Experience." He writes, "Cultural nationalists have, in the past, perceived American social structures (which are seen as monolithic) as contrary to the 'essential' values of Puerto Ricans (who are, in turn, also seen as a cohesive and unitary group) and thus have upheld any and all influence as a threat."[15]

These scenarios are set against a backdrop of economic dependence on tourism, including international gay tourism, and a hyper-nationalism that both magnifies and obscures the omnipresence of U.S. legal, economic, military, and political interests on the island. All of these factors, stated and unstated, formed part of the political currents that needed to be finessed in order to wage an effective media campaign. As the firestorm surrounding the case grew, other elements also came into play including the upcoming 2004 gubernatorial elections, an official review of Puerto Rico's Penal Code and the U.S. Supreme Court's decision to hear arguments in the case of *Lawrence v. Texas*, an attempt to overturn *Bowers v. Hardwick*, and make state sodomy laws unconstitutional. These events added questions of party platforms, public hearings, and judicial sovereignty to the issues needing to be strategized.

In her essay, "Not Just (Any)*Body* Can Be a Citizen: The Politics of Law, Sexuality and Postcoloniality in Trinidad and Tobago and the Bahamas," Jacqui Alexander documents how newly emerging postcolonial states use the law to create a hetero-normative national narrative that moors the state's authority to rule. She writes that during the process of decolonization and restructuring

> Not just (any)*body* can be a citizen anymore, for *some* bodies have been marked by the state as non-procreative, in pursuit of sex only for pleasure, a sex that is non-productive of babies and of no-economic gain. Having refused the heterosexual imperative of citizenship, *these* bodies, according to the state, pose a threat to the very survival of the nation.[16]

Like the postcolonial Caribbean nations Alexander describes, in Puerto Rico we see the figure of the homosexual as a symbol for that which is—or should be—outside the configuration of nation. Inspiring one fundamentalist Christian commentator, Jorge Raschke, to claim that "In this country we have more shame than in other parts of the world, they [homosexuals] should go somewhere else, they should go to Miami."[17] On May 12, 2002 Carlos Vizcarrondo Irizarry, president of the House of Representatives of Puerto Rico, reaffirmed and validated this sentiment and the legislature's commitment to upholding the existing sodomy statute stating,

> The values, the way of thinking and feeling of our Puerto Rican people within the context of Caribbean and Latin American life is different from the way of life of North American Anglo-Saxons. . . . What might be fine for the United States, in terms of liberalizing penal codes, is not necessarily fine in Puerto Rico, where we have visions and values that are directly rooted in our Christian spirit of life and in that sense the laws that we have at this time respond to those visions.[18]

Vizcarrondo Irizarry's statement makes clear that although the United States is irrevocably implicated in Puerto Rico's political and legal structures, Puerto Ricans will forever be culturally and sexually different from their Northern neighbors. In the process he performs the homogenization of both sites that La Fountain-Stokes describes: Puerto Rico becomes the embodiment of a "Christian spirit of life," and the United States becomes a nation of liberal Anglo-Saxons.

Appearing before the 2003 Senate Commission reviewing the Penal Code, Superintendent of Police Víctor Rivera González made evident the underlying motive of the law as one of symbolic subjugation and social control when he declared that even though he thought it improbable that the law would be enforced, "el código Penal es la herramienta vital para mantener el orden en la sociedad" (the Penal Code is the vital tool needed to maintain order in the society). He also chose to confer on the proposed Penal Code, including the provision making same-sex sexual acts illegal, the ultimate in nationalist praise, dubbing it as "contemporáneo y bastante criollo"[19] (contemporary and quite *criollo*).

Codes such as *Artículo 103* have framed in law a continual state surveillance that serves as the threat that is always ready to be unfurled against those that rail against it. Reverend Sánchez de León was threatened with arrest, threatened to have the power of law exerted against her precisely because she dared to come forward to demand her rights as a disenfranchised citizen. The threat, even in the absence of a sustained history of enforcement, is intended to do the work of the state by having citizens discipline themselves.[20] Mildred Braulio, lawyer and spokesperson for the Lesbian, Gay, Bisexual and Transgender Human Rights Project based in San Juan, explains the far-reaching effects of the law, even in the absence of its enforcement, including the denial of access to other legal recourses.[21] The effect on the national psyche is even more insidious, however; these laws serve to legitimate a further disenfranchisement, negation, and shaming of queer national subjects. Braulio writes,

> There is no law that prohibits two people of the same sex from holding hands, dancing in public places, hugging or kissing. Yet these practices are avoided in public for fear of rejection and of physical and verbal violence. This rejection and violence, in turn, create an environment in which further demands for these kinds of prohibitions emerge.[22]

This is the panoptic effect that the state desires: minimal exertion of power with maximum subjective effect. In a Puerto Rican context, the layers of surveillance become doubled. Puerto Rican residents fall under the gaze of the bureaucrats and acting politicians of the colonial government, which in turn discipline themselves to maintain the flow of U.S. capital, and avoid the embarrassment of direct U.S. intervention that would disrupt the illusion of self-governance that both countries are invested in maintaining. Everyone knows they are being watched, and as long as all of the participants play their part, the automatic functioning of dissymmetric power is maintained. In defining the work of panopticism, Foucault's classic line announces: "Visibility is a trap."[23]

Perhaps visibility is a trap, but what Sánchez de León, her co-plaintiffs, and her many allies and supporters made visible during their campaign to have this law repealed was not the sexual behavior of island citizens, but the political, social, and economic investments of the state.[24] To counter the public appeals to Puerto Rican cultural identity as inherently heterosexual, homophobic, and in need of state surveillance and control, the Puerto Rican-based lawyers Nora Vargas Acosta and Charles Hey Maestre, ACLU-cooperating attorneys in the case, very quickly began to spin their own version of Puerto Rican patriotism in the courts and in the media. In their prepared brief, where they preemptively responded to why *Bowers v. Hardwick* should not be used as the legal measure in this case, these lawyers reminded the court and the public that Puerto Rico's Constitution goes much further than that of the United States in explicitly protecting the privacy of its citizens.[25] Section 8, of the Puerto Rican Constitution specifically states, "Toda persona tiene derecho a protección de ley contra ataques abusivos a su honra, a su reputación y a su vida privada o familiar" (All persons have the right to legal protection against abusive attacks to their honor, their reputation, or their private or family life). Furthermore, these lawyers argued that *Bowers* "was based on the US Supreme Court's analysis of Anglo-Saxon history," and thus should not be transferred to a Puerto Rican historical context (ACLU).[26]

In its extensive public education campaign on the issue, activists also made sure that the public recognized that these laws did not come into being on the island until 1902, when they were imposed by the ruling colonial government of the United States after being modeled on the Penal Code of the state of California. Pre-1898 Puerto Rico, like most countries under Spanish colonial rule, never had such civil laws. In fact, historically, in the Americas the harshest penalties for same-sex relations can be found in Penal Codes inspired or imposed by the United States and Britain.[27] By 2003, aside from Puerto Rico, the only other Spanish-speaking country in Latin America with sodomy laws on the books was Nicaragua. In a related legal twist that similarly brought together the discourses of sexual liberation, sovereignty rights, and the interests of global tourism in the Caribbean, and served as the unspoken cloud shrouding the events in Puerto Rico, in 2001 the British government unilaterally decriminalized homosexuality in its Caribbean territories, including Anguilla, the Cayman Islands, the British Virgin Islands, Montserrat, and Turks and Caicos (British).[28]

By the beginning of summer 2003, the issue had migrated from the courts, where the Puerto Rican Supreme Court was waiting to decide if the *Sanchez et al. v. Puerto Rico* could proceed, into the legislature, where the Senate presented a new draft of the Puerto Rican Penal Code, which once again failed to decriminalize sodomy, and finally into the streets. At the 2003 Pride Parade in San Juan, thousands of queer activists were out in force, many with signs demanding to be arrested, echoing the call of the Pentecostal Brotherhood and other conservative groups who were already pressing the state to enforce the existing sodomy laws.[29]

Meanwhile, along the parade route, members of the Christian coalition *Pro-Vida* videotaped and photographed the parade participants in order to collect information and images for their media campaign to preserve *Artículo 103*, and humiliate and punish their political adversaries.[30] Other interested parties, particularly those with economic interests in the sprawling tourist trade, remained quiet on the subject, but were probably already imagining the devastation a queer boycott such as that unleashed on the state of Colorado would have on the island's economy.[31] It is precisely because of its colonial relationship with the United States that Puerto Rico figures as an attractive and relatively "safe" destination for North American gay tourists, a social and economic reality that neither side wished to call attention to.[32]

By calling the state's bluff as it were, queer activists and their allies had turned the panoptic gaze back on itself and succeeded in placing the state in a lose-lose situation. If the state repealed these laws, they effectively disarmed themselves in their battle to keep queer island residents silenced, and made visible their vulnerability to the political interests of foreign capital. If they did not repeal them and were forced by both the political right and the left to enforce them, they risked the economic benefits that comes from a "don't ask, don't tell," attitude to gay tourism. In fact, what remained unstated—the influence of queer transnational capital, the omnipresence of U.S. political, economic, and judicial control, and the average citizen's desire to engage in "unnatural" sexual acts—proved as relevant and persuasive as the nationalist arguments used to sway public opinion.

With the U.S. Supreme Court decision on *Lawrence v. Texas* expected by the end of June 2003, Puerto Rican politicians were working under the threat of having a U.S. mandate on the issue imposed. For some, the shadow of *Lawrence* served as an easy way out of the political quagmire in which the legislature and courts had found themselves. In a news conference, Senator Baéz Galib, president of the Judicial Commission of the Senate, stated,

> Those who have discussed this (sodomy) have gotten ahead of themselves. When the Supreme Court of the United States decides, well then the Penal Code of Puerto Rico has to obligatorily reflect what the Supreme Court of the United States decides.[33]

Deference to colonial obligations, however, although an easy way for Puerto Rican politicians to extricate themselves from the controversy, only served to further fuel the clamor for political posturing under the banner of national self-determination and patriotic pride. Throughout the events surrounding the case, Governor Sila María Calderón tried to dodge the issue at every turn, continually deferring to the legislature and the courts.[34] With the 2004 elections drawing, activists on both sides of the issue were not being placated by these acts of evasion, and instead began to demand that politicians make their opinions on the subject public. In May 2003, Fernando Martín, the *Partido Independentista Puertorriqueño* or Puerto Rican Independence Party (PIP) Senator, came out against the preservation of the sodomy statute, terming it "injusto."[35] In June, ex-governor Pedro Rosselló of the *Partido Nuevo Progresista* or New Progressive Party (NPP) used his support for the removal of the statute from the revised Penal Code as a way to distinguish himself from Carlos Pesquera, his party's leader and his rival as the NPP gubernatorial candidate. As the summer grew hotter, it began to seem as if human rights, including the rights of gays, lesbians, bisexuals, and transgenders, became the new measure of modernity and progress on the island.[36] Finally, just three days before the *Lawrence* decision was announced, in a Senate session that ran well past midnight, the *Partido Popular Democrático* or Popular Democratic Party (PDP) majority succeeded in pushing forward a vote to eliminate the statute from the new Penal Code. While the House and governor still needed to approve the proposed code, symbolically the Senate vote signaled the elimination of *Artículo 103* as an act of political self-determination, free from direct U.S. intervention, with each of the three major parties managing to somehow align themselves with the winning side before *Lawrence* would have imposed the inevitable, publicly reaffirming the fiction of political autonomy.

In their public comments to the press afterwards, activists were quick to assert this, not as a victory against the state, but as a victory for the nation and for the people of Puerto Rico. Margarita Sánchez de León termed it a "victoria para el mundo de los derechos humanos" (a victory for the world of human rights). Ada Conde, the president of the Fundación de Derechos

Humanos, declared, "ha ganado el pueblo de Puerto Rico y su Constitución"[37] (the people and Constitution of Puerto Rico have won). In an article published in *El Nuevo Día*, human rights activist Pedro Julio Serrano wrote,

> With this historic act, the senators demonstrated that we don't need to wait for decisions from other jurisdictions to validate the rights of privacy that operate without the need for additional legislation and are guaranteed under the Bill of Rights of our Constitution.[38]

The symbolic significance of a Puerto Rican decision preempting a U.S. mandate made this victory all the more meaningful to progressive queer activists by affirming their right to be heard within the larger national debate. Yet the Senate's decision, while dismantling a legal barrier to sexual self-expression, also functions to rekindle the illusionary belief in both political and sexual autonomy, free from outside influence.

Having witnessed the *contemporáneo y bastante criollo* possibilities and limitations offered by a *jaiba* politics of seduction, ambiguity, negotiation, and re-signification, let me conclude by returning to the provocative metaphors of penetration with which I began this chapter. In his brilliantly crafted essay, "What a Tangled Web! Masculinity, Abjection, and the Foundations of Puerto Rican Literature in the United States," Arnaldo Cruz-Malavé echoes Alexander's formulation of the relationship between projects of national legitimation and the bodies of the nation's queers. He illustrates how in Nuyorican literature, the discourse of nationalist virility, and the shame of its failure, has been constituted through the body of the male homosexual.[39] He argues that in these foundational narratives of Nuyorican identity, the figure of the homosexual comes to represent the abject, a "hole" and "through that hole slips in all that otherness that the community seeks to repel—treason."[40] He continues,

> No wonder, then, the insistence on homosexuality in these texts. And if it is true that their characters and poetic personae desperately try to overcome that reversible and ghostly condition that simultaneously emblematizes homosexual practices and the Nuyorican condition, it is also true that they must assume it, incorporate it. . . . To validate masculinity with its ruin, to submit to sodomy, to "buggery," in order to construct a male national identity, there's the paradoxical foundational project that Nuyorican texts set for themselves.[41]

If the Nuyorican condition is emblematic of a tainted masculinity, validated only through a submission to sodomy, can the same also be said for the island itself? That Puerto Rico exists in a perpetual limbo vis-à-vis the United States, never legitimated as an equal part of the larger union, but also never fully allowed to realize independence from the political, economic, and military demands of its Northern overlord, publicly pronouncing its national indignity through the electoral declaration of "none of the above?" What might it mean to claim that under the existing rubric of political (im)possibilities, Puerto Rico is getting fucked?

If the writers who penned the "Introduction" to *Puerto Rican Jam* respond to the failure of a masculinized nationalism with the re-signification of feminized political practices, they also suggest a rethinking of the underlying epistemologies upon which these narratives of national sovereignty and colonial penetrations are constituted.[42] As many critics in the field have rightly noted, the impact of U.S. colonialism in Puerto Rico needs to be simultaneously interrogated through an examination of the incalculable ways that Puerto Ricans have forever transformed the social, cultural, linguistic, and political landscape of the United States. If Puerto Rico is getting fucked in the sexual metaphor that has been used to define its relationship to the United States, how has the United States been fucked in return? And perhaps more importantly, what have been the consequences of these sexualized national exchanges, what pleasures, traumas, and alterations have been produced through these metaphoric acts of fornication?

In her essay, "Recasting Receptivity: Femme Sexualities," Ann Cvetkovich offers an expansive reading of metaphors of penetration and receptivity that may be serviceable to an understanding of these colonial relations. Throughout the essay she takes on the tensions between the literal, figurative, physical, and psychic dimensions of penetration in lesbian sex to enable "new social and sexual imaginaries."[43] She writes

> Being penetrated need not always represent being topped or dominated. . . . Lesbian sexuality requires a language for penetration with dildos, fingers, or fists, and it faces the challenge of expanding the erotics of penetrating objects or body parts, which is too often limited to a focus on penises or phallic substitutes. By the same token, an erotics of how different orifices, such as anuses, vaginas, mouths get fucked would be useful in order to reveal the wide range of ways that getting penetrated is experienced, both physically and symbolically.[44]

Applied to the colonial penetrations under investigation, the erotic possibilities Cvetkovich offers create a figurative space for imagining how power and pleasure circulate in the exchange between national bodies. As a woman under a colonial regime, Sánchez de León's symbolic role as a sodomite enacts the queer social and sexual imaginary that Cvetkovich calls forth. Wearing the collar that marks her as a "man of God," a reverend, she is deploying and appropriating the privileges of masculinity on multiple levels.

Rather than the foreign gay white male tourist that the state is invested in protecting but cannot afford to publicly claim, Sánchez de León, black, female, and native, demands that if the state wants the benefits of gay white tourist dollars, the price would be the legal rights of its own queer nonwhite residents; if politicians want to profess the virtues of human rights and Puerto Rican patriotism, then they will need to extend that claim to all of the island's inhabitants.[45] Admitting to sodomy, surrendering to the state, activists like Sánchez de León, have redefined the failed masculinity of the nation as an empowered femininity that affirms the power and pleasure possible through submission, a submission that engulfs, transforms, and redeploys that

Figure 10.1 Reverend Margarita Sánchez de León, left, with her lawyer Nora Vargas Acosta. (Photo courtesy of the ACLU)

which sought to subjugate. In one photograph published by the ACLU, Sánchez de Léon is seen sitting in the courtroom, wearing a reverend's collar and dark glasses, and the smile on her face suggests that the Reverend took considerable pleasure in "fucking with the state" (see figure 10.1).

In a footnote, Cruz-Malavé suggests the kind of interpretive intervention that may account for the production of these penetrating pleasures. He writes, "One could argue that the representation of Puerto Rico's failure to constitute itself as a nation also provides the opportunity for a joyous act of self-affirmation."[46] Indeed, Puerto Rico's failure to constitute itself as a nation exposes the geopolitical interpenetrations brought about through transnational capital, as it occasions the hyper-nationalism that obscures that very reality. "None of the Above" exposes the farcical fiction of the available alternatives, as it requires that "those forced to struggle in the terrain of the adversary" perform a *jaiba* politics more akin to "All of the Above," appropriating and re-signifying the discourses and strategies at their disposal.

The price of that strategy, and of victory itself, however, may be the perpetuation of the national fiction of Puerto Rican self-determination. For now, it seems that Puerto Rico's sodomites, its queers, those abject bodies that the state and its political parties had once sought to define themselves against, have momentarily succeeded in penetrating the contours of the nation, a public triumph that validates queer claims to the joyous narration of national self-affirmation as it makes unequivocal a broader civic demand for sexual, social, and political sovereignty, a sovereignty that is always already circumscribed by other circuits of power, pleasure, and control.

Notes

I wish to thank Licia Fiol-Matta, Lawrence La Fountain-Stokes, and José Esteban Muñoz for their thoughtful responses after I presented an earlier version of this chapter at the 2003 Latin American Studies Conference in Dallas, TX. I would also like to especially thank Margarita Sánchez de León for generously sharing her thoughts with me. As usual, I am indebted to the critical and cultural astuteness of Frances Grau Brull, who carefully read and responded to several versions of this chapter.

1. All translations, unless indicated, are my own. Original Spanish: Cuatro puertorriqueños están sentados en un bar discutiendo el panorama político del país y un futuro plebiscito. El primero declara "Yo voy a votar por los Estadistas. Deberíamos ser un estado y recibir todos los beneficios que vienen con eso." Otro responde enfáticamente, "¡No! Deberíamos mantener el estatus presente: ¡Estado Libre y Asociado! Yo no quiero ser un gringo y hablar inglés." El tercero se para y contesta: "Yo voy a votar por los Independentistas. Igual nos moriremos de hambre, pero nos moriremos con dignidad." Al fin se para el cuarto y dice, "Yo voy a votar por el Partido de los Homosexuales. Si me van a dar por el culo, quiero que sean profesionales."
2. As I will argue, with the help of José Dávila-Caballero's work, the meaning and implications of the law are not limited to or defined by sodomy. Because this statute is termed as a "sodomy law" in the surrounding discourse, I have elected to cautiously use this term at points in this chapter for the sake of brevity.
3. Ramón Grosfoguel, Frances Negrón-Muntaner, and Chloé S. Georas, "Introduction: Beyond Nationalist and Colonialist Discourses: The *Jaiba* Politics of the Puerto Rican Ethno-Nation," in *Puerto Rican Jam: Rethinking Colonialism and Nationalism*, ed. Frances Negrón-Muntaner and Ramón Grosfoguel (Minneapolis: University of Minnesota Press, 1997), 1–36, 28.
4. Ibid., 28.
5. Quoted in José Dávila-Caballero, "Discrimen por orientación sexual: El denominado estatuto de sodomía de Puerto Rico," *Revista Jurídica Universidad de Puerto Rico* 69 (2000): 1185–267, 1198.
6. Quoted in Dávila-Caballero, "Discrimen," 1199–2000.
7. Original Spanish: "Toda persona que sostuviere relaciones sexuales con una persona de su mismo sexo o cometiere el crimen contra natura con ser humano será sancionada con pena de reclusión por un término fijo de diez años. De mediar circunstancias agravantes, la pena fija establecida podrá ser aumentada hasta un máximo de doce años; de mediar circunstancias atenuantes, podrá ser reducida hasta un mínimo de seis años."
8. Dávila-Caballero, "Discrimen," 1214.
9. In most newspaper articles, and in the official court record, the Reverend's surname is given as Sánchez, in her own essay, she uses de León; I have elected to use Sánchez de León to avoid confusion.
10. Please see "Prueba de fuego de una pastora a justicia," *Archivo Digital de El Nuevo Día*, May 11, 1997 and May 22, 2003, <http: //www.adendi.com/noticia.asp?nid=311646>; "Soy lesbiana: Arréstame K-bron," May 20, 2003, <http://www.geocities.com/WestHollywood/Heights/5368/margarita.html>.
11. Please see, "Soy lesbiana: Arréstame K-bron," May 20, 2003, <http://www.geocities.com/WestHollywood/Heights/5368/margarita.html>.

This website provides one of the most chronologically complete and politically discerning descriptions of the events that led up to Sánchez de León being arrested, and the events immediately following. It is published without indicating an author, but several sources, including Sánchez de León, have pointed out that it was authored by Puerto Rican activist Georgie Irizarry.

12. Margarita de León, "The Personal is the Political," trans. Lawrence M. La Fountain-Stokes, *NACLA: Report on the Americas*, 31, no. 4 (1998): 35.
13. Co-defendants named in the case included Fulana de Tal; Jose Joaquin Mulinelli Rodriguez; Sutano Mas Cual; Edgard Danielson Morales; and William Moran Berberena (ACLU, "Complaint").
14. It is worth noting that the current executive director of the ACLU, Anthony D. Romero, is a gay Nuyorican.
15. Lawrence La Fountain-Stokes, "1898 and the History of a Queer Puerto Rican Century: Gay Lives, Island Debates, and Diasporic Experience," *Centro* 11, no. 1 (1999): 91–110, 92. This exceptionally well-researched and analytically incisive essay by my friend and esteemed interlocutor La Fountain-Stokes also cites the case involving Sánchez de León but situates it within the larger historical context of queer Puerto Rican activism, specifically as it has been impacted by the colonial relationship between the island and the United States. By situating his essay within a framework of a longer narrative of on-going political and cultural debates, La Fountain-Stokes's essay serves as an invaluable complement to my own more focused theoretical intervention. I am forever indebted to him for his insights, assistance, and encouragement with my own project.

    Another valuable source of background information for this article has been the unpublished paper by Aixa A. Ardín Pauneto, "Elyíbiti: Historia del activismo LGBTT en Puerto Rico desde los 70 a mediados de los 90" (BA thesis, Universidad de Puerto Rico, 2001). Ardín Pauneto documents the history of LGBTT groups on the island using extensive archival material from the island's queer press, newsletters, oral histories, and the mainstream Puerto Rican media. The text and an accompanying video entitled "Elyíbiti" served as her Bachelors Thesis at the Universidad de Puerto Rico.
16. Jacqui Alexander, "Not Just (Any) *Body* Can Be a Citizen: The Politics of Law, Sexuality and Postcoloniality in Trinidad and Tobago and the Bahamas," *Feminist Review* 48 (1994): 5–22, 6.
17. Quoted in Dávila-Caballero, "Discrimen," 1259. Original Spanish: "En este país hay más vergüenza que en otras partes del mundo, que se vayan [los homosexuales] a otra parte, que se vayan a Miami."
18. Quoted in Fundación Triángulo, "Urgente apoyo a organizaciones de Puerto Rico pidiendo la derogación de la ley anti-sodomía y condenando amenazas (sic) contra los activistas de derechos humanos," July 17, 2002, <http://www.fundaciontriangulo.es/ddhh/e_AmenazasActivistasPuertoRico.htm>. Original Spanish: "Los valores, la forma de sentir y pensar de este pueblo puertorriqueño . . . en el marco de una filosofía de vida caribeña, latinoamericana que tiene unas diferencias de estilo de vida del pueblo norteamericano, anglosajón . . . Lo que puede ser bueno para los Estados Unidos en términos de liberalización de esquemas penales no necesariamente será bueno para Puerto Rico, donde tenemos unas visiones y valores que están directamente enraizados con nuestro espíritu cristiano de vida y en ese sentido las leyes que hay en este momento responden a esas visiones."

19. Israel Rodríguez-Sánchez, "Cautela ante el delito de sodomía," *Archivo Digital de El Nuevo Día*, May 24, 2003, <http://www.adendi.com/noticia.asp?nid=555449>.
20. For an analysis on the social impact of these laws in Puerto Rico, see also Dávila-Caballero's essay "Entre el silencio y lo criminal: la orientación sexual, el closet, y el derecho puertorriqueño," *Revista Jurídica Universidad de Puerto Rico* 68 (1999): 665–67. See also Efrén Rivera Ramos's study *The Legal Construction of Identity* for an analysis of how the judicial and social legacy of American colonialism in Puerto Rico is manifested through judicial discourse. Efrén Rivera Ramos, *The Legal Construction of Identity: The Judicial and Social Legacy of American Colonialism in Puerto Rico* (Washington, DC: American Psychological Association, 2001).
21. In June 2001, a Puerto Rican court ruled that members of same-sex couples could not file for protection under Ley 54, which deals with domestic violence. The court cited a similar 1999 ruling from the Court of Appeals, which stated "una interpretación de la Ley 54 que proteja las relaciones homosexuales sería inconsistente con la política pública que tipifica como delito la conducta homosexual" ("an interpretation of law 54 which protects homosexual relations would be inconsistent with public policy that typifies as criminal homosexual conduct"). Mario Santana, "Desestiman acusación a homosexual por Ley 54," *Archivo Digital de El Nuevo Día*, June 15, 2001 and May 22, 2003, <http://www.adendi.com/noticia.asp?nid=453193>.

    In Puerto Rico, as in Florida, same sex couples have been prohibited from adopting children. For a discussion of gay and lesbian discrimination in adoption cases in Puerto Rico, see María Inés Delannoy de Jesús, "Discrimen por orientación sexual, sin licencia para armar: prohibición de adopción a personas y parejas homosexuales y lesbianas en Puerto Rico," *Revista Jurídica Universidad de Puerto Rico* 69 (2000): 1281–342. It will be necessary to watch the courts to see how the current wave of legal changes in both the United States and Puerto Rico impact other related legal issues.
22. Mildred Braulio, "Challenging the Sodomy Law in Puerto Rico," trans. Lawrence M. La Fountain-Stokes, *NACLA: Report on the Americas* 31, no. 4 (1998): 33–34, 34.
23. Michel Foucault, *Discipline and Punish: The Birth of the Prison*, trans. Alan Sheridan (New York: Vintage Books, 1979), 200.
24. For indispensable critiques of discourses that equates visibility with liberation in a queer transnational context, see Martin F. Manalansan, IV, "In the Shadows of Stonewall: Examining Gay Transnational Politics and the Diasporic Dilemma," in *The Politics of Culture in the Shadow of Capital*, ed. Lisa Lowe and David Lloyd (Durham, NC: Duke University Press, 1997), 485–503; José Esteban Muñoz, *Disidentifications: Queers of Color and the Performance of Politics* (Minneapolis: University of Minnesota Press, 1999); José Quiroga, *Tropics of Desire: Interventions from Queer Latino America* (New York: New York University Press, 2000).
25. Initially, the state attempted to dismiss the case entirely, arguing that the plaintiffs did not have the right to challenge the sodomy law because they had never been prosecuted under it. After a series of decisions that have allowed the case to move forward, the parties submitted their briefs to the Supreme Court of Puerto Rico, who were to decide whether the case could proceed.

26. ACLU, "In Historic First, Puerto Rico Supreme Court Considers Whether Law Denies Basic Rights to Gay People," *American Civil Liberties Union Press Release*, August 11, 2000 and December 12, 2002, <http://www.aclu.org/news/NewsPrint.cfm?ID=8068&c=100>.
27. In the Americas, as of this writing aside from Nicaragua, Barbados, Grenada, Guyana, Jamaica, Saint Lucia, and Trinidad and Tobago maintain laws against homosexual, and in some cases heterosexual, sodomy.
28. Other U.S. territories that had already eliminated sodomy laws include American Samoa, Guam, Mariana Islands, the U.S. Virgin Islands, and Washington, DC. For further details, please see "British Scraps Islands' Anti-Gay Laws," *The Guardian* (London), January 6, 2001, *Lexis-Nexis*, May 28, 2003, <http: www.lexis-nexis.com>, and Dávila-Caballero, "Discrimen," 1220.
29. It is worth commenting on the fact that in a country that remains predominately Catholic, it has been the influences of both progressive and conservative Protestant forces that have pushed these debates into the foreground, an observation that La Fountain-Stokes elaborates on more fully in his previously cited essay.
30. Liz Arelis Cruz Maisonave, "Pro-Vida ficha participantes de Parada," *El Vocero*, June 2, 2003, <http: //www.vocero.com /noticias.asp?n=28840&d=6/2/2003>.
31. In 1992, Colorado voters passed Amendment 12, a state-wide antigay initiative prohibiting all branches of the state government from passing legislation or adopting policies prohibiting discrimination against lesbians and gay men based on their sexual orientation. In response, queer activists organized a national boycott that cost the state millions in lost revenues after tourists, convention planners, business contractors, and over 20 municipalities began boycotting the state. In 1996, in Romer *v.* Evans, the U.S. Supreme Court ruled Amendment 2 unconstitutional.
32. In her essay, Puar refers to Puerto Rico as "the most commonly referenced destination for European-American gay and lesbian travelers." Puar's essay entitled "Circuits of Queer Mobility" uses the controversy surrounding gay and lesbian cruise ships denied docking rights in the Caribbean to examine the relationship between queer travel, tourism, and globalization. In addition to an insightful exploration of how commodity culture, "native" and "foreign" bodies, and nation-states come together in queer travel encounters, Puar's essay includes discussion of diasporic queers "returning home," an issue that is particularly relevant to understanding queer Puerto Rican travel and migration, and the burgeoning business of activist travel. Puerto Rico has been the site of several queer Latina activist conferences, including El Tercer Encuentro de Lesbianas de América Latina y el Caribe (1992) and the Latina/Latino Lesbian and Gay Organization (LLEGO) (1997); both events received extensive coverage in the local press. For more details, see Jasbir Kaur Puar, "Global Circuits: Transnational Sexualities and Trinidad," *Signs* 26 (2001): 1039–65, 1043; Jasbir Kaur Puar, "Circuits of Queer Mobility: Tourism, Travel and Globalization," *GLQ* 8, nos. 1–2 (2002): 101–37; and Ardín Pauneto.
33. "Baéz Galib dice que la sodomía no se ha discutido en código penal," *El Nuevo Día Interactivo*, May 13, 2003, 14, <http://www.endi.com/noticiat.asp?newsid={26D51178-CDF9-4BB3-856C-8EF543DEF233}>. Original Spanish: "Las personas que han discutido esto (la sodomía) se han adelantado a los acontecimientos, cuando el Tribunal Supremo de

Estados Unidos resuelva, pues el código de Puerto Rico tiene que reflejar obligatoriamente lo que el Tribunal Supremo de EE.UU. resuelve" (qtd. in ibid.).

34. "Aguarda Calderón por la Legislatura," *Archivo Digital de El Nuevo Día*, June 25, 2003 and July 11, 2003, <http: //www.adendi.com/noticia.asp?nid=560393>.
35. Israel Rodríguez-Sánchez, "Condicionado el delito de sodomía," *Archivo Digital de El Nuevo Día*, May 14, 2003 and May 28, 2003, <http: // www.adendi.com/noticia.asp?nid=553838>.
36. My thanks to Frances Negrón-Muntaner for this crystallizing insight.
37. Israel Rodríguez-Sánchez, "Da su último aletazo el artículo 103," *El Nuevo Día Interactivo*, June 23, 2003, <http: //www.endi.com/noticiat.asp?newsid={EE38FEDE-26F8-45CA-9CEF-580B5A1503BC>.
38. Pedro Julio Serrano, "¡Al fin libres!," *El Nuevo Día Interactivo*, July 8, 2003 and July 12, 2003, <http: // www.endi.com/noticiat.asp?newsid={F7D3D5D2-0D26-4B93-9D9C-DC19D9367D8C}>. Original Spanish: "[Los senadores] demostraron con este hecho histórico que no tenemos que esperar por decisiones de otras jurisdicciones para hacer valer el derecho a la intimidad, que opera sin necesidad de legislación adicional y es garantizada por la Carta de Derechos de nuestra Constitución."
39. Frances Negrón-Muntaner's *Boricua Pop*, analyzes the function of shame in the discourse of Puerto Rican identity. In her project she describes shame as "constitutive of social identities generated by conflicts within asymmetrical power relations, not privatized pathologies." For more details, see Negrón-Muntaner, *Boricua Pop: Puerto Ricans and the Latinization of American Culture* (New York: New York University Press, 2004), 4.
40. Arnaldo Cruz Malavé, "What a Tangled Web! Masculinity, Abjection, and the Foundations of Puerto Rican Literature in the United States," in *Sex and Sexuality in Latin America*, ed. Daniel Balderston and Donna J. Guy (New York: New York University Press, 1997), 234–49, 235.
41. Ibid., 240.
42. See Grosfoguel, Negrón-Muntaner, and Georas, "Introduction: Beyond Nationalist and Colonialist Discourses."
43. Ann Cvetkovich "Recasting Receptivity: Femme Sexualities," in *Lesbian Erotics*, ed. Karla Jay (New York: New York University Press, 1995), 125–46, 133.
44. Ibid., 133.
45. Another important legal case in Puerto Rico also had an unlikely female protagonist, Dr. Rosalinda Ramos. In 1995, when the Gay Officers Action League (GOAL), a U.S.-based gay and lesbian police officers association, held their convention in Puerto Rico, they were faced with considerable opposition and harassment from local police officers. The closing night of their convention in Puerto Rico, the party they were hosting at the lesbian bar, Cups, was raided. It was later revealed that Regulation Number 29 of the Puerto Rican Police Department Disciplinary Regulations prohibited members of the PRPD from "associating with prostitutes, homosexuals or other persons of dubious reputation" (qtd. in Judith Berkan, "Discrimen por orientación sexual: Mano dura—Official Police Department Bias Takes a Hit," *Revista Jurídica Universidad de Puerto Rico* 69 (2000): 1267–81, 1273.) Lambda Legal Defense successfully brought suit to have the rule overturned. It was Dr. Rosalinda Ramos, the owner of Cups and a longtime lesbian activist on the island, who was the lead plaintiff in the case and who most often presented herself to the local press.

See Berkan's article for details in the case. Berkan's article while useful in understanding the complex legal maneuvers involved, offers very little in the way of thoughtful analysis on the ironies of a local woman "representing" gay and lesbian police officers from the United States, the attendant gender and national politics implicated, or the theoretical repercussion brought about by queer tourism in a transnational Puerto Rican context.

46. Cruz Malavé, "What a Tangled Web!" 246.

CHAPTER 11

Imagining Puerto Rican Queer Citizenship: Frances Negrón-Muntaner's *Brincando el charco: Portrait of a Puerto Rican*

Alberto Sandoval-Sánchez

"Brincar el charco" is a uniquely Puerto Rican idiomatic expression that embodies a particular way of seeing migration. Above all it makes easier the speech act of putting into words the experience of diaspora, of the massive air migration that Puerto Ricans have practiced since mid-twentieth century. "Brincar el charco" is also a cultural and ideological construction that captures the historical process of displacement as a sudden jump over the ocean by turning it into a miniature puddle.

In these terms, and in a joyous and affectionate manner, the more or less four-hour flight over the Atlantic Ocean with primary destinations to cities in the northeast (New York City, Newark, Philadelphia, Hartford, and Boston) is minimized, assimilated, and made manageable by taming the violence and trauma of the act of migration into a simple maneuver of a jump. Indeed, "brincar el charco" not only encapsulates the diasporic condition that has fractured the Puerto Rican nation, families, and identities, but it also provides a domesticated image of travel velocity, a sort of linguistic lifeboat, that makes room for agency, serves as a verbal buoyant vessel, and facilitates a shorthand slogan to migrancy.

Given that Puerto Ricans have been American citizens since 1917, the decision to "brincar el charco" does not require any visa permits or a passport. Since there are no borders, no legal restrictions, and no fears of deportation, Puerto Ricans are free to come and go to the mainland, *en un cerrar de ojos se puede brincar el charco*—one could jump the puddle in a blink of an eye." For this reason, it cannot be translated as the British expression of "crossing the pond"/"pasar el charco," that would literally mean crossing the Atlantic Ocean. For Puerto Ricans, it is not a voyage or journey, *una travesía*; rather it implies a spontaneous and impetuous act of relocation and positioning, for many, a way of life up in the air, which can even be read as a choice, or as the execution of free will and autonomy, *nada más y nada menos que* (no more and no less) guaranteed by the rights of American citizenship.

The colonial status of the island and the imperial ideological formations that condition and shape Puerto Rican identities and subjectivities are crucial in determining each particular and individual decision to "brincar el charco." That means that the personal and the political are entangled in the act of migration to such a point that it is indispensable to question if Puerto Ricans are pushed, or if they simply jump on their own. Do they really have self-governance?

It was not until I saw Frances Negrón-Muntaner's film *Brincando el charco* (1994) that I became conscious of the contradictions, limitations, and possibilities engraved in the idiomatic phrase, and of how her film examines the dynamics of migration in the context of lesbian and gay sexualities, colonialism, and diaspora. As for the gerund usage in the title, Negrón-Muntaner herself has lucidly declared, "I chose the gerund *brincando* [jumping] to signal an action that is still in progress and seemingly never ends. Our stay on the United States, permanent or not, is a curiously continuous experience that produces cultural anxiety precisely because of its ambiguities. American citizens by birth, . . . Puerto Ricans can make *el charco* seem large or small as they want."[1] Here, the filmmaker acknowledges the flexibility of displacement through a constant back-and-forth traveling and its propensity to circular migratory patterns, always signaling a process of deterritorialization and reterritorialization after which "one is never the same"[2] and always encompassing the "cultural anxiety" and "ambiguities" tied to the implications, privileges, and advantages of possessing American citizenship.

* * *

Yet, the film begins with death, the play of finality. This makes me recall my essay, "Puerto Rican Identity Up in the Air: Air Migration, Its Cultural Representations, and Me 'Cruzando el charco,' " written at a moment I thought I was about to die because of AIDS health complications after 1990. In this text, I proposed that migration is an awareness of death: "an awareness of relatives and friends dying in the place of origin while realizing the impossibility of being there, an awareness of one's own death and the choice of burial place as there or here, and even experiencing a cultural death in assimilation."[3]

Nothing could be more true than when in Negrón-Muntaner's film the protagonist, Claudia Marín, receives a phone call from her brother in Puerto Rico informing her that their father just died and that the funeral would take place in a couple of days. For any Puerto Rican migrant this is the terrifying awaited phone call that could only be followed by pain and grief, by the guilt and lamentation of being away for years from the just deceased loved one, and by the immediate purchase of a round trip ticket to attend the funeral back home. However, this is not the case in *Brincando el charco.*

When Claudia's brother asks her to return home, she reacts coldly, reluctantly, and unashamedly resistant to pay tribute to her father. Claudia's most immediate excuse for not attending the funeral is that it being Christmas season, a time for family reunification in Puerto Rico, all flights were booked. The short conversation with her brother also reveals that she has not been back in five years as a result of her confrontation with her father.[4] Her response to her brother's petition to go back home is direct and defiant: "¿Es importante para quién? Seguramente no para el difunto"[5] (It's important for whom? Certainly not for the dead one). Even her lover Ana advises Claudia to attend the funeral but she is determined in her irrevocable decision (for the time being): "Why [should I go]? Why should I? I don't owe him anything. He owed me an apology."[6]

Since this is not the opening scene of the film, until then the spectators do not know the reason for the dispute between father and daughter. They only know that Claudia is a Puerto Rican lesbian migrant with a Latina lover who is a political activist in the community and that Claudia is a photographer whose shots constitute an archive of Latino bodies, gay identities, and lifestyles. The opening scenes will not have a complete contextualization and meaning until Claudia's flashback after the news of her father's death.

The flashback is a black-and-white memory of the moment in which her father discovers that Claudia is a lesbian and angrily expels her from home. The segment starts with the focusing of an altar with statuettes of la Virgen María and a rosary. The camera then moves toward the infuriated face of her father who with an enraged tone of voice holds in his hand the photo that revealed her secret: "¡Mira, míralo, con el trabajo y el sacrificio que da criar un muchacho en este país y tú me pagas con ésto! Te voy a decir algo y óyeme bien. Si tú quieres seguir revolcándote con esas mujeres malas, porque son malas, yo no te quiero más por aquí. ¿Entiendes? Es más, ahora mismo, te me vas de aquí"[7] (figure 11.1).

Without any hesitation Claudia comes out of the closet in defiance and shamelessly confesses her lesbian love relationship to her father. Not willing to compromise, her enraged father exiles her from the sphere of the home and the domain of the nation: "¡No me contestes con esa suciedades, coño, vete, vete de aquí!"[8] (Don't answer me with that filth, damn, go, get out of here!). In this melodramatic scene Papi personifies the homophobic macho that must safeguard the sanctity of *la sagrada familia puertorriqueña*[9] (sacred Puerto Rican family) and the nation. He is not alone in his execution of power: Catholicism, patriarchy, nationalism, compulsory heterosexuality, and homophobia are his institutional allies. In his self-erected castle, which comprises the whole Puerto Rican nation, there is no room for homosexuals or for any attempt to articulate a lesbian or gay identity.

It is imperative here to center on the photograph: if for Claudia the photo constituted a validation of her lesbian identity, for her father that photo inscribed total abjection and the prohibition of a lesbian subjectivity and experience within the space of the home and the nation. For the father, a picture cannot speak a thousand words, *mucho menos*, much less enunciate the

country and you pay me back
with this! Now, listen up!

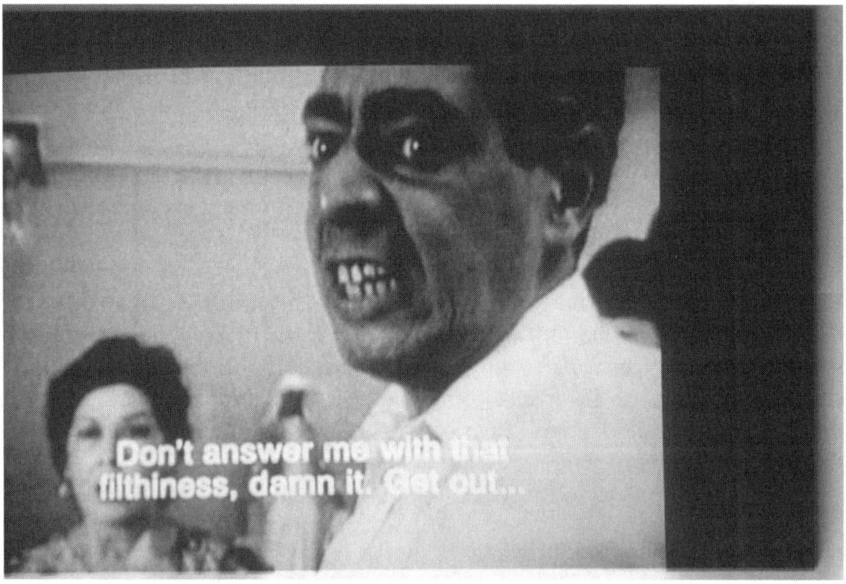
Don't answer me with that
filthiness, damn it. Get out...

Figure 11.1 "Father flashback" in *Brincando el charco.*

love that dares not speak its name, while for Claudia, as a photographer, each picture inscribes an identity, "a body with multiple points of contact,"[10] traces of scattered subjectivities. Indeed, each frame of the film—being a photo per se—embodies fragments of Claudia's partial and overlapping identities in her struggle to construct and articulate her subjectivity in process both as a lesbian and a Puerto Rican in the United States, both as a daughter and as a migrant, both as a lover and a *persona non grata*, both as a minority and a second-class citizen. In these terms, the film entails the urgency to critically approach the ontological aspect of who are Puerto Ricans, what it means to be a Puerto Rican in the island and in the United States, and what and where home is after migration. More exactly, what it means to be a queer Puerto Rican in specific political localities and junctures at home and in the mainland.

Once Claudia is s/exiled, the spectators do not need to be told that she migrates to the United States to join the Puerto Rican diaspora that started in the late 1940s for economic reasons. The film takes for granted that the viewer is aware of this fact. However, it is obvious that her sexual orientation is the reason for her migration. Given the colonial status of Puerto Rico, Claudia leaves without any state and legal bureaucratic intervention, which means that she has an open door to migration without having to apply for a visa, refuge, or asylum like so many Latin Americans do; and which is impossible for the majority of lesbian and gay *latinoamericanos*. Here, her American citizenship works in her favor: it is the passport to s/exile.

On the other hand, given that on the mainland Puerto Ricans are conceived as "people of color," she finds herself deciphering and coping with a history of racism, oppression, and marginalization. At the same time, Claudia's migration offers her the opportunity to avow and embrace her lesbianism and to take advantage of her U.S. citizenship to mobilize a Latina lesbian political practice. Claudia will benefit from the gay and lesbian movement in the United States and its granting of a queer citizenship. In such terms, the film asks audiences to problematize issues that center above all on the process of identity formation after the migration of a Puerto Rican lesbian in relationship to a homophobic father and nation, in relationship to the multiracial Latino community in the United States, and in relationship to the queer community in the United States. But there is another agenda in place: Negrón-Muntaner explores what and where home is after migration and the hardships for queers to feel at home in Puerto Rico: "Without doubt, I wanted *Brincando el charco* to provoke some type of polemic. At the same time, although the film invites the spectator to a dialogue, it also fears it. In the last instance, I expected the film to answer the question of whether it is possible to return home, or at least to return to some houses in common."[11]

How can you not be immersed in controversy when it is a lesbian who kills the symbolic father and rebels against the nation? *De todos modos*, anyhow, Negrón-Muntaner's film practice constitutes a possibility for the construction of home, that is, a safe, pleasurable, and nightmarish portable home grounded on queer difference and cultural diversity, as she states: "Given my continuous transit between diverse geographic, sexual, and creative localities, the cinematic space can enact a re-signification of home, and partially serve as its witness . . . [Yet home is still] an unresolved, fundamental, and politically charged problem because the film does not articulate a clear position regarding the political as a national project."[12] This conception of home intersects with two other queer writers—Audre Lorde and Gloria Anzaldúa—who respectively define home in the following terms: as "the very house of difference"[13] and as a bodily shelter and burden—"I am a turtle, wherever I go I carry 'home' on my back."[14]

More specifically, in Negrón-Muntaner's film, the notion of belonging is rooted in the problematization of home that "stems from the exclusion of at least four communities from the island's nationalist imagination: Afro-Puerto Ricans, homosexuals, lesbians, and U.S.-Puerto Ricans. In the insistence of representing those voices and bodies, I proposed a continuous questioning of the construction of home as the everyday practice of tolerance."[15] In this sense, the representation of home involves the questioning of boundaries and the body politic in given relations of power. The film is an attempt to shake the foundation of the patriarchal house of power. Besides being provocative and controversial by contesting nationalist discursive formations,

Negrón-Muntaner's queered notion of home, anchored in her lesbian experience and identity, procures to challenge, shock, disturb, scandalize, and haunt those who are intolerant to Otherness and have a narrow and myopic conception of nationhood.

* * *

In *Brincando el charco*, the father's death cannot simply be read as a literal patricide. It also must be understood that Negrón-Muntaner is not Claudia. Major confusion arises from the fact that Negrón-Muntaner places herself in the role of producer, director, scriptwriter, narrator, and protagonist.[16] As such, it is hard to distinguish between Negrón-Muntaner and Claudia, both are fused into one body in the film. Claudia's voice duplicates and complements Negrón-Muntaner's own. Such con/fusion is crystallized, for example, when one puts side by side the following excerpts from the film and Negrón-Muntaner's theoretical testimonial, "Beyond the Cinema of the Other or towards Another Cinema," reflecting on her s/exile: "Seven years of voluntary exile. Far from familiar faces and landscapes. Into the vulnerable protection of anonymity, detachment, indifference."[17] "Once I abandoned the paternal home, the possibilities of dwelling multiplied."[18] Negrón-Muntaner has explained the autobiographical component in her film as her "shared desire with the protagonist of multiplying the travel routes, the various ways one can come and go, without being forced to exclusively dwell within the house of the national. A conceptualization that, I believe, tends to subvert the multiple possibilities of the 'Puerto Rican' sign."[19]

No doubt that Negrón-Muntaner's political agenda and lesbian subjectivity coincide with the fictional character, however, each one's relationship with the paternal home is completely different. For Claudia, who exists in the fictional domain, the death of her homophobic and authoritarian father is the episode that unleashes a chain reaction that culminates in her decision to fly back to Puerto Rico, whether it is home anymore or not. Negrón-Muntaner thoughtfully resumes this chain reaction in the following way: "Claudia Marín's angry countenance—flared nostrils, bared teeth—is the face of expulsion, a magical mask that sets up a series of transformations, of daughters mutating into queers, queers into migrants, migrants into niuyoricans, niuyoricans into lovers, lovers into activists, activists into tourists."[20]

This succession of identitarian positions does not only convey the action of the film, it also magically registers the provisional, mutable, improvisatory, and processual aspects of identities. Now, for Negrón-Muntaner, in contraposition to Claudia, the death of the father in her 57-minute film is a premeditated and deliberate attack on Puerto Rican nationalist organic intellectuals and the nationalist party followers, as well as an assault on the figure of Luis Muñoz Marín, the founder of the *Partido Popular Democrático* (Popular Democratic Party; PDP) and mastermind for the implementation of the Puerto Rican exodus under his governorship in the mid-1940s. Negrón-Muntaner's ironic retaliation to undermine the Puerto Rican patriarch and master planner of the *Estado Libre Asociado* (Free Associated State, 1952) is fully emblematized in her baptizing of the protagonist of the film with his last name: Claudia *Marín*. In addition, another layer of irony surfaces when it is taken into consideration that the San Juan International Airport carries his name, as Negrón-Muntaner has emphasized: "no podemos olvidar que el aeropuerto mismo lleva el nombre de Muñoz Marín, y ésta es una película sobre múltiples viajes"[21] (We can't forget that the airport itself carries the name of Muñoz Marín, and this is a film about multiple trips). This act of naming shows how ingrained migration is in everyday life in Puerto Rico and in its political unconscious.

What's more, while Claudia refuses to mourn her dead father, Negrón-Muntaner perversely rejoices in killing the symbolic father. The death of the father in the film represents the death of the nationalist patriarch and paternalist discourse, in words of Negrón-Muntaner herself: "[*Brincando el charco* symbolizes a] film practice that unceremoniously sends the nostalgia of a paternalistic, racist, and classist nineteenth century to a mausoleum (or museum), and destroys the notion that every Puerto Rican's life should be a duel to death with the evil forces of colonialism."[22] Negrón-Muntaner further develops her politico-ideological proposition in an interview after the release of the film: "La película cuenta con una red densa de alusiones a los patriarcas de la cultura puertorriqueña, particularmente Antonio S. Pedreira y, acertadamente, Luis Muñoz Marín . . . la película continúa en diálogo con el legado de Muñoz Marín, pero además (simultáneamente) ensaya formas de enterrarlo."[23] (The film includes a dense web of allusions to the patriarchs of Puerto Rican culture, particularly Antonio S. Pedreira and, correctly, Luis Muñoz Marín . . . the film continues the dialogue with Muñoz Marín's legacy, but also (simultaneously) rehearses ways to bury it.)

Accordingly, Negrón-Muntaner utilizes Claudia to ventriloquize her political agenda: Claudia's rancor, let's say it plainly, death wish for the intransigent father concretizes Negrón-Muntaner's desire to counterassault nationalism and its patriarchal figures—in the paternal home and the nation per se. That ideological patricide is possible in the realm of the film thanks to the intolerance of Claudia's father who exiled her from home and the imagined national community, as she declares: "I thought he would never really die . . . away and against him, I claimed an identity, a cause, a language to remap older boundaries."[24] Definitely, her expatriation and expulsion led to an act of self-discovery and self-assurance materialized in her act of coming out of the closet. Both Claudia's defiance and resilience (like Negrón-Muntaner's in the making of the film) and lesbian consciousness have led her to a new political project that destabilizes Puerto Rican nationalism and provides her with a new space of/for political action: "I picked another way of narrating myself. No longer do I want a plate at the table on La Gran Familia Puertorriqueña."[25]

In this way, Claudia legitimizes a space for sexual difference, radical contestation, and queer insurgency, a space where *los patos y patas puertorriqueños* (the Puerto Rican queers) in their s/exile can celebrate their difference and keep in place specific strategies of resistance for their survival, even if that calls out for *ser malcriado con el padre, retarlo y desobedecerlo* (to be bad-mannered with the father, challenge, and disobey him). And, it cannot be forgotten, that if at the end Claudia boards the plane to head back home, she is going to bury him six feet under. In a way, she is a winner. She has her lover in the United States and a diasporic community to go back to. Negrón-Muntaner summarizes her return to both places as follows: "Although Claudia has agreed to accompany her family (Puerto Ricans) to bury an exclusionary culture (the father), she does so knowing that her life is in the United States and that she loves and is loved by/in the diaspora. The possibility of reconciliation entails neither abandonment of what has been struggled over nor a life lived up in the air, between two contexts. Rather, Claudia, located in the diaspora, travels to one island in the Puerto Rican archipelago, where she, perhaps, can have a place."[26] Except, I would add, given that the film ends with the freezing of the plane in mid-air, it points to the always-unfinished project and process of identity formation—suspended up in the air.[27]

Claudia's intolerant father might be dead, and she might be free to revisit her past; however, with the possibility of return, a crisis surfaces, as she says: "I don't even know how to feel." "How do I make sense now?" "How can I go back?."[28] While the killing of the father according to Negrón-Muntaner, "deja un vacío de poder que sin embargo la película no se apresura por llenar, sino más bien examinar y merodear"[29] (leaves a vacuum of power that the film, however, does not rush to fill), the protagonist in her s/exile has empowered herself in such a way that she can undo the law of the Father, tackle all kinds of prejudices and fears, and give voice to those relegated to the margins through the exploration of race, class, sexuality, and transnational identities in transit. As the film unfolds, Claudia shows how her migratory experience is part of a larger diasporic history within given social, political, and cultural junctures that make visible the complexity of layered, mutational, and contradictory identities. In this sense, the film is a broken mirror that fragments and disperses identities.

On the other hand, through activism, queer militancy, mixing of genres, bilingualism, transculturation, hybrid discursiveness, and experimental filming, Negrón-Muntaner recovers a colonial history and a diasporic experience that intersects with her fractured lesbian self. That identity is validated through the performance of lesbian and gay private and public acts in given social exchanges, relative sexual freedom and visibility, and access to queer spaces and community alliances possible in the mainland after migration. In short, the film makes spectators think critically about each one's relationship with Puerto Rico *aquí y allá* (here and there). It offers a space to raise *conscientización* about the internal agony, social abuse, and bodily violence that lesbians, gays, and transvestites undergo in their daily lives, and equips them with the necessary tools to transgress and resist. Indisputably, in *Brincando el charco* s/exile is a daring act of survival, and it goes further, as the filmmaker has stated it "makes a specifically queer location possible."[30] And, I would add, a queer citizenship is also in place.

* * *

What makes *Brincando el charco* perfectly queer? The fact that it is scandalously unapologetic in its center-staging of lesbian and gay sexualities and in its queering of the Puerto Rican nation. First of all, I use "queer" within the perspective that Michael Warner has defined the term as a resistance to regimes of the normal in *Fear of a Queer Planet*: " 'queer' gets a critical edge by defining itself against the normal rather than the heterosexual."[31] That "queer edge" I understand as the film's possibility to call into question normalizing categories, regulatory regimes, and cultural norms, as the possibility to blur boundaries and benefit from the porosity of borders, to interrogate and disrupt hegemonic (imperial and colonial) ways of seeing, to trouble, or undo, and to unsettle dominant master narratives, and to question and decenter forms of knowledge that perpetuate domination, oppression, and marginalization.[32]

When applying this alter/native critical practice to *Brincando el charco,* it is possible to visualize how the intersection and interlocking of lesbian and gay sexualities, colonialism, and diaspora have at its politico-ideological core a double agenda: foremost, to deconstruct the contradictory queer nature of American citizenship as it applies to Puerto Ricans, and, subsequently, to capitalize on the queer movement in the United States in order to question the Puerto Rican nationalist discursive domain and homophobic practices of exclusion. Accordingly, Negrón-Muntaner rethinks national belonging and proposes the possibility of a dual citizenship: an American citizenship deeply intertwined with a queer identity that destabilizes the notion of nation as a normalization category and posits queers as rightful citizens in an archipelago of comings and goings.

In spite of the birthright to American citizenship and its constitutional privileges, *Brincando el charco* traces the history of oppression, racism, violence, and discrimination that Puerto Ricans have faced in the United States. It employs archival footage and testimonials to call attention to how Puerto Ricans are marked as devalued domestic and foreign Others, always abject and suspect in the mainland. When taken into consideration that Puerto Ricans have no vote in the U.S. Congress and Senate, cannot take part in presidential elections on the island, and are under the U.S. Supreme Court jurisdiction and custom policies, further emphasis is placed on the absence of Puerto Rican sovereignty; the American surveillance, policing, patrolling, and control of its shores and subjects; and the odd and queer status of Puerto Ricans as second-class citizens and a racialized minority.

All these factors are implied in Claudia's voice over in the opening of the film: "From the moment I learned to read, I have known of Puerto Ricans asking themselves to the point of despair: Who are we? What is our common destiny? Trusting that a clear answer will undo centuries of conflict and turmoil, turning us into the owners of history. I am an echo of these questions even if I contest them."[33] The whole film is then an exploration in crescendo to the possibility to put an end to these questions and to the impossibility of finding an adequate answer. The ultimate irony is that it takes a lesbian (Claudia/Negrón) to propose from the in-between location of a minority (ethnic) within a minority (sexual) a new way of defining Puerto Rican identity and nationhood. As a result, her politics of solidarity and affinity are placed in sharp contrast to the dead-end political status of the island and its colonial condition.

Claudia has learned a new way of narrating Puerto Rican (national) history and articulating a hybrid identity from the point of view of the diaspora: "People who created new forms of struggles and solidarities; pleasures and priorities."[34] In words of poet Zulma González (in the film), the "perfectly imperfect"[35] U.S. Puerto Rican turns out to be a "purely perfect Puerto Rican."[36] The message is loud and clear: Being a U.S.-born Puerto Rican is not a good enough reason for disqualifying someone from being a member of the Puerto Rican imagined national community.

Fittingly, it is Claudia's lover who clearly exposes Puerto Rican exclusionary practices that devalue her diasporic identity, dispossess her from her right to claim her Puerto Rican belonging, and make fun of her usage of Spanglish. She had to learn how to navigate the relationship between location and identity to survive here and there: "When I'm with gringos, I say I'm Puerto Rican. When I am with real Puerto Ricans, I say I am from New York."[37] As Doreen Massey has theorized on space and identity, this statement corroborates how space and identity are socially constructed, how spaces are endowed with identities and depend on social interaction for their meanings, and I would add for diasporic peoples how spatio-national positionality is dynamic, multiple, simultaneous, relational, ever-shifting, and capable of redefining the borders of nation.[38]

The same notion of claiming a national identity applies to Evelyn Cruz, a teacher's assistant: "I am a Puerto Rican born and raised here in Philadelphia and I consider myself Puerto Rican."[39] Both cases as well show how American citizenship is subverted and contested. Not only that, but both cases attest to the subaltern's diasporic transgressions to the American national (and imperial) imaginary and to the processes of decolonization and transculturation *en las entrañas del monstruo* (the monster's entrails) that result from the identitarian geographical construction of a Puerto Rican archipelago. *Y por si fuera poco*—and if it was not enough—the politicization of abjection and difference culminates in self-empowerment, particularly when in a voice over Claudia threatens the system with her bodily presence: "My empowerment speaks a creole tongue. I can't afford any purity."[40] It cannot be dismissed that this declaration of difference goes hand in hand with the migration of people of color to El Norte and bodies struggling with AIDS. In a way, this declaration conflates the slogans "We are here because you were there" and "We are here, we are queer." The political cannot be separated from the sexual, neither the personal from the political in matters of identity formation and the positionality of hybrid subjects.

I would like to focus on a segment of a meeting of Latino/a activists in Philadelphia where identity issues are discussed and labels are questioned in the film. In a humorous display of resistance, one of the participants challenges any categorization imposed by the system by writing "Other" where it specifies to clarify ethnic, racial, or national origin: "Siempre lleno Other, porque no soy de cultura hispánica, pero no voy a dar el honor al gringo de decir iberoamericano o portugués o algo así. Lleno siempre, donde se dice Other, yo escribo Other, que se imaginen lo que soy" (I always fill in Other, because I am not from a Hispanic culture, but I am not going to give the gringo the pleasure of saying Iberonamerican or Portuguese or something like that. I always fill in, where it says Other, I write Other, let them imagine what I am).[41] This act of defiance (and independence) undermines any attempt to homogenize and classify the Other. And what is most significant, such a contestation between the lines reads "none of the above" with the purpose of undoing and unsettling the Anglo hegemonic system of power and efforts of containment. It is Claudia who straightforwardly challenges and destabilizes Anglo-American national and imperialist projects of hegemony without any reservations: "America. What a formidable fiction. We are no longer in your backyard, the rest of the world. We are in your living room making it anew."[42]

More radically, the film does not limit itself solely to redefining the American homeland. It first and foremost pushes the borders of Puerto Rico by redrawing it as an archipelago—which makes possible "a sense of belonging to multiple locations"[43] and the emergence of new inclusive and tolerant communities.[44] This is mostly possible through the intervention of queer AIDS militancy.[45] Moisés Agosto, AIDS activist and with an HIV status, based in New York City, is the one who reformulates the nation and verbalizes in a queer context the title of the film. In his political vision, Puerto Rico becomes just another barrio in the archipelago of the queered Puerto Rican nation. It is necessary to quote his lengthy intervention in the film:

> Como HIV positive viviendo en Puerto Rico, uno de los problemas que confronté es que no tenía accesibilidad a tratamiento. Tuve que brincar el charco—es una razón de sobrevivencia—como miembro de Act Up-Nueva York . . . como yo lo vizualizo es que tanto el sur del Bronx, como el barrio hispano aquí en Nueva York, son como otro pueblo más de Puerto Rico, son como una extensión . . . Y también viendo la cuestión del puente aéreo, con la facilidad que la gente de Puerto Rico viaja acá, porque saben que aquí hay un lugar de pertenencia, donde pueden venir a conseguir tratamiento y también sentirse en una atmósfera entre puertorriqueños, me justificó a mi la idea de que sí, podiamos usar ese mismo puente aéreo, para ir al otro lado del charco, donde estaba el otro barrio de Puerto Rico, que no estaba en Nueva York pero que estaba en la isla.[46]
>
> [As an HIV positive man living in Puerto Rico, one of the problems that I confronted was that I did not have access to treatment. I had to jump the puddle—an issue of survival—as a member of Act Up-New York . . . How I envision it is that the south Bronx, like the Hispanic barrio of New York, are like another town of Puerto Rico, they are like an extension . . . And also seeing the air bridge, with the ease that people from Puerto Rico travel here,

because they know that this is a place of belonging, where they can come and get treatment and also feel that they are in a Puerto Rican atmosphere, justified the idea to me that yes, we could use that same air bridge, to go to the other side of the puddle, where there was the other Puerto Rican barrio, that was not in New York but on the island.]

Clearly, there is a queer agenda here that is explicitly and effectively materialized in the film with the struggles and survival of gay men with AIDS. This agenda also entails the recognition of queer spaces like the disco, the appropriation of the dancing space by Latino voguers, the Latino/a participation in the gay parades and demonstrations, the implementation of AIDS awareness and prevention strategies, the formation of a Latino/a gay community, the decriminalization of homosexuality, and the validation of lesbian sexuality. I must put emphasis on Agosto's affiliation to Act Up because this is the organization that demanded healthcare and equal treatment for people living with AIDS and the one that founded the notion of a Queer Nation—"I pledge allegiance to the F(l)ag" is an adequate way to visualize its counter-politics agenda.

Queer Nation claimed recognition to visibility, membership in the sociocultural imaginary, and insisted on the equal rights of citizenship.[47] In challenging the exclusions, inequalities, and injustices of the nation-state, Queer Nation, as an oppositional politics and coalition movement, demanded the enfranchisement of lesbians, gays, transsexuals, and people with AIDS; publicly intervened with political disobedience, outings, die-ins, and kiss-ins; staged rituals of resistance; legitimized desire, rage, and pleasure as forms of political expression; questioned the ideologies of normalcy; and struggled for the creation of safe spaces for queers.[48] In this sense, the film itself is a safe cultural space for the constitution and articulation of Latino/a queer identities.

Needless to say, the gay and lesbian movement and Queer Nation inform Negrón-Muntaner's film. Nonetheless, it is not simply an act of assimilation. After Claudia simultaneously views the video and reads the letter that her friend Maritza sent her about the gay and lesbian parade in Puerto Rico organized by a Nuyorican transsexual perceived by many to be Anglo, she questions her own queer politics rooted in the Anglo-gay and lesbian movement of liberation: "Is the language of my sexual liberation English? Does it get translated and transformed only later, after layers of mediations?"[49] Maritza's attached letter not only exposes the institutionalized homophobia in Puerto Rico and the lack of cooperation from the police and city hall. It also brings to light the colonial condition of Puerto Rican gay and lesbians which also leads Maritza to question her own politics: "Todo el proceso me hizo cuestionarme, si un organizador del patio hubiera podido iniciarlo. Tal vez nuestra liberación es una donde primero se habla inglés y después se traduce"[50] (All that process made me question whether a local organizer could have initiated it. Perhaps our liberation is one where we first speak English and then it's translated). Maritza goes further by referring to the partial ineffectiveness of guaranteed constitutional rights for gays and lesbians in Puerto

Rico: "Subestimamos cuán civiles somos para algunas cosas; una mezcla de 'Ay bendito' y la constitución Americana"[51] (We underestimate how civil we can be about some things; a mix of "Ay Bendito" and the U.S. constitution). Her ironic statement both points to the dynamics of decolonization and the unquestionable imposition of colonial ruling under the American constitution.

The same ironic posture applies to one of the opening scenes of the film. When Claudia meets with the gay publisher to whom she submitted her book of photos for publication, he is oblivious to her investment in political and colonial issues that are fundamental aspects for her articulation of a Puerto Rican queer identity. What is worse is that he turns it into a joke: "My readers are not interested in colonialism, unless, of course, they're interested in the political implications of S/M relationships."[52] His lack of awareness and ignorance is an explicit attack on a white gay and lesbian movement that dismisses that the issues of class, racism, and colonialism for minorities go hand in hand with the challenging of heterosexism and homophobia. As Charles Fernández has stated in "Undocumented Aliens in the Queer Nation" such lack of knowledge (about genocide, slavery, colonization, imperialism, and racial hatred) renders Latinos/as invisible by ignoring ethnicity and class and by exoticizing, trivializing, and evading the personal and political implications of having multiple subjectivities.[53] And, indeed, this is the ideological agenda and radical political project that *Brincando el charco* proposes for the constitution of a Latino/a queer citizenship.

Coda

Why did *Brincando el charco* impress me so much and stay with me for days to come? Although Negrón-Muntaner has always emphasized that the father's homophobic behavior should be taken as a parody of melodrama in *telenovelas*, gay and lesbian audiences who identify with Claudia have taken it as a real and authentic experience of terror.[54] I must confess that the moment I saw him and heard his authoritarian voice *mi corazón* was bleeding. It resuscitated memories of a patriarchal and homophobic culture that shall always haunt me. That identification is possible because this is the first Puerto Rican experimental and autobiographical film to break the silence on homosexuality, to debunk patriarchal authority, and to dismantle taboos so deeply encrypted en el *corazón de la familia y la nación puertorriqueña*. As such, I would call it a foundational text that gives visibility for the first time to lesbians and gays in Puerto Rico and in the United States. For the first time the process of identification is such that *los patos y las patas* gain agency for the articulation and examination of their own relationships with the father, the family, the home, the nation, the burial place, and even with the myth of the eternal return.

What is more, in this process they become queer citizens *de la pantalla grande*, the big screen. It is the film's hybrid style and form in the blurring of the lines between fiction and reality, myth and history, narrative and documentary, archival footage and film script, processed interviews and soap opera melodrama, biographical portraits and imagined characters, and politics and entertainment that cause queer spectators to take it as a real experience and to see themselves in Claudia's position of s/exile in the United States, whether it is an imposed or voluntary one. She was pushed to jump, and so were most of the Puerto Ricans that "brincaron el charco" in the twentieth century.

Brincando el charco pone el dedo en la llaga, puts the thumb on the wound. Even I remember from my childhood the *locas* in my neighborhood that left for New York City. How can I forget el *hijo de Chacha*, Doña Isabel's grandson Liquín who became Erica, and *la loca* del beauty parlor! Negrón-Muntaner has courageously inaugurated a new discursive space and a new mode of queer representation in this film, but most important, she has filmed for posterity that primal scene of what shall always haunt *los patos y patas aquí y allá, allá y aquí*, the horror of carrying in our flesh a father's curse and the trauma of the expulsion of *nuestros cuerpos* and s/exile from a place called home once upon a time.

Notes

I am grateful to my colleagues Nancy Saporta Sternbach and Silvia Spitta for their valuable and critical suggestions in the process of writing this article. I would also like to thank Frances Negrón-Muntaner for providing me with the film and the necessary materials, *y por tener paciencia conmigo.*

1. Frances Negrón-Muntaner, "When I Was a Puerto Rican Lesbian: Meditations on *Brincando el Charco*," *GLQ* 5, no. 4 (1999): 512.
2. Ibid.
3. Alberto Sandoval-Sánchez, "Puerto Rican Identity Up in the Air: Air Migration, Its Cultural Representations, and Me 'Cruzando el Charco,' " in *Puerto Rican Jam: Essays on Culture and Politics*, ed. Frances Negrón-Muntaner and Ramón Grosfoguel (Minneapolis: University of Minnesota Press, 1997), 189–208.
4. Claudia's brother in the phone call reminds her that she has not been back to Puerto Rico in more than five years: "Hace más de cinco años que tú no pasas por aquí ni te importa nada" (For the last five years you have not come around here nor do you care about anything) (Frances Negrón-Muntaner, *Brincando el charco*, unpublished manuscript, 1994, 6). In the second scene of the film, a voice over reveals that Claudia has been in the United States for seven years: "Seven years of voluntary exile" (Negrón-Muntaner, *Brincando*, 3). In the video of the Puerto Rican gay parade in San Juan that her friend Maritza mailed her, an interviewed spectator refers to the date as 1991: "but . . . we're in 1991, and people have to be up to date in what's happening in the world" (Negrón-Muntaner, *Brincando*, 27–28).
5. Ibid., 6.
6. Ibid., 7.
7. Ibid. In English: "Look, look at it, with the work and the sacrifice that it takes to raise a child in this country and you pay me with this! I'm going to tell you something and listen up. If you want to continue to lie with those bad women, because they are bad, I don't want you around here. Understand? Actually, right now, get out of here . . ."
8. Ibid., 7–8.

9. The father also threatens his wife and son when they intervene to protect and defend Claudia. Such behavior recruits and positions spectators to see him as a villain—*el malo de la telenovela.*
10. Negrón-Muntaner, *Brincando*, 3.
11. Frances Negrón-Muntaner, "Beyond the Cinema of the Other or Towards Another Cinema" *Atzlán* 24, no. 2 (1999): 153.
12. Ibid., 150–51.
13. Audre Lorde, *Zami: A New Spelling of My Name* (Freedom, CA: Crossing Press, 1994), 226.
14. Gloria Anzaldúa, *Borderlands/La Frontera: The New Mestiza* (San Francisco: Spinters/Aunt Lute, 1987), 21.
15. Negrón-Muntaner, "Beyond the Cinema," 152.
16. Negrón-Muntaner further develops the reason for this confusion in her interview "Un cine sospechoso." See Dinah Rodríguez, "Un cine sospechoso: Conversación con Frances Negrón-Muntaner" (Interview) *Revista de Crítica Literaria Latinoamericana* XXIII, no. 45 (1997): 418.
17. Negrón-Muntaner, *Brincando*, 3.
18. Negrón-Muntaner, "Beyond the Cinema," 154.
19. Ibid., 153.
20. Negrón-Muntaner, "When I Was," 516.
21. Rodríguez, "Un cine sospechoso," 117.
22. Negrón-Muntaner, "Beyond the Cinema," 153–54.
23. Rodríguez, "Un cine sospechoso," 417.
24. Negrón-Muntaner, *Brincando*, 10.
25. Ibid., 16.
26. Negrón-Muntaner, "When I Was," 521.
27. Negrón-Muntaner has declared that her intentionality in this ending "had been to imply that the process of migrating was indeterminate, that being between locations was itself a viable identity, with specific joys and pains." (Ibid., 524.)
28. Negrón-Muntaner, *Brincando*, 7, 10, 37.
29. Rodríguez, "Un cine sospechoso," 417.
30. Negrón-Muntaner, "When I Was," 513.
31. Michael Warner, ed., *Fear of a Queer Planet: Queer Politics and Social Theory* (Minneapolis: University of Minnesota, 1993), xxvi.
32. Cherry Smith, in "What Is This Thing Called Queer?" included in *The Material Queer*, summarizes some other political suppositions in place in a queer approach: "Both in culture and politics, queer articulates a radical questioning of social and cultural norms, notions of gender, reproductive sexuality and family." See Cherry Smith, "What Is This Thing Called Queer?," in *The Material Queer: A LesBiGay Cultural Studies Reader*, ed. Donald Morton (Boulder: Westview Press, 1996), 280. I also found very helpful for my critical reading of *Brincando el charco,* David L. Eng "Out Here and Over There: Queerness and Diaspora in Asian American Studies." His notion of queerness as a "queer methodology" complements Warner's notion of "critical edge." See David Eng, "Out Here and Over There: Queerness and Diaspora in Asian American Studies," *Social Text* 52–53 (1997): 31–52.
33. Negrón-Muntaner, *Brincando*, 1.
34. Ibid., 11.
35. Ibid., 12.

36. Ibid., 15.
37. Ibid., 17.
38. Please see Doreen Massey, *Space, Place, and Gender* (Minneapolis: University of Minnesota, 1994).
39. Negrón-Muntaner, *Brincando*, 20.
40. Ibid., 30.
41. Ibid., 20–21.
42. Ibid., 33.
43. Negrón-Muntaner, "When I Was," 523.
44. The redefinition of the Puerto Rican nation is also reimagined through a process of negotiation in terms of tourism. Chloé is willing to return to Puerto Rico only as a tourist, in order to avoid any frustration or disenchantment: "No longer is this the tourism of going to the San Juan Hotel or Hyatt, but a very personal tourism of going to share with people that I love and visit places that are important to me. In that way, I can recover the surreal enchantment that Puerto Rico has for me. Because on the contrary, if I were to live there, it would become the disenchanted island." In this fashion, the film proposes new ways of approaching the nation and new ways of articulating diasporic identities in the move through partial reconciliations and flexible dispositions. Original Spanish: "Ya no es el turismo de ir al hotel San Juan o ir al Hyatt, sino es un turismo muy personal de ir a compartir con personas que yo amo y visitar lugares que son importantes para mí. De esa manera yo logro rescatar el encanto surreal que tiene Puerto Rico para mí. De lo contrario, de yo vivir allí, se convierte en la isla del desencanto." (Negrón-Muntaner, *Brincando*, 40).
45. Negrón-Muntaner's documentary *AIDS in the Barrio: Eso no me pasa a mí* (1989) specifically deals with the socioeconomic and cultural context of the AIDS epidemic in the Latino community in Philadelphia.
46. Negrón-Muntaner, *Brincando*, 33–35.
47. For an excellent article on the practices and ideological premises of Queer Nation, see Lauren Berlant and Elizabeth Freeman, "Queer Nationality," *Boundary 2* 19, no. 2 (1992): 149–89. I also highly recommend the anthology *The Material Queer*, a fabulous compilation of essays centering on queer issues and queer politics. See David Morton, ed., *The Material Queer*.
48. In two occasions Claudia refers to the notion of feeling safe: "[The disco] was the space I felt safest" (Negrón-Muntaner, *Brincando*, 22). "Glimpses of a new place where perhaps I could make myself safe . . ." (Negrón-Muntaner, *Brincando*, 31). Surely, this sense of safeness is tied to queer identity and bodies feeling at home in queer public spaces.
49. Negrón-Muntaner, *Brincando*, 29.
50. Ibid., 28.
51. Ibid., 25–26.
52. Ibid., 2.
53. Please see Charles Fernandez, "Undocumented Aliens in the Queer Nation," *Democratic Left* (May/June 1991): 9–10. This is an excellent article that questions the Anglo queer movement and challenges the privilege status of white middle-class gays and lesbians. For a similar politico-theoretical approach and the proposal of a Queer Aztlán (Nation), see Cherríe Moraga, "Queer Aztlán: The Reformation of the Chicano Tribe," in *The Last Generation* (Boston: South End Press, 1993), 145–74. Also see "Páginas

omitidas" where Luis Aponte-Parés emphasizes the sociohistorical complexities of Puerto Rican queer identities and politics in New York City. See Luis Aponte-Parés, "Páginas omitidas: The Gay and Lesbian Presence," in *The Puerto Rican Movement: Voices from the Diaspora*, ed. Andrés Torres and José. E. Velázquez (Philadelphia: Temple University Press, 1998), 296–315.

54. Negrón-Muntaner has declared her surprise about the realistic effect of this scene in Puerto Rico: "Many read this scene (and identified with it) as a call to a post-patriarchal and non-oedipal culture (in the sense of symbolically 'killing the father'). I suggested that for me the scene was always an excessive soap opera-like and surreal staging. Many students, however, actively challenged me by saying that, no, undoubtedly, that is the Puerto Rican father that they know" (Rodríguez, "Un cine sospechoso," 414). I cannot deny that I join the students in their reading and interpretation.

    Original Spanish: "Muchos leyeron esta escena (y se identificaron con ella) como un llamado a una cultura pos-patriarcal y de relaciones no-edípicas (en el sentido simbólico de 'matar al padre.') Yo comenté que para mí esa escena siempre fue una de exceso telenovelesco, surreal. Muchos estudiantes activamente me retaron diciendo que no, que sin duda ése era el padre puertorriqueño que ellos conocían."

CHAPTER 12

Exposed Bodies: Media and U.S. Puerto Ricans in Public Space

Frances R. Aparicio

The Puerto Rican Day Parade in New York demonstrates the value that performances of cultural affirmation have for *boricuas* in the diaspora. As Winn has observed,

> a joyous occasion and a vibrant parade, with drum majorettes dressed like Middle Americans but moving to syncopated Caribbean rhythms exemplifying the mix of North and Latin American that is today's "Nuyoricans," or New York Ricans. . . "We are here to show our pride in being Puerto Rican and to celebrate our culture," one man in the crowd explained as others nodded in agreement. "We are both Americans and Puerto Ricans."[1]

This public performance of Puerto Rican identity, which began on April 15, 1956 as the *Desfile Hispano*, has been developing as a social and public institution for more than 40 years. Throughout the history of its organization and planning, the parade has been characterized by tensions between paradigms of *hispanismo* and *puertorriqueñismo*, that is, between integration and the underscoring of cultural difference. The parade also embodies the simultaneous articulations of Puerto Ricans as both an ethnic group and as a nation. However, whether through integration, difference, or both, the main effect of this collective ritual has been to inscribe the presence of the Puerto Rican subject in U.S. public space and to institutionalize our visibility and our agency as historical minorities in dominant society.

Yet, after almost half a century of such collective efforts, the Puerto Rican Day Parade has been the object of an invigorated racialized discourse in mainstream media, particularly on television. In the last three years, for instance, this major cultural event has been used as the background for prime time television shows such as *Seinfeld* and *Law and Order*. In the next to the last episode of the *Seinfeld* series (aired in May 1998), Puerto Ricans appear as a mob when they respond to one of the show's characters who accidentally burns the Puerto Rican flag and stomps on it to put out the fire. On January 24, 2001, NBC aired a *Law and Order* episode based on the June 11, 2000 events referred to as the Central Park "wildings." Titled "Sunday in the Park with Jorge," the NBC narrative represents young Puerto Rican men as savages outside of "civilization."

As it is widely known, the "wildings" refer to a series of incidents that took place in 2000. After the successful completion of the Puerto Rican Day Parade, a group of men sexually attacked more than 50 women passers-by. Due to the media coverage and use as a narrative thread in popular television drama shows, the so-called wildings have since become associated with the parade, with the Puerto Rican community, and with Puerto Rican masculinity in particular, triggering a series of discursive associations in television, newspapers, and the Internet that metonymically linked the parade with sexual violence, with mobs, and with criminality.

These representations have also created a chain of images and associations in the U.S. popular imaginary that has recirculated the public image of U.S. Puerto Ricans—and the Puerto Rican male—as an internal enemy, as an alien savage who challenges the forces of law and order and that is a menace to white, middle-class Americans.[2] Furthermore, this visual economy establishes an underlying binary logic that situates whites as the embodiments of Reason and men of color (read Puerto Rican men) as its absence or opposite: irrationality and barbarism.

This racializing discourse is of course not new. Instead, it is a current articulation of a several centuries' old Western discourse in which the definitions of Reason and of rationality are themselves embedded in racist logics of differentiation and subordination. In fact, the present case study brings to the surface what David Theo Goldberg has called "the sedimented significations" of the social constructs of the primitive and of savagery.[3] Rather than trace or historicize said constructs, it is perhaps more important to ask ourselves why these European, colonial, racist constructs and images are being deployed at this particular historical, cultural, and political juncture in the United States?

I would argue that U.S. Puerto Ricans, despite the fact that many are born and raised in the United States, continue to be seen as Racial Others who need to be contained, supervised, and controlled by the state, and its institutions. In contrast to earlier junctures, the current criminalization of U.S. Puerto Ricans needs to be understood in the larger context of the demographic shifts of U.S. Latinos in the late twentieth century and the politics of space, containment, and transgression that are emerging throughout major urban centers that are, not coincidentally, also Latino cities. Moreover, the common deployment of the term "mob" in reference to Puerto Ricans across these three dominant discursive texts clearly suggests that these media representations are articulating a class and race-informed anxiety and fear for the supposedly transgressive presence of collective bodies of color in U.S. public spaces.

Race is not, however, the only pivotal category as gender plays a major mediating role in this process of racialization. Triggered by the media representations of the Central Park wildings, the criminalization of Puerto Rican or "brown" masculinity is itself the result of a constructed narrative about brown/Puerto Rican men attacking white women, a narrative that disturbingly echoes the logic of lynching in the South during post-Emancipation and that informs, in turn, the fictional narrative of the *Law and Order* episode. In this chapter, I will then trace the discourses of race and gender that are evoked by these two television programs and by the debates and discussions around the Central Park attacks, focusing on the ideologies behind them, on their function on this particular historical moment, and on the social effects that this process of racialization has had, or could have, on both the dominant society and the U.S. Puerto Rican subjects.

The Puerto Rican Parade and the Ethno-Nation

The current Puerto Rican Day Parade emerged out of the efforts of the *Organización del Desfile Puertorriqueño*, which began in the 1950s, together with other similar organizations such as the *Congreso del Pueblo*, in order to "develop community support for the working class and to reaffirm the need to confront the immediate socioeconomic problems faced by Puerto Ricans."[4] The symbolic, commercial, and political dimensions of the current parade have partially shifted from these original goals. The Puerto Rican Day Parade has been institutionalized as a major ethnic, public event in New York, exemplifying the state-sanctioned celebrations of ethnicity and cultural diversity and partaking in the multicultural politics of the city. However, many continue to understand it as a performance of cultural and political opposition or contestation.

If during the 1950s and 1960s the principal floats were subsidized by the social, hometown clubs of the island and the diaspora, since the 1980s the parade has been significantly commercialized. Floats announce commercial products and labels mediated by the presence of Puerto Rican and Latino/a actors and actresses, singers, salsa groups, rap, merengue and *jíbaro* music, school bands, and politicians, from Puerto Rican aldermen to the New York City mayor and the island governor. The visibility of the parade, which is aired on television and through the Internet, offers those invited to participate a higher level of cultural capital and social value; in turn, famous movie stars and personalities add to the social attraction of the parade itself.

Yet the parade marches through and politically traverses the most exclusive and rich sectors of New York City's elite and economic capital, thus subverting the power dynamics and socioeconomic divisions between white capital and the *boricua* community in El Barrio. The performance of Puerto Rican culture, its inscription in public space, also depends on the circulation of symbols and icons and on the production of meaning that these symbols trigger. For instance, the visual prominence of Puerto Rican flags—from large to small flags, worn as hats, bandanas, or scarves, on T-shirts, and painted on bodies, faces, and as nails, or inscribed as shaved haircut—signals the serious ethos of nationalism and patriotism among Puerto Ricans in the diaspora. Although this value is articulated and mediated as a commodified nationalism, it is also true that wearing the Puerto Rican flag on one's body, or "the use of T-shirts or other insignias on that day marks the body itself of the participants as Puerto Rican; it announces a collective identity by means of the symbolic value of certain images and the power of words."[5]

On the one hand, the mobility of the bodies of *boricuas*, mestizos, speakers of Spanglish, Spanish, and Puerto Rican English, and the audible sounds and rhythms of salsa, merengue, and rap, constitute a radical reaffirmation of the public and collective presence of our community, which continues to be marginalized and subordinated despite our fashionable moment in the U.S. popular imaginary. This cultural reaffirmation aims to contest dominant order, for it depends on "the persistence of collective memory through restored behavior."[6] In other words, the parade restores, reenacts, and brings into the public presence alternative forms of knowledge and being based on the "knowledge of the body, on habits and customs" that are, themselves, subordinate knowledges.[7]

On the other hand, this ritual simultaneously evinces the efforts to incorporate the Puerto Rican subject into the dominant spaces and hegemonic institutions through a public assertion of traditional values. (An example of this is the tradition of the Queen and the popularity of the police who march in the parade.) While this incorporation is not necessarily expressed as assimilation, it does require a sort of negotiation with the existing, dominant paradigms of ethnicity as a productive, acceptable alternative to the racialized, subordinated identities imposed on all Puerto Ricans. To make Puerto Ricans into an "ethnic group" is a way of entering the system that accepts the official paradigms of institutional multiculturalism. It is also a way of cleansing racialized images created by dominant society as well as the most radical, self-constructed *boricua* identities constructed from within the community.

As mentioned earlier, this cultural and political dialectic between ethnicity and nation, between acceptability and reaffirmation of cultural difference and political oppositionality, has been evident throughout the history of the Puerto Rican Day Parade's organization and planning. As Rosa Estades has written, since its beginning the *Organización del Desfile Puertorriqueño* advocated for a Puerto Rican Parade rather than a *Desfile Hispano*, thus signaling the tensions between articulating an acceptable, benign *hispanismo* or reaffirming *boricua* differential identity through *puertorriqueñismo*.[8] Since the Puerto Rican identity has been historically racialized, some members or factions within these planning committees argued that the Hispano rubric would avoid the negative stigmas of the Puerto Rican label. "In their struggle to escape a minority position, they can thus reach and borrow prestige from some larger and more favored minority."[9]

Rather than choosing ethnicity or nation, the Puerto Rican Day Parade integrates both paradigms of collective identity and social imaginaries. This doubled way of imagining ourselves is not exceptional to Puerto Ricans, but rather one of the strategies and results of our (post)colonial conditions, as Grosfoguel, Negrón-Muntaner, and Georas have analyzed.[10] If Puerto Ricans imagine ourselves as a nation by reclaiming a territory, the island (and in the struggle over Vieques), we also inscribe ourselves as an ethnic group within the United States, for we do not claim territory or our own state apparatus. While the island's statehood party refused to recognize Puerto Ricans as a nation during the congressional debates on the 1996 Young Bill, and former governor Carlos Romero Barceló stated that we were only a "community," Congressman Luis Gutiérrez, from the Chicago diaspora, argued in favor of Puerto Ricans as a nation. While it would be easy to think that the diaspora only claims ethnicity and the islanders' nationality, the fact that U.S Puerto Rican congresspersons such as Gutiérrez and Nydia Velázquez argued for our status as a nation destabilizes such binaries.

Similarly, the Puerto Rican Day Parade articulates both ethnicity and nationalism. It claims ethnicity in relation to the U.S. and city politics of multiculturalism, claiming a rightful space as an established, traditional ethnic group cleansed of racialized images (along with the Irish and Italian, for instance). Yet the strong, visual, symbolic, and political reaffirmation of *boricua* identity as oppositional to a (white)-melting-pot ideology continues to be clearly evident in the omnipresent icon of the flag and of its historical meanings of opposition and resistance, as well as in the diverse cultural performances included in the parade. Not surprisingly, it was the flag that became the stuff of television comedy in an effort to "disappear" Puerto Ricans from the tube.

Seinfeld and the Re-Signification of the Puerto Rican Flag

In May 1998, the next to the last episode of *Seinfeld* caused a controversy among Latino and Puerto Rican audiences. The episode shows Seinfeld and his friends stuck in a traffic jam on Fifth Avenue, a nuisance caused, indeed, by the Puerto Rican Day Parade. At one point, Kramer accidentally sets a Puerto Rican flag on fire and, in order to put it out, he throws the flag on the sidewalk and stomps on it. A group of Puerto Ricans see this, and one gay man shouts: "There is a man burning (or stepping on) our flag." Others around him react to this and run toward Kramer. Puerto Ricans, as a collectivity, are referred to as "a mob" whose out-of-control violence is associated with daily occurrences on the island. A previous statement regarding how "this happens everyday in Puerto Rico" is generalizable to the behavior of Puerto Ricans during the whole episode.

That Kramer accidentally set the flag on fire is not an arbitrary image, nor an exclusive strategy for characterization and humor. It serves as a metaphoric anticipation of the ways in which a Puerto Rican mob is constructed by the white cultural gaze. Immediately after Kramer tries to put out the fire in the most politically incorrect way—by stepping on the flag—the one voice is heard: "Someone is burning our flag," a claim that sparks the constructed collective and irrational violence of this particular mob. Like a tinderbox, Puerto Ricans as a group could explode at any moment given a specific trigger.

Unlike the representation of other mobs or collective groups—such as union labor movements and strikes in which the collectivity needs to be warmed up onto action, and organized action usually—this brown mob reacts irrationally at a gesture that is justified artistically through the naturalization of humor and through the already established expectations of Kramer's behavior. While the nature of comedy and humor has been evoked to justify this particular episode—"it's only entertainment"[11]—it is precisely comedy, as genre, and humor as discourse that frames Puerto Rican patriotism or identity as irrelevant, not serious enough of an issue to warrant a responsible representation on the part of the show writers and producers.

The *Seinfeld* episode also underscores the fragile nature of intercultural knowledge and the process of re-signification that ensues from it. As a cultural outsider, Kramer's relationship to the Puerto Rican flag—politically and in terms of identity—is very different from the meanings that the flag holds for those Puerto Ricans who attended the parade. The fact that the Puerto Rican flag has been, historically, the major symbol of pride during this event, and that it has been inscribed in multiple ways and in multiple sites—including *boricua* bodies—reveals that the flag is a signifier of cultural nationalism and political opposition to the dominant Anglo society and, at times, also to the U.S. government. While there are many pro-statehood Puerto Ricans who may not necessarily equate these values with the flag, they are still reaffirming and performing an oppositional identity that resides in the historical meanings that the flag has carried since the nineteenth century on. For Kramer, more immediate, nonpolitical ones displace the cultural meanings of the flag. It is a metonymic reference to Puerto Rican culture, to the parade; it is an adornment at most and a piece of fabric, at the least.

The gap in cultural semantics evident in this episode also informs the response of NBC to the protests articulated by the National Puerto Rican Coalition and other groups.[12] In a survey conducted through Latino Link (1998) after the episode, various respondents shared their negative reactions and outrage at these racialized images of Puerto Ricans as violent, savage subjects who are out of control.[13] They also joined in a written statement by William Santiago demanding an apology from NBC.[14]

Although at the time NBC executives insisted that the show did not insult or stereotype the community, two years later—as a result of the controversial *Law and Order* episode—they finally promised not to air the show again.[15] The fact that these television executives and producers could not recognize or validate the negative impact of these representations—in light of the lack of other, more complex representations of *boricuas* in Hollywood and on television—indicates that they did not share the same cultural and historical codes through which the Puerto Rican audience "read" the episode. Manuel Mirabal, president of the National Puerto Rican Coalition, commented; "Obviously, these executives live in another planet to think that this program would not be offensive."[16] Regardless of whether they may live in the same planet and country as half of the Puerto Rican nation, they are light years away from intercultural knowledge and understanding.

The re-signification of the Puerto Rican flag is accompanied by the recontextualization of the Puerto Rican Day Parade. The parade in *Seinfeld* was not a central event to them, but it appears only as its indirect and negative effects: the nuisance of the traffic jam, the anger of Puerto Ricans at the burning of the flag, and the threat that Seinfeld and his friends feel at the so-called "mob." Seinfeld is not interested in representing the parade as a space of cultural affirmation, for such images would imply the ideal of an integrated Puerto Rican body politic in New York. Thus, the parade could only appear as context, as indirect reference, as background. The semantic gap between the value of the parade for Puerto Ricans and the (anti)social meanings that are revealed in the *Seinfeld* episode suggests that as Puerto Ricans gradually integrate themselves into the mainstream, dominant institutions such as media and TV will attempt to dismantle this through the colonialist discourse of the Manichean allegory.

The Central Park Wildings: The Discursive Lynching of Puerto Rican Men

The Manichean allegory is an economy of representation that transforms "racial difference into moral and even metaphysical difference."[17] The representation of Puerto Ricans as a "mob" in *Seinfeld* reappears during the media coverage of the Central Park attacks on June 11, 2000, thus evincing the power that this colonialist discourse had on the average U.S. television audience. It is then recirculated as a gendered and racialized trope that, indeed, duplicates the role of colonialist texts, yet in the current context of race and the city. As JanMohamed suggests,

> If such literature can demonstrate that the barbarism of the native is irrevocable, or at least very deeply ingrained, then the European's attempt to civilize him can continue indefinitely, the exploitation of his resources can proceed without hindrance, and the European can persist in enjoying a position of moral superiority.[18]

Two years after the *Seinfeld* episode, Anne Peyton Bryant, one of the white women attacked by a group of male youth in Central Park, was interviewed in the *Geraldo Rivera Show*. In her initial comments she made explicit reference to the *Seinfeld* episode in order to refer, according to her, to the sort of violence that we can expect from the Puerto Rican Day Parade in New York.

While the controversy that Geraldo Rivera was discussing, and that the media at large was exposing, had to do with the sexism, the violence against women and this society's lack of systematic recognition of it, and particularly the indifference of the New York police to these crimes, Peyton Bryant's comment reveals the long-term impact that the *Seinfeld* episode had on its viewers. By establishing a direct association between the Puerto Rican Day Parade and sexual criminality, Peyton Bryant reproduced the colonialist politics of the *Seinfeld* episode, adding a gendered racialization to the collectivity of Seinfeld's Puerto Rican mob. In direct response, on June 16, the National Congress for Puerto Rican Rights issued a statement denouncing the youth who attacked more than 50 women that afternoon, the abuse against women, and the racism that was articulated by associating such crimes with the Puerto Rican Day Parade.[19] This association is also evident in the fact that in a web search to the Puerto Rican Day Parade one of the first links that appears is "Women's Rights/Central Park Attacks."

On September 15, 2000, Chris Rock made the following joke in his television show: "Big News in New York: The founder of the Puerto Rican Day Parade died last week. The viewing was on Monday from 3 to 6, and the groping was from 7 to 12." This joke reveals that within three months of the parade and the Central Park attacks, the U.S. popular imagination has already cemented the direct relationship between the parade and the attacks. This is based on a certain logic: all Puerto Rican men are complicit, even if a priori, of sexual crimes, and any Puerto Rican community event, including a wake, will be characterized by sexual abuse.

The documentation on the arrests of the youth who participated in the Central Park attacks reveals a variety of racial and cultural groups: The men arrested "ranged in age from 16 to 33 and included a barber, a minister's son and a father of two."[20] Yet the stereotype of the Latin Lover and the macho resurface in these cultural texts. Moreover, the female victims were represented as white women—although 40 out of 60 victims were women of color—and white women were selected by the media to act as representatives of all victims during public interviews and coverage. This inverse representation of the female victims constructed the image of the Latino male as a public (although not necessarily private) threat to white women, to the institution of the U.S. family, and, ultimately, to the masculinity of white men.

The fact that the media did not identify women of color as the targets of these attacks reveals that our bodies are invisible to dominant society unless we are objects of intercultural desire and of physical or discursive exploitation. By identifying only white women as victims, Puerto Rican men and Latino male subjectivity in general become generally suspect in public space, thus opening the path for a collective fear against urban youth of color as potential agents of violence and criminality. The image of brown/black men attacking white women is not new, as it echoes the dominant logic and social phobias behind lynching in the South.

Thus, the authority and moral superiority of the state—embodied in the NYPD—and of dominant society is further reaffirmed in the continuous replay of the Central Park attacks on television news programming. Like the reiterated television images of the Los Angeles Riots in 1992, these visual narratives "elicit negative emotions" among viewers and are more "readily remembered . . . than the information contained in accompanying narration."[21] The visual reiteration, then, helps cement the criminalization of young Latinos and simultaneously justifies increased vigilance, police authority, and containment of collective bodies of color in open, public spaces. At a time when police authority, judgment, fairness, and power were publicly contested and questioned as a result of the repeated cases of abuse and outright murder of people of color—the Amalou Diallo case was still fresh in the minds of New Yorkers—the indifference of the police toward women's sexual victimization was explained precisely as a strategy to correct the image of an abusive, irrational, and barbaric police force.

But the laissez-faire attitude toward sexual crime was not all-pervasive on June 11, 2000. Members of the police department arrested two musicians who were drumming on Bethesda Fountain, an open space preferred by *congueros*, *rumberos*, and other street musicians. If the police ignored women's pleas against the very acts of fondling, undressing, grabbing, and even penetration by hand they surely did not ignore the potentially transgressive meanings of conga playing that Afro-Caribbean drumming has historically articulated, even in current, postmodern urban spaces. In other words, while gender issues seemed unimportant, race and subordinate cultural expressions were not.

The fear of informal groups of people of color in public spaces continues to motivate the politics of containment and repression that characterizes U.S. urban centers. The new urban policies against Latino street vendors in Los Angeles and New York and against the "esquineros" (literally "corner workers"), who wait for a day of labor in Los Angeles, the complaints against *quinceañera* parties in the suburbs, and noise ordinances all constitute what Mike Davis has called the "guerrilla warfare" against the tropicalizing presence of Latinos in this country's public, urban spaces.[22]

In this larger context, the New York police ignored the women, but as a response to its public criticism and outcries, then showed all of its force in investigating and arresting the youth who appeared in the video footage. With the help of the media—headlines that spelled in red letters "WANTED" and the photos of the men in the video as fugitives from old Western movies—the NYPD tried to vindicate its judicial authority and to reclaim its power as the state's embodiment of Reason and moral authority, an identity that historically has been contingent on its structural differentiation with the Racial Other, the Puerto Rican/Latino male.

"Sunday in the Park with Jorge" or, The (Un)reason/able Whiteness of *Law and Order*

"Sunday in the Park with Jorge," aired on January 24, 2001, reveals how Reason and whiteness, inextricably interwoven, are discursively embodied in the judicial system. In its eleventh season, *Law and Order* constitutes the most extensive dramatic series on current television. It received an Emmy Award in 1997 for Outstanding Drama and has received the highest consecutive number of nominations in this category. Surveys indicate that this program has produced a total of 16.3 million viewers in the past eight years, which makes it the most valuable program for NBC.[23]

This high level of popularity and visibility suggests that its narratives and discourses of representation will have an enormous potential impact. However, its intertextual scripts and stories mostly explain the popularity of the program. The writers, under the direction of its creator, Dick Wolf, choose real cases and events as inspiration for the episodes, thus producing not only fictional drama but also the effects of a docudrama. This generic blending adds to the possible conflation, in the viewers' minds, of historical events and fictional renderings, one that exacerbates the social impact of the racialized identities of Puerto Ricans in the diaspora.

In "Sunday in the Park with Jorge," detectives Briscoe and Green investigate the murder of a white woman whose body was found at the edge of the lake in Central Park during the Puerto Rican Day Parade. The husband of the victim, a young dot-com millionaire and his partner are the first suspects when it is revealed that their impending divorce would have threatened the financial stability of the company. But evidence leads to other suspects, and the detectives finally arrest Nestor, a young Brazilian man described as extremely shy with a low IQ.

Without further ado, the trial reaffirms his guilt. Nestor finally confesses that he swam to the boat where the woman was and, reacting to her aggression, hit her head against the boat a number of times. Thus, the crime is explained away as an arbitrary, senseless (without any particular meaningfulness or purpose) reaction on the part of Nestor, who acted this way so that his Latino peers would not make fun of him. Thus, the white woman's murder is the direct result and consequence of the folly of reaffirming a public Latino masculinity. Nestor, as an individual, becomes a metaphor for the threatening, collective Latino male subject, the true culprit in this murder.

The racialization of Latino and Puerto Rican males and of their sexuality is structured around a visual and discursive binary. At the onset of the program, the sexual attacks in Central Park—represented by numerous men of color identified as Puerto Rican by their T-shirts and bandanas with the Puerto Rican flag—are juxtaposed to the idyllic scene of an Anglo, professional couple in a rowboat making out. This couple discover the body of the victim, and later we find out that they are engaged in an extramarital affair. Thus, the illegitimacy of white sexuality—undermined by a joke about a putative adultery squad—is represented at the level of the individual and of the quasi-private realm, in contrast to the public savagery and out of control behavior of the *boricua* males.

This binary logic continues throughout the episode. The Puerto Rican male suspects are all referred to as "punks," "mob," and liars. The only one rendered a proper name, Kiki Morales, who later helps to identify Nestor, has a criminal record, has been in juvenile prison, and turns out to be an unreliable witness. The only *boricua* with an individualized identity is portrayed as an unredeemable, untrustworthy delinquent. In contrast, the white suspects and all those related to them have a proper name, are individuals identified with a particular job or profession, and they play a specific role within the narrative. Seth, the business partner, and the first suspect during the investigation, even has a rational motive for murdering the victim. The detectives reaffirm that his motive, money, is a very strong one. Indeed, it is a significant, rational, meaningful motive in contrast to Nestor's senseless aggression.

Nestor's actions, which constitute second-degree manslaughter, are represented as the consequences of an instance of the lack of reason and of common sense. He arbitrarily succumbed to what he perceived as the pressure of manliness, yet what stands out in the episode is the fact that there was a lack of premeditated, reasonable cause behind his actions. This binary representation echoes the Western discourse on Reason and rationality, through which modernity justifies racism by using Reason as a basis for group differentiations and subordination. If under modernity and industrial capitalism, Reason is located in the dominant subject, Racial Others are then justifiably exploited since their lack of Reason constitutes their lack of humanity, and thus, their lack of rights. As Goldberg has written, "Subject assume value, then, only in so far as they are bearers of rights; and they are properly vested with rights only in so far as they are imbued with value."[24]

Yet the devaluing of the Puerto Rican and Latino males in this episode, which certainly adds to the already problematic Hollywood images of Latinos as gangsters, criminals, and urban delinquents, also serves as the Other through and against which the whiteness and Reason of those in the judicial system is constructed.[25] The closing arguments of both lawyers during the trial, and the closing scene of the episode, clearly reinforce this discursive binary. While the Puerto Rican, mulatto lawyer with an accent provides a passionate and political defense of Puerto Ricans and of Nestor in particular, it is the prosecutor Jack McCoy (Sam Waterston) who makes a rational argument by reminding the jury about the responsibilities and consequences of individual actions. Again, the liberal emphasis on individuality is the logic for finding Nestor guilty, although the narrative continues to rely on the collectivity and generalizability of peoples of color.

McCoy also attempts to de-racialize the definitions of the "mob," partly to locate the accountability on the individual, and partly to present the judicial system as color-blind, a representation that Dolores Inés Casillas identifies throughout the whole investigative process:

> In naming a white male businessman as the suspect and not a Puerto Rican, the show projects a position of impartiality. So, despite the pressure by the "corrupted" politicians and higher ranked legal enforcements to prosecute a Puerto Rican on the basis of saving their own reputation, the detectives and hence "the law" is above them by remaining "fair" and not succumbing to the city's racial politics. The conscious decision made by detectives "to follow the investigation where it takes them" characterizes the investigation as colorblind justice.[26]

The judicial system, and those who represent the law, cannot be irrational; they constitute Reason itself. The authoritative prosecutors, the detectives with integrity, and the policemen and the judicial system behave in supposedly objective and neutral, yet goal-oriented, meaningful ways. The aim of the NYPD to restore a public image of rational behavior, fairness, and justice is achieved through this episode.

In the closing scene, the three prosecutors leave the office after having resolved such a challenging and complex investigation. Their final comments, "We started off with a white guy, put a Brazilian behind bars, for what happened during the Puerto Rican Day Parade" and "New York City, the melting pot," summarize, on the one hand, the overt attempt of *Law and Order* to represent itself as a show that recognizes the multicultural diversity of New York City and its communities of color. Yet, covertly, it is the two white women who reaffirm the threat of Puerto Rican masculinity and culture to the public well-being.

While the first statement by Prosecutor Abbie Carmichael (played by Angie Harmon) on the surface summarizes the thread of the investigation, it also suggests that Nestor is behind bars "for what happened during the Puerto Rican Day Parade." This periphrastic reference to the murder—which is a fictional element yet central to the criminalizing discourse—does not have to be explicit, for viewers have already accepted and understood that "what happened during the Puerto Rican Day Parade" was a threat to white women and to the tranquility of the middle- and upper-class sector in the city. This knowledge about Puerto Ricans as Racial Others has been already internalized in the pretexts to the show; that is, in the *Seinfeld* episode, in the media representations of the Central Park attacks, newspapers, and the Internet.

Most disturbing, however, is the fact that this process of racialization systematically erases the historical reference and the community-building social meanings that the parade has constructed through its symbolisms, "restored behaviors," and appropriation of the public space. It also reaffirms the media representation of the female victims as only white, thus rendering the pain and trauma of the bodies of women of color in particular as unreal and inconsequential. Despite its overt claims to engage in cultural diversity, *Law and Order*'s erasure and re-racializing of a Puerto Rican collective, public subjectivity may have a more profound impact on mainstream audiences than what our own cultural productions and expressions in the diaspora could achieve.

Conclusions

As Henry Giroux has stated, the impact of media as public discourse needs to be foregrounded in cultural studies. Textuality is not important for its own sake, but significant for the power it holds over our imaginaries:

> Popular cultural texts can be used to demonize black and Latino youth while reproducing a consensus of common sense that legitimates racist policies of either

> containment or abandonment in the inner cities. . . . Depictions of urban youth as dangerous, pathological, and violent must be located in terms of where different possibilities of uses and effects of such representations may ultimately reside in contexts of every life that are at the forefront of multicultural struggles.[27]

Anne Peyton Bryant's comments, for instance, revealed how the dominant media discourse that criminalizes Latino males and Puerto Rican nationalism and identity has been internalized in the U.S. popular imaginary. What are the social, economic, and symbolic repercussions of this ideology for the Puerto Rican and Latino communities?

In terms of the Puerto Rican Day Parade itself, a number of sponsors have cancelled their subsidy for future events. While the parade "was no more problematic than other large parades," according to the New York Police Department, in 2001 there was increased security and policing. This, of course, reveals the tarnished image that has ensued from the Central Park attacks and its association with this collective, ethnic event. In the words of Ralph Morales, the parade's vice-president, "no doubt it has had a very negative impact." Organizers this past year were "still more focused on damage control from last year than promotion for an event that is, at heart, a celebration of heritage."

As a result, the Puerto Rican Day Parade Organizing Committee has increased its publicity and has attempted to purge this racialized construct from the event. Thus, its decision to ban rap music from its floats this past year created controversy around the issue of defining Puerto Rican culture. Rap is being banned precisely to cleanse the criminalized image of the parade and of Puerto Ricans, by association. Yet the argument used had to do with whether rap music was or was not an integral part of Puerto Rican tradition. This debate foregrounds the ways in which the parade's organizing committee struggled to integrate Puerto Ricans once more into the multicultural repertoire of traditional, middle-class ethnic groups in the United States. By banning rap music, they were dismantling the most oppositional discourses of youth from the event.

In terms of gender, it is not arbitrary that the criminalization of the Puerto Rican male by the media went hand in hand with the invisibility of women of color as victims of this sexual abuse. The visual presence of white women victims on the news and talk shows not only triggered past racial memories of lynching, but it also displaced the voice and the perspectives of women of color from being heard at the national level. This is significant in order to understand the gender implications of this analysis. A critique of the criminalization of the Latino male should not automatically imply eliding the reality of women.

Indeed, it is within this general context of struggles that Puerto Ricans continue to resist and oppose these criminalizing, dominant images of their community. Organized efforts against NBC led to the network's decision not to repeat the *Seinfeld* and the *Law and Order* shows. This symbolic victory will have some impact, hopefully, in the process of decision making in future television productions. As to the Puerto Rican community in New York, they feel "they should make a show of force after all the negative publicity."[28] By reasserting their collective presence once again in the public space, our subordinate communities continue the ongoing process of contestation that is needed to reiterate our historical and cultural agency in the U.S. imaginary. The fact that the parade organizers have considered "the Central Park attacks their worst crisis" in the history of this event reveals that the discourses produced by the media can be as powerful and problematic as history it avowedly "reflects."[29]

Notes

1. Peter Winn, *Americas: The Changing Face of Latin America and the Caribbean* (New York: Pantheon Books, 1992), 579.
2. Víctor M. Valle and Rodolfo D. Torres, *Latino Metropolis* (Minneapolis: University of Minnesota Press, 2000).
3. David Theo Goldberg, *Racist Culture: Philosophy and the Politics of Meaning* (Oxford: Blackwell Publishers, 1993), 162.
4. Virginia E. Sánchez-Korrol, *From Colonia to Community: The History of Puerto Ricans in New York City* (Berkeley: University of California Press, 1994 [1983]), 226.
5. Lawrence La Fountain-Stokes, "Queer Puerto Ricans on Parade, T-Shirts With the Flag, and the Performance of the National," *The Dirty Goat,* 9 (1998): 1–9.
6. Joseph Roach, "Culture and Performance in the Circum-Atlantic World," in *Performativity and Performance,* ed. Andrew Parker and Eve Kosofsky Sedgwick (New York: Routledge, 1995), 45–63, 47.
7. Ibid., 47; See also Michel Foucault, *Power/Knowledge: Selected Interviews and Other Writings 1972–1977,* ed. Colin Gordon (New York: Pantheon Books, 1980), 79.
8. Rosa Estades, "Symbolic Unity: The Puerto Rican Day Parade," in *Historical Perspectives on Puerto Rican Survival in the U.S.*, ed. Clara E. Rodríguez and Virginia Sánchez-Korrol (Princeton: Markus Wiener Publishers, 1986), 99–106.
9. Quoted in ibid., 99–106.
10. Frances Negrón-Muntaner and Ramón Grosfoguel, eds., *Puerto Rican Jam: Rethinking Colonialism and Nationalism* (Minneapolis: University of Minnesota Press, 1997), 17–19.
11. Herb Boyd, " 'Seinfeld' Inflames Group of Puerto Rican Protesters," *The New York Amsterdam News,* May 27, 1998, 10.
12. Associated Press, "Hispanic group protests 'Seinfeld,' " May 15, 1998, <http://www.msnbc.com/news/164409.asp>.
13. Latino Link, "Feedback on Seinfeld," 1998, <http://www.latinolink.com/feed.html>.
14. William Santiago, "Seinfeld Does the Hack," May 11, 1998, <http://www.latinolink.com/opinion/opinion98/ 0511osei.html>.
15. Robert Domínguez, "Seinfeld Episode Still Angers Puerto Ricans," *Hispanic Magazine,* August 31, 1998, 16.
16. National Congress for Puerto Rican Rights, "Central Park Attackers are Enemies of the Community," e-mail message to the author, June 16, 2000, rperez@boricuanet.org.

17. Abdul R. JanMohamed, "The Economy of Manichean Allegory: The Function of Racial Difference in Colonialist Literature," in *"Race," Writing, and Difference*, ed. Henry Louis Gates, Jr. (Chicago: University of Chicago Press, 1986), 80.
18. Ibid., 81.
19. National Congress for Puerto Rican Rights, "Central Park Attackers are Enemies of the Community," e-mail message to the author, June 16, 2000, rperez@boricuanet.org.
20. John Cloud, "The Bad Sunday in the Park," *Time*, June 26, 2000, 32–33.
21. Valle and Torres, *Latino Metropolis*, 51.
22. Mike Davis, *Magical Urbanism: Latinos Reinvent the U.S. Big City* (New York: Verso, 2000), 53–54.
23. "Law and Order: About the Show," 1998, <http:www.studiosusa.com/laworder/html/about/copy.html>.
24. Goldberg, *Racist Culture*, 37.
25. For further discussion, please see Nicolás Kanellos, *Thirty Million Strong: Reclaiming the Hispanic Image in American Culture* (Golden, CO: Fulcrum Publishing, 1998) and Alberto Sandoval-Sánchez, *José Can You See?: Latinos On and Off Broadway* (Madison: University of Wisconsin Press, 1999).
26. Dolores Inés Casillas, "On Law and Order" (Unpublished paper, University of Michigan, 2001).
27. Henry Giroux, *Impure Acts: The Practical Politics of Cultural Studies* (New York: Routledge, 2000), 82.
28. Mireya Navarro, "Chasing Last Year's Shadow from a Coming Parade," *The New York Times*, May 31, 2001, 4.
29. Ibid.

PART III

Boricua Borderlines

CHAPTER 13

Transing the Standard: The Case of Puerto Rican Spanish

Gloria D. Prosper-Sánchez

It is not necessary (but, of course, we will do it) to pronounce once again the new fashionable cliché: Utopia is dead.

Rubén Ríos Ávila, La raza cómica[1]

Over the last hundred years, Puerto Ricans have transformed the debate on national identity from one focused on founding a nation through political practices—a present impossibility—into one of cultural expression. Language has been at the center of this national debate, weaving together a discourse of cultural authenticity that equates being Puerto Rican with speaking the standard variety of Spanish, a register that eludes most Puerto Ricans, including code-switchers, nonnative speakers, "Spanglish" users, bilinguals and monolingual users of nonstandard varieties. While the legislative tug-of-war over "Official Language" policies and laws occupies most of the debate, less remarked is the fact that Puerto Rican Spanish is not the stable practice some imagine.

Although many language scholars in Puerto Rico face this complex cultural reality by deploying their linguistic cleaning and polishing tools on lexical and syntactical Anglicisms—words or structures adopted from English—the daily speech of Puerto Ricans invites more meaningful inquiries than whether millions of speakers are suffering from defective thinking when they choose "tuna" over "*atún.*" "Defective language . . . Defective thought," an already classic meme,[2] was in fact a media campaign aired so repeatedly on local broadcasts that it became as familiar and appealing as the beloved island celebrities who served as its spokespersons.[3]

In these Public Service Announcements (PSAs), sponsored by the University of the Sacred Heart since 1995 and written by professor Luis López

Nieves, celebrities like *salsero* Gilberto Santa Rosa and singer Melina León beckon the Puerto Rican viewer from television and radio spots to abandon words like "nice," "size," and "brown" in favor of "chévere," "talla," and "marrón," "castaño" or "pardo." Paraphrasing Spanish writer Miguel de Unamuno, the PSAs claim, "Language is the blood of the spirit" and admonish "defective language . . . defective thought." Translinguistic influence with English is the proposed reason why thought, language, and even the blood of Puerto Ricans have become diseased. Fittingly, the script notes used for producing the spots actually direct that the phrase "Language is the blood of the spirit" appear "IN RED CAPITAL LETTERS."

In contrast to this approach, by commenting on the representation of the standard variety or norm of Puerto Rican Spanish, my goal is to consider how the constant friction between languages, varieties, and powers of Puerto Rican Spanish generates unconventional linguistic insights and enriches the discursive options of all speakers. Building on the work of linguist Rubén del Rosario, I further argue that it is the persistent discursive negotiation of linguistic varieties and their supporters that will spark a reformulation of Puerto Rican Spanish, as well as of the register formerly known as the "Norm."

The Body

Before discussing the standard or *norma culta*, it must be underscored that when alluding to Puerto Rican Spanish I am referring to a lectal variety native to a linguistic community of well over 7 million speakers, a figure that nearly doubles the 3.8 million inhabitants of the islands of Puerto Rico by including the more than 3.8 million Puerto Ricans whose permanent residence is not in the commonwealth.[4] Imagining the Puerto Rican variety of Spanish requires one to assume that language and linguistic practices are not afraid of water.

In the decades that have passed since Tomás Navarro Tomás's foundational linguistic atlas of 1948, *El español en Puerto Rico*,[5] the size, significance, and constancy of the Puerto Rican diaspora have transformed Puerto Rican Spanish into a dialect that can no longer be described accurately as such. Puerto Rican Spanish is a geolect in transit; its practices exceed most geographical criteria. The dialectal alternations between the shores of Manhattan, Florida, and Puerto Rico, for instance, may not account for more significant differences than those observed between the speech of two island towns such as Fajardo and Maricao.

This supra-geographical premise challenges the notion of isogloss in its traditional significance,[6] where national maps, rivers, mountains and other telluric accidents determine the constitution of a speech community. It reveals a linguistic variety whose formulation is "transing," or moving from a physically determined identity to one generated by the adopted linguistic practices of its speakers. In addition to the variable of migration,[7] factors such as demographic self-identification, history, unstoppable moving,[8] ideologies, politics,[9] and colonialism should be considered when retracing the ways in which Puerto Rican Spanish is described. A commitment to everyday practice, to the "specificity of local orality" proposed by del Rosario,[10] will necessarily produce a representation of Puerto Rican Spanish populated by the heterogeneity of all speakers and their experiences.

Due to the eminently social character of language, it is unsurprising that much of the information for the description of its usage would come from the study of the constant contact, or more precisely, the relentless exchange between always changing codes, whether between two or more languages or two or more varieties of one or more languages. This never-ending status of code friction[11]—more akin to the quick play of legs intertwined in a tango than to a war or a brawl—will demand from those who study and comment on language an openness and flexibility as constant as the mobility of its speakers, and a curiosity appealing only to those interested in pursuing that which one already knows is impossible to grasp.

Linguistic Disobedience or Puerto Rican Spanish Spoken Here

In 1981, linguist Jorge Guitart defined "the standard" as the variety of a dialect that contained the least utterances judged to be undesirable by the educated people of that community.[12] Tacit preservation of the prevailing structure of social prestige notwithstanding, this claim helped to dismantle the fiction of Castilian Spanish as the natural ideal for a desired, uniform Spanish. The disarticulation of this fiction liberates Spanish American speakers, as well as users of non-Castilian varieties in Spain, of the ancestral guilt of never sounding "castizo" (with interdental [θ]). Yet Guitart very perceptively recognized that this description of the standard did not entirely capture Puerto Rican Spanish, due to a sociolinguistic trend that is even more pronounced today:

> Puerto Rico is perhaps the only linguistic community in the Hispanic world where the speech of educated speakers shows certain phonetic traits that are stigmatized by those speakers themselves.[13]

Two stigmatized phonetic traits to which Guitart refers, the pronunciation of *r* as *l* at the end of syllables and the velarization of *r* at the beginning of syllables, have gained in frequency and extension since Guitart's observations. That same year, Ana Celia Zentella noted how Germán de Granda, in his 1968 *Transculturación e interferencia lingüística en el Puerto Rico contemporáneo (1898–1968)*, warned about the "danger" posed by "the speech of a middle class that was formerly lower class becoming the standard."[14] A similar admonition came from the Institute of Puerto Rican Culture in 1973, through their edition of Samuel Gili Gaya's *Nuestra lengua materna*.[15] In the book's foreword, the renowned visiting scholar and linguist cautioned as follows:

> The most visible crack [in Puerto Rican Spanish] is that which can be observed in the semi-cultured environment of the urban population, open to foreign penetration . . .[16]

The openness of many Puerto Ricans to articulate vibrant consonants unconventionally or to adopt English vocabulary is perceived as a hole, a *grieta* that needs to be plugged, an unruly *raja* that breaches the linguistic defense. This penetration, apparently problematic because of its foreign origin, threatens to expose the traditional need for linguistic uniformity and containment as just one among many other fictions of the language.

Many visiting scholars were puzzled by practices in Puerto Rican Spanish that the available methodology could not explain. A decade later, however, Rubén del Rosario proposed different criteria for characterizing the standard-the oral practices of the community plus a trend toward simplification, which together give rise to new norms in Spanish-speaking countries. From the tradition of attempting to bridge the relationship between written and oral discourses, del Rosario defended the adoption of written "seseo" (the pronunciation of *c* and *z* as [*s*]), the deletion of the initial *h*, and the abolition of the written accent. He also advocated for the inclusion of *ch* and *ll* within the regular accommodation of the alphabet respectively under *c* and *l*, a long deferred transatlantic dream granted in 1994 by the Royal Academy of Spanish, and validated today by its implementation in the twenty-second edition of the *Diccionario de la lengua española*, published in October of 2001.[17]

The extent of del Rosario's proposition, however, transcends mere orthographic switch. Del Rosario's linguistic model, by privileging oral practices and simplification, generates a standard variety that does not merely permit, but rather, encourages speakers to turn to the most handy or precise word—or sound—as long as it contributes to the communicative exchange, no matter where the item or trait originated. Regarding vocabulary, this leads del Rosario to support the integration of generally used lexical anglicisms and expressions of popular urban lineage into cultured speech.[18] Colloquial constructions such as "Sería un cambio chévere" (It would be a cool change) and "un fracatán de variaciones" (a whole mess of variations) are frequently found in his academic work.

Concerning pronunciation, del Rosario's model manages to rescue one of the most stigmatized features of Puerto Rican speech: the velarization of the pre-nuclear *r* (*erre velar*), like in [xósa] in the word *rosa*, a variant often portrayed as one caused by "laziness" since it is less laborious in terms of articulation and air obstruction. This posteriorization of the vibrant generates the normatively undesired process commonly referred to as "dragging the *r*" (*arrastrar la erre*).[19] Despite his attempt to revalorize the velar *r* through the discourse of empirical linguistics, del Rosario found no allies in his efforts to raise the value assigned to this widely practiced phonetic departure.

Another stigmatized feature of Puerto Rican speech is the so-called confusion or equalization of liquid consonants when in syllable ending position, namely, the lateralization of the vibrant /r/, as in [amól] for *amor* (love), and the significantly less frequent rhotacism, as observed in [búrto] for *bulto* (package, bag).[20] Contrary to what is believed about most variants eschewed by the standard, this practice—also present in Dominican and Cuban varieties—[21] does not seem to be the result of economizing articulatory energy.[22] In commenting on Puerto Rican Spanish, Zamora-Munné and Guitart have proposed, as the genesis of this linguistic distinction, "the perceptual confusion introduced by the frequent appearance of a segment that sounds simultaneously lateral and vibrant"[23] an ambiguity provoked by the proliferation of a hybrid variant documented by Navarro Tomás in 1928: "Others, for their part, reduce the pronunciation of r and l to an intermediate sound that does not lend itself to classification under either of the two types."[24]

Because this phenomenon cannot be attributed to linguistic laziness, thus free of the strict moral judgment against being "lazy," lateralization enjoys a degree of immunity from the prescriptive effects of the standard, which might account for its prevalence in the speech of Puerto Rican speakers independent of conventional markers such as educational attainment, socioeconomic level, or the formality of the communicative exchange. Lateralization has resisted decades of reconditioning attempts in the schools, as well as the overwhelmingly negative attitude of Puerto Rican speakers themselves, undoubtedly reinforced by the many times they have had to listen politely to speakers of other varieties of Spanish who—not realizing the distinction between the beginning and the end of a syllable—tease by pronouncing "Puerto Rico" as "puelto lico." Yet daily practice with near impunity has shown speakers that when all share an utterance—even if officially rejected—the cost for noncompliance may not be so high after all.

But although Rubén del Rosario helped to legitimize urban popular words by acknowledging them within the norm, it is evident that, for him, the bus stopped at the city limits. He characterized rural speech as the product of isolation and lack of education and made no attempt to acknowledge rural variants other than the efficient "velar 'r.' " For del Rosario, like for Manuel Alonso in his 1849 book *El gíbaro*, rural speech may liven up the nation, but it also dampens its progress, road blocking the nation's route to modernity. This normative dichotomy between the urban and the rural is particularly evident in the unforgettable second-grade Spanish book *Del campo al pueblo* (From countryside to town), in which Rubén del Rosario is listed as one of the book's collaborators. For decades, the discourse of modernity arrived at Puerto Rican schools in the same vehicle as the acquisition of the linguistic norm, aboard the "marvelous adventures" of the little girl Rosa, her doll Finí, Lobo the dog, Mota the cat, and brother Pepín.[25]

The Cost of Laziness,[26] o *el vago trabaja doble*

A common observation on the features of unrefined speech is that speakers feel they can draw on them liberally when the context of a social exchange is more comfortable and relaxed. Casual speech, also characterized as "irreflective," "careless," and "informal," affords the vocal apparatus and its departments—air flow management, the phonation section, and the articulation division—a rest from the effort involved in suppressing spontaneous oral expression and adhering strictly to the valued varieties. Within formal settings, however, such a recess from strenuous work can be costly, even though it may not lessen communication in any way. In such refined circumstances, speakers of all varieties are instructed to bring forth only their most cultivated ways, much in the same manner we recur to our Sunday best when pressed to impress others.

In the case of Puerto Rico, since cultural authenticity depends so much upon speaking (good) (Puerto Rican) (Spanish), daily linguistic behavior is subjected to such constant scrutiny that "being Puerto Rican" ends up being a whole lot of work. Kept incessantly busy by the need to show (*enseñar*) their tongue as a sign of patriotism, it is remarkable that Puerto Ricans manage, finding the energy and time to actually say something. In this battle of the tongue where Puerto Rican cultural identity is constantly tested on the basis of standard Spanish competence, the menace is not foreign penetration; the enemy is already inside.

Simply by wanting to speak, Puerto Ricans must channel most of their will and energy into another one of what Yolanda Martínez-San Miguel has called "our daily plebiscites,"[27] at times a synonym for our daily self-boycott. The resulting exhaustion may account for the growing success of battle cries like "YO SOY BORICUA, PA' QUE TÚ LO SEPAS" (I am Puerto Rican, so you know it!), a loud shortcut in the long daily chore of being "100 percent Puerto Rican."

In his book *Divergent Modernities: Culture and Politics in Nineteenth-Century Latin America*,[28] Julio Ramos remarks on how national discourses depended on the assignment of moral values to such practices as work/leisure and written/oral to reinforce class divisions within the modernization projects of young Latin American nations. That modernizing spirit lives on in language representation through a whole mess of analogous dichotomies that are equally effective in guaranteeing the conditions necessary to keep the national projects rolling. Formal/colloquial, refined/vulgar, and norm/usage, as well as Spanish/Spanglish, and *boricua*/anything else exemplify the oppositional pairings used to characterize accepted and stigmatized concrete language practices.

If, in Rubén Ríos Ávila's words, "One thing is certain: Puerto Rico does not insert itself meekly into the series of hard binaries with which much of the debate of recent years is usually assembled,"[29] then the language of Puerto Ricans presents a compelling case for rethinking a few more abused duets, as are native/foreign, correct/incorrect, proper/improper, and from here/from there (*de aquí/de allá*). It is also an invitation to explore the provoking possibilities that await linguistic research by transcending the uncompromising monolingual framework. It would be most fitting that some inspiration to alter the values assigned to language use through a more open and inclusive variety configuration could be found precisely in the unpinnability of Puerto Rican Spanish.

Meanwhile, in the event of Puerto Rican language, anybody with hopes of being invited to show up somewhere in the national discourse (as something other than a bad example) must work very hard to show "boricuity" (Puertoricanness), for on the soundtrack of local language, he who does not sound authentic gets dubbed out of the recording.[30] But the problem goes beyond erasure: language institutions—induced by their high dependency on scientific validation—have found themselves juggling a discourse of diversity (sociolinguistics happened, after all), with the self-perpetuating need to keep national linguistic prestige under their grip.[31]

This apparent contradiction compels cultural entities to construct a national linguistic narrative in which all speakers are presumed to enjoy equal access to the standard linguistic form, a hard sell in the case of Puerto Rican Spanish, a linguistic variety whose normative definition excludes over half its speakers, as well as the non-Puerto Rican population of the islands. Daily practice proves that (good) (Puerto Rican) (Spanish) is not the only way to get through the *peaje* (toll booth) of cultural authenticity, yet language institutions keep posting signs to the contrary.[32] As it did in the nineteenth century, the "eloquent" minority continues to conduct the show while the efficient majority, expected to do all the work, is constantly being told that it cannot afford the price of the ticket.

"Cleans, Fixes, and Gives Splendor" or the Royal Academy of Spanish

It is difficult to conclude this discussion on the representation of the standard and the institutionalization of Puerto Rican Spanish without dedicating a few comments to the most official institution of them all: the Academies of the Spanish Language.[33] If one examined the list of members of the Academies of the Spanish Language throughout the world, one would be left with the impression that the institution is not an academy of the language, but an academy of the norm. Composed mostly of respected writers, linguists, lawyers, judges, and doctors, the Academies continue to reproduce the nineteenth-century structure of the Learned Republic, where the privileged members shared "the common authority of eloquence."[34]

Although Spanish language institutions will readily recognize that, during the journey from the nineteenth century to the present, relationships between varieties and users have evolved and multiplied as well as become more unconventional, such admission—which explains the fanfare with which many "Latin Americanisms" have been recently "admitted" into the canon—will give most speakers no satisfaction, because it leaves untouched the structure of linguistic prestige. In the case of the Academy of the Spanish Language, while the legitimacy of the inducted is backed by a fairly wide range of disciplines, it is also true that membership and resource allocation for institutionally-sponsored projects remain unrepresentative of the local communities, and deaf to the concretions of local linguistic routines.

While many disciplines have been studying the Dominican and Cuban migrations to Puerto Rico for years, a similar breadth of interest and projects needed to enlighten these debates on Puerto Rican practices from a linguistics framework has yet to emerge. Institutional enthusiasm is dedicated to validating cultured Spanish by portraying it as a variety worthy of being cleaned, pinned down, and polished. This "patriotic" act of discursive benevolence does nothing to transfigure the official bodies or to disturb the uniform dominant values that they replicate and defend. This is perhaps the royal or real tragedy of Puerto Rican Spanish: the official cultural denial of the possibility that the language utopia and other national contents may have shifted during flight.

This reading does not contemplate whether there should or should not be a norm or an Academy of the Language. Such a debate could lead to a deafness to linguistic diversity that would erase the traces of movement, hybridity, plurality, and friction all over again. That detour would ultimately be a distraction that sounds very close to just another daily plebiscite.[35]

Far from exploring the possibility or desirability of erasing or concealing speech differences, my argument considers how illuminating it would be to represent language contrasts and the infinite set of variations, varieties, and voices that they generate without feeling a need to claim authority over them. Assuming that a particular variety (in reality, its speakers) must be inherently authentic or superior stigmatizes linguistic creativity and leaves one to wonder about the undocumented sounds, words, and practices that linguists would have time to acknowledge if the discipline were not so busy rationalizing,[36] articulating, and enforcing national tongue control.

In 1989, Rubén del Rosario wrote, "*El uso le da la espalda a la Academia*"[37] (Usage turns its back on the Academy). Del Rosario's metaphor represents usage and the Academy as divorced from each other and going their separate ways, but there is another reading of his statement: "Usage gives the Academy its backbone." From del Rosario's words, translation draws out a second meaning to validate daily practices and legitimize all speakers by insisting on the specificity of local orality as one of the main factors in the constitution of the norms.

For too long now Puerto Ricans have had their hands full. One hand is "wrestling with *el difícil*"[38] (the difficult one, meaning the English language), understood to be a required skill to succeed in life. The Puerto Rican nickname for English, *el difícil*, refers not only to the language's trying learning process, but also to the history of its imposition and ideologically charged pedagogy. The other hand is kept busy polishing Spanish, in order to affirm Puerto Rican adherence to the Hispanic heritage. And Puerto Ricans have done these acts simultaneously for long enough to prove that the two skills are not mutually exclusive, and that neither by itself would be enough to account for the Puerto Rican language experience of today.

Another way to defend Puerto Rican Spanish is to make it a more inclusive variety, by teaching it and studying it in its linguistic and extralinguistic complexities. Also, by considering a standard in which the link between moral soundness, national authenticity, and competence in the Norm is examined, questioned, and discussed. If Puerto Ricans hear themselves in the formal variety of their dialect, they will be more willing to defend it, more enthusiastic about studying it and enjoying its literature, and less compelled to apologize for what they have been told is broken or defective, their *español "pateao"* ("sloppy" Spanish). As envisioned by del Rosario, in the case of Puerto Rican Spanish, the standard variety should comprise a combination of words and sounds in which those who feel Puerto Rican can find themselves.

Notes

For Yolanda Martínez-San Miguel, gracias. I would also like to thank Frances Negrón-Muntaner and Ismalia Gutiérrez-Gálang for the translation and editing of this chapter, as well as Ada Haiman for her comments.

1. Rubén Ríos Ávila, *La raza cómica: del sujeto en Puerto Rico* (San Juan: Ediciones Callejón, 2002). Original Spanish: "No es necesario (pero lo vamos a hacer, por supuesto) anunciar una vez más el nuevo clisé de moda: la Utopía ha muerto." Translation ours.
2. "A unit of cultural information, such as a cultural practice or idea, that is transmitted verbally or by repeated action from one mind to another." *The American Heritage® Dictionary of the English Language*, 4th ed. (Boston: Houghton Mifflin Company, 2000).
3. For further commentary, see Carlos Pabón, *Nación postmortem: ensayos sobre los tiempos de insoportable ambigüedad* (San Juan: Ediciones Callejón, 2002). For the complete script of the discussed PSA, please see <http://www.ciudadseva.com/otros/guioymin.htm.pdf>.
4. According to U.S. Census Bureau, Census 2000, of the 35.3 million Latinos who live in the 50 states of the United States, 9.6 percent identified as Puerto Rican. For purposes of the census, persons who indicate that they are "of Puerto Rican origin" could either have been born in Puerto Rico or be of Puerto Rican ancestry. See U.S. Dept. of Commerce, Economics and Statistics Administration, Bureau of the Census. <http://factfinder.census.gov/servlet/BasicFactsTable?_lang=es&_vt_name=DEC_2000_PL_U_GCTPL_ST6&_geo_id=04000US72> and <http://factfinder.census.gov/servlet/QTTable?_bm=y&geo_id=01000US&-qr_name=DEC_2000_SF1_U_QTP9&-ds_name=DEC_2000_SF1_U&-_lang=en&-redoLog=false&_sse=on>.
5. Tomás Navarro Tomás, *El español en Puerto Rico: contribución a la geografía dialectal hispanoamericana* (Río Piedras: Universidad de Puerto Rico, 1948). Although published in 1948, Navarro Tomás's atlas is based on field studies he conducted during the academic year of 1927–28 as a visiting professor at the University of Puerto Rico.

6. "A geographic boundary line delimiting the area in which a given linguistic feature occurs." *The American Heritage Dictionary of the English Language.*
7. In *Caribe Two Ways: cultura de la migración en el Caribe insular hispánico* Yolanda M. Martínez-San Miguel shows how the irrepressible migratory movement of the Caribbean population generates cultural representations that the traditional nationalist narratives of Latin America cannot contain. See Yolanda M. Martínez-San Miguel, *Caribe Two Ways: cultura de la migración en el Caribe insular hispánico* (San Juan: Ediciones Callejón, 2003). This chapter would not have been possible without having read her manuscript and without the generous and frequent conversations we shared.
8. For a study of the effect that speakers who come back to live in Puerto Rico have on the local level of bilingualism, see Amílcar Antonio Barreto, "Speaking English in Puerto Rico: The Impact of Affluence, Education and Return Migration," *Centro Journal* 12, no. 1 (Fall 2000): 5–17.
9. On the ideological and political factors, see Roamé Torres González, *Idioma, bilingüismo y nacionalidad: la presencia del inglés en Puerto Rico* (Río Piedras: Editorial de la Universidad de Puerto Rico, 2002).
10. Rubén Del Rosario, *La lengua de Puerto Rico* (Río Piedras: Editorial Cultural, 1975), 26.
11. From "Foundational f(r)ictions: apuntes sobre multilingüismos y roce de lenguas," a paper I presented at the 2002 "Interdisciplinary Symposium on Bilingualism y Biculturalism" organized by UPR professor Juan Gelpí of the College of Humanities. The paper engages in a dialogue with Doris Sommer's *Foundational Fictions: The National Romances Of Latin America*, and with her article "El contrapunteo latino entre el inglés y el español: notas para una nueva educación sentimental." See Doris Sommer, *Foundational Fictions: The National Romances of Latin America* (Berkeley: University of California Press, 1991); "El contrapunteo latino entre el inglés y el español: notas para una nueva educación sentimental," *Revista Iberoamericana* 66, no. 193 (October–December 2000): 863–76. I would like to thank Professor Sommer for her insightful feedback on that paper, as well as everyone who participated in the session's discussion.
12. I take this opportunity to express my gratitude to professor Guitart for faxing me his article as soon as we spoke and to professor Zamora-Munné for putting us in contact, and for his generous and always pertinent feedback.
13. Jorge M. Guitart, "The Pronunciation of Puerto Rican Spanish in the Mainland: Theoretical and Pedagogical Considerations" in *Teaching Spanish to the Hispanic Bilingual*, ed. Guadalupe Valdés, Anthony G. Lázaro, and Rodolfo García Moya (New York: Teachers College Press, 1981), 49.
14. Ana Celia Zentella, "Language Variety Among Puerto Ricans," in *Language in the USA*, ed. C.F. Ferguson and S.B. Heath (London: Cambridge University Press, 1981), 224. For an almost immediate critical response to de Granda's study, see Paulino Pérez Sala, *Interferencia lingüística del inglés en el español hablado en Puerto Rico* (San Juan: Inter American University Press, 1973). *Interferencia* is the 1973 publication of his doctoral thesis, directed by Rubén del Rosario.
15. See Samuel Gili Gaya, *Nuestra lengua materna* (San Juan: Instituto de Cultura Puertorriqueña, 1973). This text is the product of Gili Gaya's stints as visiting professor at the University of Puerto Rico during the academic years of 1929–30 and 1958–59.

16. Ibid., 7. Original Spanish: "La grieta más visible es la que se observa en el ambiente semiculto de la población urbana, abierto a la penetración extraña . . ." Translation ours.
17. In 1997, Gabriel García Márquez called for the simplification of orthography in "Botella al mar para el dios de las palabras," his opening speech at the First International Conference on the Spanish Language, held in Zacatecas, Mexico. See reprint at <http://cvc.cervantes.es/obref/congresos/zacatecas/inauguracion/garcia-masquez.htm>.
18. Professor Rafael Bernabe has recognized in this gesture much more than a stylistic choice, and has commented on how del Rosario not only defends, but validates, it with his practice. See Rafael Bernabe, " 'Un Puerto Rico distinto y futuro': lengua, nacionalidad y política en Rubén del Rosario," *Revista de Estudios Hispánicos* 1 (1997): 221–36.
19. For a recent discussion of velarization, see Hilton Alers-Valentín, "La r velar en Puerto Rico: a 50 años del atlas lingüístico de Tomás Navarro Tomás," *Revista Horizontes* 80 (1999): 189–210.
20. I have argued before that far from being two cotyledons of one phenomenon, lateralization (r > l) and rhotacism (l > r) are two independent processes that happen to be very similar in their surface representations. Certainly it would have been impossible for Navarro Tomás to ascertain this distinction; his theoretical framework conflated underlying laterals and vibrants into one category (liquids), thus missing the implications brought forth by the significant statistical differences in the behavior of these phonemes. See Gloria D. Prosper-Sánchez, "Neutralización homofonética de líquidas a final de sílaba: Aspectos sociolingüísticos en el español de Puerto Rico" (Ph.D. dissertation, University of Massachussetts, 1995).
21. See Orlando Alba, *Nuevos aspectos del español en Santo Domingo* (Santo Domingo: Librería La Trinitaria/Brigham Young University, 2000); J. Vitelio Ruiz Hernández and Eloína Miyares Bermúdez, *El consonantismo en Cuba* (La Habana: Editorial de Ciencias Sociales, 1984). In the latter, this phenomenon is characterized as "bartering" (*trueque*).
22. See Humberto López Morales, "El fenómeno de lateralización en las Antillas y en Canarias," in *II Simposio internacional de lengua española*, ed. Manuel Alvar (Madrid: Ediciones del Excelentísimo Cabildo insular de Gran Canaria, 1984).
23. Juan Clemente Zamora-Munné and Jorge M. Guitart, *Dialectología hispanoamericana*, 2nd ed. (Salamanca: Publicaciones del Colegio de España, 1988), 123.
24. Original Spanish: "Otros, por su parte, reducen la pronunciación de *r* y *l* a un sonido intermedio que no se deja clasificar bajo ninguno de ambos tipos" (Navarro Tomás, El Español en Puerto Rico, 76). Translation ours.
25. A few lines from the story "A Book of Marvels": "–Dad is going to buy a refrigerator. Why don't we tell him to buy one of these refrigerators?—said Rosa. Ring, ring, ring! sounds the telephone. Rosa ran to see who was calling and said:—Mom, come to the telephone. Dad is calling you. Bye, Dad. Many kisses. Later we want you to see the refrigerators from the book. . . . Pepín and Rosa looked at the televisions in the book. There were brown, yellow and silver televisions." Original Spanish: "Un libro de maravillas": "Papá va a comprar una nevera. ¿Por qué no le decimos que compre una de estas neveras?—dijo Rosa. ¡Lin, lin, lin! Se oye el teléfono. Rosa corrió a ver quién llamaba y

dijo:—Mamá, ven al teléfono. Te llama papá. Adiós, papá. Muchos besitos. Después queremos que veas las neveras del libro. . . . Pepín y Rosa vieron los televisores del libro. Había televisores de color marrón, amarillo y plateado." Carmen Gómez Tejera, Rosa Guzmán Vda. de Capó and Ángeles Pastor, *Del campo al pueblo* (River Forest, IL: Laidlaw Brothers Publishers, 1971), 104–5. Translation ours.

26. This section, "The Cost of Laziness," dialogues with the title of Arcadio Díaz-Quiñones's opening address, "The Price of the Ticket," for Rutgers University's symposium "None of the Above: Puerto Rican Politics and Culture in the New Millennium," where I read the first version of this chapter. The symposium, held on April 11–12 of 2001, was organized by Rutgers alumni Frances Negrón-Muntaner and sponsored by the Department of Puerto Rican and Hispanic Caribbean Studies and The Center for Latino Arts and Culture.
27. Yolanda M. Martínez-San Miguel, "Caribes boricuas/boricuas caribes: o nuestro otro plebiscito diario . . . ," *Diálogo* (November 2003): 18–19.
28. Julio Ramos, *Divergent Modernities: Culture and Politics in Nineteenth-Century Latin America*, trans. John D. Blanco (Durham, NC: Duke University Press, 2001).
29. Ríos Ávila, *La raza cómica*, 294. Original: "Una cosa es segura: Puerto Rico no se inserta dócilmente en la serie de binarismos duros con que se suele armar mucha de la discusión de los últimos años . . ." Translation ours.
30. For a discussion on the language statutes in Puerto Rico (1991, 1993) as a simulacrum of the struggle for political power in the colony, see Frances Negrón-Muntaner "English Only Jamás but Spanish Only Cuidado: Language and Nationalism in Contemporary Puerto Rico," in *Puerto Rican Jam: Rethinking Colonialism and Nationalism*, ed. Frances Negrón-Muntaner and Ramón Grosfoguel (Minneapolis: University of Minnesota Press, 1997).
31. For a discussion of these and other related issues, see José Del Valle and Luis Gabriel-Stheeman, eds., *The Battle over Spanish between 1800 and 2000. Language Ideologies and Hispanic Intellectuals* (London: Routledge, 2002).
32. As observed by Jorge Duany in "Cuestión de idioma," the primacy of language to national identity is called into question when 61.4 percent of the population in Puerto Rico claim to speak English, including 14.4 percent that speak English only. See Jorge Duany, "Cuestión de idioma," *El Nuevo Día*, December 10, 2003, 83.
33. Although not stressed so much these days, the motto of the Royal Academy of Spanish is still "Limpia, fija y da esplendor."
34. Julio Ramos, *Desencuentros de la modernidad en América Latina* (México: Fondo de Cultura Económica, 1989), 41.
35. On the inescapability of normativization, see Deborah Cameron, *Verbal Hygiene (Politics of Language)* (London: Routledge, 1995).
36. About rationalizing ideology, see Belford Moré, "La construcción ideológica de una base empírica: Selección y elaboración en la gramática de Bello," in *The Battle over Spanish between 1800 and 2000. Language Ideologies and Hispanic Intellectuals*, ed. José del Valle and Luis Gabriel-Stheeman (London: Routledge, 2002).
37. Rubén del Rosario, *La reforma del español* (San Juan: Centro Gráfico del Caribe, 1989), 6.
38. Ana Lydia Vega, "Pulseando con el difícil" in *Esperando a Loló y otros delirios generacionales.* (Río Piedras: Editorial de la Universidad de Puerto Rico, 1994).

CHAPTER 14

Boricua (Between) Borders: On the Possibility of Translating Bilingual Narratives

Yolanda Martínez-San Miguel

In what language do we remember?
Is it the language we use when
we speak with friends and family
in our everyday lives? Or does our
choice of a language of memory
involve a transposition, a
translation in the literal sense
of moving across: trasladar,
"de un lado a otro"?

Juan Flores, "Broken English Memories"[1]

Textos Ilegibles (Unreadable Texts)

Puerto Rican literature and culture earned its place within Latin American and Hispanic Caribbean Studies after a long, and sometimes heated, debate. This debate centered around the ambiguous nature of Puerto Rican claims to nationhood, based on a cultural discourse that has produced a strong definition of a national identity without having some of the basic and traditional elements of a sovereign status.[2] Given its close contact with the United States, Puerto Rican cultural practices were not, simply put, considered to be strictly "Latin American" or "Hispanic" by scholars of these disciplines.

While Puerto Rican Studies in the United States became for some critics synonymous with studies of migration, *boricua* diasporic culture and writing has had a very fragile relationship with Puerto Rican literature produced in the island. Examples of the frailty of these relationships are the contested reception of U.S. born writers such as Nicholasa Mohr and Esmeralda Santiago in Puerto Rico, the parodies of island-based writers Ana Lydia Vega and Magali García Ramis featuring Nuyorican characters, and the debate around Rosario Ferré's novels and essays in English.[3]

The study of Puerto Ricans as part of Latino Studies, a relatively young field when compared with Latin American and Caribbean Studies, poses yet another interesting problem—namely, how the Puerto Rican experience in the United States could be studied along Latino populations that cannot be considered internal migrations within a colonial network as Puerto Ricans are.[4] This state of affairs has led critics such as José Quiroga to propose "Latino American" as a new category of study, a more productive intersection between North and South in the Americas that will break the tradition of "the North always providing the theory for the South's cultural practice."[5]

One way to examine Puerto Rican literature's liminal location is by referring to Tato Laviera's book, *AmeRícan*.[6] Rooted in the diaspora, this book of poems questions a central motif in Latin American racial discourse—"miscegenation"—by creating a Caribbean subjectivity in transit, produced in New York City, which established a broad array of relationships with other immigrant groups living in "El Barrio." The text begins with a section entitled "Ethnic Tributes," and it includes graphic and discursive representations of a wide variety of ethnic groups—such as *Boricuas*, Arabs, Blacks, Chinese, Cubans, English, Greeks, Irish, Italians, Jamaicans, Japanese, Jewish, Russians, and Spanish—challenging traditional links between nationality and territory by proposing a complex set of interactions among different ethnic groups living in the United States.

The second section, entitled "Values," includes key cultural and linguistic Puerto Rican categories such as coffee, sports and race; the use of the phrase "ay bendito;" and the definition of a "jíbaro," seen by many as the quintessential symbol of Puerto Ricanness. The text invokes these categories to transform them in yet another element of a Latino and Rícan discourse that is, however, produced from another location, beyond the culture and language of the island, and without the nostalgic desire of coming back to recover an originary Puerto Rican identity.

The final section of the book, entitled "Politics," is an attempt to unify a Puerto Rican past in the island with a present that needs to incorporate the diaspora as a dynamic element of contemporary Puerto Ricanness. The book ends by proposing a hybrid and transnational identity synthesized in two words that are used as titles of two poems: "Commonwealth" and "AmeRícan." The first title refers to the political status of the island, and uses this ambiguous and debated concept to propose an identity that lives in between various limits: "i'm still in the commonwealth / stage of my life, observing / the many integrated experiences / we took everything / and became everybody else."[7]

The second term, "AmeRícan," uses linguistic hybridization by fusing and confusing the word used to refer to U.S. natives, "American," with the word used to call Puerto Ricans living in the United States, "Rícan." This reading depends heavily on Laviera's performance, because he employs an intermediate pronunciation—typographically signaled by his interesting use of capitalization and a grammatical accent—that mixes Spanish and English, producing a neologism that sounds very similar to the phrase "I'm a Rican," and also looks like a reconfiguration of the phrase "a Rícan me" following Spanish grammar: "a me Rícan" (un yo Rícan). This interlingual noun allows him to create a new national or ethnic name (in Spanish, *gentilicio*) that simultaneously acknowledges his belonging to both Puerto Rican and American societies. As a result, "AmeRícans" are proposed as a new identity produced and defined in a context of continuous transit and transition: "AmeRícan, across forth and across back / back across and forth back / forth across and back and forth / our trips are walking bridges!"[8]

I would also like to comment the poem—"Ay bendito"—included in the second section of this book as an example of a text that even resists the bilingualism and translatability of most of the pieces included in the rest of the compilation. This is a text that explores the limits of signification of any language, as the narrative proposed in the poem is constructed by a series of fragmented expressions well known in the Puerto Rican colloquial dialect, but that are literally impossible to translate into standard English:

> oh, oh, ¡ay virgen!
> fijese, oiga, fijese.
> ay bendito.
> pero, ¿qué se puede hacer?
> nada, ¿verdad?
> ave maría.
> ah, si, ah, sí, es así.
> pues, oiga,
> si es la verdad.
> pero, ¿qué se puede hacer?
> nada, ¿verdad?
> fijese, oiga, fijese.
> mire, mire.
> oh, sí, ¡hombre!
> oiga, así somos
> tan buenos, ¿verdad?
> bendito.
> ¡ay madre!
> ¡ay, Dios mío!
> ¡ay, Dios santo!
> ¡me da una pena!
> ay, si la vida es así, oiga.
> pero ¿qué se puede hacer?
> nada, ¿verdad?
> fijese, oiga, fijese.
> oiga, fijese.[9]

"Ay bendito" is composed of "interjecciones" or verbal expressions that are used in moments of intense or sudden emotion. Interjections are basic grammatical elements that convey a verbal message that is almost irrational or instinctive; they could be metaphorically conceived as emotional onomatopoeias. Translating this text, then, will go beyond finding the literal meaning of each word to identify and convey very specific cultural contents for each term. For example, the title of the poem is a short phrase—"Ay bendito"—that would require a contextual explanation of how these two words incorporate a religious background into a social meaning that is very specific for Puerto Rican speakers.

Therefore, it is surprising that Laviera is able to construct a narrative or a poetic text that expresses a "feeling" or message closely linked to an acute sense of a subaltern—yet unique—identity among Puerto Ricans. The lyrical voice of this text expresses Puerto Rican resignation to the constant difficulties faced in everyday life. The use of interjections, however, links language to a very idiosyncratic use of verbal communication, while at the same time points out the ethnic appropriation of Spanish by a Puerto Rican community. In the context of the collection of poems—*AmeRícan*—this poem is included in the section entitled "Values," which plays with the representation, translation, and re-signification of the core of Puerto Ricanness from the island to produce an identity that is portable, and functions as a dynamic element in contemporary cultural manifestations among "Nuyorícans," Diaspo-Ricans, or Puerto Ricans living in the United States.[10]

Taking into consideration how early on Laviera explores the limits of a transnational and globalized identity, I would like to use this text as a point of departure to think about the "problematic" place of a Diaspo-Rícan literature and to analyze the difficulties of reading some of these texts based on notions of disciplinary and linguistic purity, particularly academic contexts organized around a single language as a defining paradigm of ethnic and national identities.[11] I would like to think about the problems posed by a set of texts that question the foundational place assigned to language in literary studies and in other disciplines such as Ethnic, Latino/a, and American Studies, translation departments, and in the cultural components within Migration Studies programs.

In many cases, there is an implicit criticism of a hesitating or unstable language as a main characteristic of Latino/a literature that is used as a pretext not to study the intrinsic multilingual nature of many of these cultural productions. The untranslatability of some of these texts is also problematical, since it suggests that there are limits to the globalized exchanges within a multicultural society, and that there are significant areas within contemporary American cultures in the United States that cannot be easily rendered in English. Furthermore, many of these Latino cultural productions make us realize that linguistic hesitation or untranslatability cannot be understood as incompetence or lack of control over communicative skills, but quite to the contrary, as a discursive strategy that forces us as readers to reconsider our basic notions about the relationship of language and cultural identity.[12] What is at stake in this disciplinary debate is also the urgency of reconfiguring the field of cultural and literary studies, to make multiculturalism mean a new way of reading, interpreting, and understanding cultural difference.

I would also like to propose that Laviera's text is an excellent example of an "unreadable" literature. "Unreadability" is a common notion used to refer to Latino/a writing in a wide range of situations.[13] As a professor of Latin American literature, I have quite often experienced how the inclusion of Latino/a texts in courses is questioned based on disciplinary arguments—"can we consider Latino/a writings as a part of Latin American literature?"—or linguistic and pedagogical concerns—"in which language are you going to read/teach the text? are you using the 'original' version or a translation?" or "what are you going to do with all the spelling mistakes and/or the grammatical errors included in some of these texts?"

These concerns frequently raise an even more difficult question, and that is the lack of recognition of Puerto Rican and Latino/a writing and culture as a legitimate topic to be studied within U.S. college curricula.[14] One of the main problems posed by these texts is their intrinsic bilingualism and biculturalism, because in many cases this contact or convergence of languages implies a process of continuous and reciprocal translation that goes against the basic definition of a Hispanic or American national literature. Thus, I would like to propose a critical analysis of the trope of translation, and the relationship between original and translated versions of some of these works.

Textos intraducibles (Unstranslatable Texts)

The fascination of translation, as Roman Jakobson suggested, is that it poses the central question of "equivalence in difference."[15] Sherry Simon has further noted that "[t]ranslation is not only an operation of linguistic transfer, but also a process which generates new textual forms, which creates new forms of knowledge, which introduces new cultural paradigms."[16] The question I explore here is, then, what happens when a bicultural/bilingual text becomes untranslatable?

Puerto Rican and Latino writing are excellent cases to revisit traditional definitions of translation and the relationship between an original language and a secondary language in Latino/American discourses. The text itself, for instance, can be seen as a bilingual narrative, and as such there is an exercise of constant translation that is fundamental to understanding its multiple levels of meaning. It could be said, then, that many Latino texts propose a place of linguistic articulation that could be located "beyond translation," as the consistent interdependency of languages make some of these texts nearly untranslatable. If a text depends on the bilingualism of its audience, what happens when the rendition in one language literally eliminates the interlinguistic structure of a text? It seems, then, that what Bruce-Novoa describes as "interlingual writing" in Latino texts requires a new conceptualization of diglosia, bilingualism, and translation:

> These are pieces written in a blend of Spanish and English. They are not bilingual in that, in the best examples, they do not attempt to maintain two language codes separate, but exploit and create the potential junctures of interconnection. This results in a different code, one in which neither monolingual codes can stand alone and relate the same meaning. Translation becomes impossible, and purists from either language deny its viability. Monolinguals, from either side of the border, often react as if they were being personally insulted.[17]

In some of these texts the interaction of Spanish and English can be superficial—such as in the cases in which the author uses vocabulary from both languages—or it can be the basis of the internal semantic and grammatical structure—such as Sandra Cisneros's use of the diminutive in English to express affection in the same way it is done in Spanish, or the "calques" (literal translations of Spanish idioms and colloquial phrases) in the works of Víctor Hernández Cruz studied by Frances R. Aparicio. An example of these "calques" are the literal translation of Spanish names, like when Hernández Cruz refers to his hometown Aguas Buenas as "Good Water," or when a popular saying is literally translated into English: "What doesn't kill you gets you fat"[18] (lo que no mata engorda). Juan Flores and George Yúdice also study the formation of a "border vernacular" that is attained by "the crossing of entire language repertoires,"[19] as for example when Louis Reyes Rivera uses "sonrisa" and "sunrise" to create a new interlingual vocabulary in his poem "Problems in Translation."

Another relevant case is Esmeralda Santiago's *When I Was Puerto Rican/Cuando era puertorriqueña*, a text written and published, almost simultaneously, in Spanish and English. According to linguist Gloria D. Prosper-Sánchez, who studied both versions of the novel to compare the texts in lexical, phonological, and morphosyntactic terms, Santiago has native competence in academic English and colloquial Spanish. As a result, in the English version, the narration is rendered in formal English, while the dialogues are translations from colloquial Spanish. In the Spanish version, the narration is a translation from the English text, and the dialogues represent Santiago's native command of colloquial Spanish.[20] Therefore, in this case, both texts are an original version and a translation of a primary autobiographical narrative. Texts like Santiago's could also be a paradigmatic example of those "other ways of knowing" that take place between languages and that critic Walter Mignolo has described as "bilanguaging."[21]

The use of internal—and imperfect—translations in "El cuento de la mujer del mar" (The Story of the Woman of the Sea) by Manuel Ramos Otero represents yet a different type of phenomena. This text narrates the final crisis of a love relationship between two immigrant men who create a story of a woman of the sea who is constantly traveling between different cities. Angelo, an Italian American, and his Puerto Rican lover invent two parallel characters—Vicenza Vitale and Palmira Parés—and each narrator adds a chapter to the life of this imaginary women using their family histories and their personal experiences and cultural referents. The story of the woman of the sea—narrated in Spanish, English, and Italian by this couple living in New York City—becomes a pretext to postpone the ending of their dying love relationship.

Due to the different cultural backgrounds of the main characters, internal translation becomes a predominant gesture of this narrative, and fiction becomes the *lingua franca* that keeps both narrative voices sharing a communicative space within the text. The narrator uses two strategies of translation in this story, which I would like to analyze here. The first one is to present imagination as a space of encounter and coincidence for the narrator and his lover in a terrain where they can continue communicating even though their relationship is in a moment of crisis. As the Puerto Rican narrator declares,

> Contra la noche y el fuego de la yerba, contra la noche y la ventana abierta de nuestro cuarto en el Hotel Christopher, siempre uno llegando al otro como un amante que llega de repente de una tierra remota, y entre vino y amor comenzaba a contar misteriosamente de una mujer y del mar. . . . Amándonos en la zona de un inglés callejero.[22]
>
> [Against the night and fire of the grass, against the night and open window of our room in Christopher Hotel, always one arriving on the other as a lover who suddenly appears from a remote land, between wine and love I/he* began to mysteriously tell the story of a woman and the sea. . . . Loving each other within the realm of our English from the streets.] (*The Spanish version is ambiguous here in terms of the subject of this phrase.)

Storytelling keeps Angelo and the narrator together throughout the story. It becomes the dialogic space that calls on them to come together, even though their love is gradually fading.

Fantasy and imagination are like a space for a truce, as in the classical story of *One Thousand and One Nights*, the (pre)text that postpones their final separation, produced either by death or the end of love, or by their disintegration as a couple of two migrant men who become exiled "en el amor como en las ciudades"[23] (in love as in cities). Fiction is their only connection, and that is why the narrator insists on saying that "entre nosotros se alarga como un puente invisible la Mujer del Mar"[24] (between us the Woman of the Sea extends herself as an invisible bridge).

The second strategy is the constant translation and transfer of the story of the woman of the sea between narrative voices. This process of transposition sometimes results in the fusion of Palmira Parés and Vicenza Vitale in one single character that leads the life of both narrators:

> Uno es tanta gente a la misma vez. Yo sólo puedo contar el cuento de la Mujer del Mar (la historia nunca antes contada de la poeta manatieña Palmira Parés) y Angelo sólo pudo contar "**the story of the woman of the sea**" (tanto escuchó

> la historia de Vicenza Vitale . . . : la viajera había iniciado el viaje en un puerto de Napoli, detrás de un pasaje del Vesubio, venía de los parrales de Giocavaran llena de polvo, inmóvil en la popa de un velero—"**immobile . . . on the orange aft of a vaporous vessel**," contaba el amado inmóvil, atardeciendo—había atracado en Casablanca y en las Islas Azores había zarpado camino del mar a las Antillas; con otros campesinos del agua salada, en el agosto caluroso de 1913 llegó a San Juan). El orden de sus vidas iba diluyéndose en las palabras memoriosas de los cuentos.[25]
>
> [One can be so many people at the same time. I can only tell you the story of the Woman of the Sea (the story never told before of the poet from Manatí, Palmira Parés) and Angelo could only narrate "**the story of the woman of the sea**" (he heard Vicenza Vitale's story so many times [. . .]: the traveler began her journey in a port in Naples, behind a passage of the Vesuvius, she came from the vineyards of Giocavaran, covered with dust, immobile on the aft of a sailboat—"**immobile . . . on the orange aft of a vaporous vessel**," the immobile lover narrated, as the sun was going down—the vessel docked in Casa Blanca and the Islas Azores, it had departed in route to the Antilles's sea; with other sea water peasants she arrived to San Juan, on the hot August of 1913. The order of their lives was diluting in the memorious words of the stories.]

Ramos Otero includes different languages in his narrative without marking or separating them. In these quotes from Ramos Otero's short story I am adding emphasis to distinguish the original languages of the text (English is in **bold**, Italian will be identified in *italics*, and Spanish as the predominant language is represented in regular typeface). In the story, the narrator translates, rather freely, Angelo's phrases in English. It is noticeable that there is not a desire to achieve an "exact" transfer of ideas; instead, an approximate exchange of narratives is proposed.

This "imperfect translation" happens again in other parts of the story:

> " '**my father was born in Providence, in an old house inhabited by witches, purified by fire, and the aged memories of a remote Italy, full of dust** . . .' (una casona habitada por brujas purificadas en la hoguera y los recuerdos añosos de una Italia . . . de la que sólo quedaba la imborrable virilidad de las mujeres y el mudo secreto de los hombres)" [" '**my father was born in Providence, in an old house inhabited by witches, purified by fire, and the aged memories of a remote Italy, full of dust** . . .' (an old house inhabited by witches purified by fire, and the aged memories of a remote Italy . . . from which the only remains were the indelible virility of women and the mute secret of men)].[26]

The process of translation is not exact, but not because it is imprecise, rather because the narrator chooses different selections of both narratives that coincide only partially. The Spanish version translates some of what Angelo has just said in English, but it includes more of what has already been quoted from his story of Vicenza Vitale. In this text the translation from one language to another is consciously inaccurate, as if to suggest that meanings can be partially exchangeable, or as if the narrative voice carelessly chose portions of each of the two versions, producing a single story composed of the interlocking pieces of the narrations in different languages.

In this sense, both versions of this story are simultaneously original texts and translations of the final story of the woman of the sea. This gesture of free and imprecise transferences reminds us of the way in which Walter Benjamin describes the task of the translator:

> Even when all the surface content has been extracted and transmitted, the primary concern of the genuine translator remains elusive. Unlike the words of the original, it is not translatable, because the relationship between content and language is quite different in the original and the translation. While content and language form a certain unity in the original, like a fruit and its skin, the language of the translation envelops its contents like a royal robe with ample folds.[27]

On other occasions each lover uses his own cultural referents to reconstruct the story produced by the other narrator, to translate the story from the narrator's discourse to the listener's imaginary:

> "Él me hablaba todavía de aquella Vicenza Vitale . . . y yo sólo veía puertos grises y mares solitarios, él hablaba de esas arrugas profundas (*'solcari profondo . . .'*) como si fueran surcos de una Italia remota quel exilio había convertido en callejones, y yo sólo veía un cementerio de islas, las tumbas verdes de Atlántida" [He would speak to me about that Vicenza Vitale . . . and I only saw gray ports and lonely seas, he spoke about those deep wrinkles (*'deep furrows . . .'*) as if these were furrows of a remote Italy that exile had transformed in alleys, and I only saw a cemetery of islands, the green tombs of Atlantis].[28]

In this case, the reader witnesses a translation that parallels an interpretative process that makes possible or impossible the communication between these two storytellers and lovers. By incorporating each narrator's referents, the rendition of the story from one language to another also implies the transference and exchange of cultural imaginaries, so, as Joseph Pivato suggests about the process of translation, "[t]he same events are recalled in a different language and each time are changed."[29]

Thus, fiction becomes an alternative "native tongue" that allows a communication that is not based on the commonality of referents that characterizes those who speak the same tongue and/or dialect, but that instead is based in a process of constant interpretation and acknowledgment of diverging cultural referents. Imagination provides a space in which translation becomes a "site for dialogue,"[30] instead of pretending to be a transparent mode of transmission of ideas between speakers. This new "mother tongue" is not a regional or specific code, but a broad and mutating discourse, as polysemic and boundless as that sea crossed by Palmira/Vicenza to complete their endless travels. Fiction forges a fragile community of emotions and imaginaries that transcend conventional or unique interpretations, so in this creative realm it is possible to promote a deeper and more intimate communication than the one that usually takes place between the speakers of the same national language. In this case, sharing imaginaries seems to be a stronger bond than the one supplied by a common language.

De Boricua a Latino: Reconfiguring Latino/American Studies

I would like to conclude by returning to one of the first concerns posed in this chapter by raising the following question: In which kinds of academic contexts do these Rícan and Latino texts become "readable"? If, as Mignolo points out, "changing linguistic cartographies implies a reordering of epistemology,"[31] what kind of productive relationship can Latino/a literature establish with Departments or Programs of English, Spanish, Comparative Literature, Translation, Linguistics, American, Ethnic, Latin American, and Migration Studies?

One of the most interesting features of this corpus of texts is its resistance to be read, as a consequence of the difficulty posed by the multilingual nature of many of their referents. As Julio Ramos points out, Latino intellectuals and critics redefine the traditional limits of Latin American Studies as a discipline by destabilizing notions such as linguistic purity, or the fixed and univocal relationship with a place of origin or a native tongue.[32] Thus, Rican and Latino/a writing problematizes one of the key coordinates in the definition of a national and ethnic identity by proposing a variable and mutable relationship between the subject and his/her native tongue.[33] By destabilizing the connection between a mother tongue and a national or cultural identity, these texts question the epistemological paradigms of many of the language and literature departments, as well as some of the limits separating disciplines or programs, such as English, American Studies and Latin American Studies, among others.[34]

By the same token, due to the interstitial nature of its production, Latino/a literature questions the geopolitical limits and the imaginary cartographies of what is currently defined as Latin American literature. Thus, it is no surprise that *The Cambridge History of Latin American Literature* ends with two sections devoted to Latino Literature: "Chicano Literature" and "Latin American (Hispanic Caribbean) Literature Written in the United States."[35] Ana Pizarro also includes Chicano literature in her anthology *América Latina: Palavra, Literatura e Cultura. Volume 3: Vanguarda e Modernidade.*[36] Even though Rícan and Chicano literatures and cultures are still the two foundational traditions in the configuration of contemporary Latino Studies, it has become increasingly evident that there is a U.S. pan-Latino culture and discourse that makes possible a common set of questions that I would like to explore in the final section of this chapter. For example, it can be said that the limits of Latin American Studies have been actively reconceived as a result of the dialogues currently established between Latin American and Latino/a literatures and cultures. Furthermore, Latino bilingualism has also functioned as a provocative counterpoint to rethink Latin American cultural traditions by studying linguistic contacts as a crucial element in many canonical texts, such as the *Comentarios reales, Los ríos profundos* or Rigoberta Menchú's testimony, not to mention the debates on bilingual education in México, Paraguay, and Perú. At the same time, Latino

Studies has reconfigured some of the most recent definitions of Caribbean and Puerto Rican Studies by making possible new questions on the significance of location, displacement, and multiculturalism that redefine the limits of cultural practices and traditions.

On the other hand, as a result of the internal bilingualism and the constant work with internal and external translations, Latino texts also explore some of the problems posed by translation as a discipline. For example, many of these works incorporate more than one language, or are published in both monolingual versions of English and Spanish. In some cases the same authors do the translations of their work (Esmeralda Santiago and Rosario Ferré, for example).[37] In these cases the difference between the original and the translation becomes problematic, because in some of the monolingual versions there are sections that are translated from another language while others function as a narrative with native competence. The existence of multiple works that are all original versions, or the emergence of texts that are partly original versions and partly translations, could pose an interesting set of questions in translation and comparative literature departments or programs, since many of them legitimate their field of study by stressing their usage and analysis of the "original" versions of many literary texts. What happens when we have more than one original version of the same narrative, and when each version proposes a different set of meanings depending on the language in which they are rendered or even remembered?

Moreover, Latino/a literature poses a question that can be crucial in the revitalization of the relationship existing between literature and linguistic departments. By questioning the privilege given to linguistic purity and the use of a standard language, Latino/a literature brings forward a whole new set of studies on the usage of popular language,[38] as well as on the incorporation of orality and colloquial variants of both Spanish and English, so linguistic readings become crucial to study and interpret many of these ethnic narratives. Linguistic competence, code-switching, and linguistic registers all become productive areas of study to unravel the complexity of these texts.

Latino/a literature also reassesses the relationship between sociological studies of migrant populations and the study of their cultural productions. More than refurbishing the traditional readings of literature from a sociological perspective, these writings make evident the need to reconceptualize the way we define the limits between fields of study. Interdisciplinarity or multidisciplinarity is not only crucial when addressing ethnic cultures,[39] but in this case it seems that one thing Latino/a literature points out is the importance of disciplinary "contact zones"—to remember here Mary Louise Pratt's illuminating concept—as a condition of possibility for new questions.[40] For example, Saldívar uses Chicano Studies to consider "the effects of shifting critical paradigms in American Studies away from linear narratives of immigration, assimilation, and nationhood."[41] Sommer also proposes that a "bilingual aesthetic" can broaden the areas of research of a variety of intellectual fields.[42]

Finally, Frank Bonilla explores the productive "interdependence" between Latino/a and Latin American Studies by rethinking the usefulness of interdisciplinary approaches.[43] I would like to suggest that the comments I am including in this last section are all a result of the questions that arise when we explore new readings that are made possible by the disciplinary contacts promoted by Latino/a writing, due to its marginalized position within the American and Latin American curricula. I am not questioning the need for Latino/a studies as a separate field of study, because it is clear there are both institutional and academic needs for these kinds of programs.[44] More than opposing the goals and objectives of each one of these disciplines to define a specific object of study[45] or trying to find a home department or program to study Latino/a culture in all its complexity, I am proposing that one way to take advantage of the "floating" nature of this cultural production is by exploring the new questions that these texts propose, especially those related to the variable and dynamic relationship existing between language and subjectivity.

The incorporation of Latino/a literatures into a broad range of courses and programs can become an opportunity to promote interdisciplinary dialogues as a crucial element in the reconfiguration of academic institutions and disciplines from within. Perhaps, by looking at the disciplinary, linguistic, and cultural contacts, and sometimes the oppositions that these writings make possible, we could begin to explore the multiple translatability that Latino/a literature promotes and calls for within American and Latin American universities. Beyond the academic world, Latino cultural productions—along with other ethnic and minority discourses present in many U.S. creolization and melting pots—push the limits of the working notion of a multicultural and globalized identity. In this context, unreadability and untranslatability become, more than a source of isolation or anxiety, an invitation to share real and fictional imaginaries as a point of departure to explore "equivalence in difference."[46]

Notes

I would like to thank Ben. Sifuentes-Jáuregui for providing insightful comments and suggestions on a previous version of this article.

1. Juan Flores, "Broken English Memories: Languages in the Trans-colony," in *From Bomba to Hip-Hop: Puerto Rican Culture and Latino Identity* (New York: Columbia University Press, 2000), 56.
2. Ramón Grosfoguel, Frances Negrón-Muntaner, and Chloé S. Georas, "Introduction: Beyond Nationalist and Colonianist Discourses: The *Jaiba* Politics of the Puerto Rican Ethno-Nation," in *Puerto Rican Jam: Rethinking Colonialism and Nationalism*, ed. Frances Negrón-Muntaner and Ramón Grosfoguel (Minneapolis: University of Minnesota Press, 1997), 10–19; Jorge Duany, *The Puerto Rican Nation on the Move. Identities on the Island and in the United States* (Chapel Hill: University of North Carolina Press, 2002), 15–18.
3. For more information, please see the debate between Nicholasa Mohr and Ana Lydia Vega about her short story "Pollito chicken" (in *Vírgenes y mártires* (*cuentos*), [Río Piedras: Editorial Antillana, 1983], 73–79) included in Mohr's

essay entitled "Puerto Rican Writers in the United States, Puerto Rican Writers in Puerto Rico: A Separation Beyond Language" (*The Americas Review* 15, no. 2 [Summer 1987]: 87–92); and the discussions on bilingualism and Puerto Rican literature in the case of Esmeralda Santiago (Gloria D. Prosper-Sánchez, "Washing Away the Stain of the Plantain: Esmeralda Santiago y la constitución del relato autobiográfico bilingüe," in *Actas del "Congreso en torno a la cuestión del género y la expresión femenina actual."* [Aguadilla: Universidad de Puerto Rico, 1998], 131–138) and Rosario Ferré ("On Destiny, Language, and Translation, or, Ophelia Adrift in the C. & O. Canal," in *Voice-Overs. Translation and Latin American Literature*, ed. Daniel Balderston and Marcy E. Schwartz [Albany, NY: SUNY Press, 2002], 32–41). Magali García Ramis also published a controversial text on the motives for Puerto Rican migration, entitled "Los cerebros que se van, los corazones que se quedan" (in *La ciudad que me habita* [Río Piedras: Editorial Huracán, 1993] 9–19). This same uneasy dialogue between Puerto Rican literature and culture produced in the island and the U.S. was the central topic in the Second Annual Conference of the Puerto Rican Studies Association held in San Juan Puerto Rico in September of 1996.

4. Ramón Grosfoguel, "The Divorce of Nationalist Discourses from the Puerto Rican People: A Sociohistorical Perspective," in *Puerto Rican Jam: Rethinking Colonialism and Nationalism*, 66–70.
5. José Quiroga, *Tropics of Desire: Interventions from Queer Latino America* (New York: New York University Press, 2000), 8. Frances Aparicio has also noted Diana Taylor's coinage of the term "Latin(o) America" in her book *Negotiating Performance* (1994) to integrate Latin American and U.S. Latino cultural spaces and practices (Frances R. Aparicio, "Latino Cultural Studies," in *Critical Latin American and Latino Studies*, ed. Juan Poblete [Minneapolis: University of Minnesota Press, 2003], 3–31).
6. Tato Laviera, *AmeRícan* (Houston: Arte Público Press, 1981).
7. Ibid., 80.
8. Ibid., 94.
9. Ibid., 45.
10. Jorge Duany has noted that, "scholars cannot even agree on a common terminology to refer to Puerto Ricans in the United States. The papers for the 1996 Puerto Rican Studies Association Conference in San Juan suggested the following alternatives: Neo-Rican, Nuyorican, Niuyorrican, *nuyorriqueño*, mainland Puerto Rican, U.S.-born Puerto Rican, Boricua, Diaspo-Rican, and even Tato Laviera's curious neologism *AmeRícan*—but never that hyphenated mixture, Puerto Rican-American" (*The Puerto Rican Nation on the Move: Identities on the Island and in the United States* [Chapel Hill: University of North Carolina Press, 2002], 28).
11. See Walter Mignolo, "Bilanguaging Love: Thinking in Between Languages," in *Local Histories/Global Designs: Coloniality, Subaltern Knowledges and Border Thinking* (Princeton, NJ: Princeton University Press, 2000), 222; Doris Sommer, "El contrapunteo latino entre el inglés y el español: notas para una nueva educación sentimental," *Revista Iberoamericana* 66, no. 193 (October–December 2000): 866; Julio Ramos, "Genealogías de la moral latinoamericanista," in *Nuevas perspectivas desde/sobre América Latina: el desafío de los estudios culturales*, ed. Mabel Moraña (Pittsburgh, PA: Instituto International de Literatura Iberoamericana, 2002), 224.

12. This is one of the main arguments to devalue bilingual speakers who use code-switching during spontaneous speech. This view of alternation of linguistic codes as a deviation that "indicated a speaker's inability to separate the two languages at her or his disposal" is now recognized as a "functional linguistic behavior which demonstrates the speaker's ability to manipulate the grammar and lexicon of two languages at the same time" (Holly Cashman, "Language Choice in U.S. Latina First Person Narrative: The Effects of Language Standardization and Subordination," *Discourse* 21, no. 3 [Fall 1999]: 132–50). This same view is presented by Lipski in his essay entitled "Spanish-English Language Switching and Literature: Theories and Models," *The Bilingual Review/La revista bilingüe* 9, no. 3 (September-December 1982): 191–212, and in Ana Celia Zentella's foundational book, *Growing up Bilingual: Puerto Rican Children in New York* (Malden, MA: Blackwell, 1997).
13. I use "unreadable" here as the "unintelligible," in the sense proposed by Butler in *Gender Trouble*: "To what extent do *regulatory practices* of gender formation and division constitute identity, the internal coherence of the subject, indeed, the self-identical status of the person? To what extent is 'identity' a normative ideal rather than a descriptive feature of experience? And how do the regulatory practices that govern gender also govern culturally intelligible notions of identity? In other words, the 'coherence' and 'continuity' of 'the person' are not logical or analytic features of personhood, but, rather, socially instituted and maintained norms of intelligibility" (Judith Butler, *Gender Trouble: Feminism and the Subversion of Identity* [New York: Routledge, 1990], 16–17). I propose extending Butler's reflection on gender to the ways in which ethnic identity is constructed within American and Latin American interpretations of Latino cultures.
14. See Frances R. Aparicio, "Reading the 'Latino' in Latino Studies: Toward Re-Imagining Our Academic Location," *Discourse* 21, no. 3 (Fall 1999): 5, 15; Nina Scott, "The Politics of Language: Latina Writers in United States Literature and Curricula," *Melus* 19, no. 1 (Spring 1994): 57; Margaret Villanueva, "Ambivalent Sisterhood: Latina Feminism and Women's Studies," *Discourse* 21, no. 3 (Fall 1999): 49; Marcus Embry, "The Shadow of Latinidad in U.S. Literature," *Discourse* 21, no. 3 (Fall 1999): 78; Frances R. Aparicio and Susana Chávez-Silverman, "Introduction," in *Tropicalizations: Transcultural Representations of Latinidad*, ed. Frances Aparicio and Susana Chávez-Silverman (Hanover, NH: Dartmouth College, 1997), 14; Pedro Cabán, "The New Synthesis of Latin American and Latino Studies," in *Borderless Borders. U. S. Latinos, Latin Americans, and the Paradox of Interdependence*, ed. Frank Bonilla et al. (Philadelphia: Temple University Press, 1998), 203; Suzanne Oboler, "Anecdotes of Citizen's Dishonor in the Age of Cultural Racism: Toward a (Trans)national Approach to Latino Studies," *Discourse* 21, no. 3 (Fall 1999): 25.
15. Roman Jakobson, quoted in Sherry Simon, "Rites of Passage: Translation and its Intents," *The Massachusetts Review* 31, no. 1–2 (Spring–Summer 1990): 97.
16. Ibid., 96–97.
17. Juan Bruce-Novoa, "Spanish-Language Loyalty and Literature," in *Retrospace: Collected Essays on Chicano Literature Theory and History* (Houston: Arte Público Press, 1990), 49. This topic has sparked the interest

of cultural critics and linguists. Frances Aparicio calls this interaction of English and Spanish common in Latino text a "tropicalization" of North American poetic discourse ("On Sub-Versive Signifiers: Tropicalizing Language in the United States," in *Tropicalizations: Transcultural Representations of Latinidad*, 204–5), while Juan Flores and George Yúdice refer to this process of intercultural transferability as "Transcreation" ("Living Borders/Buscando América: Languages and Latino Self-Formation," in *Divided Borders: Essays on Puerto Rican Identity* [Houston: Arte Público Press, 1993], 219–20). John Lipski, on the other hand, has approached this same topic as a linguistic issue and has proposed the existence of a "bilingual grammar" (William Luis, "Latin American (Hispanic Caribbean) Literature Written in the United States," in *The Cambridge History of Latin American Literature, Volume 2: The Twentieth Century*, ed. Roberto González Echevarría and Enrique Pupo-Walker [Cambridge, NY: Cambridge University Press, 1996], 208). I use Bruce-Novoa's definition because it refers directly to the problem of translation that I am analyzing in this section of the chapter.

18. Frances R. Aparicio, "On Sub-Versive Signifiers: Tropicalizing Language in the United States," in *Tropicalizations: Transcultural Representations of Latinidad*, 203–6.
19. Flores and Yúdice, "Living Borders/Buscando América: Languages and Latino Self-Formation," 221.
20. For more information, see Gloria D. Prosper-Sánchez, "Washing Away the Stain of the Plantain: Esmeralda Santiago y la constitución del relato autobiográfico bilingüe," in *Actas del "Congreso en torno a la cuestión del género y la expresión femenina actual."* [Aguadilla: Universidad de Puerto Rico, 1998], 131–138.
21. Walter Mignolo, "Bilanguaging Love," 264.
22. Manuel Ramos Otero, "El cuento de la mujer del mar," in *Cuentos de buena tinta* (San Juan: Instituto de Cultura, 1992), 219–20.
23. Ibid., 221.
24. Ibid.
25. Ibid., 213–14; All emphases are mine.
26. Ibid., 226–27.
27. Walter Benjamin, "The Task of the Translator," in *Illuminations*, ed. Hannah Arendt (New York: Schocken Books, 1969), 75.
28. Manuel Ramos Otero, "El cuento de la mujer del mar," 226.
29. Joseph Pivato, "Constantly Translating: The Challenge for Italian-Canadian Writers," *Canadian Review of Comparative Literature* 14, no. 1 (June 1987): 69. This link between a vital experience and the language in which it is recalled or narrated is also explored by Edward Said in his autobiography entitled *Out of place: A Memoir* [New York: Alfred A. Knopf, 1999], 4) and by Esmeralda Santiago in her introduction to *Cuando era puertorriqueña* (New York: Vintage Books, 1994), a self-translation of her autobiographical narrative *When I was Puerto Rican* ([New York: Vintage Books, 1994], xv–xvii). In both cases the contention is that for the exiled or migrant narrator some experiences occur in a particular language, and that problematizes the process of producing a monolingual account of their lives. I explore this topic in more detail in my article entitled "Bitextualidad y bilingüismo: reflexiones sobre el lenguaje en la escritura latina contemporánea," *Centro: Journal of the Center*

for Puerto Rican Studies 12, no. 1 (Fall 2000): 19–34. Ramos Otero's writing, however, proposes the formation of one single narrative between two different narrative voices and explores how the process of intermingling of languages and imaginaries can produce a space of commonality that promotes a communication that transcends the limits of the native or national tongues ("El cuento de la mujer del mar").

30. E.D. Blodgett, "Translation as Dialogue: The Example of Canada," in *Cultural Dialogue and Misreading*, ed. Mabel Lee and Meng Hua (Broadway, Australia: Wild Peony, 1997), 149.
31. Mignolo, "Bilanguaging Love," 247.
32. Julio Ramos, "Genealogías de la moral latinoamericanista." Paper presented at the Department of Romance Languages and Literatures, Princeton University, April 1998.
33. Martínez-San Miguel, "Bitextualidad y bilingüismo," 29.
34. In "Capitalism and Geopolitics of Knowledge," Walter Mignolo extends this question to include the location from which knowledge is produced by proposing a comprehensive comparative history of the ideological and epistemic foundations of Latin American and Latino Studies in the United States to point out the problematic relationship with studies on Latin American culture conducted in Latin America. One of his most interesting proposals is the connections he establishes between Latino scholars and intellectuals in Latin America, because they both live immersed in the political and cultural practices they study (in *Critical Latin American and Latino Studies*, ed. Juan Poblete [Minneapolis: University of Minnesota Press, 2003], 43).
35. See Luis Leal and Manuel Martín-Rodríguez, "Chicano Literature," in *The Cambridge History of Latin American Literature, Volume 2: The Twentieth Century*, 557–86; William Luis, "Latin American (Hispanic Caribbean) Literature Written in the United States," 526–56.
36. See Ana Pizarro, ed., *América Latina: Palavra, Literatura e Cultura, Volume 3: Vanguarda e Modernidade* (São Paulo: Editora da Unicamp, 1995).
37. Rosario Ferré reflects on the difficulties she has faced when translating her own works in her essay "On Destiny, Language, and Translation, or, Ophelia Adrift in the C. & O. Canal," in *Voice-Overs.*
38. See Frances R. Aparicio, "La vida es un Spanglish disparatero: Bilingualism in Nuyorican Poetry," in *European Perspectives on Hispanic Literature of the United States*, ed. Genvieve Fabre (Houston: Arte Público Press, 1988), 147; Cashman, "Language Choice in U.S. Latina First Person Narrative, 135; William Luis, "Latin American (Hispanic Caribbean) Literature Written in the United States," 540.
39. Frank Bonilla, "Rethinking Latino/Latin American Interdependence: New Knowing, New Practice," in *Borderless Borders: U.S. Latinos, Latin Americans, and the Paradox of Interdependence*, 222, 227.
40. See Mary Louise Pratt, *Imperial Eyes. Travel Writing and Transculturation* (London: Routledge, 1992).
41. José David Saldívar, *Border Matters: Remapping American Cultural Studies* (Berkeley: University of California Press, 1997), 1.
42. Sommer, "El contrapunteo latino entre el inglés y el español," 866.
43. Bonilla, "Rethinking Latino/Latin American Interdependence," 221–28.
44. See Juan Poblete, ed., *Critical Latin American and Latino Studies* (Minneapolis: University of Minnesota Press, 2003).
45. Cabán, "The New Synthesis," 206–12.
46. Jakobson, quoted in Simon, "Rites of Passage," 97.

CHAPTER 15

The Diaspora Strikes Back: Nation and Location

Juan Flores

Many of us who were there that night still hold vivid recollections of the historic Town Hall Meeting that took place in El Barrio a few years back, on September 26, 2002. The subject was El Museo del Barrio, and an animated gathering of neighborhood residents, artists, educators, writers, elected officials, and community activists showed up to voice their views and vent their frustrations over the direction that community institution has taken in recent years. Some of the Museo's trustees were present, as was its former executive director, as speaker after speaker stepped to the microphone to lament the growing distance between the institution and its community, between the Museo and El Barrio. "It's a people's museum and it belongs to the people, not to the corporate sponsors and the elite art world." "It's our museum and you can't take it away." "We are watching you!" "Community participation in programming and decision-making." "I'm Puerto Rican from New York and I don't have an identity complex."

Such were some of the positions taken, and as the evening progressed a strong sense of unity and determination emerged, even among people who had differed in the past on a range of other issues. The Museo's origins and history were continually raised: how it had emerged in the late 1960s as part of the New York Puerto Rican community's cultural and political awakening of those years, and how for decades, in order to remain true to its mission, that artistic community had been forced to resort to its own limited resources in order to gain self-expression because of its systematic exclusion from the mainstream American, as well as island Puerto Rican, cultural institutions. This local grounding and specific—though not exclusive—Puerto Rican focus are what the institution has always been about, and what those in attendance felt it should continue to be about. Of course there have been important changes in the intervening decades, having to do with transnational cultural flows and the dramatic growth and diversification of the Latino population in El Barrio and the rest of the city and country. And needless to say, the Museo like so many other community-based organizations has faced the challenge of establishing a stable financial base from which to develop programs, and thus has had to turn to public and private philanthropic sources.

But under the aegis of a board and executive directorship comprised mainly by a corporate and art-world elite from Latin America and Puerto Rico, and with little or no consultation from the Barrio community or its artists, El Museo has moved further and further away from the interests and talents of the community that gave it birth, devoting itself to handsomely funded exhibits and high art from Latin America, and leaving its educational and artistic programs and other community service dimensions largely untended. Symbolically, there was even thought of changing the institution's name to Museo Latino, or "Museum of Latin American Art," though sensing community displeasure helped to dispel that idea. But the thrust of erasing the barrio roots and history of the museum is still there, and the Town Hall Meeting made clear that the New York Puerto Rican community, still underrepresented and still militantly outspoken, knows about the wiles of privilege and resists being ripped off and tricked into compliance.

The aspect of this struggle that is most interesting for the theme of diaspora and cultural identity, and what most caught my attention at that energizing assembly, is that the continual appeal to the Puerto Ricanness of the institution's social roots and raison-d'étre, which brought the inevitable charge of ethnocentrism and narrowness, were actually qualified in two important ways so as to signify something other than straight-out cultural nationalism. First off, the "Puerto Rican community" in this usage refers not only to ethno-national identification, but equally and inextricably to social class: El Barrio is not only mainly and historically Puerto Rican, but it is poor and working class. Indeed, some of the speakers and the host of the meeting were African American, and the moderator was Dominican. Social deprivation and discrimination were as basic to this "Puerto Rican" experience as the reference to nationality, and charges of racism and elitism were sounded as much as anti-Puerto Rican treatment, and often synonymously.

Second, in that setting being "Puerto Rican" generally meant, even for those who are from the island, "de aquí"; it signified Puerto Rican identity from the perspective of the diaspora. The diaspora perspective entails a heightened sense of belonging and connecting to Puerto Rico and Puerto Ricanness, however nostalgic and mythical, and at the same time an equally insistent affirmation of a formative location and social experience in the United States. Each of these impulses is forged in response to ongoing pressures to marginalize and erase that identity, manifestations of social power that would make that identificatory position invisible or untenable.

The intense national affiliation stems from both the tendency of U.S. culture to incorporate and domesticate difference by reducing national or racialized experience to ethnic labels, including of course the pan-ethnic Latino label, and at the same time it also stems from the tendency of the cultural gatekeepers on the island with their smug claims to cultural authenticity, purity, and entitlement, to dismiss, deny, or patronize diaspora Puerto Ricans. Furthermore, the strong identification with a U.S.-based cultural formation is sounded as a response to the rampant Othering of Puerto Ricans as "foreigners" in spite of their long-standing status as citizens and direct contributions to U.S. society. At the same time it is a response to the blurring or ignoring of that specific location when it is treated as a mere (and unfortunate) extension of the culture of the island, without any specific dynamic or historical agency of its own.

Yet, as the Town Hall Meeting further attested, the diasporic way of being and thinking Puerto Rican is not merely a responsive, reactive, defensive one, though the multiple and powerful pressures mentioned do of course elicit a strong, defiant holding of ground. If the traditional, territorially based concept of Puerto Rican identity rested on the idea of Caribbean creolization or the syncretistic transculturation of indigenous, African, and Iberian cultural traditions, the diasporic identity formation is in our time caught up in a comparable process of re-creolization, a new type and level of cultural interaction and fusion that involves, for Puerto Ricans, all of those cultural experiences with which they come into contact and share in the most direct and democratic way. That has meant for U.S. Puerto Ricans, their relationships, say, with Caribbeans of diverse backgrounds, with other Latinos (especially Caribbean Latinos), with Asian Americans, Italians, Irish, and Eastern Europeans, and, as I emphasize in my writings, very tellingly and profoundly with African Americans.

These exchanges and convergences are not ancillary to the diasporic cultural formation but integral to and definitive of it: Puerto Ricans "de aquí" are new creoles, new not for their cultural hybridity but certainly hybrid in new and intricate ways, and as articulated from the base of working-class experience. It is ironic, and symptomatic in this regard, that for all his controversial and at times irreverent laying bare of Puerto Rican nationalist theory, Carlos Pabón, in his book *Nación postmortem* (2002), pays the usual scant attention to the diaspora experience, certainly the most substantive challenge in modern Puerto Rican history to the traditional theory of the nation.[1] Interesting, too, that his main way of differentiating Nuyoricans from those on the island is that they are considered "híbridos," as though those in the home territory are somehow pure.

Now this re-territorialized and subaltern perspective generated by the Puerto Rican diaspora experience constitutes not just an extension of inherited theories of national culture, however innovative or subversive, but a direct and radical defiance of accepted wisdom. Both the continuities and the disjunctions with the territorially circumscribed cultural concept exert a deeply unsettling effect, shaking up cherished assumptions about the race, gender, and class parameters of national cultural self-definition. Most obviously, the long and harsh social experience of a colonial diaspora takes the glow out of the wishful annexationist prospect, while at the same time helping to point up the denial and hypocrisy typical of even the most strident *independentismo* on issues of blackness and sexual equality.

We should recall that in the early 1970s, when some of the prominent elite intellectuals from the island were parachuted in to serve as visiting faculty for the fledgling Puerto Rican studies departments at City University of New York (CUNY), many of the Nuyorican students were disappointed and angered at what they felt to be a racist and elitist disdain toward them, and in the name of anti-Yankee nationalism at that. The history of those early confrontations, which lie at the heart of the founding of Puerto Rican Studies, has yet to be told and subjected to the due analysis, and has yet to be incorporated into present-day projections of the future of our field of study. And, of course, much the same clash of values and perspectives on Puerto Rican identity have colored the cultural dimension of return migration and the experience of diasporicans on their many sojourns and relocations to the island, with Nuyoricans often cast as the criminalized, racialized other in their own beloved ancestral homeland.

Can there be any wonder, then, that *the diaspora strikes back* by way of forcing a radical rethinking of national identity as a whole, an intellectual "moving of the center," to borrow the great Kenyan writer Ngûgî wa Thiongo's very pertinent phrase, "From the territorially circumscribed to a transnational frame of reference?"[2] The Puerto Rican case is of course not alone in this regard, but sets the pace in important ways for cultural processes symptomatic of the current global–local conundrum. It is clear that Dominicans in the United States have stood to learn a great deal from the Puerto Rican diaspora experience, and their quest for cultural redefinition exhibits similar patterns of continuity and innovation. But perhaps Nuyoricans have something to emulate in Dominican cultural awakening as well; it is telling that an established Dominican historian like Frank Moya Pons can articulate in sharp unequivocal terms the profound transformative impact of return migrants on the very self-conception of Dominican nationality.

In Moya Pons's words,

> The discovery of Dominican negritude was not the result of an intellectual campaign as had been the case with Haiti and Martinique, after Jean Price-Mars and Aimé Césaire. The real discovery of Dominican black roots was a result of the behavior of returning migrants. . . . Many arguments for this new racial and national stance come from the urban centers of the United States and have been imported by the migrants, especially by the younger generation who have been raised in the cities of the East and have grown up with colored Puerto Ricans, West Indians, and Black Americans. . . . Racial and cultural denial worked for many years, but migration to the United States finally cracked down the ideological block of the traditional definition of Dominican national identity."[3]

Similar thoughts, in chapters like "La diáspora piensa . . . ," "Los beneficios del éxodo," and "Los ausentes como amenaza cultural," are set forth by Silvio Torres-Saillant in his significantly titled book *El retorno de las yolas*,[4] perhaps more transparently than in the case of Nuyoricans, but in line with the same patterns of transnational cultural flows, here again *the diaspora strikes back*.

Traditionally, it has been the national territory that has been thought of as the fount of cultural perspectives that are alternative and oppositional to hegemonic metropolitan cultures of domination, and that this contestatory culture of resistance then informs the cultural perspective of the nation's diaspora within the metropolis. It is now becoming evident that the flow may also travel in the opposite direction, and that the colonial diaspora itself may well generate a culture of resistance to elite national domination. Translocated by means of the *guagua aérea* of circular migration and the ubiquity of contemporary communications technology, those "cultural remittances," as it were, then implode in the national territory as something foreign, and yet in their relevance not so foreign after all. Particularly when the focus is on popular culture—in the sense of community and street experience and working-class expression—and on youth culture, this multidirectional kind of cultural movement and impact comes most clearly into view.

The book on postcolonial literature, *The Empire Writes Back*—whose title suggested that of my present intervention—cites Guyanese writer Wilson Harris on the power of the new kinds of creolization transpiring in today's Caribbean diasporas: "The paradox of cultural heterogeneity, or cross-cultural capacity, lies in the evolutionary thrust it restores to orders of the imagination, the ceaseless dialogue it inserts between hardened conventions and eclipsed or half-eclipsed otherness, with an intuitive self that moves endlessly into flexible patterns, arcs or bridges of community."[5] As strikingly evident in cultural practices such as hip-hop, slam poetry, graffiti writing, dress styles, and even language usages, street youth in the diaspora and in the home country now form a new and interesting example of such "flexible patterns, arcs or bridges of community"; Robin Cohen's book *Global Diasporas* offers a lucid description of this re-creolization among diasporic youth:

> Aesthetic styles, identifications and affinities, dispositions and behaviours, musical genres, linguistic patterns, moralities, religious practices and other cultural phenomena are more globalized, cosmopolitan and creolized or "hybrid" than ever before. This is especially the case among youth of transnational communities, whose initial socialization has taken place with the cross-currents of more than one cultural field, and whose ongoing forms of cultural expression and identity are often self-consciously selected, syncretized and elaborated from more than one cultural heritage.[6]

Puerto Rican youth culture in our times offers rich examples and articulations of these transformed cultural relations and crosscutting, multidirectional influences. Victor Hernández Cruz, Sandra María Esteves, and Tato Laviera among many other diasporic poets give ample testimony to the new cultural mixing and blending in the transnational setting, what I have elsewhere called "creolité in the 'hood." Laviera's poem "nuyorican," with its angry yet loving tone directed at the island and its attitudes, may well be the signature statement of the diaspora striking back, getting even for the disdain and unfounded claims to cultural authenticity.[7] Mariposa's unforgettable "Ode to the Diasporican" is a prime example of transposed, re-localized cultural identity, with its classic refrain "No nací en Puerto Rico, Puerto Rico nació en mí."[8] And finally, so as to show that the translocal Puerto Rican imaginary works in both directions, there is the verse by the young, island-based poet "Gallego" (José Raúl González), who in recognition of all that he has learned from the diasporicans, takes his cue from Mariposa by proclaiming, "No nací en Nueva York, Nueva York nació en mí."[9]

It is clear, then, that "revisiting" that age-old identity conundrum, "¿qué somos y cómo somos?" in our times must begin by addressing the further question, "¿dónde estamos?" One key to the nation is the sense of location. And as became clear in so many ways at that historic Town Hall Meeting in El Barrio on September 26, 2002, the answer can in no way be strictly geographical.

Notes

A version of this chapter was presented at the panel, "*Qué somos y cómo somos* Revisited: Perspectives from the Diaspora," at the 2002 conference of the Puerto Rican Studies Association in Chicago.

1. Carlos Pabón, *Nación postmortem: Ensayos sobre los tiempos de insoportable ambigüedad (San Juan: Callejón*, 2002).
2. Ngûgî wa Thiongo, *Moving the Centre: The Struggle for Cultural Freedoms* (London: Heinemann, 1993).
3. Frank Moya Pons, "Dominican National Identity in Historical Perspective," *Punto 7 Review* (1996): 23–25.
4. Silvio Torres-Saillant, *El retorno de las yolas* (Santo Domingo: Ediciones Librería La Trinitaria and Editora Manatí, 1999).
5. Wilson Harris, cited in *The Empire Writes Back: Theory and Practice in Post-Colonial Literatures*, ed. Bill Aschcroft, Gareth Griffiths, Helen Tiffin, and Sarah Menin (London: Routledge, 1989).
6. Robin Cohen, *Global Diasporas* (London: Routledge, 2001).
7. Tato Laviera, "nuyorican," in *AmeRícan* (Houston, TX: Arte Público, 1985), 53.
8. Mariposa (María Fernández), "Ode to the Diasporican," *Centro Journal* 12, no. 1 (Fall 2000): 66.
9. My thanks to Mariposa and others for referring me to this unpublished poem, and to Gallego himself for discussing it with me.

CHAPTER 16

Will the "Real" Puerto Rican Culture Please Stand Up? Thoughts on Cultural Nationalism

Raquel Z. Rivera

Few polemicists set out to prove that their ancestors invented blood sacrifice, the sexual double standard, or the ambush.

Sidney Mintz, Caribbbean Transformations[1]

Hay cultura establecida y cultura estableciéndose. [There is established culture and culture establishing itself.]

Vico C, Interview with Author[2]

Few people will disagree that *arroz con gandules* is part of Puerto Rican culture, but few will agree that *mangú* or rape are also a part of it. Are *reggaetón*, hip-hop, and punk as much a part of Puerto Rican culture as *danza, plena*, and *jíbaro* music? Is *boricua* culture a selective agglomeration of our collective virtues or does it also include our worst vices? How do we deal with the fact that what looks like a "virtue" to one person can appear as a "vice" to another? The answers to these questions vary greatly as arguments regarding what Puerto Rican culture is have been (and are still) central to the most cohesive discourse of *boricua* community building, namely, cultural nationalism.

Regardless of one's location, cultural nationalism has profoundly impacted the life of Puerto Ricans in the island as well as in the diaspora. Its twentieth- and twenty-first century–versions have operated as direct responses to U.S. colonialism. But despite its potentially apparent conceptual unity, cultural nationalism has been anything but a monolithic force and has been formulated from diverse quarters: popular culture, literature, the pro-independence movement, and the colonial government, among other sectors.

For *independentistas*, cultural nationalism has been intricately tied to the struggle for national sovereignty. The "defense" of Puerto Rican culture has been viewed by most *independentistas* as a means, as well as an end, of attaining political independence from the United States.[3] According to this perspective, a vibrant national cultural identity will further the goal of independence, and, at the same time, the attainment of independence for the island will insure the preservation of a vibrant national culture. From this point of view, a strong and distinct Puerto Rican culture is theorized as inassimilable to U.S. culture.

Cultural nationalism has also been championed by sectors that do not favor independence, including the Puerto Rican government itself (in both its pro-statehood and pro-commonwealth manifestations). Incidentally, the local colonial government has at times been the most influential promoter of the dominant strand of cultural nationalism, with all its racist, classist, xenophobic, patriarchal, and homophobic shortcomings. In these cases where cultural nationalism is not linked to the project of political independence, the "defense" of Puerto Rican culture is an end unto itself and serves a multiplicity of interests and institutions.[4]

The use of culture as a consensual mechanism has been the object of much critique over the last decade. As Carlos Pabón points out, pro-independence cultural nationalists have been guilty of defining Puerto Rican culture in highly problematic terms—which oftentimes can barely be differentiated from the positions of anti-independence cultural nationalists.[5] However, as Luis Fernando Coss rightly retorts, it is also true that the pro-independence camp has been the driving force behind the scholarship dedicated to documenting workers' and environmental struggles, the student and women's movements, migration, and racism.[6] Just like Puerto Rican culture is not homogenous or monolithic, neither is cultural nationalism—not even the brand of cultural nationalism coming from *independentistas.*

Despite their differences, a basic tenet of all cultural nationalists is "defending," celebrating, or nourishing the national culture, a struggle that has most often been described as preserving and nurturing Puerto Rican customs and traditions—the "roots" of Puerto Rican culture. But how those roots are defined and defended, which roots are reclaimed, which roots are suppressed, and which roots are invented has varied greatly depending on the specific cultural nationalist discourse that has been deployed, and there has been little discussion about these important differences. In this chapter, I explore the various ways—often contradictory—in which Puerto Rican culture has been defined from within the ranks of cultural nationalism.

Cosa Nuestra de Barrio (Our Barrio Thing)[7]

One of Puerto Rico's better-known rappers, Vico C, proudly said in his 1993 hit "Base y fundamento":

> Yo no me paso copiando de los morenos, señor
> Si todos saben que lo que yo tengo es mucho sabor

> Hago su moda, pero es a mi estilo, tú ves
> Por eso tengo navaja de doble filo, bebé.
>
> [My music is not just a copy of that of African Americans
> Everyone knows I've got plenty of flavor
> I follow the trend they started, but I do it in my own style
> That's why my blade is double-edged.]

Vico C's statement was undoubtedly a direct response to the frequent criticism directed by narrow-minded cultural nationalists—which were, and still are, numerous—toward rap music in the island: that it was a foreign product that local young people had mindlessly copied, a tool of U.S. imperialism that was corrupting the national culture. Vico rebuffed their charges by arguing that rap music had ceased to be "foreign" once he, and artists like him injected their local flavor and style into it.

In a song released shortly after "Base y fundamento," another island-based rapper, Eddie Dee, tackled the same cultural nationalist criticisms, making reference to Vico's song, but building a completely different argument.

> Yo sí copio de los morenos
> Porque si no copio de ellos
> De quién voy a copiar
> ¿De Tavín Pumarejo?
>
> [I do copy African Americans
> Because if I don't copy them
> Who am I going to copy?
> Tavín Pumarejo?]

Instead of trying to assuage the cultural nationalists' fears, Eddie confirmed them. However, he dismissed their accusations as unimportant. After all, he needed to draw musical inspiration from somewhere, and what had been officially defined as national culture—which he mockingly equated to the clownish *jíbaro* TV character made popular by Tavín Pumarejo—was certainly not providing it. The *jíbaro* imagery flaunted by the dominant strand of cultural nationalism as the epitome of Puerto Rican culture meant nothing to him. If being truly Puerto Rican is being like a *jíbaro*—meaning not urban and, at least in the case of the mythical *jíbaro*, white—then Eddie preferred to model himself and his music in the image of African Americans.

Cultural nationalism was undoubtedly an influence for all parties involved in this example. The criticisms aimed at rappers were based on an approach to cultural nationalism that branded locally-produced rap as foreign, inauthentic, impure—a threat to the "real" Puerto Rican culture. But Vico's and Eddie's rebuttals were also informed by a century-long legacy of cultural nationalism under U.S. colonialism.

The value that Vico placed on Puerto Rican cultural expression and his belief that a worthy musical product cannot be a mere mimicry of a "foreign" cultural expression, but must be reworked through local "style" and "flavor," is a product of cultural nationalism. So is the way in which he upheld in that song his working-class origins as an integral part of Puerto Rican culture. ("Tengo mi *clase*, mi base y fundamento.") Vico's lyrics are an example of how cultural nationalism has fostered the creation of a local youth and class-based musical expression in the form of rap, which draws linkages with similar social sectors outside the island's borders, but consciously building upon a local cultural foundation. There is pride in the local legacy, but also an openness to incorporating selected cultural influences from outside of the island's borders.

Ah . . . but then we have Eddie Dee who explains his preference for African American culture through his inability to identify with the mythical *jíbaro* figure, which certain strands of cultural nationalism have proclaimed as the ultimate symbol of Puerto Ricanness. This is an example of how cultural nationalism has promoted a mythology based on racial hierarchies that has led this young man to reject part of the cultural legacy of Puerto Ricans. By upholding that mythical white *jíbaro* imagery and marginalizing Puerto Rican blackness, cultural nationalism has led young Puerto Ricans like Eddie Dee to search for their blackness outside the realm of Puerto Ricanness. Blackness is indeed hard to recognize and celebrate when "we think of ourselves as Europeans, as indigenous people, anything but black," as *bomba* singer Nelie Lebrón Robles says.[8]

Twenty-something-year-old Iván Ferrer explains his musical career as being partly a search for himself as a black Puerto Rican. A former member of island-based hip-hop (rap) group Boricua Bomb Squad, he is currently part of the New York-based *bomba* group Alma Moyó. In his words:

> Through hip hop, I was trying to connect to my blackness. But in order to connect to that blackness, I felt I couldn't fully connect to my Puerto Ricanness. Through bomba I feel like I can connect to both.[9]

Like Eddie Dee, Iván Ferrer also felt compelled to look outside the realm of narrowly defined "real" Puerto Ricanness for a vehicle of artistic expression that better allowed room for his experiences. Rap music's close identification with blackness, defined in terms of the African American experience, for years served the purpose for him. Years later, Ferrer found *bomba* music and dance to be an even more appropriate vehicle to fully explore his black Puerto Ricanness.

Raíces (Roots)[10]

Let's now consider *bomba* as another example. A musical and dance tradition that emerged among Africans and their descendants in Puerto Rico around the seventeenth century, its contemporary fate can serve to further illustrate the debates regarding the "real" and "authentic" expressions of Puerto Rican culture.

How would *bomba* be different today had the Instituto de Cultura Puertorriqueña (Institute of Puerto Rican Culture) not taken it upon itself decades ago to promote and "preserve" it? Perhaps it would have died out by now. But do we know that for sure? Is there a shred of a possibility that, without governmental intervention, *bomba* might be even stronger and richer than what it is today? Although difficult to say, these questions point to a specific conundrum: In order to "preserve" the tradition, *bomba* had to be defined. And that definition, which was to celebrate *bomba* as a national cultural product, came from a select few intellectuals, bureaucrats, and cultural practitioners.

One problem was that the most important "folkloric" groups chosen to represent *bomba* hailed from Santurce and Loíza. Thus, an extremely rich music and dance form with pronounced regional variations started being equated with the version of Santurce and Loíza traditions that these groups presented to the public. But this homogenization of *bomba* has not gone unchallenged.

Current practitioners of *bomba* such as J. Emmanuel Dufrasne González (writer and director of the musical group Paracumbé) and Isabel Albizu Dávila (director of the Ballet Folklórico Bambalué) have focused their efforts on documenting and cultivating the *bomba* styles of the southern coast of Puerto Rico.[11] The goal has been to celebrate the differences among regional *bomba* styles and, particularly, to counter the notion that all *bomba* must fit the Loíza and Santurce mold.

These concerns have been growing among *bomba* practitioners. I attended an open-air concert in Mayagüez in January of 2002 and was struck by the fervor with which one of the members of Félix Alduén y Sus Tambores, a *bomba* group from Mayagüez, kept reminding the audience that the music this group plays might not sound like that of Loíza and Santurce, but it is, nevertheless, *bomba*. The Primer Congreso Nacional de Bomba (First National Congress of Bomba), held in late April 2004 and organized by the Fundación Rafael Cepeda, featured practitioners from Loíza, Ponce, Santurce, Mayagüez, and "the Diaspora" (in this case, from New York and New Jersey). From the podium, the congress organizers often voiced their concern that *bomba* not be viewed as monolithic and that its various regional variations be recognized.

There were a few other problems that stemmed from the Instituto de Cultura Puertorriqueña taking *bomba* under its wing. First, in order to be presented on stage, *bomba* had to be removed from its social context. It was no longer a communal gathering, where everyone participated to varying degrees and important social interactions took place. Instead, it was transformed into a colorful spectacle to be watched. Second, "authentic" *bomba* was portrayed as static. Since the aim was purportedly to rescue Puerto Rican traditions, the past had to be faithfully "recreated," and *bomba* was thus frozen in time. Third, this musical and dance tradition also became divested from its spiritual/religious dimensions and pronounced as purely secular.[12] Halbert Barton notes some of these trends in his study of *bomba* and the often-problematic effects of folklorization: "The designation of particular cultural practices as 'folkloric' all too often is used as part of a temporal distancing scheme . . . which renders them anachronistic and/or frozen in time, and thus of little relevance to a world of rampant cultural change."[13]

Though some *bomba* practitioners embrace the genre's folklorization, others are ambivalent or even outright opposed to it. For example, New York-based band Yerbabuena is described in their website as follows: "Yerbabuena is an important part of the struggle to develop and promote identity through living Puerto Rican musical traditions such as *bomba, plena* and *música jíbara*. Yerbabuena reclaims the Puerto Rican music branded 'folkloric,' refusing to accept its packaging as frozen-in-time museum pieces, only vaguely connected to contemporary culture. Instead, they make gorgeous music that incorporates past and present. Yerbabuena taps right into the core of who we are."[14]

Both folklorists and their critics are concerned with identifying, understanding, and nourishing the "roots" of *bomba*. But while some are most interested in the preservation of the past (not that there is always consensus on what things looked like then, or even exactly when and where "then" was) others focus on the integration between past and present so that *bomba* is not merely an attempt to recreate a tradition but an actual "living tradition."

Throughout the 1990s and even to this day, various groups in Puerto Rico—made up in large part by people in their twenties—have taken it upon themselves to promote *bombazos*, in order to rescue the interactive element that was neglected for so many years but is at the heart of *bomba*.[15] Here, the defense of the "roots" promoted by cultural nationalism injects greater vibrancy to the *bomba* traditions being promoted by encouraging greater audience participation.

Nevertheless, problems persist. Because wide, heavy, ankle-length skirts were promoted for decades by the official definition of *bomba* as a requisite for women dancers, some women today do not dance at *bombazos* unless the "right" kind of skirt is available. In other words, *bomba* is not perceived as a come-as-you-are affair, because you need a costume (inspired by nineteenth-century plantation garb) in order to participate. Here is an example where cultural nationalism's attempts to rescue the roots and define authenticity freezes the tradition in time and hampers spontaneity. In this case, the long skirt requisite in a society where most women are not wearing one at a given time kills what should be one of the most important aspects of *bomba*—dancing your heart out to the beat of the drums (figures 16.1, 16.2, and 16.3).

DiaspoRicans

The appeal by the dominant strand of cultural nationalism to mythical roots where our African heritage is marginalized has fostered and perpetuated racial inequalities among Puerto Ricans.[16] Ironically, it is also partly responsible for rap and reggae's vibrancy in Puerto Rico. Since racial pride and the acknowledgment of contemporary urban realities was hindered by the *jíbaro* mythology and the marginalizing of black culture, then young Puerto Ricans longing to come to terms with their blackness sought cultural alliances with

Figure 16.1 Obanilú Iré Allende, a member of Yerbabuena and Alma Mayó, dances at a *bombazo* at El Maestro Cultural and Educational Center, October 2004, The Bronx. Photo by Raquel Z. Rivera.

African Americans, New York Puerto Ricans, and other people from the Caribbean.

And speaking of New York Ricans, cultural nationalism—despite its shortcomings—has proved key in the way in which *boricuas* have survived in the United States and made sense of their experiences. Though the Eurocentrism of the first generations caused friction between them and African Americans, the effect has decreased over time. As the second and third generations of Puerto Ricans in New York came up, influenced by their interactions with African Americans and the larger U.S. society, they largely spliced the Puerto Rican cultural nationalist discourses with the legacy of the civil rights and black power movements. Out of that history, hip hop culture and rap music developed in 1970s New York City, with the foundational participation of Puerto Ricans, African Americans, and West Indians.

U.S.-based hip-hop culture and African Americans have greatly influenced the racial, ethnic, and national consciousness of young Puerto Ricans in the last three decades, both in the United States and in Puerto Rico. Conversely, the racial, ethnic, and national identities of Puerto Ricans have left a deep imprint on U.S.-based hip-hop culture and African Americans.

New York Puerto Rican rap artists may have grown up away from the island, but cultural nationalism has still been a central influence in their lives.

Figure 16.2 Julia Loíza Gutiérrez-Rivera dances at a *bombazo* at El Maestro Cultural and Educational Center, October 2004. To her right, Camilo Molina-Gaetán responds to her movements on the *primo* drum. To Camilo's right, his mother, Mercedes Molina, looks on, smiling. In front of the flag, Julia's father, Juango Gutiérrez, director of Los Pleneros de la 21, plays the güiro, and Jorge Vázquez plays the *buleador* drum. Photo by Raquel Z. Rivera.

The outcome has been internationally known New York Puerto Rican artists like Fat Joe (Joseph Cartagena) using Afrocentric Muslim religious and philosophical imagery in his songs, and at the same time choosing the image of a cockfight for his 1995 album's front cover, and visibly participating in the movement to get the U.S. Navy out of Vieques.[17] That is how we can have artists like Tony Touch, also known as the Taíno Turntable Terrorist, sampling Albizu Campos's voice at the beginning of his commercially

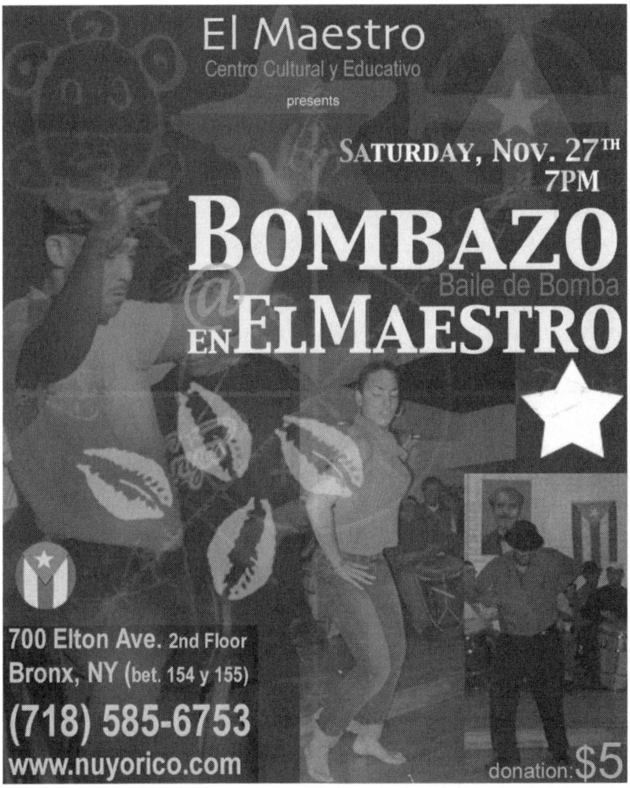

Figure 16.3 Promotional flyer for a *bombazo* at El Maestro Cultural and Educational Center, November 27, 2004, The Bronx, NY. Dancing, from left to right, Pedro "Unico" Noguet, Julia Loíza Gutiérrez-Rivera, and Obanilú Iré Allende. Flyer design by Tato Torres for Yerbabuena, Inc.

successful album *The Piece Maker* and claiming a Taíno identity, and the late rap star Big Pun (Christopher Ríos) using a few lines from "La Borinqueña" in his hit song titled "100%."[18] Cultural nationalism also informs Hurricane G and La Bruja's celebration of *espiritismo* and *santería* traditions as links to their peoples, roots, and ancestors.

These artists' identities as Puerto Ricans, however, do not preclude them from also sharing with African Americans an ethno-racial and class-based identity as people of color living in the United States' inner cities. And while many Puerto Ricans identify this way, others go a step further in breaching the most commonly held assumptions regarding the boundaries between African Americanness and Puerto Ricanness.

Don Divino, a Puerto Rican rapper who is currently affiliated with the very politicized African American duo Dead Prez and who used to be part of the Shanghai Assasinz hip-hop group in Puerto Rico, identifies himself as a black person who shares a common blackness with African Americans.[19] The same goes for hip-hop journalist Edward Rodríguez and dancer Rocafella

(Ana García-Dionisio). In their view, identifying as black, an identity category shared with African Americans, takes nothing away from their Puerto Ricanness.

Likewise, some African American hip-hop artists and enthusiasts talk of Puerto Ricans as "their people" or as fellow black people. Davey D, an African American DJ and writer who grew up in New York and has for years lived on the West Coast, says in an article discussing the ethno-racial dynamics within hip-hop:

> Oftentimes when people from NY say Black they were automatically including Puerto Rican. For the most part there are many Puerto Ricans who aside from the language looked Black as far as the mainstream was concerned. The relationship between the two groups has always been tight. Hence when Hip Hop first emerged it naturally included our Puerto Rican brothers and sisters who participated on all levels. Historically speaking that relationship had always been tight because of our shared drum based culture. It wasn't coincidental that you had a Puerto Rican brother, Felipe Luciano who was down with the original Last Poets. NY is such that Blacks and Puerto Ricans find they have each other in their family.[20]

M-1 and Sticman of Dead Prez put it the following way in an interview with *In the House Magazine*: "The people of Puerto Rico are African descendants, in the same way that the so-called slaves that they brought to [the United States of] America. That's why we understand we are the same people and we are happy to see our brothers representin' themselves."[21]

The most common versions of cultural nationalism, both among Puerto Ricans and among African Americans, usually do not envision African American and Puerto Rican identities as intersecting. But since culture and identity are not circumscribed to assumptions about what should be, in practice these identity categories do intersect. They have historically fed off of each other and continue to do so.

Of course, once again we go back to the effects of this legacy of cultural nationalism often pulling in different directions. While cultural nationalism has made it possible for U.S.-raised Puerto Ricans who participate in hip-hop art forms not to be ashamed of the legacy and history of their ethnic community, the racist streaks in certain approaches to cultural nationalism are partly responsible for many of the unnecessary and debilitating frictions existing between African Americans and Puerto Rican hip hop enthusiasts.[22]

Us and Them

> *Lo importante para el nacionalismo es*
> *la creación de un "nosotros" que pueda*
> *oponerse a un otro, un reverso negativo,*
> *de cuyo repudio dependa la afirmación*
> *de la identidad nacional.*

[What is important for nationalism is
the creation of a "we" that can stand
in opposition to an other, a negative reverse,
so that through rejection national
identity can be affirmed.]

Carlos Pabón, "De Albizu a Madonna"[23]

Track 20 of Sietenueve's debut album *El progreso* (2003) is called "Jí-baro-jop."[24] It starts with the first few notes of a *danza* that comes to a jarring stop with a record needle scratch. A few more introductory bars featuring strings and a flute interspersed with the characteristic sound of the *coquí* and a gravely voice singing a barely melodic "*le lo lai le lo le la*" are cut off by a sound reminiscent of machine gun fire. The song's chorus comes in:

Es claro soy de campo
Un jíbaro de lejos
Pero estás bien jodío
Si te crees que soy pendejo
Sietenueve, EA Flow
Las dos ceibas musicales
Comenzó la revolución de jíbaros reales.

[Clearly, I'm from the countryside
A *jíbaro* from far away
But you're really mistaken
If you think I'm a fool
Sietenueve, EA Flow
The two musical *ceibas*
The revolution of real *jíbaros* has begun.]

In the first verse, EA Flow reminisces about growing up in the Caguas countryside. He celebrates the linguistic peculiarities of the area and constructs rich metaphors from images of the landscape and neighborhood residents. The chorus then comes in once again. The second verse is Sietenueve's turn to shine:

Al yankee no me arrodillo
Ni le he rendío respeto
Si aquel Domingo de Ramos
No me lo saco del pecho
Y no es cuestión de racismo
Pero yo dao no me quedo
Si doy el tajo al racimo
Y después el fruto no veo.

[I don't kneel in front of the Yankee
I've never given him respect
Because I can't tear from my heart
That Palm Sunday
It's not a question of racism
But if you hit me, I'll hit you back

If I cut down the fruit
But then its taken away.]

At this point in the song, it is clear that both Puerto Rico-based artists are proponents of cultural nationalism and *pro-independence* politics. We may think we know more or less where the song may be heading, until a few verses later when Sietenueve proudly announces,

Que un cibaeño aguzao en esto no come cuento
Coño, despierta boricua, a construir nuestro sueño
¿Porqué juzgar al vecino?
Si el que nos da de comer echa en mi patio el veneno.

[This quick-witted man from El Cibao won't hesitate
Damn it, wake up Boricua, let's build our dream
Why judge the neighbor?
If the one feeding us is spilling poison in my backyard.]

A Puerto Rican-born child of Dominican parents thus highlights his commitment to Puerto Rican national liberation by boasting that he is a *cibaeño aguzao*—a sharp-witted man from El Cibao, Dominican Republic. Considering the rampant discrimination and ill feelings existing toward Dominicans in Puerto Rico, it is doubly significant that Sietenueve actually opts for flaunting his Dominicanness. To add even more complexity to the matter, Sietenueve is not explaining that he is Puerto Rican, though his parents are Dominican. He is proudly celebrating that he is Puerto Rican and Dominican—not any less of one, because he is also the other. Hundred percent *jíbaro real.* Hundred percent *cibaeño aguzao.*

The song concludes with lighthearted banter from both artists. Sietenueve dedicates the song to all the "*jibaritos y jibaritas y los cibaeños aguzaos,*" and he proceeds to commend the latter for knowing how to appreciate "*un buen plátano*" (plantains) "*con mantequilla, su cebollita, quesito frito, salami . . .*" (with butter, onions, fried cheese, and salami . . .). We can imagine Sietenueve salivating as his voice trails off with sweet recent memories of his *mangú*-filled gastronomic reality as a *jíbaro real/cibaeño aguzao* in his "Borinquita bella."

Dominicans frequently find themselves placed by Puerto Ricans in the "them" category, but not always, as the song by Sietenueve and EA Flow shows.[25] For these young cultural nationalists, "us" and "them" can in this case be transformed into a loving and combative "us," an "us" unafraid to explore differences but, more than anything, interested in establishing commonalties and solidarities. This tendency is not only to be found in Puerto Rico; it is also flourishing in New York.

Borinquen and *Quisqueya* on the Hudson

During the last four years, there has been a renewed interest among young New York Puerto Ricans in *bomba*, very much premised upon cultural nationalism's championing of our roots. But breaking with the stifling assumptions of the dominant approaches to cultural nationalism, New York *bomberos* have cultivated close musical and personal relationships with Dominican *paleros,* whose music is often featured at *bomba* events and vice versa.

An event in 2002 in honor of deceased Dominican traditional musician and dancer Santiago "Chago" Villanueva—tragically murdered that same year by New Jersey police officers while he suffered an epileptic seizure—featured *palos* and *salves* by Pa' lo Monte, Palo Mayor, and La 21 División, and concluded with a *bomba* set by Yerbabuena. These groups have (or have had at one point or another) members of the *other* ethnicity. The presence of Dominican *paleros* at the Rincón Criollo (also known as La Casita de Chema) in the Bronx has come to be regularly expected, either to play *palos* during *bombazos* or to participate in the *bomba* jam. Likewise, Dominican *paleros* are often featured at the Julia de Burgos Cultural Center and Carlito's Cafe in El Barrio at events organized by Puerto Ricans and where Puerto Rican music tends to be the main attraction.

In order to celebrate *bomba*, Dominican musicians or Dominican music need not be excluded from the mix. On the contrary, through their close musical interaction, Puerto Rican and Dominican musicians have begun to honor the similarities between the traditions. *Palos* songs to Candelo intimately connect with the sensibilities of Puerto Rican *espiritistas.* Singers and composers explore through their creative output the possible existing links between Anaízo in Puerto Rico and the spirit called Anaísa in the Dominican Republic. Drummers study the striking resemblances between the rhythmic patterns of the drum known as *catalié* in Dominican *gagá* and certain variations of the *holandé* rhythm in Puerto Rican *bomba.* Nearly half of *bomba* group Alma Moyó's members are Dominican; the same is true of the all-women's musical collective Yaya—of which I am a member—dedicated to both *bomba* and Dominican *salves.*

In July 2003, one of the musicians that shined the most at master *bomba* drummer Tito Cepeda's homage at The Point community center in the Bronx was a 23-year-old woman named Manuela Arciniegas. A blossoming *primo* (lead drum) player and a student of Cepeda, it was the first time that many of the masters present had seen her play. Those present emotively celebrated her accomplishments and progress with affection and pride. More experienced drummers such as Camilo Molina-Gaetán (a 13-year-old virtuoso) and Obanilú Allende (another young master drummer, 21 years old) stepped away from the *primo* so that she could play. They both danced for her, challenging and also encouraging her with their looks and gestures. Out of all the women present—very few of whom can play drums—Manuela was the only one bestowed the honor of playing the *primo.* She is also a Dominican woman raised in the Bronx.

National identity and traditions are sometimes celebrated by both New York Puerto Ricans and Dominicans, but without neglecting the connections (historical, present, and potentially future) among Caribbean nations.

Will the "Real" Puerto Rican Culture Please Stand Up?

Cultural nationalism has been often formulated from perspectives that promote inequality, repress creative expression, and do not contribute to the formation of a more just, fun, diverse, and fulfilling society. But that does not mean that the proverbial baby needs to be thrown out with the bath water. As long as U.S. colonialism exists and as long as Puerto Ricans identify as Puerto Ricans, cultural nationalism can potentially serve as a valuable means and ends.

I am all for cultural nationalism's defense of Puerto Rican traditions and roots as long as the past is viewed with a critical perspective and not a delusional nostalgia. As long as patriarchy, class exploitation, racism, xenophobia, and homophobia do not keep being reproduced. As long as we acknowledge that contemporary culture is what it is, not what we would like it to be. As long as we recognize that culture is not static and that in order to grow and respond to a community's needs, it changes continually. And I am all for celebrating our Puerto Rican "roots" as long as we accept that there has not been, there is not, and there will never be a homogenous Puerto Rican culture.

National identity and the diverse expressions of Puerto Rican culture are what they are, regardless of our opinions or approval. That does not mean that we cannot argue for or against a certain existing aspect of Puerto Rican culture (whether a long-standing tradition or a recent addition). What does not make sense is arguing that because we do not approve of it, a certain phenomenon is not part of the "real" Puerto Rican culture—which, unfortunately, has been a frequent strategy deployed by cultural nationalists. Sexism and homophobia are long-standing traditions within Puerto Rican culture. Just because they are traditional and our forebears practiced them does not mean that they are venerable or that we need to follow them.

"If men define situations as real, they are real in their consequences," said W.I. Thomas. True indeed. Puerto Rican culture, like any other national culture, may be a social construction, but it is also absolutely real. And it is a contested terrain in perpetual flux.

Notes

1. Sydney Mintz, *Caribbean Transformations* (New York: Columbia University Press, 1990).
2. Vico C., Interview by author, March 1993.
3. The pro-independence movement has also included proponents who are not nationalists, but internationalists. Examples include the Socialist Party of the early twentieth century and the contemporary Taller de Formación Política.
4. Jorge Duany, *The Puerto Rican Nation on the Move: Identities on the Island and in the United States* (Chapel Hill: University of North Carolina Press, 2002).
5. Carlos Pabón, "Posmodernismo y nacionalismo: ¿debatir la nación?" in *Segundo Simposio del Caribe 2000: hablar, nombrar, pertenecer*, ed. Lowell Fiet and Janette Becerra (Rio Piedras: Caribe, 2000), 128–42 and "De Albizu a Madonna: Para armar y desarmar la nacionalidad," *bordes* 2 (1995): 22–40.

6. Fernando Coss, *La nación en la orilla (respuesta a los posmodernos pesimistas)* (San Juan: Editorial Punto de Encuentro, 1996).
7. "Cosa nuestra de barrio" is the title of a song by Vico C.
8. Nelie Lebrón Robles, "Prólogo," in *Puerto Rico también tiene . . . ¡tambó!: Recopilación de artículos sobre la plena y la bomba*, ed. J. Emanuel Dufrasne González (Rio Grande, Puerto Rico: Paracumbé, 1994), iii.
9. Iván Ferrer, in-class presentation for the course Puerto Rican Culture, Hunter College, New York, 2003.
10. *Raíces* is the title of a 2001 Banco Popular documentary dedicated to the two Puerto Rican musical genres most closely related to Afro-Boricua traditions: *bomba* and *plena*.
11. J. Emanuel Dufrasne González, *Puerto Rico también tiene . . . ¡tambó!: Recopilación de artículos sobre la plena y la bomba* (Rio Grande, Puerto Rico: Paracumbé, 1994).
12. Interview, Alberto "Tito" Cepeda, 2002; Interview, Héctor "Tito" Matos, 2003; Carlos "Tato" Torres and Ti-Jan Francisco Mbumba Loango, "Cuando la bomba ñama . . . !: Religious Elements of Afro-Puerto Rican Music," 2001, unpublished manuscript.
13. Halbert Barton, "The Drum-Dance Challenge: An Anthropological Study of Gender, Race and Class Marginalization of Bomba in Puerto Rico" (Ph.D. dissertation, Cornell University, New York, 1995).
14. http://www.yerbabuena.biz/index.html.
15. Halbert Barton, "A Thousand Soberaos: CICRE and the Bombazo Movement, Cultural (con)Fusion? [Transcaribbean Performance and Performers]" *Simposium IV*, ed. Lowel Fiet and Janet Becerra (Río Piedras: Caribe, 2000), 35–47.
16. Duany, *Puerto Rican Nation on the Move.*
17. Fat Joe, *Jealous One's Envy.* Relativity 88561–1175–4. Cassette, 1995.
18. Tony Touch, *The Piece Maker*, Tommy Boy Music. TBCD1347. Compact Disc, 2000.
19. Don Divino, in-class presentation for the course Puerto Rican Culture, Hunter College, New York, 2004.
20. Davey D., "Why is Cleopatra White?" *The FNV Newsletter*, May 21, 1999, <http://www.daveyd.com/fnvmay21.html 1999>.
21. DJ Robert, "Dead Prez," *In the House Magazine* 11 (1999), 34.
22. Raquel Z. Rivera, *New York Ricans from the Hip Hop Zone* (New York: Palgrave Macmillan, 2003).
23. Carlos Pabón, "De Albizu a Madonna: Para armar y desarmar la nacionalidad," *bordes* 2 (1995): 22–40.
24. Sietenueve, *El pro-greso.* ARS Records. Independent release. Compact Disc, 2003.
25. Eugenio García Cuevas, *Mirada en tránsito: dominicanos, haitianos, puertorriqueños y otras situaciones en primera persona* (San Juan: Isla Negra Editores, 1999) and Yolanda Martínez-San Miguel, *Caribe Two Ways: Cultura de la migración en el Caribe insular hispánico* (San Juan: Ediciones Callejón, 2003).

CHAPTER 17

Salsa, Bad Boys, and Brass

José Quiroga

Always in flux, salsa plays with bodies in space—it throws you out, pulls you in, spins and makes you sweat, turns you into mush, leaves you gasping for air. It is predicated on something that turns liquid—a mess, a condimented thickness—a can of Goya tomato sauce, so thick the spoon will not move on the pot. *Salsear* as a verb involves at some point forgetting what you did—not in the sense of losing control but in a form of dancing that is all about mediated control, where the step rules and the partners figure it out with each other—who's doing the turn, what arm goes where, who's moving the hip and in what angle, so the double flip and turn can take place.

Even (or because) it is music predicated on dancing, salsa celebrates collective identifications—the other, your partner, groups of people swaying to the music, conga players who lose it while they hit the taut skin of the drums. This identifying is related to the music that names the beat, and that is the reason why the name of the genre refers to food; food and music pivot around each other in salsa.[1] As a name, salsa stands at the *sofrito* level of signification—it is the fried base that needs to be there for the thing itself to be concocted. But at the same time it crowns the dish, when the sauce is poured ("échale salsita") out of the pot and onto the plate. Salsa creates the dish but it also ends it. It is not the dish in itself but its conduit. One does not "eat" salsa but rather pours it in.

In terms of Latino music, salsa for many years was seen as a kind of "gumbo" (or Louisiana "jambalaya" or Cuban "ajiaco")—a genre that depended upon many musical ingredients for it to develop into something that was always a hybrid created out of something else. The history (or histories) of salsa concerns how *salsómanos* (salsa addicts) reheated the genre. This is important considering that, for many years, and depending on your point of view, salsa itself was not a genre but rather, a deformation. Cubans, in particular, insisted on this: Salsa was a variant of the *son montuno*, with horns and brass and commercial appeal added in the city of New York when the vital links to Cuba where cut off.

Some Cubans (in spite of the status of the very Cuban Celia Cruz as the "Queen of Salsa") never recognized salsa as something other than a kind of bastardization of what was, in nationalist terms, *música cubana*. The *salsero* Willie Colón, however, set things straight when he clarified that "salsa is a genre, not a rhythm, collecting elements from Cuban music, from the Caribbean in general, from South America, North America, all of which we Puerto Ricans—more than anybody else—began to combine until we came up with salsa."[2] Puerto Ricans embraced and even concocted salsa, but for many Puerto Ricans the issues became whether the salsa in itself was produced in the island or in New York—whether it stuck close to a "native" form of music, or whether it felt "deracinated," smooth, or even too jazz-oriented for the dancer and consumer of the Caribbean society.

Yet, the communities created around salsa where multilingual and crossed over boundaries—"translocal," to use Mayra Santos Febres's term. The different communities that participated in the salsa craze turned it into a mode of language, a kind of conversation. With its pan-geographical referents, its culturally hybrid situations, its brass competing with the stringed *cuatros*, or the flutes playing along with the congas, salsa allowed a new generation of peoples from the Caribbean to communicate. Puerto Ricans, Cubans, and African Americans found themselves fusing, experimenting, and jamming with each other in the barrios of New York City to an extent that has only been reproduced recently—to a certain degree—with the multiethnic, multilingual communities organized around rap, in New York, Los Angeles, San Juan, and Santo Domingo. Where salsa as a genre was once seen as a kind of hybrid, as a bastardized construction, it now stands as one of the founding moments of the contemporary Caribbean diasporic location. A founding moment, of course, predicated and plagued by the consciousness of its own status as a copy, a "simulacrum" of something else.

In making this argument, however, I am not interested in fashionably arguing a "postmodern" status for salsa as celebration of difference but in exploring how that difference only appears with a regulatory mechanism that intervenes and also defines the genre in itself. I want to point out that in salsa there is interplay between a politics of resistance and a politics of regulation that is also part and parcel of the genre.

What I mean by a politics of resistance concerns the ways that salsa constructed identity and identification—the links that salsa had to "el pueblo," "el público salsero," or "el barrio" as a whole. Salsa understood itself as the music of resistance because identity was defined as a term of resistance. This is the sense in which I understand writer Mayra Santos Febres's comments on the coded language of salsa: "Salsa language sings of street philosophy, prototypes of el barrio, and about music itself as an act of signifying through a code, a clave that is unrecognizable to those who do not inhabit the spaces delimited by salsa music."[3] This code is there, though I think it is more accessible than what Santos Febres's imagines it to be. Resistance entails organization, and salsa was a concerted effort at responding to issues of marginalization as well as to capitalist economic dislocation.

Simultaneously, it is important to understand how these politics intersect with the politics of regulation—the gender constructions that salsa mobilized, and also with the diasporic "translocality" of the genre. Salsa was by no means the first trans-Caribbean or even transcultural musical genre, but it placed itself alongside political situations that it had the motivation and the courage to address. What I would like to put forth then is that the fact that salsa argued itself as an invasive identitarian politics could only be sustained by a regulatory mechanism that ascertained normative sexual identities. The broader implications of this statement concern precisely whether it is necessary to construct a politics of regulation in order to resist, or whether this regulation in particular shows that resistance is always a futile and exclusionary project.

Gendering Our Latin Thing

Before moving forward, I should clarify from the onset the sheer historical "datedness" of the term salsa, like a stellae from a past that I am allowing myself to revisit. Like bolero, I would argue that salsa does not exist in the 1990s as a meaningful term, but rather as a point of reference. The grid marked by the reference entails a sense of temporality (the 1960s, 1980s, and perhaps the 1990s) bisected by spatial dispersion (New York, San Juan, or Caracas). It is not that the term has been rendered useless because the rhythm is no more. What has happened is that time has remotivated and has changed the political struggles, and certainly the sense of imminent hope, that accompanied the term's origins.

The loss of "politics" in the 1980s; new hybrids such as "*salsa* romántica"; the trans-Caribbean craze for merengue; the success of women on the stage as powerful *salseras* or *merengueras*; along with new artists such as Marc Anthony or Manny Manuel, already belie that something different has happened to the genre. For example, if Willie Colón, as quoted above, defines such as translocal genre as salsa in nationalist terms, the strict equation between music and national consciousness has suffered important changes in the last 10 or 15 years. We can speak of merengue in terms of Dominican national consciousness, but we should also take note of the fact that some of the major *merengueros* (La India, Manny Manuel, Olga Tañon, Giselle, Ashley, and Jailene Cintrón) are Puerto Rican, and that enormously popular forms of merengue, such as meren-rap, are sung by—among others—Francesca and Lisa M., who are not necessarily born and bred in the Dominican Republic.

Although we can say that musical genres belong to a particular form of national consciousness, to examine music solely by means of nationalities is at this point sometimes a tricky proposition. Forms of validation may originate in the national arena—it makes a lot of sense for Olga Tañón to insist on the validation given her form of merengue in Santo Domingo, the cradle of merengue as a form—but it is also clear that Puerto Ricans derive much satisfaction and national pride from the sheer fact that Olga Tañón, as a Puerto

Rican woman, has been able to triumph in what was perceived as the musical arena of the "other"—Santo Domingo. The case of merengue, of course, is by no means an isolated one. One may be tempted to make a distinction between more rhythmical or danceable forms, such as salsa or merengue, and more lyrically inflected forms such as *bachata*, or even *vallenato*, and think that rhythm is exported, while more lyrically inflected forms remain within their countries of origin. The same can be said of salsa, for at the time registered in the most famous salsa documentary of all times, Fania's *Our Latin Thing*, it was clear that the fusion was translocal and Caribbean. But it was also clear that its breeding ground was the Puerto Rican barrios in New York and San Juan.

Identification in terms of ethnicity is the central and most important argument that *Our Latin Thing* makes. This identification starts at the beginning of the film, which opens with a camera that follows a kid who guides us through the labyrinth of back alleyways, arriving in front of a giant scaffolding where a bunch of kids and adolescents are playing a ferocious street rumba with bottles and cans. These shots are meant to insist on how tradition is maintained within a world that corrodes and destroys it. The use of children throughout the film—in the opening shots, but also, toward the end, when the flutist Larry Harlow guides an army of them through the streets of New York with his flute—is meant to point out the particular fragility in which this tradition exists. Childhood is fragile but resilient, like culture. The movie is at pains to show the community in these binaries, like the one from the concert hall to the barrio, that come together in the figure of the defiant adolescent or the prankster child.[4]

Only in New York could this community of the disenfranchised come together, as César Miguel Rondón remarked. What he does not point out is that the message precisely comes from the epitome of the capitalist setting, and that in the film the notion of community is also juxtaposed to a masculine notion of competition. The *salsero* is the one, as Ray Barreto says at one point in the film, who wants it all for himself. Not the one who has lost it, but rather the one who still wants it and makes a spectacle out of wanting it. This competition appears within a universe that is populated only by males and where women—witness the case of Celia Cruz—can participate only by positioning themselves as the "link" to the "roots."

The sensibility that best defines the *salsero* in *Our Latin Thing* is that of street-smartness. The *salsero* as performer is a conduit for the group, the mass, and the people. He disappears in the best of circumstances to allow salsa itself to rule. Where an audience is transported, when it has become a dancing "audience," the *salsero* has accomplished his mission. The *salsero* regulates the orchestra, while also allowing it to explore. The orchestra is the site for this war—for the competing jams, the improvisatory interventions, and the fugues of each of its players. As a musical entity, the orchestra plays the part of representing the war that is also taking place in the streets of New York. Identification is a difficult process that needs to allow not only for explosion but also for the regulation of its outbursts.

Not coincidentally, salsa players may have bodies, but in *Our Latin Thing* what they really have, fundamentally, are faces—they are not shot at medium range but rather close-up, so you can see their expressions of joy. It is the most direct form of appeal, for the whole point in the film is having the ability to see (or not to see, which is the same thing) the very face of pleasure. The facial registers of salsa—its commotion, its emotive frenzy—are at the center of this film. But this joy needs a center of stability that allows it to have some meaning. It is no wonder then that Leon Gast chose the conga player Ray Barreto as the charismatic figure at the center of the action.

The facial registers of the *conguero* are the most complex—his figure is at the center of the film. It is from that joy that the circuitous routes of pleasure are meant to take shape—a circuit that goes from *sonero* to dancing audience, and that entails to beckon the "passive" audience that is watching the film. This face regulates the limits of the permissible in many ways. It identifies the musician and allows us to engage in the circuitous routes of identification, but it also, in many ways, manages our pain. One may identify with the pain of a bolero singer, but one wants to participate in the joy of the one who is playing the conga, even when that joy is predicated upon the pain caused by so much economic poverty existing within the richness of soul or tradition. By jump-cutting between scenes of poverty and the concert hall, the film identifies pain but also regulates it—in order to better identify the roots and reasons for struggle.

Salsa's pain is simultaneously meant to be suffered, rejoiced in, and danced to, but this is always done collectively, as if dialectically opposed to the more individualized suffering of the bolero. Salsa does not preclude moments of regulated sadness, but in *Our Latin Thing*, this sadness is meant to sustain a call for action. This can be seen in a scene in the film when a man is playing an old and beaten-down Spanish guitar on a stoop. There is a woman singing next to him—actually, she is not singing but trying to recall the words of an old bolero—and there is a man in front of the guitar player, also attempting to recall those words. The three of them are presented in a decayed setting, and they are obviously drunk or stoned.

Although most of the action in the film is staged (in the most literal sense of this term), there is the effort to make this an authentic-looking scene. This moment stands isolated in the film as a warning sign. We are meant to understand that the triumphant masculinities that one sees throughout the film in the faces of the *conguero*, or in the competitive jams of the different members of the orchestra, which are always on the verge of degenerating into this: a moment of convulsive beauty and absolute sadness. This sadness, one feels, is unsustainable in this setting. There is a risk entailed in remembering too much. It turns people into sad and passive members of a community. Homeland, or even nostalgia for the homeland, needs to be regulated. This is different from repressing nostalgia; it is not a question of repression but of managing it, allowing it to appear so that it can then disappear.

If pain is regulated, a more important regulation comes via gender. As pointed out earlier, in *Our Latin Thing*, *salseros* have faces whereas women have bodies. Their reactions to the music are similar to that of the male *salseros*, except that women dance and the *salseros* play or sing. The camera definitely takes the male angle of vision—at one point it almost penetrates a trombone; at another point it changes focus, from the *piragüero* crushing ice, to the breast of a woman who is watching the action. Its angles of vision for women's bodies are meant to emphasize the exuberance of hips, behinds, and breasts, whereas the face is merely of secondary interest. This is reproduced in the overwhelmingly male-centered universe constructed around salsa. The promise for a future announced at the beginning of the film is bound directly specifically and exclusively to boys, not girls.

Santos Febres explains that salsa creates a "translocal community," defined as "a community of urban locations linked by transportation, communication technologies, and the international market economies."[5] But for Santos Febres, salsa "does not search for the formation of any structures of power, but attempts to mark out new spaces for improvisation, for those acts of violence inherent in questioning, pushing against, and threatening the limits of any structure."[6] Aside from the brilliance of Santos Febres's work, I think that to deny salsa the search for structures of power is to misread what salsa, in its heydays in the early 1970s, was all about. For the struggle for power was an important component in the history of salsa. And by this I mean not only the "translocalized" search for power, but also a more specific form of power—of men and boys over women and girls, and of conga players over melancholic guitar players.

I agree with Santos Febres that the task of salsa was the construction of a community that was "larger than national and broader than ethnic," but I think that this construction was strictly regulated from within, to the extent that the regulation is inscribed within the very creative acts of fashioning translocal communities.[7] Ethnicity in *Our Latin Thing* is the ruling paradigm, to the extent that it regulates all others at its expense. The film does not offer a radical, as opposed to a liberal, possibility. Its choices are embedded within the very contradictions of capitalism: It is choice between ethnicity and gender, a choice that creates a politics of resistance based upon ethnicity, while consequently sustaining this within a politics of regulation based upon gender.

If we look at the roots of the genre in itself—not that I am arguing for historical exactitude here—the vision that we have of it may be more in line with the critique that we may produce in terms of a general politics of identity, one that seeks expression by means of regulating and consigning "other" spaces to a secondary role. That this is meant to be done for the sake of a "politics of action" is not a reason for decrying what in effect is a "method" that produces a rationalized theory. For, in a sense, it was the perceived regulation that brought about, in my view, the demise of the salsa space—particularly in its New York variant. It failed to take into account other modes and means of contact, other forms of community interaction.

Given the fact that it was a commercial enterprise sustained in many of its facets by white record promoters, it could see only "jazz" as its reasonable point of contact—even if the jazz angle ran the risk of having it lose its links with a "people" who were not only intermarrying but that in effect had women occupying roles that would come to light only much later, in the rise of new figures such as La India or Jailene Cintrón. But many of these figures are associated with merengue—the only other Latino genre that at present has undertaken to create linkages with multiple other multilingual communities.

The continuing histories of salsa have served to illuminate the systems of control that were always involved in its very production. It is clear that the setting up of these two systems side by side is the surest route for failure of any political or progressive project. For the politics of resistance will always collapse because the very weight of the systems of regulation that it sets up will fall short in terms of the very representation that it seeks to bring forth.

It is interesting, however, to note what has happened between 1971 and 2002. Let us recall that the young Willie Colón, who appears in the film, is the producer of La India's first chart-topping recording and that Jerry Masucci, who died recently in Buenos Aires, was about to release a New Fania record label and was starting to sign up Havana bands that play what is now called *sonido cubano*. Only Cuba now serves as the last bastion of nationalism, while other countries desperately search for a national idiom in order to counteract the ransacking of musical tradition. While merengue has become more and more *puertoricanized*, Dominicans have turned to "bachata" in order to safeguard national sentiment.

Notes

1. Juan Carlos Quintero Herencia recalls José Arteaga's history of the word from the work of Fernando Ortiz, the Cuban Ignacio Piñeiro's son "Echale salsita" from 1928. However, he also clarifies that salsa as the name of a commercial genre was born with the film *Our Latin Thing*, which chronicles the concert of August 21, 1973 at the Cheetah ballroom, and with the later movie *Salsa*. See Juan Carlos Quintero Herencia, "Notes Toward a Reading of Salsa," in *Everynight Life: Culture and Dance in Latin/o America*, ed. José Esteban Muñoz and Celeste Fraser Delgado (Durham, NC: Duke University Press, 1997), 189–222, 219–20.
2. Interview with Frank Parilla, quoted in Quintero Herencia, "Notes," 196.
3. Mayra Santos Febres, "Salsa as Translocation," in *Everynight Life: Culture and Dance in Latin/o America*, ed. José Esteban Muñoz and Celeste Fraser Delgado (Durham, NC: Duke University Press, 1997), 175–88.
4. For Rondón, this focus can mean only one thing: "De manera tajante se nos dice que la salsa no es más que eso, la prolongación de la misma tradición de siempre amoldada y parida en los predios de una cultura extraña." See *El libro de la salsa*, 63.
5. Santos Febres, "Salsa as Translocation," 180.
6. Ibid., 179.
7. Ibid.

CHAPTER 18

[a. k. a.: The Sex/Salsa/ Identity Show]

Félix Jiménez

There's a hole in my soul/
You can see it in my face/
It's a real big place.

Robbie Williams, "Feel"

A ambiciones y anhelos
no renunciaré/
Seguiré insistiendo/
No me rendiré.

Luis Omar, "Venceré"

[Ambitions and yearnings
I will not give up/
I will continue to insist/
I will not give in.]

The Cut

As national identities and sentiments are being placed and misplaced, defended and crossed over in pan-Caribbean "tropical" musical genres, somewhere in the recesses of a record company's warehouse, thousands of CDs rest untouched and unplayed. The silence of those CDs mark the unsettling end to the short and footnoted career of Puerto Rican salsa singer Luis Omar, the man who—had it not been for one night in October 2001—would have been anointed as heir to the sexy tropical crooners that populate and copulate the polisexual Caribbean rhythm island.

The then 27-year-old entertainer was poised to enter the attitudinal universe of made-for-salsa suits, sensual posturing, and flamboyant choreography.

His career script was mired in its predictability: Armed with a multinational record distribution deal with Sony, the singer—or so it was predicted—would succeed in procuring airplay, light the musical fires of the Puerto Rican patron saint festival party circuit, secure better contracts, cross over North and South, establish his credentials as a major player as publicized and acclaimed as Marc Anthony, and fantasize about coasting to a Grammy Awards ceremony and winning one or two gramophones himself. It had been done before.

But on October 25, 2001, just months after Luis Omar's first cut hit the airwaves of his native island, the singer quietly vanished, not as a casualty of celebrity culture, but as an exceptional Houdiniesque survivor of the musical underworld. Gone—perhaps forever, it was then thought—Luis Omar became a celebrity cult, and his invisibility (enhanced by the disappearance of his only musical production from record stores) so confounded the Puerto Rican media that the story of his downfall has never been aired or printed on the island.

When Luis Omar vanished, his body and his presence were being requested by his newfound fans; TV and concert bookings awaited the "*salsero* for the new century"; websites from Turkey to Italy to Japan peddled his record. But instead of riding the preordained wave to crossover success, he ended up as a fugitive in the most wanted list in several states from California to Florida. No one knew what he had done or where he had gone, but two things are now clear: the criminal past and the penchant for self-sabotage of this prodigal son who will never step on any of the stages he had framed in the exacting dimensions of his desire and ambition. The painstakingly calculated *making of* a candidate for salsa iconography was thwarted by the secrets that still remain to be uncovered.

The day Luis Omar fled the California house in which he lived with his lover, he had been planning his first promotional tour after one of the songs from his debut CD, *Así así*,[1] climbed the charts in Puerto Rico and Latin America. He had worked hard for this moment. But the fame-hungry singer also had been lavishly caressed by the marked gods of music. In the summer of 2001, his physique in a dark blue suit and tailored white shirt adorned many of the billboards that surround the strip that welcomes tourists to the Luis Muñoz Marín International Airport in Puerto Rico. His face was a welcoming mat of sorts, as befits an island that promises the enchantments of music and abandon as selling points for the Caribbean pseudo-cultural fantasy of massified tourism.

For the casual passersby, the billboards signaled the nascent career of a salsa hunk who complied with all the basic requirements and attendant accoutrements of a Latin male music megastar: muscle tone, attitude, Euro-style wardrobe, evident metrosexuality, and an unflinching attention to detail, all in a six-foot-two frame. His first album served to promote the singer as a musical *wunderkind*—he had authored five of the songs of his debut recording, served as co-executive producer, and financially underwritten the enterprise that would launch his career. For his flirtations with stardom, his chameleon-like Mediterranean looks had been packaged for the kill.

But though many had seen him, few had actually heard of him before his splashy salsa tune moved up in the tropical music charts in a concerted effort by his record company, MP Productions, to saturate the airwaves. Money, it seemed, was not the issue. Wallpapered around San Juan, the mere image of Luis Omar as the ultimate performer, as a walking provocation, seemed ready for cultural consumption and belied no trace of the pathologies about sexual and national identities that later would be layered and attached to the mystery of his rise and fall from a career that never was.

The questions that Luis Omar's disappearance posed went beyond the music and media worlds precisely because his ubiquitous public presence created unusually high expectations for his career. Moreover, the anticipation surrounding this previously unknown musical personality was accompanied by unsubstantiated rumors about his sexuality, lending an air of mystery to the singer's publicity, and an opportunity for niche commodification.

As a newly minted star-to-be, Luis Omar stood as the absent center of a well-worn rags-to-riches sequence. But it was a sequence with a twist—he had to act with passion and proceed with caution. He was forced to keep himself at a distance—albeit a *participating* distance—from the paths taken by his own artistic creation toward fame and fortune. While he targeted Puerto Rico as his natural main market because of his Puerto Rican identity, he stood outside the intersections of his own fabricated self as an overseer of the risks that his sexual and criminal personas could inject into the island's music scene through a tropical music genre. As if the twin preoccupations of Puerto Rican identity and sexual identity were not enough, Luis Omar had to contend with the other secrets he carried within that, if discovered, could spell instant disaster.

That guarded past finally caught up with Luis Omar's ambitions as his interstate and transnational acts of commission surfaced on national television. The singer became known as the "Salsa Swindler" just nine months after his disappearance, when the story of his short-circuited career was recounted by the TV show *Unsolved Mysteries* as a senseless collusion of deception and ambition in which his musical talents and devious entrepreneurial audacity paid for every desire and every whim. In the retrospective messiness accorded to this one-record-wonder who was on his way to the construction of a "disaffirmative artistic model,"[2] music stands as the key to his identitary hole in the soul. It turns out that music (the making of, the teaching of, the selling of) was Luis Omar's legal occupation and documented illegal vocation.

Who was this wannabe star who so laboriously constructed his palatability only to surrender to a life of forced anonymity in a hide-and-seek game with the police? Once a used-car salesman in Puerto Rico, Omar Adalberto Arroyo moved to California from Puerto Rico to collect the missing pieces of a well-focused dream: a hit record and a luxurious life. Disenchanted with the delay in his career plans, the singer relied on his looks and talents to devise a simple fraud to con "simple people." Luis Omar's ritzy Arcadian existence in Los Angeles was paid for by his best kept secret: a network of music schools in Southern California that offered accordion classes and musical instruction packages to children of unsuspecting families (mostly migrant, mostly Mexican) who never imagined that the suave Puerto Rican and his Costa Rican business and life partner, pianist Mario Yunis, were collecting their credit information to live off their credit cards. Those interethnic crimes netted an estimated $2 million in a two-year period, before Luis Omar was permanently and publicly scarred the night of July 3, 2002, when FOX's *Unsolved Mysteries* carried the story and his face to millions of viewers in the United States. He had finally attained the fame he desired, but he was not around to witness how his elaborate assemblage had crumbled, and how his fictions and poses careened his life outside his sphere of control.

The program notes narrate the story of how the singer's meticulously constructed world collapsed, when one of his clients—one of the "simple people" he targeted—discovered what he and his business partner had been doing unchecked for years in several California locations.

> Martha Gallardo bought one [music] package for her daughter that included the purchase of an accordion, to be billed over a three-year period, and lessons for three different instruments over a three-year period. However, the ink was barely dry on the contract when everything fell apart. Early one morning Martha dropped off her daughter for her weekly lesson but nobody was there. The first thing that came to Martha's mind was the possibility of fraud. According to police, Martha's instincts were right. When Martha Gallardo received her credit card bill, she found a single charge for the entire cost of the accordion—more than eighteen hundred dollars. Allegedly, it was a cheap import worth about three hundred dollars. However, many other unsuspecting families—unaware of laws designed to protect consumers from credit card fraud—were reportedly hit much harder. Some had credit card bills totalling $20,000.[3]

The subplots of fraud, grand theft, identity theft, and false representation underscore the singer's evident multiplicities. The show concentrated on the slippery financial transactions masterminded by Luis Omar on his way to instant success. But the web of deception that led to the singer's ultimate escape was directly and solely linked to Luis Omar's sexuality in the Spanish language U.S. media, which only briefly exploited the desperate, passionate, and calculatedly somber route that led him from wannabe star to mug shot material. Univision's tabloid news show *Primer Impacto* framed the complex story in the convenient and palatable storyline of "confused sexual identity," portraying the singer's criminal actions and subsequent disappearance as a *Dog Day Afternoon*-ish Latin sequel in the West Coast, as a story that would perhaps mirror the storyline of *Plata quemada*, the Argentinean film based on the real-life heist and flight of two "dashing gay bandits" who, after a 1965 bank robbery, fled from Buenos Aires to Montevideo.[4]

After the media's initial surprise and cursory interest in the singer's sexual persona, the Hispanic networks calibrated the facts and seemed to shy away from the story, deeming the Latino-on-Latino crime unworthy of its newscasts and tabloid shows. Perhaps the ratings-savvy networks feared they would further cheapen their TV "news" formats with a story that fit the strictures of a made-for-TV movie with a simple Latin storyline: A Puerto Rican and a Costa Rican stealing from Mexicans, discovered and eventually punished for trafficking with migrant musical dreams.

How attractive was a story that included the identity theft, hybridity, and diasporic entanglements of a "bogus" Latino with eight aliases (Luis Omar, Luis Omar Ferre, Adalberto Arroyo, Miguel Rodríguez Hernández, Carlos Tomás Santiago Rivera, Alberto Miranda, Omar Ferret, Omar Adalbert Arroyo) who had frequent run-ins with police since he was 17 years old and had been arrested numerous times? The Los Angeles Police Department, responsible for Luis Omar's search, dispatched numerous bulletins and updates with the singer's photograph and a seven-sentence summary description: "1. Sings karaoke. 2. Drinks Corona beer. 3. Weight fluctuates. 4. Has been known to get liposuction. 5. May have had plastic surgery. 6. Has two daughters, Desi and Dyni. 7. Police say he is bisexual."[5]

It was evident to the police that Luis Omar was a king of transformations, an expert in obstructing views of himself, suggesting veils, a human illusion so perfect that it concealed its solicitation; an illusion that ultimately dictated what could be seen, whether anyone was watching or not. The singer's entrepreneurial skills fueled his desire to bridge his tattered past with a triumphant present in a perversely risky enterprise, using his past to become impermeable in the future. In the process, he devised tricks that used his biography as the raw material for its own concealment.

The logo for his record company, DesyDyni Records, featured a sepia-toned miniature photograph of his two daughters from a previous marriage. But while the CD's visual package attempts to link the singer to a world of placid heterosexual, pan-Latino interactions, the encoded messages inscribe his lyrics in a queer environment. The record, after all, had been coproduced by Maryleen Cohen Spielberg, the singer's transsexual lover, in her first post-operative professional endeavor. As props for Luis Omar's heteronormative performance, the models for his logo, daughters Desy and Dyni, had been conveniently relocated to California, helping the couple complete the required fantasy of familial perfection and portray the singer as a robust pater. To operate in a heterosexual paradigm, one of his two minority identifications (Puerto Rican or bisexual) would have to be erased. And to not be in a subordinate position, the singer was willing to re-inscribe his identities through sequential transgressions and identity layerings. If identity is "constantly destabilized by what it leaves out,"[6] Luis Omar willingly destabilized the facts and sequence of his real biography to accommodate his diasporic heterosexual lie.

So that was how Luis Omar was lost and found and lost in the Woodland Hills section of Los Angeles: multicultural, multinamed, multitalented, and multicornered, losing his soon-to-be-a-star status, any claim to his eight aliases, and refusing to be caught after bringing in and leaving out pasts, criminal and sexual, to attain success. Yet music afforded him the financial possibilities for his record cut, and also provided for Mario Yunis's surgical cutting up of his male past and his male organ. After the travesty schemed by the couple, the only trace of their quest to fulfill dreams and fill the hole in the soul, the only material creation that remains is a unique recording—a coming out CD, the first Puerto Rican salsa trans love album.

Packaging Promises and Faking It

> Yo quiero crearte un mundo/
> y regalártelo después.
>
> [I want to create a world/
> And give it to you later.]
>
> Luis Omar, "Contigo"

What to make of a song that sifts through the air like any other tune, except that it flaunts the false exceptionality of a fake? Did the singer really have something to say? Was there something there, in Luis Omar's CD, beyond standard fare for dance-hall regulars? Why didn't anyone notice—or care about—the disappearance of a hyperpublicized face that carried a tune to the charts, or identify his songs in the key of queer?

For a salsa singer in Puerto Rico to publicly (homo/bi/tran)sexualize his music still is a formidable task. Tropical music lives to tell the story of hetero-dominance and betrayal, and so salsa lyrics commonly attain wide oral and aural circulations through the iteration of traditional gender patterns. Without the added traceable and intentional queerness of his lyrics, Luis Omar's career perhaps would have followed the conventions and patterns of salsa music, with its musical tensions and market conditions.[7] Manicured, exfoliated, beautified salsa singers (as opposed to the always primped appearance of merengue bands) have been and still are rarities in the traditionally male province of salsería.

Traditional salsa is a rough terrain inhabited by tough faces (Willie Colón, Héctor Lavoe, Fania All Stars, El Gran Combo, Apollo Sound, Sonora Ponceña, Oscar de León). Merengue, as practiced in Puerto Rico for the last two decades, resembles a beauty factory, a drag-as-you-will atmosphere that starts at the gym and ends in the bank. This beautified formula has yielded long-lived and established groups such as Limi-T-21 and Grupomanía, the equivalent of U.S. boy bands that, unlike their counterparts, live forever in their ability to find fans in all age groups with their tropical sounds. In this environment, Luis Omar's choice of musical genre—salsa instead of merengue—signified not only a possible musical preference, but also a self-inflicted challenge—his immersion into a market much more difficult to approach and conquer than others, an obstacle even more unsurmountable than his somewhat timid vocal range.

The mechanics of the Puerto Rican music star system benefits the creation of instant starts, as evidenced by Luis Omar's potential competitors in the salsa market. The 1990s music factory had revitalized salsa with the advent of younger singers such as Michael Stuart, Víctor Manuelle, and Jerry Rivera, who were sold and bought as the musical markers of the New Salsa Masculinity, to counterbalance the explosion of hip-hop and rap that saturated and dominated the island's music market and the selling power of merengue, which had displaced salsa as the tropical genre of choice in Puerto Rico. But Stuart, Víctor Manuelle, and the other, younger *salseros*—now fashion trendsetters, influential award-winners, and habitual gold record-sellers—would not or could not go beyond the obvious gay-baited and-styled CD cover shot or the ambiguous sexual undertones that are standard fare in their concerts and musical videos. The creation of their public remained an exercise in inclusivity.

Even if objectified as part of the specular economy of music, these singers' choices provoke no gender panics or identity anxieties, for they strive to maintain a comfortable flexibility in their audience base. As salsa singers, they labor in the creation of a "poetic public," and the limits of their discourse follow the strictures imposed by their audience, as "all discourse or performance addressed to a public must characterize the world in which it attempts to circulate, projecting for that world a concrete and livable shape, and attempting to realize that world through address."[8]

Against this ironic backdrop of ambiguous and sophisticated remasculinization of Puerto Rican salsa, Luis Omar's strategy aspired to reverse that logic. While his visual presentation—more conservative and less playful than, for example, Stuart's or Víctor Manuelle's—was designed to play the heterosexual card in public, his lyrics attempted to privately address a more limited target audience. There was no trace of self-sabotaging tendencies in his music; the lyrics of his songs skillfully push the boundaries of a perfect identity bubble: Cognizant of the logic of the Latin market—and of its unspoken prohibitions—Luis Omar quietly assembled a compilation of love songs for his transsexual lover. He wrote "Contigo" and "Todo lo que haces por mi" and included love songs by other well-known Latin composers—"Yo nací para amarte" (Kike Santander) and "Me estoy enamorando" (Armando Larrinaga).

The surface strategic blandness of Luis Omar's music belied a more ambitious project of seduction—a melodramatic sequence of queer-coded salsa lyrics with gender-neutral layers that would shield his "constructedness" inside the musical world and outside of it. Songs such as "Venceré" and "Mentira" trumpet his melancholy battle to succeed, prevail, and conquer, but romanticize his life at the margins, his pose of relentless warrior, the power of music as marginal battlefield, and reasserts his marginality as "a site one stays and clings to even, because it nourishes one's capacity to resist."[9] But if Luis Omar's hidden agenda was to puncture the heterosexual normativity of his chosen musical genre and shatter the artificial divide of gender and genre (the word for both in Spanish is *género*), he ran out of time.

Unimpeachable Void

Do we ever kneel before something that is not a composite, a fragmented frame, a facade, an inauthentic marker? In this case, the excess accumulation and accentuation of private ambiguities that this musical production forces upon the listener clashed with the macho posturing of the cover, which portrays the singer as a svelte model-like figure in a dark suit, gesturing to the camera in an ever-so-slight rapper pose. If Luis Omar had been able to slowly puncture the bubble of salsa, its fastidious gender demarcation, then perhaps the hybrid sense of self that his CD cover announced would have found a public, and Luis Omar would have been his last assumed name. That did not happen. He had morphed into his own screening device, selling a uniqueness that was there, but not for the reasons the singer and his publicists advertised. For a brief moment in time, billboarded, he was the unimpeachable *salsero*. And since he never performed live, the purloined, criminally-financed CD was the performance of a lifetime.

Yet, the possibilities of writing about the man, the person, the entertainer, diminish with Luis Omar's forced silence. The eight-men-in-one Luis Omar was enveloped by a lack: no record of his words, no utterances, no question and answer sessions, no in-depth interviews, no evidence of his opinions, no record of his talking voice. The star-to-be, as he once was, miscalculated the importance of his silences, which protected his criminal persona, but hindered the creation of his artistic self and turned him into a cipher. His non-singing voice never reached the media in an atypical absence of opinion, of words, and of facts about the man behind the record. Thus, only his unreadable void of celebritydom survives. He never had stares on him as a performer; viewers could stare at him only after he could no longer perform.

Could his real-life antics compensate for that silence? Luis Omar proved to be the man who would enact a salsa fantasy prevalent since the 1970s, for he would become the real deal, the dangerous *boricua* that turned into reality the outlaw aesthetics of that decade. The most outlandish example of the *faux* delinquent salsa esthetics is the cover of Willie Colón's album *The Big Break* (1971), which displays mock mug shots of the mustachioed Colón, "The Hustler," his fingerprints, his "Criminal Record" ("known to kill people with little provocation with their exciting rhythm without a moment's notice") and a mock word of warning: "ARMED WITH TROMBONE AND CONSIDERED DANGEROUS."

In his analysis of Colón's album covers, Juan Otero Garabís asserts that they "reproduced the image of the delinquent that the dominant culture stereotypically assigned to Puerto Ricans, transforming it into a positive element of ethnic and community identity."[10] In his discussion of Héctor Lavoe's mythical life-after-death fame, Wilson Valentín-Escobar concentrates on Puerto Rican singers' playful appropriations of the "bad-boy masculine image," mimicking urban myths and perhaps foreshadowing "similar images adopted by many rappers from the late seventies to the current period."[11] As "trans-Boricua imaginations," he concludes, "the album covers signify other masculine-driven representations of national mythologies and identities . . . Album covers become more than textual self-representations but are also self-reflexive meta-performances of diasporic identities and musical style."[12]

Luis Omar's CD sported a cover that also was a *real* cover up and a *real* coming out. The *Así, así* album cover made no grandiose statements, did not play with stereotypically assigned identities or delinquent-type images. The real "Salsa Swindler" did not need that publicity. It was the Los Angeles

Police Department that in its real "most wanted" bulletins granted that imprimatur to this bad bi boy: "WARNING: Do not attempt to apprehend this subject yourself. If seen contact your local police department immediately."[13] The warning, however, intended to protect citizens from someone who was rewriting the stereotypes and queering salsa's history.

Then again, why the media's silence? Luis Omar's embodied ambiguities managed to escape the media radar. Were his subtle gender-bending moves too subtle? Was his story unworthy of attention? The Puerto Rican media's blackout of the "Salsa Swindler" story seems ironic because the island's media frequently surprise and arouse readers with lifestyle profiles that feature same-sex couples playing with their dogs in seaside penthouses and full-length features of lesbian mothers-with-child on Mother's Day. The gender-bending media star, the trans-diva of the twenty-first century forever recurring in magazines, newspapers, and TV talk shows is fashion designer Verona (née Orlando Martínez Didier), who in 2000, with one simple request to a journalist ("From now on, call me a she") startled the media and saw his lifelong wish fulfilled: to be *nominally* a woman even before the first of two dozen operations that would eventually render him physically so. The island's media complied, no one complained, and the acquiescence turned the until-then-little-known fashion personality into gender-bending royalty. In a 2003 fashion show by the sea, in which Verona wore a wedding dress, the designer went even further, telling journalists that he preferred to be addressed as *una dama*—"a lady."

For its part, Puerto Rican television for decades has lived in a perennial culture of transvestite worship. In 2003, the top 20 television shows had a total of 36 prime time gay and drag characters.[14] Highlights of the 2003 television season in Puerto Rico included the two-part series "Me castré para ser mujer" and a sports challenge that kept TV audiences tuned in for a once-in-a-lifetime treat—a Puerto Rican gay volleyball team versus an all-star straight male volleyball team battling it out in prime time, broadcast through the local Telemundo affiliate.[15]

The selective silences of the singer/delinquent/fugitive intervened. He could not speak, or else he would have spoken and would have been talk-show and newscast material in Puerto Rico. But the strands of the tale were always there to provide the backbone for a story—Luis Omar's evidential masculinity, contoured by his multiplicities, his CD, his crimes, the men and women who searched for him in California, Florida, Mexico, Puerto Rico, and Costa Rica, the journalists who had hailed him as a "welcomed voice" in the salsa world, the record company once congratulated for its presence of mind in nabbing a singer with star quality. There was the Puerto Rican fantasy of music as the vehicle for the actualization of financial possibilities, for the margin-to-center course that turns rags into riches, like boxing or baseball. They were all ignored when he became the stuff of scandal in the fracas that ultimately led to his disappearance.

The media were unable and unwilling to assign the cultural value of his songsex, or locate him in postcolonial identity traumas. As an exotic creature that fleshed out his contradictions, Luis Omar "[n]ever escape[d] the condition of continually restaged marginality," and his music "fail[ed]to clear a space for its nominally transgressive energies, arguably falling back instead on a reinscription of the manufactured cultural hierarchies, dictated largely by the fashion of the moment."[16]

Men Don't Leave: An Ethnic Drag

> (Mimicry) is like camouflage, not a harmonization or repression of difference, but a form of resemblance.
>
> Homi Bhabha

> Mentira, todo era mentira/
> Cuando me jurabas que me querias/
> Mi amor te entregué sin condición/
> Y hoy me pagas con una traición/
> Y aunque mi corazón está destrozado/
> No voy a desearte mal/
> La vida continúa/
> Que tengas felicidad.
>
> [Lies, everything was a lie/
> When you swore that you loved me/
> I gave you my love unconditionally/
> And now you pay me with treason/
> But even if my heart is destroyed/
> I wish you well/
> Life goes on/
> Be happy.]
>
> Luis Omar, "Mentira"

Mario Yunis was desired. That is why he became Delia León. And Delia León was loved, or she thought she knew she was loved. The songs in Luis Omar's first and only recording were dedicated to her. So she became Maryleen Cohen Spielberg, content in floating from minority to minority, identity to identity, resembling other bodies and souls in the entertainment capital, enjoying a new house and an instant family, portraying the role of a 1950s housewife with a Jewish identity and a perfectly fashionable (and recognizable) surname. Yunis's constant "efforts at alignment"[17] collided with the veneer of sophistication in the world of entertainment, and also collided with the constant police surveillance that led to her arrest the same day her lover fled. Her assumed identity was her own private California: to become a Spielberg, a coproducer of dreams, the housewife of a house where dreams were fabricated—and where she was caught justifying the comings and goings of a lover with salsa and grand theft in his résumé. But in the end, Luis Omar was the one who got away, to become Mario somewhere else. Or more precisely, to become Mario in Mario's homeland of Costa Rica.

The end of the story weighs in with full-circle simplicity, and the presence of the ghost of a past identity. Luis Omar became Mario. Identity is all that he took from his loved triad of Mario, Delia, and Maryleen, and for some time he tasted freedom, the partial efficacy of deceit and the rewards of inauthenticity under his ninth—and last—known alias. Luis Omar lived placidly for a year under the assumed name of Mario Yunis, tending to his business of music schools in San José, Costa Rica, protecting his transnational identity. He assumed his lover's previous male identity and continued with his musical frauds until his arrest on August 30, 2003.[18] For 12 months, his former lover's identity was his place of impunity.

Between sex and salsa, what or where was the real mystery? For all the identities lost and found in the twin passions of music and sex, Mario Yunis a.k.a. Delia a.k.a. Maryleen was sentenced to 12 years in federal prison in December 2003.[19] Luis Omar a.k.a. Mario Yunis had his encounter with Costa Rican authorities as the Costa Rican man he helped turn into a Jewish woman. Underneath it all, he still was a karaoke singing, Corona drinking, bisexual Puerto Rican submerged in silence, forever performing his own erasure.

Notes

1. Musical Productions Inc., MPPK-5-6363, 2001.
2. The term is Bennett Simpson's, and is applied mainly to art bands whose musical contraptions acquire an unusually large following, blending the expectations of the band as art and the music as commodified success. See Bennet Simpson, "From Noise to Bueys," *Artforum* (February 2004): 59.
3. *Unsolved Mysteries*, Lifetime TV, Program Notes, July 3, 2002. The "carefully crafted sales pitch" included lying to the school staff as well: "Reportedly, Arroyo and Yunis even duped their own employees—lying about the credit card scheme and paying them with bogus checks."
4. *Plata quemada* (Burnt Money), Marcelo Piñeyro (Dir.), Alfa Films and Filmax, 2001.
5. "Wanted Fugitives," December 21, 2002, <http://www2.amw.com/site/thisweek/A/ArroyoOmar/arroyoindex.html>, also "Wanted by the LAPD," Los Angeles Police Department Financial Crimes Unit, October 2002, <www.lapdonline.org/get_involved/most_wanted/fcd/mw_arroyo_omar.htm>.
6. Stuart Hall, "Who Needs 'Identity'?," in *Questions of Cultural Identity*, ed. Stuart Hall and Paul Du Gay (London: Sage Publications, 1996), 33.
7. See Frances R. Aparicio, *Listening to Salsa: Gender, Latin Popular Music and Puerto Rican Cultures* (Hanover, NH: Wesleyan University Press, 1998); also Peter Manuel, "Gender Politics in Caribbean Popular Music: Consumer Perspectives and Academic Interpretation," *Popular Music and Society* 22, no. 2 (1998): 11–30.
8. Michael Warner, "Publics and Counterpublics," *Public Culture* 14, no. 1 (2001): 81.
9. bell hooks, "Marginality as Site of Resistance," in *Out There: Marginalization and Contemporary Cultures*, ed. R Ferguson et al. (Cambridge: MIT Press, 1990), 341.
10. Juan Otero Garabís, *Nación y ritmo: "descargas" desde el Caribe* (Río Piedras: Ediciones Callejón, 2000), 127.
11. Wilson Valentín-Escobar, "Nothing Connects Us All But Imagined Sounds: Performing Trans-Boricua Memories, Identities and Nationalisms Through

the Death of Héctor Lavoe," in *Mambo Montage: The Latinization of New York*, ed. Agustín Laó-Montes and Arlene Dávila (New York: Columbia University Press, 2001), 212.

12. Ibid., 213.
13. "Wanted by the LAPD," Los Angeles Police Department, in <http://www.lapdonline.org/get_involved/most_wanted/fcd/mw_arroyo_omar.htm>.
14. Mediafax Annual TV Ratings Report, San Juan, December 2003.
15. Noel Algarín Martínez, "Aceptado el reto de los voleibolistas gay," *Primera Hora*, May 30, 2003, 98.
16. Graham Duggan, *The Post Colonial Exotic: Marketing the Margins* (New York: Routledge, 2001), 99.
17. See Judith Butler, *Bodies That Matter* (London: Routledge, 1993), 227.
18. A.M. Costa Rica, "Man Wanted in $1.5 Million Fraud Caught Here," September 1, 2003, <http://www.amcostarica.com>.
19. Sharyn Obsatz, "Music School Scam Yields 12-Year Term," *Press-Enterprise*, December 12, 2003, Riverside Metro Section, 1.

PART IV

Coda

Living La Vida Global: The Case of Jose Padilla/Abdullah Al Muhajir

Frances Negrón-Muntaner

Jose Padilla makes poor martyr material.

Miles Harvey, "The Bad Guy"[1]

There may be no better case to survey the potential and peril of the global era than that of Jose Padilla a.k.a. Abdullah Al Muhajir. A Puerto Rican "ethnic" who identified himself as an African American, a baptized Catholic who came to prefer the company of Muslims, and a U.S. citizen trying to escape the American Dream by moving to Egypt, Padilla/Al Muhajir was arrested at Chicago's O'Hare International Airport on May 8, 2002. Initially held as a material witness in relation to a 9/11 investigation, a month after his detention Padilla was designated an enemy combatant and accused of being an al Qaeda operative bent on making radioactive "dirty bombs" to destroy cities across the United States. Shortly after, U.S. President George W. Bush called him a "bad guy" and banished him to a South Carolina Navy Brig without charges and without free access to a lawyer or family members.

During his three and a half-year captivity, the state continued to make public well-timed and inconsistent accusations against Padilla through the mass media. While Attorney General John Ashcroft, for instance, claimed that Padilla was planning to detonate bombs in supermarkets and gas stations, Deputy Defense Secretary Paul D. Wolfowitz stated that Padilla did not have "a specific target" nor did he have "an actual plan."[2] Regardless, holding Padilla was allegedly necessary to protect American lives because, as Deputy Attorney General James Comey put it, if Al Muhajir were charged in federal court, "he would likely have ended up a free man."[3]

Despite the potential embarrassment of seeing Padilla released by the courts, the Bush administration finally decided to charge him in late 2005. Not surprisingly, the final indictment had little resemblance to earlier accusations.

If initially the state had portrayed Al Muhajir as a domestic threat, now Padilla emerged as a distant menace, one that "may have been planning to use gas lines to destroy apartment buildings" but, most importantly, had "fought American forces in Afghanistan alongside Qaeda colleagues."[4] Padilla and four others are also accused of "conspiracy to murder, kidnap and maim people in a foreign country, conspiracy to provide material support to terrorists and providing, material support to terrorists."[5]

In the end, the most concrete accusation made against Padilla to date is that he allegedly arrived in Chicago with $10,000 in his suitcase and a couple of days worth of "explosives training."[6] Evidently, the eyes had been on another prize. As journalist Mike Whitney has observed, "It's the precedent that's paramount; the go-ahead to toss citizens in jail at the whim of the president and to dispose of enemies without recourse to the law."[7] But given the possibly infinite number of men who could have served just as well, why *this* "bad" guy?

Purely Perfect Puerto Rican

In a compelling essay, cultural critic Juan Duchesne Winter has argued that it was Al Muhajir's ethnic, racial, and national ambiguities that kept Padilla incommunicado in a navy brig for nearly four years.[8] But while ambiguity is an important part of the Padilla story to which I will return, his case also

Mugshot of Jose Padilla following his October 1991 arrest in Broword Country (CBS/AP)

suggests that it is the evocation of specific colonial, racial, and global identities—and not only his perceived ability to shape-shift—that has elicited the required consent to imprison him without any significant opposition outside of legal scholars, constitutionalists, and human rights activists.

Born Jose Padilla Ortega to U.S.-raised Puerto Rican parents in Brooklyn on October 18, 1970, little Pucho, as he was nicknamed for being chubby, grew up in a "rough" Puerto Rican Chicago neighborhood where his father was reportedly killed by a police officer. Like many other second- and third-generation inner city youths, Padilla joined a street gang, the Maniac Latin Disciples, when he was in his early teens. At age 15, he was convicted as a juvenile for his role in a petty robbery that ended up in the fatal assault of a Mexican immigrant, Elio Evangelista.[9] After his release at the age of 18 from Illinois Youth Detention Center, Padilla was arrested several more times for a wide range of infractions including attempted theft, battery, resisting an officer, obstructing police, criminal trespassing, and unlawful use of a weapon.[10] Following his move to Lauderhill, Florida, in 1991, Padilla was sentenced for nearly a year on three felony charges related to a traffic violation in Broward County.[11]

Up to this point, Padilla's early life story offers all the plot elements necessary to imagine him as a natural born terrorist. Padilla's past as a gang member—even when he has not been part of a gang since he was in his early teens—immediately positions him as inherently hazardous to national law and order, or in literary critic Monica Brown's words, as "the threat from within."[12] Furthermore, to the extent that in the aftermath of 9/11, gang activity and terrorism are imagined as "analogous" practices in journalistic stories, government research, and in state and federal legislation, Padilla's gang past and alleged terrorist present appear as mutual confirmation of his guilt. The equation of gangs and fundamentalist groups facilitates the labeling of gang members, who are often racialized, as terrorists or enemies of national security.[13] This is dramatically evident when a *Time* magazine commentator describes Padilla's ties to al Qaeda as those of "a former street hoodlum desperate to join a new gang."[14]

To insinuate that Padilla is a *Puerto Rican* gang member, however, offers additional discursive possibilites to imagine him as a danger to the national community. On the one hand, Padilla's "enemy combatant" status recalls the island's political subordination as an unincorporated territory: Both are entities produced by legal discourse, at once "outside of the law, yet inside of the sovereign's power."[15] On the other hand, the racialization of U.S. Puerto Ricans further positions Padilla on the margins of the nation. While in any of the 50 states Puerto Ricans are legally considered full-fledged U.S. citizens, the fact that they are racialized and are perceived as eternal immigrants has made the enjoyment of citizenship, understood as the aspiration to fully participate in one's governance, virtually impossible. In the words of Linda Basch, Nina Glick Schiller, and Cristina Szanton Blanc, "Immigrants, permanently foreign, are the enemy within and constitute a threat to national well-being—even survival."[16]

A symptom of Padilla's tenuous claim to U.S. citizenship status is that although the mainstream media and the state often described him as an "American," his deviance from this identity is accentuated by the constant use of descriptive words or phrases such as "Puerto Rican," "Muslim convert and former Chicago street gang thug,"[17] or "former Chicago street gang member and alleged Al Qaeda recruit."[18] In fact, most of the time that Padilla is referred to as an "American," this declaration is accompanied by a photograph or statement connoting either his "Latinness" or "Arabness." As conservative commentator Georgie Ann Geyer succinctly put it, "Whoever and whatever Jose Padilla was—and is—he is indeed an immigrant between ideologies, between ways of life and surely between loyalties."[19]

Moreover, the fact that some Puerto Ricans have engaged in violent political acts against the United States for which neither the media nor the state provides any context also makes the idea of a Puerto Rican terrorist, even one that does not want to be *boricua*, a credible threat. The historical relationship between Puerto Rican identity and terrorism is evident in the rhetoric of antistatehood advocates such as Pat Buchanan for whom, "to attempt to absorb and assimilate this independent island people could trigger a renewal of the terrorism of recent decades."[20] That Padilla grew up in Chicago, a city that is known for its Puerto Rican nationalist activism, further strengthens this link. During the 1980s, for instance, the pro-independence, Chicago-based *Frente Armado de Liberación Nacional* (FALN) claimed responsibility for several bomb attacks in Chicago and New York that injured or killed many people.[21] From early to mid-1990s, Chicago witnessed several other conflicts around nationalist Puerto Rican politics, including a major debate about the placement of a statue of Nationalist leader Pedro Albizu Campos, considered by some Puerto Ricans and U.S. authorities to be a terrorist.

Yet, in these times when communications are not accessory to power but one of its key axes, the viability of Padilla/Al Muhajir as a virtual terrorist also rests in the way his un-American identities efficiently activate a history of representation by and through the mass media. This allows the state to draw Padilla as a "dangerous" character without spectators needing to hear him speak or to see him except in carefully selected mug shots or in candid photos released and commented on at appropriately dramatic moments by state functionaries in the press and on television.[22] If the state's objective was to inspire the maximum amount of fear with the least amount of effort and political backlash in the aftermath of 9/11, Padilla/Al Muhajir offered what white enemy combatants such as John Walker Lindh and Saudi terrorists on the run such as Osama bin Laden could not: a man whose actual body the state could vanish while showing his "criminal" face wherever it pleased.

A comparison between Padilla and Walker Lindh, a young man who was captured by U.S. military forces while in Afghanistan fighting on the side of the Taliban, is quite useful here. Dubbed the "American Taliban" to Padilla's "enemy citizen," Walker was granted access to a lawyer and a constitutional trial in an open court in less than two months. Sources as diverse as CNN and the World Socialist website consistently portrayed Walker, unlike Padilla, as a "sweet" but confused boy playing out an adolescent spiritual quest in a faraway land. Significantly, although the Justice Department illegally and routinely released prejudicial information about the defendant, Walker Lindh's photos were of a victim: stripped, strapped, and hungry.[23] As a result of the media's relative sympathy and his parents' ability to hire a first-rate trial lawyer (and later a legal team), the state balked at declaring Walker an enemy combatant; the most serious charge against him—conspiracy to kill American nationals abroad—was also eventually dropped.

In addition, even though the "American Taliban" did eventually receive a 20-year sentence, federal prosecutors expressed "no objections to Walker Lindh's request to serve prison time near his family."[24] The glaring difference in process and outcome did not escape Padilla's mother, Estela Ortega Lebrón. "That John Walker Lindh. They didn't make him disappear, take away his rights. I guess maybe because his father's a lawyer. He's white, whatever."[25] As journalist Miles Harvey noted, unlike Lindh, "Padilla can count on little support from his family—which . . . includes a half brother in jail on first-degree murder charges and a homeless sister."[26] In order to best hit the desired demographic, middle-class America, the star of the "war on terror" production would ideally be a "domestic" minority with no family or political resources, whose drama would present itself as the equivalent of a rerun—with a twist.

Virtually *Boricua*

Uncannily, Padilla's story evokes several widely available sites of Puerto Rican identity construction in the United States, including the Broadway musical and film *West Side Story* (1957/1961); the trial (later also a Broadway show) of Salvador "The Capeman" Agrón, a 14-year-old Puerto Rican gang member who was involved in the murders of two white youths in 1959; and ex-con Piri Thomas's highly publicized 1967 memoir, *Down These Mean Streets*.[27] In portraying gang members as a threat to the American sexual, social, and/or symbolic orders, these texts have also contributed to shaping how Puerto Ricans are visualized in the mass media, clearing the way for Padilla to appear as "naturally" criminal and irrational, a ready-made image for public consumption.

West Side Story, the first major mass media product to represent Puerto Ricans as a distinct U.S. ethnic group with specific racial, linguistic, and bodily dispositions, directly forged a link between *boricua* ethnicity and gang membership.[28] From then on, Puerto Rican men would not only be assumed to be gang members unless proven otherwise, but also consumable as spectacles that reassured the nation of its values and inner stability. The film also underscored the racialized nature of Puerto Rican citizenship when it included *boricuas* in the overall picture as outsiders, and not an integral part of the "national" gang.[29]

Significantly, if less remarked, the musical also faced a critical problem of representation whose solution was to have a long-lasting effect. Since Puerto Ricans are a "racially" mixed group and not always visually distinguishable from either whites or African Americans, the film insisted on the need to see "brownness" as a marker of *boricua* visibility, in distinct opposition to "whiteness," which in *West Side Story*'s context is largely connoted as "blondeness."[30] This meant that the "American" characters were not only light skinned but light haired, and the "Puerto Rican" actors were either cast for looking brown or were made-up to look brown, as was the case of white actors playing Puerto Rican characters like George Chakiris (who had played a Jet in a stage production), or passing Puerto Rican actors like Rita Moreno.

The fact that Padilla's image only appears for seconds on television or in small photographs in print makes his brownness a particularly important asset in the projection of Puerto Rican criminality. It allows for the immediate reading of what anthropologist Ellen Moodie called the "criminal icon," whose biggest crime is often to look the part.[31] As a former Puerto Rican gang member who comes across as brown, Padilla can then be effortlessly seen as the next incarnation of *West Side Story*'s Chino, the character who kills the white protagonist Tony for the love of Maria. A comparison of the close-up on Chino when he is being arrested and Padilla's mug shots reveals an uncanny resemblance, virtually lodged on the skin.

If *West Side Story* lays the film foundation for seeing brown, the media frenzy that surrounded the Salvador "the Capeman" Agrón case contains other important elements that encourage the visualization of Padilla as another Puerto Rican in a long line-up of mass-mediated criminals. Different from *West Side Story*'s gang members but similar to Padilla, Agrón was often represented as inarticulate, irrational, and heartless. In accounts concerning Padilla's participation in the murder of Evangelista, for example, he is repeatedly described as saying that he kicked his victim in the head "because he felt like it."[32] This recalls Agrón's infamous comments plastered across all the New York newspapers: "I don't care if I burn. My mother can watch me."[33]

Equally important, the extensive print and broadcast coverage of the Agrón trial tended to characterize Puerto Ricans as prone to "foreign" identifications, in excess of their ethnic identity *as* foreign. To this end, stories highlighted that Agrón was often seen wearing a black cape with red satin lining and carrying a Mexican dagger, and that, as a member of a teenage gang named The Vampires, he called himself Dracula. In this regard, Puerto Ricanness, from its eruption as a stereotype in the mass media to its present articulations, is not only constituted as violent and brown but also as capable of embodying a wide range of social fears, from blood-sucking flamboyant migrants like Agrón to foreign-identified terrorists wearing "Arab" robes and calling themselves Abdullah like Padilla.

The first memoir by a U.S. Puerto Rican writer to achieve mass distribution, Piri Thomas's *Down These Mean Streets*, both offers a counternarrative to these gang stereotypes and adds additional elements to the visualization of Puerto Rican men. While *West Side Story* emphasized brownness and the

Agrón trial underscored foreignness, *Down These Mean Streets*'s narrator is actually uncertain whether he is Puerto Rican or African American, a question that Padilla resolved for himself in a defining way. In the stories of both Thomas and Padilla, the subject is first unable to recognize himself in U.S. racial schemes, and then attempts—but fails—to deploy violence as a means to destigmatize his racialized masculinity. In the end, both subjects reject the rule of earthly governments and swear allegiance to the higher authority of God.

Yet, unlike Thomas or Agrón, ex-convicts who became model citizens and/or icons of oppressed *boricuaness*, Padilla settled not on a Christian religion but on Islam; he re-affirmed himself not as a Latino, a Nuyorican, or an Afro-Rican, but as a black Muslim. Although, as hip-hop historian Raquel Rivera argues (chapter 16), it is not uncommon for Puerto Ricans to identify with African Americans, Padilla's embrace of Islam does not appear invested in empowering blacks in the United States or even in directly critiquing racism in American terms. Different than pre-Mecca Malcolm X, Padilla is born again to escape the nightmare of America and disrupt the very logic that makes him a bad (Latino) American guy but an ideal subject of global terror.

Straight from Central Casting

The common assumptions that Puerto Ricans are not real Americans (hence potentially disloyal) and are likely to carry out spectacular—if politically marginal—anti-American actions make Padilla a useful shorthand in convincing the public that terrorists are already—and inexplicably—among us. But a Puerto Rican who is taken for a Mexican and calls himself Al Muhajir presents additional advantages for the state at a time that it aims to redefine the geographical and legal parameters of warfare by synthesizing the internal Latino others (the "violent" Puerto Rican and the "illegal" Mexican) as well as the new target of national repulsion, the global "terrorist" Muslim. Or in *Time* magazine's words, "For incarnating the sum of our fears, the former Chicago-thug-turned-terror suspect is our person of the week."[34]

The construction of Padilla's Mexicanness begins with the fact that he worked in the purportedly Mexican fast-food eatery Taco Bell in South Florida before moving to the Middle East. This last detail would likely be insignificant if it were not for the fact that it was at Taco Bell that he came into contact with Islam through his wife-to-be, Cherie Maria Stultz, a Jamaican-born Muslim convert, and his boss, Mohammad Javed Qureshi, a prominent Muslim in South Florida. It was this convergence of food and religion that apparently prompted conservative commentator Laura Ingram to call Padilla the "Tortilla Terrorist," wrapping both Latino and Muslim identities into a perfect ideological enchilada. Yet Ingram was not the only pundit to cook this up. A web columnist made a similar connection among Padilla, Mexican food, and terrorism as an explosive combo. "Back in the good old days, your biggest concern about the guy behind the counter at Taco Bell was that he might spit in your burrito. But this is the 21st century, and nowadays you have to worry about whether he's working for Osama bin Laden instead of a talking Chihuahua: Yo quiero uranio enriquecido."[35]

A second important space to imagine Padilla as connected to both Mexicans and Muslims is the U.S.-Mexico border. Several media stories explicitly place Padilla at the border in the company of the Mara Salvatrucha or MS-13, a gang that operates transnationally across the Americas.[36] In the words of CBN.com News terrorism analyst Erick Stakelbeck, "Ironically, before converting to Islam and volunteering his services to Al-Qaeda, Padilla belonged to the Chicago chapter of the Latin Kings—like MS-13, a violent Hispanic criminal gang."[37] Although according to U.S. and Central American officials, there is "no evidence linking gangs like the Mara Salvatrucha to terrorist activity," the insistence on the connection between racialized identity, gang membership, and terrorism serves to elide the difference among the three, and underscore their danger to "America."[38]

Significantly, the fear of Latino immigrants is not only about the possibility of terrorism. It is also about the fear that the OTMs—Other Than Mexicans—or SIAs—Special Interest Aliens—can pass and blend in as Mexicans, producing identity uncertainty among the American authorities: "They pay to learn Spanish language skills, and by the time they reach the U.S., they're acting and talking like Mexicans to fool border agents."[39] The anxiety produced by interethnic morphing underscores that it is the articulation of presumably fixed identities in new combinations and with the potential for reversibility that ultimately got Padilla his star status.

Not surprisingly, in the majority of stories about Padilla the most used photographs are his mug shots, already coded to denote Puerto Ricanness as inherently criminal, and a photo of him wearing a keffiyeh, a headdress closely associated with Palestinian nationalism and usually seen on American television on the head of the late Palestinian Liberation Organization founder Yasser Arafat, considered by many to have been a terrorist. In these visual texts, the stereotype of the "Latino armed with a blade" is not so much replaced by "robed Arab terrorist,"[40] but rather the two are fused into a single unstable menace. In the impeccable words of the Solicitor General of the United States Paul Clement, Padilla is "a latter-day citizen version of Mohammed Atta,"[41] referring to one of the chief executioners of the Twin Towers attack.

It is then Padilla's paradigmatic "Puerto Rican" story, "Mexican" misrecognition, and "Arab" refashioning that are critical to understanding his political fate as a virtual villain whose potential for evil is considered to be so great that most people in the United States—80 percent according to a 2002 Gallup poll—are willing to exchange a feeling of "safety" for "some" of their civil rights.[42] In this light, Al Muhajir appears as both a reanimation of a colonial body of stereotypes and also the frightful new subject of globalization, one who cannot be pinned down in terms of race, ethnicity, nationality, religion, territory, geography, or citizenship. Given this, one could say that well before Padilla allegedly "thought" of creating a dirty bomb, he had already committed several crimes of identity that made him an undesirable subject of any national discourse: He is a U.S. Puerto Rican, he has chosen to be a Muslim, and he has affirmed not his country, family, or ethnic gang but instead his location as everywhere a foreigner.

Oh, Jose Can't You See? Politics Besides Identity

Wearing a keffiyeh and wandering between Miami, Chicago, Egypt, Afghanistan, Yemen, and Pakistan, Padilla refashions himself as a global nomad, rejecting any naturalized boundaries of identity. For Padilla, joining al Qaeda rather than an American gang like the Marines may have offered a way to, as Monica Brown has argued in another context, re-signify his relationship to the United States and recuperate "the subjectivity conferred by citizenship."[43] As a Muslim, Padilla could free himself from the binaries that have historically structured his specific social possibilities and join what for many African American and Latino converts is a color-blind brotherhood, "a universal faith where people of all walks of life pray together."[44] Under Allah's gaze, he is neither Puerto Rican nor American, ex-con nor minimum wage worker; indeed, he is born again, a "new" man.

Padilla's status as America's domestic terrorist poster boy (dressed in a " 'three-piece-suit'—shackles, leg irons, and a metal belt"[45]) however suggests that although people do mix and match themselves into new subjectivities, the state still relies on the idea that people are born with God-given identities, including gender, nationality, and race, and exploits the one most likely to cause fear at a given moment. Regardless of Al Muhajir's multiple identifications, when needed, the U.S. conservative commentators "stripped" him back to "Jose Padilla," his presumably "real" ethnic self. In the succinct words of Georgie Ann Geyer: "He is a Puerto Rican who lived on the American mainland, and a Roman Catholic by his parents' training . . . the name of things are crucially important, and his real name is Padilla."[46] Whereas he was initially wanted as Al Muhajir, he will now be tried as Padilla.

Importantly, pegging Padilla as a Puerto Rican is executed not by overt racist allusion but by "factual" description. This is why white conservatives clearly see Padilla as the latest in a long line-up of Puerto Rican men who embody a threatening internal enemy, while most community leaders have suggested that the Padilla case is not a "Puerto Rican" issue. According to a leading attorney, "Most Puerto Rican organizations are involved in issues such as housing, employment, and health, poor people issues. Civil rights cases are white people's law."[47] This division of labor is quite evident in the "nine inch thick friend-of-the-court briefs" filed in Padilla's 2003 appeal to the 2nd Circuit Court of Appeals in Manhattan by such "white" Left, Right, and libertarian organizations as the American Bar Association, Cato Institute, Rutherford Institute, the Constitution Project, People for the American Way, and Center for National Security Studies.[48]

The question of why most Latinos, and Puerto Ricans in particular, have remained largely indifferent to his case is as politically urgent as the question of why the state targeted Padilla in the first place.[49] In the United States, after all, as sociologist Suzanne Oboler comments, it is the responsibility of the affected racialized or ethnic group to protect its own against the abuses of the state.[50] U.S. Puerto Ricans also have a sophisticated machinery to address matters of racial discrimination, police brutality, and political injustice. In fact, Puerto Rican activists evicted the U.S. Navy from the Puerto Rican island of Vieques[51] claiming that the United States transformed all *viequenses* into potential political prisoners, as well as militarized the entire social space. But the same issues as they apply in the Padilla case have been virtually ignored.[52]

Arguably, this is the case for several, interlocking reasons. Padilla exposes the state's latest technologies of control that hail and order racialized people in a different way. In this "globally" applicable paradigm of natives and foreigners, Latinos and "Arabs" can under certain conditions appear as two sides of the same coin, allowing for the slippage in current conservative discourse between a "war on terror" waged through foreign policy in the Muslim and Arab "worlds" and a "war on immigrants" waged on Mexicans and Mexican Americans. The new model is then not only based on a paradigm along the black/white axis that served as the norm for most of the twentieth century, but also along the native/foreign one prevalent in the aftermath of September 11. Articulated with the imagined threat of Mexican hordes taking the United States "back" and the disloyal Puerto Ricans always ready to be ungrateful are the Arabs, generally perceived as a "menace to society, degenerates from an uncivilized culture."[53]

The general indifference that Latino organizations have shown toward Padilla is a sign of the state's success in persuading racialized populations to define themselves as law-abiding "natives" who may also happen to be racially or culturally different, but heartily resist being conflated with those who insist on being "bad niggers." Or in the terms used by Miguel Nogueras, executive director of Chicago's Puerto Rican Chamber of Commerce: "We support this country fully in the war against terrorism . . . I see [Padilla] as an aberration."[54]

The potential for harm by the state has a disciplining effect in which nonwhite U.S. citizens who wish to be rewarded, or at least not targeted, must perform as unconditionally patriotic Americans and distance themselves from Latino criminalized sectors. As literary theorist Michael Hardt and philosopher Antonio Negri have observed, fear, after all, is the "primary mechanism of control that fills the society of the spectacle."[55] This dynamic has reached its apex with President Bush's latest appointment for attorney general, the Mexican American Alberto Gonzalez. Known for his conservative record, Gonzalez is also infamous for providing counsel to the White House in which he argued that, "[the] new paradigm renders obsolete Geneva's strict limitations on questioning enemy prisoners."[56] Not surprisingly, Gonzalez was ecstatic about the 2005 decision upholding the state's right to detain Padilla. "As the court noted today . . . the authority to detain enemy combatants like Mr. Padilla plays an important role in protecting American citizens from the very kind of savage attack that took place almost four years ago to the day."[57] The wording of this statement is remarkably telling; obviously, Padilla is not an American citizen.

By buying into the idea that we all "act our race," nativist and ethnic groups have accepted the state's logic: By sacrificing Padilla the rest of us will be safer. In self-determination advocate José E. Aponté's words, "Padilla is accused of an action linked to the destruction of 9/11, so there is an issue of personal safety. People are giving the government the benefit of the doubt."[58] The irony of this convergence is that Puerto Ricans do not care about Padilla because he does not proclaim himself or is not only framed as a *boricua*, while mainstream America is happy to accept Al Muhajir's fate precisely because he is a "Hispanic" criminal. The treatment of Padilla reminds many upwardly mobile, middle-class Latinos of something that they may want to forget: that citizenship for nonwhites is contingent and that under the current model of racialization, Latinos, including Puerto Ricans, are particularly vulnerable as "essentially 'un-American' and potentially 'enemies within.' "[59]

The perception of Padilla by the island mass media as yet another celebrity capable of bringing either good or bad publicity to Puerto Rico also misreads the island's precarious place in the current cartography of power on a global scale. When the local press immediately dubbed him the "Puerto Rican Taliban," it was fully enjoying the connotations of anti-Americanism, an outlaw pose, and the inscription of Puerto Ricans into global events. If, in the United States, Padilla sat at the edge of the nation's definition of itself, in Puerto Rico, cultural nationalist discourse turned al Muhajir into another famous *boricua* just like boxers, baseball players, beauty queens, entertainers, and other outlaws: "Wanted" people who, through their magnificent celebrity status, confirm that Puerto Ricans exist and transform the world in both trivial and important ways, especially against any apparatus that connotes or exercises legalized authority.

In this context, the tendency of Puerto Ricans to almost exclusively organize as ethno-national and ethno-racial subjects may be the most effective where it matters least. Compare, for instance, the amount of attention and efficacy in the mobilization of Puerto Ricans around the anti-Latino comments of transvestite humorist Dame Edna in *Vanity Fair*, in which she criticized the Spanish language as not as sophisticated as French, or the outpouring of writing when the Puerto Rican basketball team beat the U.S. team in the 2004 Olympics, with the amount of concern and activism about Padilla. It is evident that a nationalist discourse based on *boricua* cultural pride is inadequate to engage with the forms of power currently deployed by the state.

"Al Muhajir"—more than "Padilla"—represents a critical challenge to Puerto Rican and all nationalist politics. Unlike the imprisoned nationalist warriors that Puerto Rican "progressives" consensually defend and often successfully lobby for, Al Muhajir does not appear to identify as *boricua*, whether they are imagined as an ethnic group, a nation, or an ethno-nation. He has cast his lot with Allah. Moreover, as César Perales, executive director of the Puerto Rican Legal Defense Fund, commented, "The difference between Padilla and the political prisoners is that the prisoners were part of the community and they had a base. Organizations like ours received a lot of pressure to take action. There are not very many Puerto Ricans beating a drum about Padilla."[60] The fact that the state has not explicitly linked his political identity to his ethnicity but rather allow the media to index it continuously makes Padilla unattractive as a martyr for the national cause. In Aponte's direct prose, "If Padilla is not described as a Puerto Rican, there is nothing major to gain."[61] If what "really" matters in Puerto Rican politics is that Puerto Ricans be recognized and be valued *as* Puerto Ricans, then Al Muhajir is not a political concern for *boricuas.*

At this point, Puerto Ricans may identify as American, hence native, as native Puerto Rican, Latino, Taíno, and/or as a dissident to these categories. Yet, what is important is not what is "essentially" there in any of these locations. In this "none of the above" world, where the center is disputed and the exception becomes the rule, the most compelling reason to care about Al Muhajir is not his uncomfortable Puerto Rican ethnicity, his second-class U.S. citizenship, or his "Pucho of Arabia" hybrid identity. The biggest threat of all, however we identify ourselves, may well be the state's and the media's nearly unencumbered capacity to make their version of "Jose" out of any of us.

Notes

This essay is based on my Oscar Micheaux lecture delivered at the University of Chicago on February 18, 2004. I would like to thank Prof. Jacqueline Stewart for her invitation and the opportunity to share this essay.

1. Miles Harvey, "The Bad Guy," *Mother Jones*, March/April 2003, 1–5, 5, <http://www.motherjones.com/commentary/notebook/2003/03/ma_293_01.html>.
2. "Lawyer: Dirty Bomb Suspect's Rights Violated," June 11, 2002, *CNN.com*, CNN.com/2002/US/06/11/dirty.bomb.suspect/
3. "Transcript of News Conference on Jose Padilla," CNN.com, June 1, 2004, http://www.cnn.com/2004/LAW/06/01/comey.padilla.transcript/index.html.
4. Ibid.
5. Terry Frieden, "Court Delays Padilla Transfer from Brig," *CNN.com*, November 30, 2005, <http://www.cnn.com/2005/LAW/11/30/padilla.transfer/>.
6. Shannon McCaffrey, "Terror Suspect Stashed in S.C. 'Black Hole,' " *The State*, June 6, 2003, <www.thestate.com/mld/thestate/news/local/6046311.htm>.
7. Mike Whitney, "Free Jose Padilla," *Counter Punch*, May 23, 2005, <http://www.counterpunch.org/whitney05232005.html>.
8. Juan Duchesne Winter, " 'Cualquiera' es mi nombre: el caso de Abdullah al-Muhajir / Jose Padilla," *WebIslam*, <http://www.webislam.com/numeros/2003>.
9. Cam Simpson, Eric Ferkenhoff, and Kim Barker, "Cops Say Padilla Was a Just a Small-Time Thug," *Chicago Tribune*, June 11, 2002, 1.

10. Cam Simpson and Kim Barker, "Padilla's 2nd Life Began in Florida," *Chicago Tribune*, June 12, 2002, 1.
11. For further details, see Simpson, Ferkenhoff, and Barker, "Cops Say Padilla was a Just a Small-Time Thug."
12. Monica Brown, *Gang Nation: Delinquent Citizens in Puerto Rican, Chicano, and Chicana Narratives* (Minneapolis and London: University of Minnesota Press, 2002), xiii.
13. For further discussion on several sides of these debates, please see Jessica Glicken Turnely and Julienne Smrcka, "Terrorist Organizations and Criminal Street Gangs: An Argument for an Analogy" and Michelle Garcia, "N.Y. Using Terrorism Law to Prosecute Street Gang."
14. Tony Karon, "Person of the Week: Jose Padilla," *Time*, June 14, 2004, <www.time.com/time/pow/article/0,8599,262269,00.html>.
15. Charles Venator Santiago, "From the Insular Cases to Camp X-Ray: Agamben's State of Exception and United States Territorial Jurisprudence and Policy" in *Sovereign Acts*, ed. Frances Negrón-Muntaner (Cambridge, MA: South End Press, forthcoming, 2007).
16. Linda Basch, Nina Glick Schiller, and Cristina Szanton Blanc, *Nations Unbound: Transnational Projects, Postcolonial Predicaments, and Derritorialized Nation-States* (London and New York: Routledge, 2000), 289.
17. Clarence Page, "Punishment First, Then the Crime," June 21, 2002, http://www.jewishworldreview.com/0602/page062102.asp.
18. Cam Simpson, "Court Takes Padilla Case," *The Chicago Tribune*, February 21, 2004, 1.
19. Georgie Anne Geyer, "Rootless Young Men Everywhere are Prime Terrorist Fodder," *Chicago Tribune*, June 14, 2002, 31.
20. Pat Buchanan, "Let Puerto Rico Remain Puerto Rico," *The Internet Brigade*, September 15, 1998, <http://www.buchanan.org/pa-98-0915.html>.
21. Edmund Mahoney, "Clinton Offer Includes Mastermind of 1983 Wells Fargo Robbery," *Hartford Courant*, August 12, 1999, A1.
22. Another classic example is that of a Libyan exile, Omar Deghayes, who was labeled an enemy combatant and incarcerated at Guantánamo. Despite the fact that Deghayes's right eye was damaged when he was four as a result of an accident involving a sword, "European agencies circulated a mug shot purporting to be Deghayes that portrays a goggle-eyed black-haired Chechen fighter." Carol Rosenberg, "Captives Tell Their Side," *The Miami Herald*, March 31, 2005, <www.miami.com/mld/miamiherald/news/11272290. htm>.
23. "The Case of the Taliban American," *CNN.com*, <www.cnn.com/CNN/Programs/people/shows/walker/profile.html>; David Walsh, "The *New York Times* and the Case of John Walker," World Socialist Website, <http://wsws.org/articles/2001/dec2001/walk-d22.shtml>.
24. Ibid.
25. Deborah Sontag, "Jose Padilla—Terror Suspect's Path from Streets to Brig," New York Times, April 25, 2004, 1–12, <http://middleeastinfo-org/article4357.html> 1–12, 9.
26. Harvey, "The Bad Guy," 1–5, 4.
27. Piri Thomas, *Down These Mean Streets* (New York: Vintage, 1997).
28. Frances Negrón-Muntaner, *Boricua Pop: Puerto Ricans and the Latinization of American Culture* (New York: New York University Press, 2004), xvi.

29. Alberto Sandoval-Sánchez, "A Puerto Rican Reading of the America of *West Side Story*," in *José, Can You See?: Latinos On and Off Broadway*" (Madison and London: University of Minnesota Press, 1999), 62–82, 66.
30. For further commentary, see Sandoval-Sánchez, "A Puerto Rican Reading of the America of *West Side Story*," 68.
31. Ellen Moodie, " '¡Agente! Fíjense en estas caras!' Discipline, Control and Biopolitics in 1930s El Salvador," Presented at 1932 Symposium, Columbia University, 2004, 1–15, 3.
32. Deborah Sontag, "Jose Padilla."
33. Quoted in George Spiegler, "The Capeman Murders," <http://www.hellskitchennyc.com/html/capeman.htm>.
34. Tony Karon, "Person of the Week: Jose Padilla."
35. "Jose Padilla," <http://www.rotten.com/library/bio/crime/terrorist/jose-padilla/>.
36. Erick Stakelbeck, "Unholy Border Alliance," *FrontPageMagazine.com*, January 3, 2005, October 27, 2005, <www.frontpagemag.com/Articles/ReadArticle.asp?ID=16509>.
37. Ibid.
38. "El Salvador Gang Member: I'm No Terrorist," *Miami Herald*, February 24, 2005, reprinted in <http://www.americas.org/item_18122>, website for Resource Center of the America.org.
39. Ibid.
40. Suzanne Oboler, "Nuevas formas/viejos moldes: la discriminación racial contra los Latinos en los Estados Unidos, después del 11 de septiembre 2001," unpublished manuscript, 20. Original Spanish: "el racial profiling de gente de descendencia árabe coincide y casi reemplaza el estereotipo anterior del latino armado con una navaja."
41. Linda Greenhouse, "Court Hears Case on U.S. Detainees," *New York Times*, April 29, 2004, reproduced in the *Puerto Rico Herald*, <www.puertorico-herald.org/issues/2004/vol8n18/Media1-en.shtml>.
42. Alan Keyes, "Liberty and Security," *Catholic Exchange*, June 19, 2002, <http://www.catholicexchange.com/vm/index.asp?vm_id=1&art_id=14071>.
43. Brown, *Gang Nation*, 83.
44. Ibrahim Gonzalez, quoted in Lisa Viscidi, "Latino Muslims a Growing Presence in America," *Washington Report in Middle East Affairs* 22, no. 5 (June 2003): 56, 58–59, <http://hispanicmuslims.com/articles/latinogrowth.html>.
45. Kari Lundgren, "Wartime Powers," *Mother Jones*, <www.motherjones.com/news/dailymojo/2004/04/04_538.html>.
46. Georgie Anne Geyer, "Rootless young men everywhere are prime terrorist fodder," *Chicago Tribune*, June 14, 2002, 31.
47. Phone Interview, César Perales, August 18, 2004.
48. Tom Brune, "Court Filings Rip Bush on Padilla Case," *Chicago Tribune*, August 6, 2003, 11.
49. An exception was the play "The Peculiar Case of Jose Padilla" by Ramon Florez. Produced by La Compañía de Teatro de Albuquerque, the play was produced in early 2005 in New Mexico. For a review, see Matthew Chavez, "Play challenges misconceptions," *The Daily Lobo*, February 17, 2005.
50. Oboler, "Nuevas formas/viejos moldes," 17.
51. Duchesne Winter, " 'Cualquiera' es mi nombre," 1.

52. For further elaboration on the militarization of civil society, see Juan Duchesne Winter, "La Guerra de las banderas en Puerto Rico," July 1, 2002, unpublished manuscript.
53. Narmeen El-Farra, "Arabs and the Media," *Journal of Media Psychology*, 1, no. 2 (Spring 1996), <www.calstatela.edu/faculty/sfischo/Arabs/html>.
54. Dan Mihalopoulos and James Janega, "Terror Suspect's Arrest Puts Hispanics on Edge" *Chicago Tribune*, June 12, 2002, <hispanicmuslims.com/articles/onedge.html>.
55. Michael Hardt and Antonio Negri, *Empire* (Cambridge, MA: Harvard University Press, 2000), 323.
56. Michiko Kakutani, "Following a Paper Trail to Roots of the Abuse Scandal at Abu Ghraib Prison."
57. Neil A. Lewis, "Court Gives Bush Right to Detain U.S. Combatant," *New York Times*, September 10, 2005, A1, A10.
58. Phone interview, José Aponte, August 17, 2004.
59. Nicholas De Genova and Ana Y. Ramos-Zayas, *Latino Crossings: Mexicans, Puerto Ricans, and the Politics of Race and Citizenship* (New York: Routledge, 2003), 48–49, 217.
60. Phone interview, César Perales, August 18, 2004.
61. Phone interview, José Aponte, August 17, 2004.

Notes on Contributors

Silvia Alvarez-Curbelo is a professor at the Graduate School of Communication of the University of Puerto Rico and director of the Communications Research Center. She is the coeditor of *Senado de Puerto Rico. Ensayos de historia institucional* (1992), *Del nacionalismo al populismo* (1993), *Historias vivas* (1996), *Ilusión de Francia: Arquitectura y afrancesamiento en Puerto Rico* (1997), and *Hispanofilia; Arquitectura y vida en Puerto Rico* (1998), and editor of *Etica y retórica en la comunicación política* (2001). She is also the author of *Un país del porvenir: el afán de modernidad en Puerto Rico* (2001). She is currently writing a history of the Puerto Rican soldiers in the Korean War.

Frances R. Aparicio is professor and director of the Latin American and Latino Studies Program at the University of Illinois, Chicago (UIC). She is the author of *Listening to Salsa: Gender, Latin Popular Music and Puerto Rican Cultures* (1998) and coeditor of *Tropicalizations* (1997), *Musical Migrations* (2003), and the forthcoming *Hibridismos Culturales* (2005). At UIC, she helped to establish the new *Latino Studies Journal* and created the Lectures in the Community Series and a new publication series with University of Illinois Press on Latinos in Chicago and the Midwest.

Jaime Benson Arias is a professor at the Economics Department of the University of Puerto Rico, Río Piedras.

Christina Duffy Burnett is the coeditor of *Foreign in a Domestic Sense: Puerto Rico, American Expansion, and the Constitution* (Duke University Press, 2001) and the author of "The Case for Puerto Rican Decolonization," *Orbis: A Journal of World Affairs* (Summer 2001). She holds a JD from Yale Law School, an M.Phil. in political thought and intellectual history from Cambridge University, and a master's degree in American history from Princeton University, where she is completing a doctorate on the legal history of American expansion. She served as a law clerk on the Second Circuit Court of Appeals in 2000–1, and on the U.S. Supreme Court in the October 2004 term.

Jorge Duany is professor of Anthropology at the University of Puerto Rico, Río Piedras. He has published extensively on transnational migration, national identity, and popular culture, especially in the Caribbean and Puerto Rico, and among Latinos in the United States. His latest book is *The Puerto*

Rican Nation on the Move: Identities on the Island and in the United States (Chapel Hill, NC: University of North Carolina Press, 2002).

Juan Duchesne Winter is the author of three books on literary and cultural criticism: *Narraciones de testimonio en América Latina* (1992), *Política de la caricia* (1996), and *Ciudadano Insano* (2001). He codirected two independent theoretical journals, *Postdata* (1989–92) and *Nómada* (1995–2000), and cosponsored, with Carlos Pabón, *Radio Alicia*, an experiment in bringing cultural theory to the radio (1999–2003). He currently teaches literature in the Department of Spanish, School of General Studies, University of Puerto Rico.

Juan Flores is a professor at Hunter College and the CUNY Graduate Center. His publications include *Divided Borders* (1993), *From Bomba to Hip-Hop* (2000), *La venganza de Cortijo* (1997), *Memoirs of Bernardo Vega* (1984), and *Cortijo's Wake* (2004).

Félix Jiménez is professor of communication and cultural studies at Universidad del Sagrado Corazón in Puerto Rico. He studied comparative literature at Yale, and is a former CNN editorial producer and contributor to *The Village Voice* and *The Nation*. He is the author of *Vieques y la prensa* (2001) and *Las prácticas de la carne: construcción y representación de las masculinidades puertorriqueñas* (2004).

Yolanda Martínez-San Miguel is an associate professor in the Department of Romance Languages at the University of Pennsylvania. She has published two books, *Saberes americanos: subalternidad y epistemología en los escritos de Sor Juana* (Iberoamericana, 1999) and *Caribe Two Ways: cultura de la migración en el Caribe insular hispánico* (Callejón, 2003), and a compilation of essays, coedited with Mabel Moraña, *Nictimene . . . sacrílega. Estudios coloniales en homenaje a Georgina Sabat-Rivers* (Claustro de Sor Juana and Iberoamericana, 2003).

Marianne Mason, translator, is an assistant professor of modern languages and linguistics at the Georgia Institute of Technology. Her publications on the analysis of covert speech have been featured in the *Journal of Pragmatics* and *Police Quarterly*. At present she is working on a manuscript that examines the linguistic structure of psychic readings.

Frances Negrón-Muntaner is an award-winning writer, filmmaker, and scholar. She is the author of *Boricua Pop: Puerto Ricans and the Latinization of American Culture*, a 2004 Choice Outstanding Academic Title, coeditor of *Puerto Rican Jam: Rethinking Colonialism and Nationalism* (1997), and editor of the forthcoming volume, *Sovereign Acts* (South End Press). Her films include *Brincando el charco: Portrait of a Puerto Rican* (1994), and *For the Record: Guam and World War II* (2007). Negrón-Muntaner is also a founding member and chair of NALIP, the National Association of Latino Independent Producers. For her various achievements, *Hispanic Magazine* named her as one of the nation's "Most Influential Hispanics" in 2005. She currently teaches at Columbia University.

Laura L. Ortiz-Negrón is currently Researcher at the Social Science Research Center at the Río Piedras Campus of the University of Puerto Rico. Her book, *Al filo de la navaja: Los márgenes en Puerto Rico* (1999) examines the subject of post-work culture and those sectors excluded from the world of work identified as the margins. Her most recent project is the video *Arcadas de las estaciones 20–21: Visiones sobre los centros comerciales en Puerto Rico* (2005). Currently she is writing a book on consumer culture in Puerto Rico, a work that casts a trenchant look at Puerto Rican society.

Carlos Pabón teaches at the University of Puerto Rico-Río Piedras. He has published essays on national identity, globalization, history, and postmodernism. He is the author of *Nación postmortem: Ensayos sobre los tiempos de insoportable ambigüedad* (San Juan, Ediciones Callejón, 2002) that was awarded first prize in the essay category by Puerto Rico's Pen Club.

Fernando Picó is a professor of History at the University of Puerto Rico, Río Piedras campus. He has published several books on Puerto Rican history, including *Puerto Rico 1898: The War After the War* (2003).

Gloria D. Prosper-Sánchez is a linguist and professor of Spanish at the University of Puerto Rico at Río Piedras. She received her Ph.D. in Hispanic Linguistics at the University of Massachusetts at Amherst. In addition to her research on the sociolinguistic aspects of homophonetic neutralization of liquids in Puerto Rican Spanish, she has published essays exploring the intersections of linguistic theory and literature. She is currently working on a book, *F®icciones de la lengua*, an examination of the use of linguistics by normative institutions in the constitution of the standard variety of Puerto Rican Spanish.

María Isabel Quiñones Arocho has conducted fieldwork in Barbados, Ghana, and Puerto Rico. Her main interests are cultural theory, the shifting boundaries of the imaginary in a globalized world, gender relations in the Caribbean, the beauty industry, and the production of the self. Author of several articles and essays, she has recently published *El fin del reino de lo propio: ensayos de antropología cultural* (Siglo veintiuno editores, 2004), which won the 2003 *Pensamiento caribeño* competition sponsored by the University of Quintana Roo, Mexico and UNESCO. Currently she is full professor in the Department of Social Sciences, General Studies Faculty, University of Puerto Rico, Río Piedras Campos and coordinator of the Women and Gender Studies Program at the same institution.

José Quiroga is professor and chair of the Department of Spanish and Portuguese at Emory University. He is the author of *Understanding Octavio Paz* (1999) and *Tropics of Desire: Interventions from Queer Latino America* (2001). His latest book is *Cuba Palimpsests* (2005).

Raquel Z. Rivera is a writer and a professor at the Department of Sociology at Tufts University. As a Mellon postdoctoral fellow, she is presently conducting research on gender roles and generational dynamics in traditional

Caribbean music. Her book, *New York Ricans from the Hip Hop Zone*, was published by Palgrave Macmillan in 2003. A freelance journalist, her articles have been published in numerous magazines and newspapers including *Vibe, One World, El Diario/La Prensa, El Nuevo Día*, and *The San Juan Star*. Her academic work has been published in books and journals such as *Puerto Rican Jam: Rethinking Colonialism and Nationalism* (1997), *Revista de Ciencias Sociales* (1998), *Mambo Montage: The Latinization of New York* (2001), and *Latina/Latino Popular Culture* (2002). A writer of fiction and poetry, she is also a member of the music group Yaya, a collective of women paying homage to Dominican salves and Puerto Rican *bomba*. Born and raised in San Juan, Puerto Rico, she has lived in New York City since 1994 and is a resident of East Harlem.

Juana María Rodríguez is the author of *Queer Latinidad: Identity Practices, Discursive Spaces* (2002) and is currently completing a new manuscript entitled *Queer Law: Cultural Readings of Contemporary Jurisprudence.* Currently, she is associate professor of Women and Gender Studies at the University of California-Davis.

Alberto Sandoval-Sánchez is Professor of Spanish and U.S. Latino literature at Mount Holyoke College. He has published numerous articles in books and journals on Latin American, Spanish, and U.S. Latino theatre, Puerto Rican migration, and images of Latinos in film and Broadway. He is the author of *New York Backstage/Nueva York Tras Bastidores* (Chile: Cuarto Propio, 1993), *José, Can You See?: Latinos On and Off Broadway* (University of Wisconsin Press, 1999), and coeditor of *Puro Teatro: A Latina Anthology* (University of Arizona Press, 2000, in collaboration with Nancy S. Sternbach from Smith College). His latest book is *Stages of Life: Transcultural Performance and Identity in Latina Theatre* (University of Arizona Press, 2001, also in collaboration with Sternbach).

Index